SELECTED STUDIES ON
DEUTEROCANONICAL PRAYERS

CONTRIBUTIONS TO BIBLICAL EXEGESIS AND THEOLOGY

Angela Kim HARKINS and Barbara SCHMITZ (eds.)

SELECTED STUDIES ON DEUTEROCANONICAL PRAYERS

PEETERS

LEUVEN – PARIS – BRISTOL, CT

2021

A catalogue record for this book is available from the Library of Congress.

© 2021 — Peeters, Bondgenotenlaan 153, B-3000 Leuven

ISBN 978-90-429-4387-2
eISBN 978-90-429-4388-9
D/2021/0602/6

TABLE OF CONTENTS

ACKNOWLEDGEMENTS

This collection would not have been possible without the assistance of the following individuals: Verena Sauer, Maximilian Häberlein, Franziska Reichert, Lara Mayer, Lea Brenner, and Hayden G. Cowart who assisted in various ways with the editing of the essays. The editors also wish to acknowledge the cooperation of the two SBL program committees who were involved with the initial plans for a joint session on deuterocanonical prayers in 2018. The co-chairs and steering committee of the Deuterocanonical and Cognate Literatures program unit were Kristin De Troyer, Barbara Schmitz, and Frank Ueberschaer (co-chairs), Gerhard Karner, Renate Egger-Wenzel, and Benjamin Wright; and the co-chairs and steering committee of the Prayer in Antiquity program unit were Daniel K. Falk and Angela Kim Harkins (co-chairs), Ruth Langer, Mika S. Pajunen, Eileen M. Schuller, and Michael Swartz. The completion and final editing of this volume took place during the global pandemic in 2020. The editors wish to express their gratitude to their own families, to the contributors, and to all of the families and communities of the contributors of this volume for their support during such an unusual and unprecedented time.

ABBREVIATIONS

AB	Anchor Bible
ABRL	Anchor Bible Reference Library
AJEC	Ancient Judaism and Early Christianity
AnBib	Analecta Biblica
ANESSup	Ancient Near Eastern Studies Supplement Series
ANRW	*Aufstieg und Niedergang der römischen Welt*
AOAT	Alter Orient und Altes Testament
ArBib	Aramaic Bible
ATD	Altes Testament Deutsch
AVL	*Arbeitsbericht des Vetus Latina-Instituts*
BASOR	*Bulletin of the American School of Oriental Research*
BBB	Bonner Biblische Beiträge
BBRSup	Bulletin for Biblical Research, Supplements
BEATAJ	Beiträge zur Erforschung des Alten Testaments und des antiken Judentums
BETL	Bibliotheca Ephemeridum Theologicarum Lovaniensium
Bib	*Biblica*
BibInt	Biblical Interpretation Series
Bijdr	*Bijdragen: Tijdschrift voor filosofie en theologie*
BIOSCS	Bulletin of the International Organization for Septuagint and Cognate Studies
BJS	Brown Judaic Studies
BN	*Biblische Notizen*
BZAW	Beihefte zur Zeitschrift für die alttestamentliche Wissenschaft
BZNW	Beihefte zur Zeitschrift für die neutestamentliche Wissenschaft
CBET	Contributions to Biblical Exegesis and Theology
CBQ	*Catholic Biblical Quarterly*
CBQMS	Catholic Biblical Quarterly Monograph Series
CEJL	Commentaries on Early Jewish Literature
CHANE	Culture and History of the Ancient Near East
CP	*Classical Philology*
CRINT	Compendia Rerum Iudaicarum ad Novum Testamentum
DCLS	Deuterocanonical and Cognate Literature Studies
DCLY	Deuterocanonical and Cognate Literature Yearbook
DJD	Discoveries in the Judean Desert
DSD	*Dead Sea Discoveries*
ECDSS	Eerdmans Commentary on the Dead Sea Scrolls
EHAT	Exegetisches Handbuch zum Alten Testament
EJL	Early Judaism and Its Literature
FAT	Forschungen zum Alten Testament
FC	Fathers of the Church

FCB	Feminist Companion to the Bible
FRLANT	Forschungen zur Religion und Literatur des Alten und Neuen Testaments
FSBP	Fontes et Subsidia ad Bibliam Pertinentes
HBAI	*Hebrew Bible and Ancient Israel*
HBS	Herders Biblische Studien
HCS	Hellenistic Culture and Society
HThKAT	Herders Theologischer Kommentar zum Alten Testament
HTR	*Harvard Theological Review*
ICC	International Critical Commentary
Idt	Iudith (Vulgate)
Int	*Interpretation*
JAAR	*Journal of the American Academy of Religion*
JANER	*Journal of Ancient Near Eastern Religions*
JAOS	*Journal of the American Oriental Society*
JBL	*Journal of Biblical Literature*
JJS	*Journal of Jewish Studies*
JNES	*Journal of Near Eastern Studies*
JQR	*Jewish Quarterly Review*
JSHRZ	*Jüdische Schriften aus hellenistisch-römischer Zeit*
JSJ	*Journal for the Study of Judaism in the Persian, Hellenistic, and Roman Periods*
JSJSup	Journal for the Study of Judaism Supplement Series
JSOT	*Journal for the Study of the Old Testament*
JSOTSup	Journal for the Study of the Old Testament Supplement Series
JSP	*Journal for the Study of the Pseudepigrapha*
JSPSup	Journal for the Study of the Pseudepigrapha Supplement Series
JTISup	Journal of Theological Interpretation Supplement Series
LCL	Loeb Classical Library
LHBOTS	The Library of Hebrew Bible/Old Testament Studies
LSTS	The Library of Second Temple Studies
MSU	Mitteilungen des Septuaginta-Unternehmens
NEchtB	Neue Echter Bibel
NETS	New English Translation of the Septuagint
NIB	*The New Interpreter's Bible*
NIDB	New Interpreter's Dictionary of the Bible
NICOT	New International Commentary on the Old Testament
OBO	Orbis Biblicus et Orientalis
OCM	Oxford Classical Monographs
ORA	Orientalische Religionen in der Antike
OrChrAn	Orientalia Christiana Analecta
OTE	*Old Testament Essays*
OTL	Old Testament Library
PO	Patrologia Orientalis
PSBA	*Proceedings of the Society of Biblical Archaeology*
RAC	*Reallexikon für Antike und Christentum*
RBén	*Revue Bénédictine*

RBS	Resources for Biblical Studies
RevQ	*Revue de Qumran*
RivB	*Rivista biblica italiana*
SAPERE	Scripta Antiquitatis Posterioris ad Ethicam Religionemque pertinentia
SBLDS	Society of Biblical Literature Dissertation Series
SBLSymS	Society of Biblical Literature Symposion Series
SCS	Septuagint and Cognate Studies
StBibLit	Studies in Biblical Literature (Lang)
STDJ	Studies on the Texts of the Desert of Judah
TLZ	*Theologische Literaturzeitung*
TWNT	*Theologisches Wörterbuch zum Neuen Testament*
UBS	United Bible Societies
VL	Vetus Latina: Die Reste der altlateinischen Bibel
VTSup	Supplements to Vetus Testamentum
WMANT	Wissenschaftliche Monographien zum Alten und Neuen Testament
WUNT	Welt und Umwelt des Neuen Testaments
ZDPV	*Zeitschrift des deutschen Palästina-Vereins*

INTRODUCTION

This collection of essays reflects recent changes in the discipline of biblical studies, which have led to renewed interest in two long neglected areas of study: early Jewish prayer and the deuterocanon, a collection of texts known from the ancient Greek translation of the Jewish Scriptures—the Septuagint. New energy surrounding the study of the deuterocanonical books and its associated literature is illustrated in part by the creation of the *International Society for Deuterocanonical and Cognate Literature* (ISDCL) in 2002 in Salzburg, Austria and the *Deuterocanonical and Cognate Literature Studies* series devoted to such topics published by de Gruyter press.[1] In the past five years, two SBL program units have been newly formed. The *Deuterocanonical and Cognate Literature* unit was founded in 2016 by Barbara Schmitz, Kristin De Troyer, and Frank Ueberschaer; and the *Prayer in Antiquity* unit was founded in 2015 by Rodney Werline and Daniel Falk. The latter began as a consultation that sought to examine the phenomenon of early Jewish prayer, a long neglected subject that was inadequately addressed by traditional historical-critical approaches, which focused on the canonical psalms alone. Interest in early Jewish prayer can be seen in the SBL "Penitential Prayer Consultation" in 2003–2005, which produced three volumes of collected essays that raised important methodological questions for future study.[2]

---

[1] Recent publications dealing with prayer from that series which may be of interest to readers of this collection are Stefan C. Reif and Renate Egger-Wenzel (ed.), *Ancient Jewish Prayers and Emotions: Emotions Associated with Jewish Prayer in and Around the Second Temple Period*, DCLS 26 (Berlin: de Gruyter, 2015) and Nuria Calduch-Benages, Michael W. Duggan, and Dalia Marx (ed.), *On Wings of Prayer. Sources of Jewish Worship. Essays in Honor of Professor Stefan C. Reif on the Occasion of his Seventy-fifth Birthday*, DCLS 44 (Berlin: de Gruyter, 2019). Other recent publications from that series are Kristin De Troyer and Barbara Schmitz (ed.), *The Early Reception of the Book of Isaiah*, DCLS 37 (Berlin: de Gruyter, 2019) and Kristin De Troyer, Barbara Schmitz, Joshua Alfaro, and Maximilian Häberlein (ed.), *The Early Reception of the Torah*, DCLS 39 (Berlin: de Gruyter, 2020).

[2] Mark J. Boda, Daniel K. Falk, and Rodney A. Werline (ed.), *Seeking the Favor of God: Volume 1, The Origins of Penitential Prayer in Second Temple Judaism*, EJL 21 (Atlanta: SBL, 2006); Boda, Falk, Werline (ed.), *Seeking the Favor of God: Volume 2, The Development of Penitential Prayer in Second Temple Judaism*, EJL 22 (Atlanta: SBL, 2007); Boda, Falk, Werline (ed.), *Seeking the Favor of God: Volume 3, The Impact of Penitential Prayer beyond Second Temple Judaism*, EJL 23 (Atlanta: SBL, 2008).

Since that consultation, the study of early Jewish prayer has steadily gained momentum, pushing past historical-critical, form-critical, and tradition-critical methodologies, which tend to reduce prayer to its canonical instantiations and textual forms. The *Prayer in Antiquity* program unit has also featured papers that use new methodologies to produce a "thick" cultural analysis so as to better understand prayer in specific contexts of lived experience and embodied practices.

Under the leadership of the co-chairs, Barbara Schmitz and Kristin De Troyer, and Angela Kim Harkins and Daniel Falk, these two SBL program units embarked on a fruitful collaboration that led to two joint sessions on prayer in the deuterocanonical books held at the SBL meeting in Denver, Colorado in 2018. We are grateful for the high quality of the papers in those sessions, many of which have been expanded and edited to become the core of this volume. Seven essays from these two joint sessions have been revised and expanded for publication in this volume: those of Samuel Balentine, Andrew Krause, Jennie Grillo, Beate Ego, Larry Wills, Barbara Schmitz, and Noah Hacham. In addition to the contributions from that 2018 SBL collaboration, this volume also includes contributions by Joseph P. Riordan, Matthew E. Gordley, Bradley C. Gregory, and Werner Urbanz.

The creation of the *Deuterocanonical and Cognate Literature* and *Prayer in Antiquity* SBL program units highlights the monumental shift in the study and understanding of the Second Temple period that has taken place in the twentieth-first century, effects of the 1947 discovery of the Dead Sea Scrolls. This discovery opened the door to a renewed interested in a time period that had been long overlooked. The full publication of this corpus in 2009 has made an enormous body of primary texts available to a readership that now reaches beyond Scrolls specialists. The 1947 discovery of the Scrolls also revitalized the study of many different kinds of Jewish literature that stood outside of the Hebrew Bible, resulting in increased scholarly attention to the Septuagint, a name given to different ancient Greek versions of the biblical books.[3] While these Greek versions were well known to scholars prior to the discovery of the Scrolls, they were regarded as tendentious translations and insignificant for textual criticism. The Septuagint was the ancient Scripture that was used by early Christians and Jews, and scholars viewed it as a translation with strong ideological or theological tendencies. These

---

[3] Timothy Michael Law, *When God Spoke Greek: The Septuagint and the Making of the Christian Bible* (New York: Oxford University Press, 2013).

views of the Septuagint have been upended by Scrolls scholarship of the
past generation.[4]

The biblical Dead Sea Scrolls have shown that early scholarly models
of textual development dramatically oversimplified the complex process
of transmission and underestimated the Septuagint as an ancient version.
The most famous of these early models was Frank Moore Cross's Theory
of Local Texts, which presumed three text types according to geographi-
cal regions: (1) the Palestinian, represented by the Samaritan Pentateuch;
(2) the Babylonian, a very early branching of the Palestinian text tradition
that continued to develop independently in Babylonia, represented by the
Masoretic Text (MT); and (3) the Egyptian, represented by the Septuagint. Just as the Septuagint is a term that stands for a number of different
versions of the ancient Greek, so too is the MT. While Cross's theory
was an early attempt to process and synthesize this new data from the
Scrolls, it has long been recognized as inadequate for understanding
the diversity of texts and traditions from the Second Temple period.
Cross's model has since been replaced by others that better account for
the great diversity of textual traditions in use prior to the destruction of
the Second Temple. In the process, questions have been raised about the
goals of textual criticism and the original text that it aims to reconstruct.
One of the major outcomes of these text-critical studies is a renewed
appreciation for the Greek versions known as the Septuagint and an
awareness of the undue scholarly bias toward the MT. Eugene C. Ulrich
writes, "Should not the object of the textual criticism of the Hebrew
Bible be not the single (and textually arbitrary?) collection of Masoretic
texts of the individual books, but the organic, developing, pluriform
Hebrew text—different for each book—such as the evidence indicates?"[5]
For example, the Qumran copies of Jeremiah from Cave 4, one of the last
Caves to be published, demonstrates that various textual traditions com-
fortably co-existed in the late Second Temple period. The Scrolls known
as 4QJer[b,d] exemplify how the Qumran discovery decentered the MT in
text-critical discussions and simultaneously transformed how the Septuagint was understood by scholars.

---

[4] Eugene C. Ulrich, "Double Literary Editions of Biblical Narratives and Reflections on
Determining the Form to Be Translated," in *The Dead Sea Scrolls and the Origins of
the Bible*, SDSSRL (Grand Rapids: Eerdmans, 1999), 34–50; Emanuel Tov, "The Qumran Hebrew Texts and the Septuagint—An Overview," in S. Kreuzer et al. (ed.), *Die
Septuaginta: Entstehung, Sprache, Geschichte* (Tübingen: Mohr Siebeck, 2012), 3–17.
[5] Ulrich, "The Community of Israel and the Composition of the Scriptures," in *The Dead
Sea Scrolls and the Origins of the Bible*, 15.

All of the essays in this collection deal in some way with the prayers known principally from the ancient Greek versions known collectively as the Septuagint, the study of which has changed dramatically in the past fifty years.[6] More specifically, these essays examine texts that are known as the deuterocanon, a name given to the books found in the Septuagint that are not found in the medieval Hebrew MT. While the nomenclature implies that these writings were additions to the ancient Greek versions and never a part of the Hebrew text tradition, it is the case that a first-century Hebrew copy of the deuterocanonical book of Sirach was discovered at Masada and the Hebrew text is also attested in the Cairo Genizah.[7] Qumran has also yielded five Semitic fragmentary copies of the book of Tobit from Cave 4 (4Q196–200).[8] The seven deuterocanonical books and additions are frequently grouped with other writings under the broader category of Apocrypha. Since the majority of essays in this volume began as conference papers in two joint sessions of the *Deuterocanonical and Cognate Literature* and *Prayer in Antiquity* program units, we, the editors, have chosen to use the more narrow designation "deuterocanonical studies" in the title.

Changing understandings of the Second Temple period during the twentieth and twenty-first centuries have also led to the realization that early Jewish prayers—texts that constitute nearly twenty percent of the Dead Sea Scrolls—were a significant but largely neglected area of study in classical biblical scholarship. The study of prayers and their ritual and emotional experiencing have long been overlooked in favor of more predictable inquiries into the literary forms and rhetorical structures of prayer studied as literature. In his book, *Prayer in the Hebrew Bible* (1993), Samuel E. Balentine describes the scholarly preference for rational intellectual analysis and the aversion to ritual or forms of piety.[9] Balentine offers some reasons for the systematic neglect of prayer in biblical studies, one of which is the scholarly preference for texts that more easily provide data needed for historical investigation. While inquiry into historical origins was a strong driver of the early scholarship

---

[6] Many of the recent changes to the field of Septuagint studies are described well by Law in *When God Spoke Greek*.

[7] Pancratius C. Beentjes, *The Book of Ben Sira in Hebrew: A Text Edition of All Extant Hebrew Manuscripts and a Synopsis of All Parallel Hebrew Ben Sira Texts*, VTSup 68 (Leiden: Brill, 1997).

[8] Joseph A. Fitzmyer, *Tobit*, CEJL (Berlin: de Gruyter, 2003), 18–27.

[9] Samuel E. Balentine, *Prayer in the Hebrew Bible: The Drama of Divine-Human Dialogue*, OBT (Minneapolis: Fortress, 1993), 10.

on the Qumran texts, the 1980s witnessed a significant decline in opti-
mism over what could reasonably be reconstructed of the Second Temple
period from the discovery.[10] The re-dating of the Qumran settlement from
the second century to the first century has also influenced the historical
study of the Scrolls.[11] The changing understandings of history have
opened the door to new approaches to studying prayer texts that might
make allusions to historical events but ultimately frustrate any attempt to
reconstruct history from them.[12] The essays in this volume offer exegetical and theological insights into these deuterocanonical prayers, paying
close attention to the way these prayers reflect and interact with their
larger narrative contexts. This consistent focus makes the *Contributions
to Biblical Exegesis and Theology* series an ideal venue for this
collection.

It is fitting that Balentine's contribution, "Prayer in the Hebrew Bible:
Retrospective and Prospective" stands as the lead essay in this collection.
Its title draws readers' attention to his foundational work of the same title
from 1993, a book that continues to be a crucial starting point for the
academic understanding of prayer. Balentine's discussion serves as
a bridge between the study of prayer in the Hebrew Bible and the study
of prayers from the late Second Temple period, highlighting many of the
new approaches being used today. Balentine's essay concludes with
a discussion of the horizontal dimensions of prayer—its sociological
effects—and the vertical aspects of prayer—its theological aim—when it
is understood as a means of communication with a transcendent deity.
Balentine sets the stage for Andrew Krause's essay, which focuses on
the otherworldly spatial imagery found in the Song of the Three Youths
(Dan 3:46–90 LXX). Krause places this within a wider Second Temple
milieu by comparing its cosmology to that found in certain prayers from
Qumran Cave 4, namely 4QBerakhot[a] and 4QDibHam[a].

---

[10] See Charlotte Hempel, *The Qumran Rule Texts in Context* (Tübingen: Mohr Siebeck, 2013), 5.

[11] Jodi Magness, *The Archaeology of Qumran and the Dead Sea Scrolls* (Grand Rapids: Eerdmans, 2002), 65.

[12] For a discussion of the problems with historical investigation into the prayers known as the Thanksgiving Hymns from Qumran, see Angela Kim Harkins, "Who is the Teacher of the Teacher Hymns? Re-examining the Teacher Hymns Hypothesis Fifty Years Later," in *A Teacher for All Generations: Essays in Honor of James C. VanderKam, 2 Vols.*, ed. Eric F. Mason et al., JSJSup 153 (Leiden: Brill, 2012), 2:449–67; eadem, "How Should We Feel about the Teacher of Righteousness?" in *Is there a Text in this Cave? Studies in the Textuality of the Dead Sea Scrolls in Honour of George J. Brooke*, STDJ 119, ed. Ariel Feldman, Maria Cioată, and Charlotte Hempel (Leiden: Brill, 2017), 493–514.

The remaining essays in the collection are organized into two groups, the first of which discusses how inset prayers interact with their larger narrative context. Jennie Grillo's essay, "Prayer as Mnemonic for the Book of Daniel," describes how artistic depictions of a praying figure in a place of peril play a key role in the reception of the book of Daniel. These images of a praying figure emerge from the Greek versions and the Additions to the book of Daniel, which are not present in the MT. Daniel praying in the lions' den, a scene known from the long versions of chapter 3, comes to be used for other virtuous characters of the Daniel traditions, such as Azariah in the furnace or Susanna in the garden. Grillo's essay illustrates well how this exegetical process, which includes both texts and images, pivots on the image of an individual in a posture of prayer.

Grillo's essay is followed by the essays of Beate Ego, Lawrence M. Wills, and Barbara Schmitz, all of which discuss narrative prayers ascribed to women in the deuterocanon. Beate Ego's essay evaluates the central importance of Esther's prayer in Addition C to LXX Esther by exploring how its structure and motifs interact with the larger Greek Book of Esther. She then takes up Johannes Marböck's claim that the prayer is "a sum of the Greek interpretation of the Hebrew Book" by pointing out how the motifs of sin and guilt and the complex transformation of the character of Esther constitute a rewriting of the Hebrew Esther story for audiences in the time of Antiochus IV. Ego's essay is followed by two discussions of the prayers in Judith. The first of these is Lawrence M. Wills's fresh study of the pivotal prayer in Judith 9. Building on the earlier work of Barbara Schmitz (2004), which notes the contrasting role of the prayers and speeches, on the one hand, and the larger narrative flow, on the other, Wills artfully explores how Judith's prayer could be said to exert a control on how readers understand the larger novella, and how it can be seen as an ironic commentary and even a transgression of the narrative itself. The second essay on Judith is by Barbara Schmitz, who focuses on the importance of the two prayers prayed by Judith prior to her dramatic decapitation of Holofernes in the Greek and Latin versions of chapter 13. Schmitz explores the placement, content, and function of these two prayers within the storyline of the LXX version of the book of Judith and compares them in light of the considerably different Vulgate version of the book of Judith. Schmitz notes the differences in the textual history of the Judith narrative and highlights the different theological perspectives of each version.

Noah Hacham's essay contrasts standard citations of and allusions to the verse "I did not despise them" (Lev 26:44) with its depiction in Eleazar's prayer in 3 Macc. The prayer's structure and content show that it depicts the plotline of 3 Macc by using historical precedents to allude to figures of the book. Furthermore, a close look at divine epithets and the references to gentiles, Jewish life outside the land of Israel, and epiphany provides insights into the diasporan theological view of the book's author. Overall, Eleazar's prayer and its use of the citation, "I did not despise them" is one that fits precisely into the theological and literary context. This group of essays ends with that of Joseph P. Riordan, "Long Live Zion: The Meaning of σκηνή in Tob 13:10 (G^{II}, VL)." Riordan begins with the question of the relationship between the hymn in Tob 13 and the larger narrative. His text-critical discussion of the tent imagery in Tob 13:10 argues in favor of understanding the city of Jerusalem as the "tent" of Zion. Riordan's study exemplifies how Second Temple Studies has led to the revitalization of text-critical questions about the Septuagint.

The final three essays explore the role of prayer in the deuterocanonical wisdom books. The first of these is by Matthew E. Gordley, who examines how references to prayer in the book of Wisdom interact within the larger literary work, reflecting larger cultural inflections from the Hellenistic world. His essay is an expansion of his paper that was presented in the *Prayer in Antiquity* session held at the SBL meeting in San Diego, CA in 2019. Gordley's contribution is followed by two studies of prayer and its role in moral formation in Sirach. Bradley C. Gregory's essay examines how self-control is highlighted in the first of three prayers in Sir 22:27–23:6, discussing how vice is described in this prayer and relating it to Second Temple Judaism and other classical texts. The final essay in the collection, "Spiritual Exercises in Sirach and the Role of Prayer" by Werner Urbanz, brings us back to the opening theological perspective of Samuel Balentine. Urbanz examines the specific theological significance of prayer and its didactic purpose in Sirach by outlining how prayer is set in the context of spiritual exercises, spiritual education, and the pursuit of wisdom. His essay highlights the numerous ways the author of Sirach presents prayer within a larger program of spiritual exercises that ultimately works to transform the one who prays.

The exegetical discussions of the various prayers in the deuterocanon makes the *Contributions to Biblical Exegesis and Theology* series a fitting home for these essays. We hope that this collection will be of use to students and scholars alike who desire a deeper understanding of the prayers in the deuterocanonical books, and that it would stimulate further work on these texts. We wish to express our gratitude to Peeters Press and especially to Kristin De Troyer for her support and encouragement in publishing this collection in the CBET series.

Angela Kim Harkins
and Barbara Schmitz
July 2020

PRAYER IN THE HEBREW BIBLE: RETROSPECTIVE AND PROSPECTIVE

Samuel E. BALENTINE

> It is a difficult and even formidable thing to write on prayer, and one
> fears to touch the Ark.
>
> P. T. Forsyth, *The Soul of Prayer* (1915)

It has been twenty-five years since I used these words from Scottish theo-
logian P. T. Forsyth to introduce my book, *Prayer in the Hebrew Bible:
The Drama of Divine-Human Dialogue*.[1] Writing under the death clouds
of World War I, Forsyth understood that any attempt to analyze the *soul*
of prayer—language that clearly demarcates an interior spirituality that
should leave prayer untouched by scholarly critique[2]—was bound to meet
with resistance, if not outright rejection. With the benefit of 1993 hindsight, I noted that Forsyth's judgment had been prescient.

For most of the first part of the twentieth century scholars focused on
the phenomenology of prayer, especially Friedrich Heiler's distinction
between prayer that emerges out of the free and "spontaneous utterings
of the soul," which Heiler judged to be "genuine prayer," and formal,
literary prayers, which he considered to be only "faint reflections" of the
genuine article.[3] Biblical scholars largely accepted this distinction, but
they conceptualized it as a distinction between cultic, prosodic prayers
and non-cultic, prosaic prayers. With Hermann Gunkel and Sigmund
Mowinckel, the Psalms emerged as the primary deposit of biblical

---

[1] The conference paper version of this essay took place at the annual meeting of the SBL
in 2018, twenty-five years after the publication of my book, *Prayer in the Hebrew Bible:
The Drama of Divine-Human Dialogue*, OBT (Minneapolis: Augsburg Fortress, 1993).

[2] I appropriate the language of William James, who argued that because prayer is the
movement of the soul that puts one in personal relationship with the mysterious power
of God, "we can easily see that scientific criticism leaves it untouched", see William
James, *Varieties of Religious Experience: Introduction and Notes by Wayne Proudfoot*
(New York: Barnes & Noble Classics, 2004 [originally published 1902]), 400. See
further below.

[3] Friedrich Heiler, *Prayer: A Study in the History and Psychology of Religion* (Oxford:
Oxford University Press, 1932 [1918]), xvii–xviii.

prayer,[4] and with Claus Westermann, Walter Brueggemann, and others, two particular kinds of psalmic prayer, lament and praise, provided the dominant perspective for understanding the function of prayer in ancient Israel's cultic worship.[5] Prose prayers embedded in narrative contexts, by way of contrast, were largely regarded as merely literary creations and were therefore mostly neglected, until Moshe Greenberg's short but seminal study demonstrated that they reflected authentic interhuman discourse that provided a resource for understanding the "unmediated, direct forms of popular piety."[6] My own work built upon Greenberg's discernments by offering a more expansive discussion of prose prayers as literary vehicles for the depiction of both divine and human character, for addressing theodic issues, and for conceptualizing a divine-human dialogic relationship that may be theologically constructive in the modern world. By the end of the twentieth century, after decades of scholarly neglect, study of the prayers of the Old Testament, both psalmic and non-psalmic, had moved from the periphery of our work to a place more centrally connected to our primary interests. To return to Forsyth's pithy language, biblical scholars had dared to touch the Ark.

My assignment is to offer a retrospective on where our work on the prayers of the Old Testament has gone during the course of the last twenty-five years and a prospective of where it might be going in the future.[7] Like the Roman god Janus—but without any claim to divinity—

---

[4] Hermann Gunkel and Joachim Begrich, *Einleitung in die Psalmen*, 3rd ed. (Göttingen: Vandenhoeck & Ruprecht, 1966 [1933]); ET: *An Introduction to the Psalms*, trans. Mark E. Biddle (Macon, GA: Mercer University Press, 1998); Sigmund Mowinckel, *Psalmenstudien*, 6 vols. (Kristiania: J. Dybwad, 1921–1924); ET: *Psalm Studies*, trans. Mark E. Biddle, 2 vols. (Atlanta: SBL Press, 2014).

[5] Claus Westermann, *The Praise of God in the Psalms*, trans. Keith R. Crim (Richmond: John Knox, 1965); idem, *Praise and Lament in the Psalms*, trans. Keith R. Crim and Richard N. Soulen (Atlanta: John Knox, 1981); idem, *Elements of Old Testament Theology*, trans. Douglas W. Scott (Atlanta: John Knox, 1982); see for example Walter Brueggemann, *The Message of the Psalms: A Theological Commentary* (Minneapolis: Augsburg Fortress, 1984); idem, *Israel's Praise: Doxology Against Idolatry and Ideology* (Philadelphia: Fortress Press, 1988); idem, *Theology of the Old Testament: Testimony, Dispute, Advocacy* (Minneapolis: Augsburg Fortress, 1997); cf. Leo Krinetzki, *Israels Gebet im Alten Testament* (Aschaffenburg: Paul Pattloch, 1965); Erhard S. Gerstenberger, *Der bittende Mensch* (Neukirchen-Vluyn: Neukirchener Verlag, 1980); Henning Graf Reventlow, *Gebet im Alten Testament* (Stuttgart: Kohlhammer, 1986).

[6] Moshe Greenberg, *Biblical Prose Prayer As a Window to the Popular Religion of Ancient Israel*, The Taubman Lectures in Jewish Studies 6 (Berkeley: University of California Press, 1983); cf. Adolf Wendel, *Das freie Laiengebet im vorexilischen Israel* (Leipzig: Eduard Pfeiffer, 1931).

[7] For overviews of the history of biblical scholarship on prayer, see, e.g., Samuel E. Balentine, *Prayer in the Hebrew Bible*, 13–32, 225–59; Reventlow, *Das Gebet*, 9–80;

I am to stand between past and future and look in both directions at the same time. Sometimes "what's past is prologue," as Shakespeare puts it (*The Tempest*, 2.1), and thus it sets the table for what comes next. Sometimes what's past is simply past; an insight, an observation that once seemed new and promising looks now, in retrospect, more like an artifact. And sometimes the lines between what has been and what will be are unclear. To appropriate the words of one of Hawthorne's characters in *The Scarlet Letter*, when it comes to writing prospectives and retrospectives, I find myself standing in "neutral territory, somewhere between the real world and fairyland, where the actual and the imaginary can meet, and each imparts its nature to the other."[8]

In what follows, I identify four areas of our work that seem to me important for the task before us: 1) the genealogy of lament and penitence;[9] 2) prayer as religious practice and experience; 3) cross-cultural perspectives on prayer; and 4) prayer's intellectual vulnerability. The sequencing does not imply a hierarchical order, and I make no attempt to allocate equal space to each topic. As closing thoughts (not conclusion) I will offer brief comments on a meta issue that might provide context for thinking about underlying and lingering theological issues: the lure of transcendence and the audacity of prayer.

The Genealogy of Lament and Penitence

Westermann identified praise and lament as the two primary types of prayer in ancient Israel, and he provided substantive analysis and theological commentary on both these genres. Although praise prayer has continued to receive attention in the wake of his work,[10] the lament genre, especially the evolution of lament into penitence, has emerged as a primary concern for contemporary scholars. We are indebted to Richard Bautch, Mark Boda, Daniel Falk, Judith Newman, and Rodney Werline

---

Michael Widmer, *Moses, God, and the Dynamics of Intercessory Prayer*, FAT 2/8 (Tübingen: Mohr Siebeck, 2004), 9–56; Sam Gill, "Prayer," *ER* 11:489–93. For a recent overview of prose prayer, see Suk-il Ahn, *The Persuasive Portrayal of David and Solomon in Chronicles: A Rhetorical Analysis of the Speeches and Prayers in the David-Solomon Narrative*, McMaster Biblical Studies Series 3 (Eugene, OR: Pickwick, 2018).

[8] Nathaniel Hawthorne, *The Scarlet Letter* (New York: Vintage Books, 2014 [1850]), 38.

[9] I appropriate the idea of a "genealogy" of penitence from David Lambert, *How Repentance Became Biblical: Judaism, Christianity, and the Interpretation of Scripture* (Oxford: Oxford University Press, 2015). See further the discussion below.

[10] E.g., Frank Crüsemann, *Studien zur Formgeschichte von Hymnus und Danklied in Israel*, WMANT 32 (Neukirchen-Vluyn: Neukirchener Verlag, 1969); Brueggemann, *Israel's Praise*.

for organizing the SBL Penitential Prayer consultation group, which focused on this topic over a three year period (2003–2005), and especially for their leadership in publishing three volumes setting forth new perspectives on the origin, development, and impact of penitential prayer in and beyond Second Temple Judaism.[11] I need not repeat this good work here, but I will highlight several of the important findings.

Following Westermann, discussion of penitential prayer had been limited primarily to four paradigmatic prose texts that were judged to be exemplars of a post exilic shift away from prayers of lament and complaint to prayers that accented confession of sin and petition for forgiveness: Ezra 9:6–15; Neh 1:5–11, 9:6–37; and Dan 9:4–19. The shift from lament to penitence was typically explained as the consequence of the historical trauma of the exile, which necessitated heavy reliance on the sin-punishment-repentance theology embedded in the Deuteronomic tradition.

The Penitential Prayer group analyzed a larger corpus of texts from across the wider history of Judaism and Christianity (including late antiquity and medieval periods). This more expansive diachronic trajectory problematized the narrowly focused form-critical perspective of previous work by identifying multiple contexts (liturgical, psychological, social-cultural) that shaped these prayers and the more complex ways in which they reused and reinterpreted biblical penitential traditions. It also problematized the rather simplistic theological interpretation of these prayers that Westermann and others had offered. If petitionary prayers (and prayer texts) with penitential elements are trans-historical and adaptable to diverse social and cultural contexts, then interpreting them as only or primarily theological vehicles expressing moral contrition is insufficient. On this latter point, David Lambert's recent analysis of repentance as a cultural construction for shaping communal discipline and defining communal boundaries has pointed us in new and promising directions.[12]

Lambert's argument is complex, and I cannot do it justice in this context, but I do want to single out several aspects of his hermeneutics of repentance that are pertinent for our future work on prayer. He contends that our continuing use of the form-critical designation "penitential prayer" has had the effect of nominalizing repentance in ancient Israel as a specialized form of religious speech. We have tended to import into

---

[11] Mark Boda, Daniel Falk, and Rodney Werline, eds., *Seeking the Favor of God*, EJL 21–23, 3 vols. (Atlanta: SBL Press, 2006).

[12] Lambert, *How Repentance Became Biblical*. Lambert was a participant in the 2005 Penitential Prayer consultation, but his paper ("Reconsidering the 'Penitence' in Penitential Prayers") was not included in the published volume.

these texts a spiritualized piety that they do not presuppose. Lambert's alternative approach is to examine the "logic of appeal" that is an intuitive part of everyday speech, especially in situations where pain and suffering threaten a diminishment of self. Viewed from this perspective, petitions for divine intervention presuppose a double agency: for the individual or community in distress, the petition is an autonomous, self-generated cry for help that is effective in calling an otherwise uninvolved God into action; for God, human appeal affirms that God is an agent empowered to relieve distress, if not always for altruistic reasons then at least out of self-interest.[13] The appeal is therefore essentially non-penitential; it is instead part of a natural behavioral pattern that is mutually beneficial for both parties in the relationship.[14] With his attention to the agency of petition, Lambert anticipates what I think should be an important focus for our future work. I will return to this point below.

Prayer as Religious Experience and Practice

In his seminal work published in 1903, *The Varieties of Religious Experience*, William James argued that prayer is the movement of the soul that puts one in personal relationship with the mysterious power of God. James understood this interior, intimate, unmediated communion with God to be definitively non-rational. For him, the experience and practice of prayer was effectively sequestered in subjectivity; as he put it, "we can easily see that scientific criticism leaves it untouched."[15] James's work had little impact on biblical studies, but it was enormously influential in identifying the phenomenon of prayer as an object for study within the History of Religions school (e.g., E.B. Tylor, Robertson Smith, James Frazier, Mircea Eliade).

A significant development in our work over the last twenty-five years has been the effort by biblical scholars to pry open this black box of subjectivity and reclaim the religious experience of prayer as a subject for constructive critical analysis.[16] For this work we are especially indebted to the SBL group on "Religious Experience in Early Christianity

---

[13] Ibid., 35.
[14] Ibid., 54. As Lambert puts it, "Each party acts according to the dictates of its nature (expressing pain and relieving pain, respectively). Quite apart from any discourse around morality, from these natural, social elements, a moral system emerges", ibid., 36.
[15] James, *Varieties of Religious Experience*, 400.
[16] Colleen Shantz, "Opening the Black Box: New Prospects for Analyzing Religious Experience," in *Linking Text and Experience*, ed. Colleen Shantz and Rodney Werline, vol. 2 of *Experientia*, EJL 35 (Atlanta: SBL Press, 2012), 1–16.

and Judaism" (organized in 2005), which has thus far published two volumes of essays.[17] One of the strengths of this group has been its wide-angled approach to the study of religious experience. I single out two aspects of their work that I think will continue to merit close attention: the summons for a more nuanced cultural-anthropological approach to prayer, and the call for a more rigorous integration of the work being done in the field of the Cognitive Science of Religion.

More sophisticated cultural-anthropological approaches to the study of religion have expanded our understanding of what constitutes religious experience. Whereas James focused on intensely personal encounters with the divine that were primarily mystical in nature, we now have a clearer understanding of how religious rites and practices in and of themselves become religious experiences, experiences that in turn both shape and are shaped by culturally constructed givens. Ongoing work in social and cultural anthropology provides a theoretical framework for analyzing prayer as an embodiment of cultural values deemed authoritative and necessary for the maintenance of the community.[18] Both individual and corporate prayers may be culturally constrained by regnant expectations of what is to be affirmed with praise and thanksgiving or scrutinized with lament and protest, what is to be confessed and judged as sin and what may be forgiven by divine grace. For biblical scholars, the cultural anatomy of prayer invites analysis of its use and function within the shifting political dynamics of ancient Israel and Second Temple Judaism. One objective for future research should be a comprehensive examination of the politics of prayer.[19]

On the other hand, ritual theorists have demonstrated that religious rites and practices, including prayer, enable participants to construct alternatives to present realties that can be actualized by living "as if" they can happen in historical time.[20] Biblical scholars have constructively

---

[17] Frances Flannery, Colleen Shantz, and Rodney Werline, eds., *Inquiry into Religious Experience in Early Judaism and Early Christianity*, vol. 1 of *Experientia*, SBLSymS 40 (Atlanta: SBL Press, 2008); Shantz and Werline, *Linking Text and Experience*.

[18] E.g., Clifford Geertz, *The Interpretation of Cultures* (New York: Basic Books, 1977); Pierre Bourdieu, *Outline of a Theory of Practices* (Cambridge: Cambridge University Press, 1977).

[19] On a related topic see, for example, W. S. Morrow, "The Politics of Worship," in *The Oxford Handbook of Ritual and Worship*, ed. S. E. Balentine (Oxford: Oxford University Press, 2020), 427–444.

[20] E.g., Victor Turner, *The Ritual Process: Structure and Anti-Structure* (Chicago: Aldine, 1966); Arnold van Gennep, *The Rites of Passage* (Chicago: Chicago University Press, 1960 [1909]); Roy Rappaport, *Ritual and Religion in the Making of Humanity*, Cambridge Studies in Social and Cultural Anthropology 110 (Cambridge: Cambridge

harvested the work of ritual theorists, especially in the examination of ritual texts and cultic practices like sacrifices and offerings, but thus far prayer has been an outlier in this approach.[21] Some attention has been given to prayer as "performative speech," following the work of John Austin and John Searle, but thus far this work does not seem to have gained much traction.[22]

More promising, I think, is the work on prayer as a mode of constructing identity and human agency that Carol Newsom and others have begun.[23] Of particular interest is her examination of the Qumran prayer texts known as the Hodayot or Thanksgiving Psalms and the kinds of religious experiences they induce. She focuses on the use of the first-person singular language in these prayers, which both linguistically and ideationally establishes the speaker's role as an active subject—not merely a passive object—in a "figured" or "imagined" world.[24] The "I" of the prayer constructs his own identity, claims his own experiences, and declares his own capacity for purposive action.[25] In the community at

---

University Press, 1999); Catherine Bell, *Ritual Theory, Ritual Practice* (Oxford: Oxford University Press, 1999).

[21] E.g., Roy Gane, *Cult and Character: Purification Offerings, Day of Atonement, and Theodicy* (Winona Lake, IN: Eisenbrauns, 2005); Gerald Klingbeil, *Bridging the Gap: Ritual and Ritual Texts in the Bible*, BBRSup 1 (Winona Lake, IN: Eisenbrauns, 2007); Ithamar Gruenwald, *Rituals and Ritual Theory in Ancient Israel*, BRLA 10 (Atlanta: SBL Press, 2003).

[22] E.g., Jay C. Hogewood, "The Speech Act of Confession: Priestly Performative Utterance in Leviticus 16 and Ezra 9-10," in *The Origins of Penitential Prayer in Second Temple Judaism*, vol. 1 of Boda, Falk and Werline, *Seeking the Face of God*, 69–82.

[23] E.g., Carol A. Newsom, "Religious Experience in the Dead Sea Scrolls: Two Case Studies," in Shantz and Werline, *Linking Text and Experience*, 205–22; cf. eadem, *The Self as Symbolic Space: Constructing Identity and Community at Qumran*, STDJ 52 (Leiden: Brill, 2004; repr., Atlanta: SBL Press, 2007). For further reading on the general issue of moral agency, see eadem, "Models of the Moral Self: Hebrew Bible and Second Temple Judaism," *JBL* 131 (2012): 5–25; eadem, "Moral Recipes in Deuteronomy and Ezekiel: Divine Authority and Human Agency," *HBAI* 6 (2017): 488–509; Jacqueline Lapsley, *Can These Bones Live? The Problem of the Moral Self in the Book of Ezekiel*, BZAW 301 (Berlin: de Gruyter, 2000); Brennan Breed, David Hankins, and Robert Williamson Jr., eds., "Writing the Moral Self: Essays in Honor of Carol A. Newsom," *JSOT* 40 (2015): 3–135; Anne W. Stewart, *Poetic Ethics in Proverbs: Wisdom Literature and the Shaping of the Moral Self* (Cambridge: Cambridge University Press, 2016); eadem, "Models of Moral Agency in the Hebrew Bible," in *Oxford Research Encyclopedia of the Bible*, ed. John Barton (Online Publication; November 2016; religion. oxfordre.com); Yitzhaq Feder, ed., "Moral Norm Formation and Transformation in Ancient Israel," *HBAI* 6 (2017): 383–526.

[24] On "figured worlds," see Dorothy Holland et al., *Identity and Agency in Cultural Worlds* (Cambridge: Harvard University Press, 1998), 49–63.

[25] On the rhetorical "I" and embodied subjectivity in the Hodayot psalms, see Angela Kim Harkins, *Reading with an "I" to the Heavens: Looking at the Qumran Hodayot through the Lens of Visionary Traditions*, Ekstasis 3 (Berlin: de Gruyter, 2012).

Qumran, these once-oral-now-textualized prayers provide a model for other members of the community who will recite them; they will step into the speaking self of the prayer, re-experience its thinking from the inside, and thus recalibrate their capacity to alter their circumstances. After immersing themselves in the "society of the text," community members step back into their everyday lives, now imaginatively recreated by their apprehension of alternative and transcendent realties.[26]

In the Hodayot prayers, a critical aspect of this transformation of self is a paradoxical construction of the speaker's knowledge and moral capacity.[27] On the one hand, the speaker acknowledges that his capacity for knowledge is a gift from God;[28] on the other, the speaker simultaneously recognizes that in the act of praying, he has experienced a "distinctive dynamic within his own psyche" that calls forth and intensifies his capacity not only to know about the world of God's design but also to act upon it meaningfully and reflectively. Although it is not Newsom's primary objective, I suggest that her work will seed future efforts to analyze the epistemological assumptions underlying models of moral agency in the prayers of Hebrew Bible (see further below).

A second area of research into religious experience is located in the field of the cognitive science of religion (CSR). Since the 1980s CSR has emerged as a subdiscipline of religious studies and has developed an increasingly sophisticated approach to understanding the neurobiology of religious ideation. Neuroscience provides models for understanding that prayer is not only culturally constructed and socially enacted in accord with prevailing norms and values; it is also connected in some causal way to the neural architecture of the brain, which predisposes human beings, in whatever cultural or social situation they may inhabit, to conceptualize a supernatural dimension to life.[29] Simply put, our brains are prewired

---

[26] For this way of describing the "uniquely re-utterable" aspect of ritually oriented prayers, I have appropriated the language of F. W. Dobbs-Allsopp in *On Biblical Poetry* (Oxford: Oxford University Press, 2015), 206.

[27] Newsom, "Religious Experience in the Dead Sea Scrolls," 212.

[28] E.g., "you [God] have caused me to know" (1QH XII, 28); "I know by means of the spirit that you have placed in me" (1QH V, 6); for these and other references, see ibid., 212–4.

[29] E.g., Brian J. Scholl and Patrice D. Tremoulet, "Perceptual Causality and Animacy," *Trends in Cognitive Science* 4 (2000): 299–308; Justin L. Barrett, *Cognitive Science, Religion, and Theology: From Human Minds to Divine Minds* (West Conshohocken, PA: Templeton Press, 2012), 96–112. For recent discussion, see, for example, Neil Van Leeuwen and Michiel van Elk, "Seeking the Supernatural: The Interactive Religious Experience," *Religion, Brain, and Behavior* 9 (2019): 221–75.

for prayer.[30] Until quite recently, Biblical scholars have seldom transgressed their own methodologies to avail themselves of this research, and when they have, their focus has been on the neuroscience of religious experience in a more general way, not specifically on the practice of prayer.[31]

The recent work by Judith Newman is a welcomed sign that this situation may be about to change.[32] Newman has intentionally adopted an intradisciplinary approach that draws upon anthropology, ritual theory, and neuroscience to examine the growing importance of prayer and liturgical activity in the post-exilic period. She argues that prayer provides a critical link between the engagement of scripture and an ensuing revelation from God. Before one prays there is a text to be understood, e.g., Daniel's need to decipher Jeremiah's prophecy about the length of the exile (Dan 9:1–2). After Daniel prays (9:4–19), he receives "wisdom and understanding" through divine revelation (9:22–27; cf. Bar 1:15–3:18). The practice of prayer is therefore at the center of an intellectual endeavor. It may be viewed through the lens of neuroscience as part of a cognitive process in which a person's natural self is decentered and then suspended—via a prayer addressed to a supernatural agent—in a suppositional space of possible thoughts and behaviors that will better match the needs of the moment. Ultimately, the natural self is integrated into a new self, a new self-identity, and a transformed consciousness of agency.[33] As

---

[30] Cognitive scientists distinguish between "hardwiring," which connotes fixed and non-malleable neural circuitry, and "pre-wiring," which allows for social and cultural influence on the cognitive process.

[31] E.g., István Czachesz, "The Emergence of Early Christian Religion: A Naturalistic Approach," in *Explaining Christian Origins and Early Judaism: Contributions from Cognitive and Social Science*, ed. Petri Luomanen, Ilkka Pyysiäinen, and Risto Uro, BibInt 89 (Leiden: Brill, 2007), 73–94; idem, "Filled with New Wine? Religious Experience and Social Dynamics in the Corinthian Church," in Shantz and Werline, *Linking Text and Experience*, 71–90; István Czachesz and Tamás Biró, "Introduction," in *Changing Minds: Religion and Cognition through the Ages*, ed. idem (Leuven: Peeters, 2011), ix–xvi; István Czachesz and Risto Uro, eds., *Mind, Morality and Magic: Cognitive Science Approaches in Biblical Studies* (New York: Routledge, 2013); Colleen Shantz, *Paul in Ecstasy: The Neurobiology of the Apostle's Life and Thought* (Cambridge: Cambridge University Press, 2009).

[32] Judith H. Newman, *Before the Bible: The Liturgical Body and the Formation of Scripture in Early Judaism* (Oxford: Oxford University Press, 2018).

[33] For the neuroscience of the "decentering" process, Newman draws upon the work of Patrick McNamara, *The Neuroscience of Religious Experience* (Cambridge: Cambridge University Press, 2009). McNamara refers to the "suppositional space" opened up by religious practices like prayer as the "possible world's box" (50, et passim).

I noted above, moral agency is a theme addressed by David Lambert and Carol Newsom as well.

Newman identifies this decentering process with the scripturalization of prayer and prayer texts that takes place in the Hellenistic-Roman period (e.g., Daniel, Ben Sira, Baruch, the Qumran Hodayot), but I would argue that something of the same cognitive process along with its impact on one's understanding of moral agency is at work in the prayers of the Hebrew Bible as well. Newman has demonstrated the benefit of a cross-disciplinary approach to this matter, and we may hope that future studies will follow her lead and build upon her insights.

Cross-Cultural Perspectives

During the early decades of the twentieth century, when the phenomenology of prayer was a prominent subject for investigation in the History of Religion school, cross cultural comparisons were common. When biblical scholars effectively siloed prayer inside their own methodologies, cross-cultural perspectives were largely sidelined. On the Old Testament (and deutero-canonical) side of our discipline, we contextualize the study of prayer within the cultures of the Levant; on the New Testament side, we typically expand that context to include the Greco-Roman world. In neither case have we typically placed biblical prayer in critical conversation with prayers, meditations, chants, psychic musings, or other forms of spiritual discourse that occur outside monotheistic religions or in a-theistic cultures.

An important exception has been the work of the SBL group on Lament in Sacred Texts and Cultures, especially the multiple publications by Nancy Lee, a cofounder of this group.[34] Lee has connected lament in Abrahamic sacred texts (Jewish, Christian, and Muslim) with motifs across cultures that reflect a common concern with suffering. Her objective is to examine how diverse cultures create space for lamentation in public expression or in ritual/liturgical performance. She finds that people not only participate in and conserve spiritual practices embedded in local sacred texts; they also innovate these practices by addressing

---

[34] Nancy C. Lee, *The Singers of Lamentations: Cities Under Siege from Ur to Jerusalem to Sarajevo*, BibInt 60 (Leiden: Brill, 2002); Nancy C. Lee and Carleen Mandolfo, *Lamentations in Ancient and Contemporary Cultural Contexts*, SBLSymS 43 (Atlanta: SBL Press, 2008); Nancy C. Lee, *Lyrics of Lament: From Tragedy to Transformation* (Minneapolis: Fortress Press, 2010); cf. idem, *Hannev'ah and Hannah: Hearing Women Biblical Prophets in a Woman's Lyrical Tradition* (Eugene, OR: Cascade, 2015).

suffering through contemporary poems, songs, and other lyrics of distress. From this cross-cultural perspective it becomes clear that the composition and performance of lament is a global practice. Whether in Asia, Africa, or the Americas, lamentation provides a constructive means for addressing the sociopolitical and religious challenges of the day.

Lee's work is at its core a theological summons to the community of faith to participate in a global discourse of empowerment in the face of violence and injustice in its many forms. Beyond this, however, it is also an important reminder to biblical scholars that biblical texts are not the only sacred texts in the world and that, when it comes to a critical analysis of prayer, a cross cultural perspective will likely complexify settled (Western) assessments and open them up to new and generative scrutiny.

Prayer's Intellectual Vulnerability

Underlying all of the work referenced above is what Gerhard Ebeling calls prayer's "intellectual vulnerability."[35] Ebeling refers to the essential subjectivity of prayer that places it in a category of human experience that can neither be empirically verified nor logically falsified. But it seems to me that his description of prayer can be interpreted in different ways. For those who view prayer as the quintessential encounter of the human soul with the divine, its *in*vulnerability to intellectual scrutiny is a comfort not a burden. An aphorism from the German romantic poet Novalis is apt: "Praying is to religion what thinking is to philosophy."[36] William James puts the same perspective in a slightly different way: without prayer, he says, "religion is only a philosophy." Suffice it to say that for James the equation of religion and philosophy was not a good thing.[37] However, for those who wish to examine the intellectual world in which prayer is meaningful and efficacious, its *vulnerability* to critical investigation is what makes it an interesting subject. Our work to date on more nuanced ways of understanding religious experience, including its neurocognitive aspects, has gone a long way towards opening up the

---

[35] Gerhard Ebeling, *Dogmatik des christlichen Glaubens I* (Tübingen: Mohr Siebeck, 1979), 209. For this reference, I am indebted to Widmer, *Moses, God, and the Dynamics of Intercessory Prayer*, 4.

[36] Novalis, *Blüthenstaub* (1798); cited in Heiler, *Prayer*, xiii.

[37] James, *Varieties of Religious Experience*, 400: "Born at epochs of rationalism, of critical investigations, it [philosophy] was never anything but an abstraction. An artificial and dead creation, it reveals to its examiner hardly one of the characters proper to religion."

"black box" of prayer's subjectivity, as my comments above have noted. But I suggest there is more to be discovered in this area, especially by assessing the epistemic map of prayer.

A number of recent studies have focused on biblical epistemology, but thus far prayer has not been a primary object of the investigation.[38] As we look to this as one of our future areas of work, I suggest the following questions will be pertinent:[39]

— What were assumed to be the necessary and sufficient conditions for prayer, that is, what were the epistemological assumptions in the world of the text about the nature and character of God? The nature and character of human beings? The moral order of the cosmos?
— Why, according to the text, is prayer possible, desirable, necessary, efficacious?
— What, according to the text, is prayer expected to do?
— What, according to the text, can prayer *not* be expected to do?
— What access to knowledge do people have in the world of the text?
— Is there access to knowledge apart from God?

Closing Thoughts: The Lure of Transcendence and the Audacity of Prayer

I close with a few words about a meta theological issue that should not be lost in our thinking about prayer as both a spiritual practice and an

---

[38] E.g., Yael Avrahami, *Senses of Scripture: Sensory Perceptions in the Hebrew Bible*, LHBOTS 545 (New York: T&T Clark, 2013); Michael Carasik, *Theologies of the Mind in Biblical Israel*, StBibLit 85 (New York: Peter Lang, 2006); Jaco Gericke, *The Hebrew Bible and Philosophy of Religion*, RBS 70 (Atlanta: SBL Press, 2012); Yoram Hazony, *The Philosophy of Hebrew Scripture* (Cambridge: Cambridge University Press, 2012); Mary Healy and Robin Parry, eds., *The Bible and Epistemology: Biblical Soundings of the Knowledge of God* (Colorado Springs: Paternoster, 2007); Dru Johnson, *Biblical Knowing: A Scriptural Epistemology of Error* (Eugene, OR: Cascade, 2013); idem, *Knowledge by Ritual: A Biblical Prolegomenon to Sacramental Theology*, JTISup 13 (Winona Lake, IN: Eisenbrauns, 2016); idem, *Epistemology and Biblical Theology: From the Pentateuch to the Gospel of Mark* (New York: Routledge, 2017); Ryan O'Dowd, *The Wisdom of Torah: Epistemology in Deuteronomy and the Wisdom Literature*, FRLANT 225 (Göttingen: Vandenhoeck & Ruprecht, 2009); Ian W. Scott, *Paul's Way of Knowing: Story, Experience, and the Spirit* (Grand Rapids, MI: Baker Academic, 2008); cf. Robert S. Kawashima, "Conclusion: Toward an Archaeology of Ancient Israelite Knowledge," in *Biblical Narrative and the Death of the Rhapsode* (Bloomington, IN: Indiana University Press, 2004), 190–214; Marc Van De Mieroop, *Philosophy Before the Greeks: The Pursuit of Truth in Ancient Babylonia* (Princeton, NJ: Princeton University Press, 2016).

[39] I have appropriated and reformulated questions from Gericke, *Hebrew Bible and Philosophy of Religion*, 313–6.

object of theoretical reflection. Prayer may comprise ordinary words from everyday language, but it does not aspire to conventional intrahuman discourse. Prayer is a proximate means to an ultimate end. Its volitional mode transports speakers from their natural habitus to a suppositional supernatural world where the finite may be transformed by the infinite. In the ancient world, such a move was almost certainly instinctive, or as our neuroscience colleagues would say, it was driven by a kind of neural automaticity.[40]

The discourse of prayer responds to the abiding lure of transcendence. From Gilgamesh to the primordial human beings in Eden to Odysseus, the quest for ultimate truths has summoned forth all manner of human effort—courageous, desperate, pious, impious, successful, failed, invited, forbidden—and like all such lures, one can never be certain whether the glimmer of transcendence is that of a bright and shining star that illuminates the shadows or only a shiny object that seduces one into an inescapable darkness (e.g., a fishing lure). Prayer's invocation of God transgresses the limits of human beings. Inviting, let alone commanding, God to speak may be the "acme of bardic pretention,"[41] but in the ancient world such transgression characterizes the audacity of prayer.

It is a truism to say that we no longer live in the enchanted world of the ancients, where mortals praying to God/gods was woven into the very fabric of human existence. In that world, prayer was an audacious *and* ubiquitous human practice. Ours is a disenchanted world where theorizing about such things as transcendence and prayer is virtually the default position. Our scholarly work on prayer during the last century reflects this changing ethos. Focus on the phenomenology of prayer by psychologists and historians of religion at the beginning of the twentieth century yielded to a concentrated exegesis of the forms and theological functions of prayer by biblical scholars, which has in turn now morphed into a multi-disciplinary and cross-cultural approach to the practice and experience of prayer. In the first decades of the twenty-first century, the theoretical and the theological have been joined, although depending on your

---

[40] Note, for example, the discussion of "the mind's machinery of transcendence" in Andrew Newberg, Eugene D'Aquili, and Vince Rause, *Why God Won't Go Away: Brain Science and the Biology of Belief* (New York: Ballantine Books, 2001), 140–1.

[41] I appropriate the language of Jonathan Culler, *Theory of the Lyric* (Cambridge, MA: Harvard University Press, 2015), 231. Culler uses the expression with respect to Alphonse de Lamartine's poem, "Le Lac:" "Eternity, nothingness, dark abyss, / What do you do with the days you engulf? / Speak, will you give us back these sublime ecstasies / That you ravish from us?"

disciplinary location you may regard this as either a healthy merger or a hostile take-over.

And yet, for all these shifts and changes, we remain "language animals," as Charles Taylor reminds us in his latest work.[42] To crib together a sentence out of the titles of his seminal works: we live in a "secular age" where the "sources of the self" are to be found in the generative language of dialogue, not the descriptive language of monologue. In his words, "Language doesn't just develop inside individuals, to be then communicated to others. It evolves always in the interspace of joint attention, or communion."[43] Taylor calls upon the Romantic poets, especially their attention to the constitutive role of imagination, to develop his understanding of what is necessary if this dialogic communion is to produce a transformed self.

To conclude this essay, I want to suggest that as we ponder our future work on prayer, we might focus on the "interspace of joint attention" where the human and the divine meet, where the rational and the non-rational are joined, where the theoretical and the theological are intertwined. For work in this place, the cultivation of our imagination will be a premium. On this point, I too want to call on the Romantic poets for help. Wordsworth, who was both the center and the circumference of eighteenth-century Romanticism, describes imagination as "Reason in her most exalted mood" ("The Prelude," Book 14, 190). We might consider a rephrasing of this discernment without compromising Wordsworth's fundamental insight: Prayer is reason in her most exalted mood.

Bibliography

Ahn, Suk-il. *The Persuasive Portrayal of David and Solomon in Chronicles: A Rhetorical Analysis of the Speeches and Prayers in the David-Solomon Narrative*. McMaster Biblical Studies Series 3. Eugene, OR: Pickwick, 2018.

Avrahami, Yael. *Senses of Scripture: Sensory Perceptions in the Hebrew Bible*. LHBOTS 545. New York: T&T Clark, 2013.

Balentine, Samuel E. *Prayer in the Hebrew Bible: The Drama of Divine-Human Dialogue*. OBT. Minneapolis: Augsburg Fortress, 1993.

Barrett, Justin L. *Cognitive Science, Religion, and Theology: From Human Minds to Divine Minds*. West Conshohocken, PA: Templeton Press, 2012.

---

[42] Charles Taylor, *The Language Animal: The Full Shape of the Human Linguistic Capacity* (Cambridge, MA: The Belknap Press of Harvard University Press, 2016). See further, idem, *Sources of the Self: The Making of the Modern Identity* (Cambridge, MA: Harvard University Press, 1989); idem, *A Secular Age* (Cambridge, MA: The Belknap Press of Harvard University Press, 2007).

[43] Taylor, *Language Animal*, 50.

Bell, Catherine. *Ritual Theory, Ritual Practice*. Oxford: Oxford University Press, 1999.

Boda, Mark, Daniel Falk, and Rodney Werline, eds. *The Origins of Penitential Prayer in Second Temple Judaism*. Vol. 1 of *Seeking the Favor of God*. EJL 21. Atlanta: SBL Press, 2006.

Boda, Mark, Daniel Falk, and Rodney Werline, eds. *The Development of Penitential Prayer in Second Temple Judaism*. Vol. 2 of *Seeking the Favor of God*. EJL 22. Atlanta: SBL Press, 2007.

Boda, Mark, Daniel Falk, and Rodney Werline, eds. *The Impact of Penitential Prayer beyond Second Temple Judaism*. Vol. 3 of *Seeking the Face of God*. EJL 23. Atlanta: SBL Press, 2008.

Bourdieu, Pierre. *Outline of a Theory of Practices*. Cambridge: Cambridge University Press, 1977.

Breed, Brennan, David Hankins, and Robert Williamson Jr., eds. "Writing the Moral Self: Essays in Honor of Carol A. Newsom." *JSOT* 40 (2015): 3–135.

Brueggemann, Walter. *The Message of the Psalms: A Theological Commentary*. Minneapolis: Augsburg Fortress, 1984.

Brueggemann, Walter. *Israel's Praise: Doxology Against Idolatry and Ideology*. Philadelphia: Fortress Press, 1988.

Brueggemann, Walter. *Theology of the Old Testament: Testimony, Dispute, Advocacy*. Minneapolis: Fortress Press, 1997.

Carasik, Michael. *Theologies of the Mind in Biblical Israel*. StBibLit 85. New York: Peter Lang, 2006.

Crüsemann, Frank. *Studien zur Formgeschichte von Hymnus und Danklied in Israel*. WMANT 32. Neukirchen-Vluyn: Neukirchener Verlag, 1969.

Culler, Jonathan. *Theory of the Lyric*. Cambridge, MA: Harvard University Press, 2015.

Czachesz, István. "The Emergence of Early Christian Religion: A Naturalistic Approach." Pages 73–94 in *Explaining Christian Origins and Early Judaism: Contributions from Cognitive and Social Science*. Edited by Petri Luomanen, Ilkka Pyysiäinen, and Risto Uro. BibInt 89. Leiden: Brill, 2007.

Czachesz, István. "Filled with New Wine? Religious Experience and Social Dynamics in the Corinthian Church." Pages 71–90 in *Linking Text and Experience*. Edited by Colleen Shantz and Rodney Werline. Vol. 2 of *Experientia*. EJL 35. Atlanta: SBL Press, 2012.

Czachesz, István and Tamás Biró. "Introduction." Pages ix–xvi in *Changing Minds: Religion and Cognition through the Ages*. Edited by István Czachesz and Tamás Biró. Leuven: Peeters, 2011.

Czachesz, István and Risto Uro, eds. *Mind, Morality and Magic: Cognitive Science Approaches in Biblical Studies*. New York: Routledge, 2013.

Dobbs-Allsopp, F. W. *On Biblical Poetry*. Oxford: Oxford University Press, 2015.

Ebeling, Gerhard. *Dogmatik des christlichen Glaubens I*. Tübingen: Mohr Siebeck, 1979.

Feder, Yitzhaq, ed. "Moral Norm Formation and Transformation in Ancient Israel." *HBAI* 6 (2017): 383–526.

Flannery, Frances, Colleen Shantz, and Rodney Werline, eds. *Inquiry into Religious Experience in Early Judaism and Early Christianity*. Vol. 1 of *Experientia*. SBLSymS 40. Atlanta: SBL Press, 2008.

Gane, Roy. *Cult and Character: Purification Offerings, Day of Atonement, and Theodicy*. Winona Lake, IN: Eisenbrauns, 2005.

Geertz, Clifford. *The Interpretation of Cultures*. New York: Basic Books, 1977.

Gericke, Jaco. *The Hebrew Bible and Philosophy of Religion*. RBS 70. Atlanta: SBL Press, 2012.

Gerstenberger, Erhard S. *Der bittende Mensch*. Neukirchen-Vluyn: Neukirchener Verlag, 1980.

Gill, Sam. "Prayer." Pages 489–93 in vol. 11 of *Encyclopedia of Religion*. Edited by Mircea Eliade. New York: Macmillan; London: Collier Macmillan, 1987.

Greenberg, Moshe. *Biblical Prose Prayer As a Window to the Popular Religion of Ancient Israel*. The Taubman Lectures in Jewish Studies 6. Berkeley, CA: University of California Press, 1983.

Gruenwald, Ithamar. *Rituals and Ritual Theory in Ancient Israel*. BRLA 10. Atlanta: SBL Press, 2003.

Gunkel, Hermann and Joachim Begrich. *Einleitung in die Psalmen*. 3rd edition. Göttingen: Vandenhoeck & Ruprecht, 1966 [1933]. ET: *An Introduction to the Psalms*. Translated by Marc Biddle. Macon, GA: Mercer University Press, 1998.

Harkins, Angela Kim. *Reading with an "I" to the Heavens: Looking at the Qumran Hodayot through the Lens of Visionary Traditions*. Ekstasis 3. Berlin: de Gruyter, 2012.

Hawthorne, Nathaniel. *The Scarlet Letter*. New York: Vintage, 2014 [1850].

Hazony, Yoram. *The Philosophy of Hebrew Scripture*. Cambridge: Cambridge University Press, 2012.

Healy, Mary and Robin Parry, eds. *The Bible and Epistemology: Biblical Soundings of the Knowledge of God*. Colorado Springs: Paternoster, 2007.

Heiler, Friedrich. *Prayer: A Study in the History and Psychology of Religion*. Oxford: Oxford University Press, 1932 [1918].

Hogewood, Jay C. "The Speech Act of Confession: Priestly Performative Utterance in Leviticus 16 and Ezra 9-10." Pages 69–82 in *The Origins of Penitential Prayer in Second Temple Judaism*. Vol. 1 of *Seeking the Face of God*. Edited by Mark Boda, Daniel Falk, and Rodney Werline. EJL 21. Atlanta: SBL Press, 2006.

Holland, Dorothy, William Lachicotte Jr., Debra Skinner, and Carole Cain, eds. *Identity and Agency in Cultural Worlds*. Cambridge: Harvard University Press, 1998.

James, William. *Varieties of Religious Experience. Introduction and Notes by Wayne Proudfoot*. New York: Barnes & Noble Classics, 2004 [1902].

Johnson, Dru. *Biblical Knowing: A Scriptural Epistemology of Error*. Eugene, OR: Cascade, 2013.

Johnson, Dru. *Knowledge by Ritual: A Biblical Prolegomenon to Sacramental Theology*. JTISup 13. Winona Lake, IN: Eisenbrauns, 2016.

Johnson, Dru. *Epistemology and Biblical Theology: From the Pentateuch to the Gospel of Mark*. New York: Routledge, 2017.

Kawashima, Robert S. "Conclusion: Toward an Archaeology of Ancient Israelite Knowledge." Pages 190–214 in *Biblical Narrative and the Death of the Rhapsode*. Bloomington, IN: Indiana University Press, 2004.

Klingbeil, Gerald. *Bridging the Gap: Ritual and Ritual Texts in the Bible.* BBRSup 1. Winona Lake, IN: Eisenbrauns, 2007.

Krinetzki, Leo. *Israels Gebet im Alten Testament.* Aschaffenburg: Paul Pattloch, 1965.

Lambert, David. *How Repentance Became Biblical: Judaism, Christianity, and the Interpretation of Scripture.* Oxford: Oxford University Press, 2015.

Lapsley, Judith. *Can These Bones Live? The Problem of the Moral Self in the Book of Ezekiel.* BZAW 301. Berlin: de Gruyter, 2000.

Lee, Nancy C. *The Singers of Lamentations: Cities Under Siege from Ur to Jerusalem to Sarajevo.* BibInt 60. Leiden: Brill, 2002.

Lee, Nancy C. *Lyrics of Lament: From Tragedy to Transformation.* Minneapolis: Fortress Press, 2010.

Lee, Nancy C. *Hannev'ah and Hannah: Hearing Women Biblical Prophets in a Woman's Lyrical Tradition.* Eugene, OR: Cascade, 2015.

Lee, Nancy C., and Carleen Mandolfo, eds. *Lamentations in Ancient and Contemporary Cultural Contexts.* SBLSymS 43. Atlanta: SBL Press, 2008.

McNamara, Patrick. *The Neuroscience of Religious Experience.* Cambridge: Cambridge University Press, 2009.

Morrow, William S., "The Politics of Worship." Pages 427–444 in *The Oxford Handbook of Ritual and Worship*. Edited by Samuel E. Balentine. Oxford: Oxford University Press, 2020.

Mowinckel, Sigmund. *Psalmenstudien.* 6 vols. Kristiania: J. Dybwad, 1921–1924; ET: *Psalm Studies.* Translated by Marc E. Biddle; 2 vols. Atlanta: SBL Press, 2014.

Newberg, Andrew, Eugene D'Aquili, and Vince Rause. *Why God Won't Go Away: Brain Science and the Biology of Belief.* New York: Ballantine Books, 2001.

Newman, Judith H. *Before the Bible: The Liturgical Body and the Formation of Scripture in Early Judaism.* Oxford: Oxford University Press, 2018.

Newsom, Carol A. "Religious Experience in the Dead Sea Scrolls: Two Case Studies." Pages 205–22 in *Linking Text and Experience*. Edited by Colleen Shantz and Rodney Werline. Vol. 2 of *Experientia*. EJL 35. Atlanta: SBL Press, 2012.

Newsom, Carol A. *The Self as Symbolic Space: Constructing Identity and Community at Qumran.* STDJ 52. Leiden: Brill, 2004. Repr. Atlanta: SBL Press, 2007.

Newsom, Carol A. "Models of the Moral Self: Hebrew Bible and Second Temple Judaism." *JBL* 131 (2012): 5–25.

Newsom, Carol A. "Moral Recipes in Deuteronomy and Ezekiel: Divine Authority and Human Agency." *HBAI* 6 (2017): 488–509.

O'Dowd, Ryan. *The Wisdom of Torah: Epistemology in Deuteronomy and the Wisdom Literature.* FRLANT 225. Göttingen: Vandenhoeck & Ruprecht, 2009.

Rappaport, Roy. *Ritual and Religion in the Making of Humanity.* Cambridge Studies in Social and Cultural Anthropology 110. Cambridge: Cambridge University Press, 1999.

Reventlow, Henning Graf. *Gebet im Alten Testament*. Stuttgart: Kohlhammer, 1986.

Scholl, Brian J. and Patrice D. Tremoulet. "Perceptual Causality and Animacy," *Trends in Cognitive Science* 4 (2000): 299–308.

Scott, Ian W. *Paul's Way of Knowing: Story, Experience, and the Spirit*. Grand Rapids, MI: Baker Academic, 2008.

Shantz, Colleen. "Opening the Black Box: New Prospects for Analyzing Religious Experience." Pages 1–16 in *Linking Text and Experience*. Edited by Colleen Shantz and Rodney Werline. Vol. 2 of *Experientia*. EJL 35. Atlanta: SBL Press, 2012.

Shantz, Colleen. *Paul in Ecstasy: The Neurobiology of the Apostle's Life and Thought*. Cambridge: Cambridge University Press, 2009.

Stewart, Anne W. *Poetic Ethics in Proverbs: Wisdom Literature and the Shaping of the Moral Self*. Cambridge: Cambridge University Press, 2016.

Stewart, Anne W. "Models of Moral Agency in the Hebrew Bible," in *Oxford Research Encyclopedia of the Bible*. Edited by John Barton. Online Publication; November 2016; religion.oxfordre.com.

Taylor, Charles. *The Language Animal: The Full Shape of the Human Linguistic Capacity*. Cambridge, MA: The Belknap Press of Harvard University Press, 2016.

Taylor, Charles. *Sources of the Self: The Making of the Modern Identity*. Cambridge, MA: Harvard University Press, 1989.

Taylor, Charles. *A Secular Age*. Cambridge, MA: The Belknap Press of Harvard University Press, 2007.

Turner, Victor. *The Ritual Process: Structure and Anti-Structure*. Chicago: Aldine, 1966.

Van De Mieroop, Marc. *Philosophy Before the Greeks: The Pursuit of Truth in Ancient Babylonia*. Princeton, NJ: Princeton University Press, 2016.

Van Gennep, Arnold. *The Rites of Passage*. Chicago: Chicago University Press, 1960 [1909].

Van Leeuwen, Neil, and Michiel van Elk. "Seeking the Supernatural: The Interactive Religious Experience." *Religion, Brain, and Behavior* 9 (2019): 221–75.

Wendel, Adolf. *Das freie Laiengebet im vorexilischen Israel*. Leipzig: Eduard Pfeiffer, 1931.

Westermann, Claus. *The Praise of God in the Psalms*. Translated by Keith R. Crim. Richmond: John Knox, 1965.

Westermann, Claus. *Praise and Lament in the Psalms*. Translated by Keith R. Crim and Richard N. Soulen. Atlanta: John Knox, 1981.

Westermann, Claus. *Elements of Old Testament Theology*. Translated by Douglas W. Scott. Atlanta: John Knox, 1982.

Widmer, Michael. *Moses, God, and the Dynamics of Intercessory Prayer*. FAT 2/8. Tübingen: Mohr Siebeck, 2004.

CREATIONAL BLESSINGS IN SECOND TEMPLE PRAYER AND PSALMODY

Andrew R. KRAUSE

Creation accounts are, by nature, political statements. In Genesis 1, the God of Israel is said to stand above the water unchallenged while forming and filling that which is *tohu wa-bohu*, unlike gods of other nations who are equally matched to the various sea monsters. In the Enuma Elish, Marduk acts as the paragon of kingliness and the city of Babylon is the center of all that is created. So too in subsequent retellings and reinterpretations of Genesis' initial, priestly creation story, the structure and contents of the literature, as they represent the structure and contents of the cosmos, make fundamental claims regarding religio-political truth.[1]

The Song of the Three Youths (Pr Azar 23–68 // Dan 3:46–90 LXX) enumerates a series of creational blessings that begin in the heavenly throne room and work their way down to increasingly earthly regions. This basic structure is also found in the call for all of creation to praise God in Ps 148. Moreover, the Song's serialized benedictions are not unique amongst Second Temple literature, as we find similar, though shorter, parallels in 4QBerakhot[a] and the Thanksgiving Hymn for the Sabbath in 4QWords of the Luminaries (4QDibHam[a] 1–2 recto VII, 4–9). By comparing the rhetoric of the various prayers and hymns in this literary form, we stand to clarify the purpose of this purportedly secondary

---

[1] For discussion of the rhetorical meanings of creation accounts, see Gabriel Gösta, *enūma eliš – Weg zu einer globalen Weltordnung*, ORA 12 (Tübingen: Mohr Siebeck, 2014); Andrea Seri, "Some notes on *enūma eliš*," *JAOS* 137 (2017): 833–8. According to Seri, "*enūma eliš* … includes a parallelism between the idea of kingship of the gods and the socio-political concept of kingship, a resemblance between Marduk and the king, and also the claim of Babylonian hegemony. The ultimate political concept then is that the ideal kingship is (con)centrated and centralized, stable and stabilizing." (pg. 838). While Seri seeks a socio-political understanding, I will push further into a more ideologically conceived religio-political understanding of these phenomena, in terms of both ritual and authority exercised in these texts. On the influence of this text on early Israelite authors, see Kenton L. Sparks, "'Enūma Elish' and Priestly Mimesis: Elite Emulation in Nascent Judaism," *JBL* 126 (2007): 625–48.

Danielic composition. For example, while the other Second Temple Period compositions end with Sheol, the Song of the Three Youths appears to omit this chthonic space. However, its place is taken by the praise of the three themselves from the furnace as they give thanks for being saved from the grave, which may call into question the assertion that this singular mention of the three in the song is a clumsy interpolation. If this ironic correspondence is true, the (supposed) grave itself praises God, as it does in 4QWords of the Luminaries. Conversely, Sheol (or Abaddon as in 4QCurses) is only spoken of in subsequent curses as the place of Belial in 4QBerakhot. This alterity in other such texts raises questions of whether the Song of the Three Youths is likewise a self-glorification for a specific group and thus implicitly cursing others, despite the seeming universalism of a unified, praising creation. Spatializing the blessings of God systematically is in many ways a purposeful ordering of the cosmos to suit the authors and their perceived communities. Much like the earlier Mesopotamian creational accounts, these blessings render the entire cosmos as a ritual site.

In this essay, I will argue that the various creational blessings provide examples of groups assembling a meaningful cosmology that complements their theologies, and in ways that are amenable to the apocalyptic thought and tropes of the time. In order to do so, I will begin with a brief discussion of the literary and historical contexts of the Song of the Three Youths. Following this, I will survey the various exemplars of such blessings, in terms of both how they cohere to the formal elements and how they adapt them to their needs. Finally, I will conclude with a more detailed analysis of how these adaptations relate to the religio-political needs of a given community or movement, especially the Danielic one in which we find the deuterocanonical version of the Song of the Three Youths.

The Song of the Three Youths in Literary and Historical Context

The Song of the Three Youths is a constituent part of the Prayer of Azariah, which is an addition to LXX Daniel between what in the MT is demarcated Dan 3:23 and 24. The Prayer of Azariah (Pr Azar 1–22) and a short narrative bridge between the two poetic sections (Pr Azar 23–28) account for the rest of the addition. Contra Carey Moore, the Song itself is not divisible into two separate compositions, an Ode (vv. 29–34) and a Psalm (vv. 35–68), despite a change in poetic metrical pattern and a move from declarative praise of God to an imperative call for creation to praise

God;[2] as John Collins aptly states, "nothing is gained by treating it [i.e., the Ode] as a separate composition."[3] Indeed, as I will argue, we have good literary reasons to see these two sections as purposefully parallel. The original language of composition was almost certainly Hebrew,[4] though some have previously claimed that the Aramaic version of the work in the medieval *Chronicle of Jerahmeel* is the basis for the Theodotion text.[5]

This Song evinces a clear, repetitive structure, though one containing a great deal of nuance and creativity. Each unit begins with εὐλογημέ-νος, εὐλογητός, or εὐλογεῖτε in a call to bless or praise God, as either declarative or imperative. Each unit is then followed by the antiphonal refrain ὑμνεῖτε καὶ ὑπερυψοῦτε αὐτὸν εἰς τοὺς αἰῶνας (excepting 33b: καὶ αἰνετὸς καὶ δεδοξασμένος εἰς τοὺς αἰῶνας), with only minor variations, similar to the antiphonal refrain of Ps 136. These lines follow strict metrical patterns of either 4/4 (declarative section; 29–34) or 2+2/3 (imperative section; vv. 35–68).[6] At the compositional level, the song is easily split into three distinct sections: Heavenly, declarative praise (29–34), creational call to praise (35–60), and the national call to praise (61–65),[7] each beginning with a summative line in the first instance:[8]

Blessed are you, O Lord God of our ancestors	Εὐλογητὸς εἶ, κύριε ὁ θεὸς τῶν πατέρων ἡμῶν (29)
Bless the Lord, all you works of the Lord	εὐλογεῖτε, πάντα τὰ ἔργα τοῦ κυρίου, τὸν κύριον (35)
Bless the Lord, O Israel	εὐλογεῖτε, Ισραηλ, τὸν κύριον (61)

---

[2] Carey A. Moore, *Daniel, Esther, and Jeremiah: The Additions*, AB 44 (New York: Doubleday, 1977), 40–4.

[3] John J. Collins, *Daniel: A Commentary on the Book of Daniel*, Hermeneia (Minneapolis: Fortress Press, 1993), 207.

[4] Curt Kuhl, *Die drei Männer im Feuer*, BZAW 55 (Giessen: Töpelmann, 1930), 89–100, 111–54. Kuhl's forensic translation of the Prayer of Azariah has shown that the text contains sufficient Hebraisms and can be retroverted to a workable, metrically-comparable Hebrew text. See also Matthias Henze, "Additions to Daniel," in *Outside the Bible: Ancient Jewish Writings Related to Scripture*, ed. Louis H. Feldman, James L. Kugel, and Lawrence H. Schiffman (Lincoln: University of Nebraska Press, 2013), 122–39, 129; Collins, *Daniel*, 199, 207; Moore, *Additions*, 44–6.

[5] See Moses Gaster, "The Unknown Aramaic Original of Theodotion's Additions to the Book of Daniel," *PSBA* 16 (1894): 280–317.

[6] See Moore, *Additions*, 48, 75–6.

[7] Most scholars signal the break between vv. 59 and 60, with "Bless the Lord, sons of men" (εὐλογεῖτε, οἱ υἱοὶ τῶν ἀνθρώπων, τὸν κύριον) as the summative first line, though it seems a better ending to the previous section, following all the birds of the air and the wild animals and livestock of the ground. Given that all of the people listed in vv. 62–65 are clearly Israelites and Judaeans, v. 61 is a more fitting summative first line.

[8] See Henze, "Additions," 133.

The final three verses of the song are almost exclusively viewed by scholars as a later, clumsy attempt to incorporate Shadrach, Meshach, and Abednego at the end in order both to incorporate this likely pre-existing, cultic song into the Danielic tradition and to place the praise of God in the mouth of the Jews being saved rather than in the mouth of the Babylonian king who placed them in the furnace, as in MT Dan 3:28. Later tradition is notably divided on this point, as prayers are credited to the three youths in b. Pesaḥ. 118a, while they are silent in b. Sanh. 92b. However, as I will argue below, while the Song itself was likely pre-existent, the addition of the final three verses is far from clumsy.

Structurally, the general movement in this song is continually descending from Heaven and its functionaries to the creation from the sky down to the depths, and finally God's elect nation, much like we find in Ps 148, though with significantly greater detail. This movement downward is nuanced, according to Raija Sollamo and Mika Pajunen, with the ordering of the Priestly Creation Narrative (Gen 1:1–2:3), as birds are followed by wild animals, cattle, and humanity in vv. 51–59.[9] However, we should note that in both cases the authors are treating the Song as a parallel example of this phenomenon in other texts, Jubilees for Sollamo and 4QBerakhot[a] for Pajunen. It is also noteworthy that the OG and Theodotionic versions contain different ordering, especially in vv. 44–51, though Sollamo also notes that both evince questionable logic and therefore likely contain glosses and confused ordering.[10] Unfortunately this latter point is difficult to adjudge without further manuscripts, though it does not necessarily create many problems. Thus, while I would certainly agree that Genesis 1 influenced the Song of the Three Youths, I would argue that it remains secondary to the downward, spatial structuring principle in this composition.

While a full commentary of the text is beyond the scope or requirement of the current chapter, a few important inclusions and placements are notable. First, the inclusion of 'angels of the Lord' (ἄγγελοι κυρίου) in v. 37 has been variously interpreted. According to Collins, this group

---

[9] Raija Sollamo, "The Creation of Angels and Natural Phenomena Intertwined in the *Book of Jubilees* (4QJub[a])," in *Biblical Traditions in Transmission: Essays in Honour of Michael A. Knibb*, ed. Charlotte Hempel and Judith M. Lieu, JSJSup 111 (Leiden: Brill, 2006), 273–90, esp. 280–2; followed by Mika S. Pajunen, "Creation as the Liturgical Nexus of the Blessings and Cursings in 4QBerakhot," in *Ancient Readers and their Scriptures: Engaging the Hebrew Bible in Early Judaism and Christianity*, ed. John Anthony Dunne and Garrick V. Allen, AJEC 107 (Leiden: Brill, 2018), 27–39.

[10] Sollamo, "Angels," 281.

is analogous to Angels of the Presence, as we find them in 4QShirShabb[a] 1 I, 1–2, 4, 8; however, in comparing the Song of the Three Youths to *Jubilees*, Sollamo rejects the notion that this refers to the attending angels.[11] Further, the mention of 'powers of the Lord' (δυνάμεις κυρίου) in v. 39 is ambiguous, as it likely translates 'hosts' (צְבָאוֹת), which may variously be interpreted as angels (Ps 148:2), an army (Gen 21:22), celestial bodies (Dan 8:10; Ps 33:6), or potentially all of the above.[12] This definition is made all the more difficult given the aforementioned inclusion of angels in v. 37 and the subsequent mention of celestial bodies in vv. 40–41. Further, while few literary connections exist other than the narrative placement of the Prayer of Azariah and the Song of the Three Youths, the specific mention of 'dew' in v. 46 is significant given the role of dew in the cooling of the furnace in v. 27. Regarding the sea monsters in v. 57, this follows Pss 148:7 and 106:26 in having the Leviathan brought into the domain of God's creation rather than portraying it as a creational or eschatological foe, as in Isa 27:1 or in Job 41 in which God tames the Leviathan in order to make it his servant.[13] Finally, in the purportedly secondary ending, following the mention of the three youths by name, we are told that they praise God for saving them from Hades, death, and the furnace (v. 66b), which Collins compares to Ps 16:10 and 1QH[a] 9:20.[14] However, as I will argue in section 3, it is important to note that, like the furnace itself, Hades and death intriguingly continue the downward movement into chthonic spaces. In each of these examples, and indeed in each verse, we find clear clues of how this Song constructs a detailed cosmology.

The creativity of this cosmology, however, is not made of whole cloth; the text's intertextuality is clear. Firstly, in Tob 8:5 Tobias declares:

> Εὐλογητὸς εἶ, ὁ θεὸς τῶν πατέρων ἡμῶν,
>   καὶ εὐλογητὸν τὸ ὄνομά σου τὸ ἅγιον καὶ ἔνδοξον εἰς τοὺς
>   αἰῶνας·
> εὐλογησάτωσάν σε οἱ οὐρανοὶ καὶ πᾶσαι αἱ κτίσεις σου.

> Blessed are you, O God of our ancestors,
>   and blessed be your holy and glorious name for the ages.
> Let the heavens and all your creatures bless you. (NETS)

---

[11] Collins, *Daniel*, 206; cf. Sollamo, "Angels," 281.

[12] On the ambiguity of this reference, see Moore, *Additions*, 71.

[13] Collins, *Daniel*, 206.

[14] Collins, *Daniel*, 207. Regarding the latter parallel, Collins cites the Sukenik placement of this text, in III 19.

We thus find both the opening line of the Song followed by a description of the first two sections. While Moore assumes that the entire Song was an elaboration on this verse, Collins rightly questions this notion, as it is just as likely that the Song of the Three Youths was the inspiration of Tob 8:5 as the other way around or that both were inspired by more diffuse hymnic traditions.[15] Likewise, the Song concludes with a near quotation of Ps 136:1–3, which further connects the Song to Ps 136, to which most scholars have compared the antiphonal refrain. Regarding the connections to Pss 136 and 148, however, Collins is more decisive. Despite the similar structuring of downward-moving blessings—including similar ordering of elements wherever possible and the difficulty in dating Psalms—Collins notes the much higher levels of intricacy, the development of the themes from Ps 148, and the intertextuality with several other Psalms (e.g., Ps 136 and the antiphonal refrain) in arguing that the Song almost certainly followed Ps 148 with influences from Ps 136.[16]

However, as a final note on the genre of this text, it must be acknowledged that this descending movement in such lists is not unique to Jewish liturgy. As several scholars have indicated, this text is at least related to the *Listenwissenschaft* of Wisdom literature. We find similar structuring in sapiential texts such as Job 38–41 and Sir 43, which are often viewed as having been influenced by earlier Egyptian wisdom lists.[17] Such works offer a speculative ordering of creation meant to present it as intrinsically ordered and complete. This phenomenon has been identified in apocalyptic and exegetical texts, as well, by Michael E. Stone and Shani Tzoref, respectively.[18] For Stone, this sense of comprehensiveness

---

[15] Moore, *Additions*, 47, 69; Collins, *Daniel*, 205.

[16] Collins, *Daniel*, 207. Similarly, Moore, *Additions*, 75.

[17] The term was coined by Wolfram von Soden and later applied to biblical studies by Albrecht Alt. See Wolfram von Soden, "Leistung und Grenze sumerischer und babylonischer Wissenschaft: Die Welt als Geschichte," *Zeitschrift für universalgeschichtliche Forschung* 2 (1936): 411–64, 509–57; Albrecht Alt, "Die Weisheit Salomos," *TLZ* 76 (1951): 139–44; Gerhard von Rad, "Hiob 38 und die altägyptische Weisheit," in *Wisdom in Israel and the Ancient Near East,* ed. Martin Noth and Winston Thomas, VTSup 3 (Leiden: Brill, 1955), 293–301; Michael E. Stone, "Lists of Revealed Things in Apocalyptic Literature," in *Magnalia Dei: The Mighty Acts of God*, ed. Frank Moore Cross, Werner E. Lemke, and Patrick D. Miller, Jr. (New York: Doubleday, 1976), 414–52, esp. 435–39; Markus Hilgert, "Von ‚Listenwissenschaft' und ‚epistemischen Dingen': Konzeptuelle Annäherungen an altorientalische Wissenspraktiken," *Zeitschrift für allgemeine Wissenschaftstheorie* 40.2 (2009): 277–309.

[18] Stone, "Lists," 414–52; Shani Tzoref, "4Q252: *Listenwissenschaft* and Covenantal Patriarchal Blessings," in *Go Out and Study the Land (Judges 18:2): Archaeological,*

and speculative ordering in texts such as 2 Bar. 59 seem similar, though offer very little additional clarity in understanding their uses. Such listing continues in Late Antique Jewish texts, notably in blessing and cursing texts. However, as Michael Swartz has argued, the sense of comprehensiveness was replaced in the Rabbinic Period by both a more ornate aesthetic in such so-called magical texts (i.e., 'jewelled style') and a desire to objectify the created elements being blessed or cursed as the practitioner claims authority over them.[19]

Thus, in the Song of the Three Youths, we find an intricately composed song of blessing or praise to God with a sweeping, comprehensive movement from the Heavenly throne room to the Land of Israel, and even down to the grave. This listing of creation makes significant use of other Psalms and the Priestly Creation Narrative of Genesis 1. However, much remains unclear from the above discussion. What precisely was meant by the blessing and what precisely did the redactor of this text mean to say with its inclusion in the Danielic Narrative? What was the ultimate goal of this list's ordering? Fortunately, the Song is not entirely unique amongst the liturgical works of the Second Temple Period. Most notably, 4QBerakhot[a], as reconstructed by Bilhah Nitzan,[20] and the extremely fragmentary text of the Sabbath praise of 4QWords of the Luminaries (4QDibHam[a] 1–2 recto VII, 4–9) are similar enough to act as instructive parallels.

Other Creational Blessing Lists

As stated in the previous section, Ps 148 and other texts share the basic structure of descending blessings of God and call for all of creation to join in this blessing or praise. We are thus left to question precisely how these texts are related. Even more broadly, what are these blessings

---

Historical, and Textual Studies in Honor of Hanan Eshel, ed. Aren M. Maier, Jodi Magness, and Lawrence H. Schiffman, JSJSup 148 (Leiden: Brill, 2011), 337–57.

[19] Michael D. Swartz, "The Aesthetics of Blessing and Cursing: Literary and Iconographic Dimensions of Hebrew and Aramaic Blessing and Curse Texts," *JANER* 5 (2006): 187–211, 191. Cf. Martin S. Jaffee, "Deciphering Mishnaic Lists: A Form Critical Approach," in *Text as Context in Early Rabbinic Literature*, ed. William Scott Green, vol. 3 of *Approaches to Ancient Judaism*, BJS 11 (Chico: Scholars Press, 1981), 19–34; Jaffee opines almost complete continuity between these texts. As I will argue in the following section, texts such as 4QBerakhot[a] provide a medial position.

[20] See Bilhah Nitzan, "4QBerakhot A-e (4Q286-290): A Covenantal Ceremony in the Light of Related Texts," *RevQ* 16 (1995): 487–506; eadem; "Berakhot," in *Qumran Cave 4, VI: Poetical and Liturgical Texts*, ed. Esther Eshel et al., DJD 11 (Oxford: Clarendon, 1998), 1–74.

meant to accomplish? In what sense might they be considered ritually efficacious? What rhetorical purpose is served by the inclusion of such comprehensive blessing lists? Unfortunately, the various texts in this small list are in various states of repair, which will problematize the comparison, though not sufficiently to question the results. The present section will seek to move beyond generalized comments of form and genre in order to clarify the rhetorical differences in texts that describe the features of the cosmos in such a systematic fashion.

But what do ancient writers and ritual functionaries mean when they command people—let alone sea monsters and snow—to bless or eulogize God? According to James Aitken's deservedly influential study on blessings in this period, when humans are blessed by God, the term expresses divine approval or election, though when humans bless God, the meaning is 'to praise'.[21] However, Jutta Jokiranta has, in my opinion, convincingly argued that this understanding lacks phenomenological and historical rigor. According to Jokiranta, Aitken's use of speech-act theory is instructive, though it must go further. She advocates understanding blessings as both communication and ritual action with several meanings, purposes, and behavioral expectations that ultimately generate power through their intended purposes and behavior.[22] Ultimately, such acts are magical insofar as they are predictive and they seek to effect a specific change through set formulas, especially in terms of transforming the mundane domain through proximity to the divine domain.[23] Jokiranta differentiates 'agent-based' agency in blessing, in which the object is blessed through the ritual authority and virtuosity of a specific functionary, from 'action-based' agency, in which the actions themselves enact the desired change.[24] For our purposes, the most important takeaway involves the recognition of the multiple agencies and purposes of these ritual acts, even within a single work. To this we might also add the extended ritual use of 'eulogy' as a term for honoring or memorializing in modern funerary rites. Blessing was not a static category that had to do merely with

---

[21] James K. Aitken, *The Semantics of Blessing and Cursing in Ancient Hebrew*, ANESSup 23 (Leuven: Peeters, 2007), 96–102.

[22] Jutta Jokiranta, "Towards a Cognitive Theory of Blessing: The Dead Sea Scrolls as a Test Case," in *Functions of Psalms and Prayers in the Late Second Temple Period*, ed. Mika S. Pajunen and Jeremy Penner, BZAW 486 (Berlin: de Gruyter, 2017), 27–47.

[23] Jokiranta, "Towards," 33–5. Here, Jokiranta follows Jesper Sørensen, *A Cognitive Theory of Magic* (Plymouth: Altamira Press, 2007), 95–139. Sørensen argues that magic may entail either manipulative behavior in which the deity is coerced or transformative behavior in which the mundane is changed through relation to the divine.

[24] Jokiranta, "Towards," 37–45.

praising another being, but rather it was intended to effect a specific change desired by the subject offering the blessing or praise. In all of these cases, we must be aware that εὐλογέω, ברך, and other related terms can carry a great deal more lexical freight and ritual efficacy than mere blessing or praise.

When we seek to compare and to clarify the rhetoric of blessings, we must specifically analyze the desired social and religio-political goals of the eulogy. Specifically, how do such ritual actions change social realities? Here it is important to acknowledge the intrinsic relationship between blessings and curses, as two sides of a single action. Jeff Anderson is correct to note the intramural nature of blessings and curses, as they communicate within specifically in-group and out-group dynamics and the ritual performer seeks to gain social control through affirming specific social norms.[25] Likewise, Christopher Frechette presents blessing as either motivating proper behavior through validation or cultivating solidarity within the performative community.[26] These goals are accomplished through the promise of divine favor for right action and the threat of divine retribution for transgressive actions as understood by the practitioner. Such incentivising and punishment are often, though not always, related to oaths or covenants. Thus, in the blessings and curses of Deut 27:11–28:19, the Deuteronomic Covenant is presented as the standard against which the congregation and eventually the nation will be judged; keeping the covenant will lead to blessings in the Land and breaking the covenant will lead to disaster at the national level or ejection from the camp or Land at the individual level. Such boundary-marking usage was taken further in the blessings and curses of the *Yaḥad* movement's Covenant Renewal Ceremony in 1QS 2:16–3:12.[27] While purportedly based on the same covenant and Torah, the *Serekh* presentation elaborated on the covenantal blessings and curses, effectively marking their

---

[25] Jeff S. Anderson, "Curses and Blessings: Social Control and Self Definition in the Dead Sea Scrolls," in *The Dead Sea Scrolls in Context: Integrating the Dead Sea Scrolls in the Study of Ancient Texts, Languages, and Cultures*, ed. Armin Lange, Emmanuel Tov, and Matthias Weigold, VTSup 140.1 (Leiden: Brill, 2011), 1:47–60, esp. 1:52–3.

[26] Christopher G. Frechette, "Blessing and Cursing," in *The Oxford Encyclopedia of the Bible and Law*, ed. Brent A. Strawn (Oxford: Oxford University Press, 2015), 59–63.

[27] Regarding the ritual construction of bound space, see Jonathan Z. Smith, *To Take Place: Toward Theory in Ritual* (Chicago: University of Chicago Press, 1987). For the creation of such bound space in these texts, see Daniel K. Falk, *Daily, Sabbath, and Festival Prayers in the Dead Sea Scrolls*, STDJ 27 (Leiden: Brill, 1998), 219–36; Andrew R. Krause, "Community, Alterity, and Space in the Qumran Covenant Curses," *DSD* 25 (2018): 217–37.

community as not only the lone righteous group, but also the only group capable of marking divine election and rejection through their ritual performance of these blessings and curses. But what does this mean for such declarative blessing of God as is found in the Song of the Three Youths? It is notable that similar boundary-marking based on the curses of Deut 27:11–26 and the praise of Ps 148 may be found in the primary text for comparison in this section: 4QBerakhot[a]. While the notion that this text is another version of the same covenantal renewal ceremony should be rejected,[28] we find similar boundary marking in this ritual text. Despite the sense of universalism that we find in the creational blessings, the inclusion of curses and the clear stipulation that this text is meant to be performed by the "Council of the Community" (4QBer[a] 7 II, 1) construct ritual boundaries around the performing community. Thus, we must acknowledge with Anne Marie Kitz that blessings and curses have intrinsically complementary purposes of granting life or hastening death within a social system; that is, the act of demarcating those who are blessed also differentiates them from those who are implicitly cursed and vice versa.[29]

However, in some cases such boundaries can be ambiguous, as we find in the Sabbath prayer from Words of the Luminaries (4QDibHam[a] 1–2

---

[28] Many scholars have noted differences between 1QS 1:16–3:12 and 4QBer[a–e], as well as problems with defining both texts as yearly ceremonies. Carol Newsom and Daniel Falk both argue that the level of variance found in the two texts should call the equation of the two rituals without stronger connections being argued. Russell Arnold notes that the respective curses are very different in terms of what is actually adjured, as the curses of 1QS 2 focus on the wicked and dark deeds of those being cursed (ethical), whereas 4QBerakhot repudiates the wicked, guilty, and impure schemes of Belial and the association of the cursed individuals relation to these schemes (social and cosmological). Such differences cannot simply be ignored or rationalized. Andrew Krause argues that the theological imagery and spatial conceptions of the two texts are simply too divergent to be classified as the same rite. See Falk, *Daily*, 219–36; Carol A. Newsom, *The Self as Symbolic Space: Constructing Identity and Community at Qumran*, STDJ 52 (Leiden: Brill, 2004), 119; Krause, "Community," 217–37; Russell C. D. Arnold, *The Social Role of Liturgy in the Religion of the Qumran Community*, STDJ 60 (Leiden: Brill, 2006), 162. Contra J.T. Milik, "Milkî-ṣedeq et Milkî-rešaʿ dans les anciens écrits juifs et chrétiens," *JJS* 23 (1972): 95–144; Bilhah Nitzan, "Textual, Literary, and Religious Character of *4QBerakhot* (4Q286–290)," in *The Provo International Conference on the Dead Sea Scrolls,* ed. Donald W. Parry and Eugene Ulrich, STDJ 30 (Leiden: Brill, 1999), 636–56; Nitzan, "4QBerakhot A-e " 487–506; James R. Davila, *Liturgical Works,* ECDSS 6 (Grand Rapids: Eerdmans, 2000), 41; Stephen J. Pfann, "The Essene Yearly Renewal Ceremony and the Baptism of Repentance," in *The Provo International Conference on the Dead Sea Scrolls,* ed. Donald W. Parry and Eugene Ulrich, STDJ 3 (Leiden: Brill, 1999), 337–52, 342–3.

[29] Anne Marie Kitz, *Cursed are You: The Phenomenology of Cursing in Cuneiform and Hebrew Texts* (Winona Lake: Eisenbrauns, 2013), 199–204.

recto VII, 4–9). The Words of the Luminaries consist of a daily prayer cycle dominated by the petition for the Lord to remember his promises and covenants; the cycle begins on the first day with Adam and Eve, and it progresses to the Babylonian Exile on the sixth day.[30] The extant Sabbath prayer is composed of Thanksgiving and a brief call for creation to bless God (הודו; cf. Ps 148:13). This text is extremely fragmentary and is written on both sides of the parchment, but is generally regarded as non-sectarian based on the extant text.[31] For our purposes, the relevant data of Thanksgiving occurs in the Sabbath call for "all the angels of the heavenly vault/firmament" (כול מלאכי{ם} רקיע קודש) (4QDibHam[a] 1–2 VII, recto 6–7), "the earth and all its handiwork" (הארץ וכול מחשב°ה) (4QDibHam[a] 1–2 VII, recto 7), and most intriguingly, "[the] great abyss], Abaddon, and all the waters and all that [are in them]" (רבה ואבדון והמים וכֹל אשׂר [בם) (4QDibHam[a] 1–2 VII, recto 8) to give thanks. That the abyss and Abaddon are themselves included in this call is relevant, as the Song of the Three Youths specifically speaks of the grave as the place from which the three youths are saved and, as we will see, this is the place to which the Belial and his lot are consigned in 4QBerakhot[a].

As its title would suggest, 4QBerakhot (4Q286–90) is primarily a collection of liturgical blessings, though one that is matched with curses. Based on terminology and the liturgical cues at the conclusion of the blessings—"the Council of the Community, all of them will say together 'Amen, Amen'" (עצת היחד יומרו כולמה ביחד אמן אמן) in 4QBer[a] 6 1—this text has been deemed sectarian. It should be acknowledged at the outset that Bilhah Nitzan, the editor of the *editio princeps*, reconstructed and ordered fragments 1–6 of 4QBerakhot[a] based on the assumption that it is a creational blessings collection and a covenant renewal ceremony similar to 1QS cols. II–III.[32] While early scholarship followed Nitzan in this

---

[30] See Jeremy Penner, "The *Words of the Luminaries* as a Meditation on the Exile," *RevQ* 28 (2016): 175–90; Jeremy Penner, "Mapping Fixed Prayers from the Dead Sea Scrolls onto Second Temple Period Judaism," *DSD* 21 (2014): 39–63, esp. 57–8. According to Penner, the text situates the nation as still in exile and calling for God to bring them out. This text is generally dated to the mid-2nd century BCE.

[31] Esther G. Chazon, "Is Divrei ha-me'orot a Sectarian Prayer?" in *The Dead Sea Scrolls: Forty Years of Research,* ed. Devorah Dimant and Uriel Rappaport, STDJ 10 (Leiden: Brill, 1992), 3–17; Penner, "Mapping," 57. Chazon has recently nuanced this stance by arguing that the prayers were probably pre-Qumran, though the *Yahad* likely still used this collection despite some theological dissonance; Esther G. Chazon, "Prayer and Identity in Varying Contexts: The Case of the *Words of the Luminaries*," *JSJ* 46 (2015): 484–511.

[32] Nitzan, "Textual," 637.

latter identification of ritual context, it has been challenged and placed in doubt based on differences in imagery, theology, and ritual performance.[33] On the latter point, it is notable that the 'Council of the Community'—most likely the entire assembled congregation of the *Yaḥad*—recites these blessings and curses, as opposed to only the priests and Levites in 1QS 1:18–19.

While this reconstruction needs more objective reassessment based on material-philological methods such as the Stegemann method,[34] the contents of fragments 1–6 do display many of the same structural elements we find in the Song of the Three Youths, and it contains many telling parallels as it is presently ordered. For example, as in the Song, 4QBerakhot contains summative opening lines to the various sections, e.g.,

יברכו בי[ן]חֿד כולמה את שם קודשכה

all will bless together your holy name (4QBer[a] 2a–c 4)

הארץ וכול]אֿ[ן]שֿׁר]עֿליה תבל וכול[ן] יושבי בה אדמה וכול מחשביה
ארץ וכו[ל יקומה

the earth and all [t]hat is [on it, world and all] its inhabitants; ground and all its depths, the earth [and all] its living things (4QBer[a] 5a 1–2)

וכו[ל בחיריהֿמֿה

and al]l their elect ones (4QBer[a] 7a 2)

While the last of these three examples is potentially dubious given its fragmentary nature, it nonetheless summarizes the following lines, which speak of those possessing special revelation and knowledge of the psalms. Likewise, as we find in 4QBer[a] 3 2–4 (cf. Pr Azar 42–51), the description of the heavenly sphere includes a list of meteorological phenomena directly after the mention of angels, as well as a catalogue of geological features in the earthly section (4QBer[a] 5 9–12; cf. Pr Azar 53–56). In this

---

[33] See n. 27 above.

[34] See Hartmut Stegemann, "Methods for the Reconstruction of Scrolls from Scattered Fragments," in *Archaeology and History in the Dead Sea Scrolls,* ed. Lawrence H. Schiffman, JSPSup 8 (Sheffield: JSOT Press, 1990), 189–220; Hartmut Stegemann, "The Material Reconstruction of the *Hodayot,*" in *The Dead Sea Scrolls: Fifty Years after their Discovery,* ed. Lawrence H. Schiffman, Emmanuel Tov, and James C. VanderKam (Jerusalem: Israel Exploration Society, 2000), 272–84; Hartmut Stegemann, Eileen Schuller, and Carol Newsom, *Qumran Cave 1, III: 1QHodayot[a]: With Incorporation of 1QHodayot[b] and 4QHodayot[a-f],* DJD XL (Oxford: Clarendon, 2009), 13–53. For a more recent usage of this method on a comparable scroll, see Joseph L. Angel, "The Material Reconstruction of 4QSongs of the Sage[b] (4Q511)," *RevQ* 27 (2015): 25–82. Cf. Angela Kim Harkins, "Another Look at the Cave 1 Hodayot: Was CH I Materially Part of the Scroll 1QHodayot[a]?" *DSD* 25.2 (2018): 185–216. Harkins presents significant cautions regarding the assumptions and use of this method, which may lead to an undue sense of unity.

category, it is noteworthy that the phrase 'droplets of dew' (לט ילגא),
which is found in both Pr Azar 27 and 46, is also listed in 4QBer[a] 3 5
and in Job 38:28, two other instances of such creational listing.[35] Finally,
emphasis is placed on the worshipers in both the opening and the closing
of this section, allowing a symmetrical parallel between the heavenly
worshipers and God's chosen worshipers on earth.[36] However, as Nitzan
notes, 4QBerakhot goes further in this respect, as it enumerates several
calendrical elements that exhibit correspondence between the heavenly
worship and the sun-moon-stars sections of the heavenly list.[37] As
Jokiranta has recently argued, the sort of listing that we find in 4QBera-
khot[a] elicits a sense of ritualization by focusing the attention on the list
and leading to ritual action through the sense of experience that is trig-
gered.[38] Thus, "by not being able to fully comprehend [sic] the lists,
people may have become more receptive to the authoritative teaching in
how to make sense of reality."[39] I believe that the same might be said
in the other instances of creational blessings lists.

Another important area in which 4QBerakhot[a] is similar to, though
moves beyond the Song is in its spatializing language. While all of these
lists give a sense of spatiality through the descending movement of the
list and the general sense that what is listed in the heavenly or earthly
realms reside there, 4QBerakhot goes into much greater detail about the
spaces in each sphere. For example, 4QBer[a] 1a I, 6–7, which lists a series
of sapiential spaces as being present in the heavenly realms:

> a foundation of wisdom and a structure of knowledge, and a fountain
>   of insight, a foundation of prudence,
> and a (council) of holiness, and a foundation of truth, a treasury of
>   understanding, structures of justice, and places of hone[sty].[40]

---

[35] Davila, *Liturgical*, 55; Stone, "Lists," 435–6.

[36] Bilhah Nitzan, "Harmonic and Mystical Characteristics in Poetic and Liturgical Writings from Qumran," *JQR* 85 (1994): 163–83, esp. 171–6.

[37] Nitzan, "Harmonic," 176.

[38] Jutta Jokiranta, "Ritualization and the Power of Listing in 4QBerakhot[a] (4Q286)," in
*Is There a Text in this Cave? Studies in the Textuality of the Dead Sea Scrolls in Hon-
our of George J. Brooke*, ed. Ariel Feldman, Maria Cioță, and Charlotte Hempel, STDJ
119 (Leiden: Brill, 2017), 438–58.

[39] Jokiranta, "Ritualization," 458.

[40] Bilhah Nitzan, "Berakhot," 1–74, 13. While Nitzan argues that עצה should be translated
'counsel' rather than 'council,' this should be questioned. The poetics of this text follow
a pattern in which the spatial referents followed by sapiential terms in a genitival construct relationship are being enumerated; Nitzan's translation breaks this pattern. This
poetic consideration should trump outlying uses from 1QS, especially as עצה is used in
the construction 'council of the X' numerous times in 4QBerakhot (e.g., 4QBer[a] 7a I,
2, 6; 4QBer[b] 7a II, 1; 4QBer[d] I 1), thus taking precedence.

Many of these phrases are attested elsewhere in the sectarian literature, especially the Hodayot.[41] This also provides an intriguing parallel to Ps 148:5–6, which speaks of the creation and fixed bounds of the heavenly spaces. The heavenly structures may also be paralleled by the earthly fountains, foundations, and councils in 4QBer[a] 5 4–12. Such spatialization should bring us beyond the purely literary treatment of this text, as the heavenly and earthly spaces are being brought together by a movement that believed that its various communal rituals were shared with the heavenly worshippers. It also further draws attention to the ordering of the cosmos as a whole.[42]

The final element to note here is the rather obvious difference that 4QBerakhot[a] contains curses, while the Song, the Words of the Luminaries, and Ps 148 do not. However, the inclusion of those being cursed as Belial's lot continues the downward movement to the chthonic spaces of Sheol and Abaddon, where the transgressors are consigned. This boundary-marking element of the ritual recorded in 4QBerakhot also adds to the sense of spatiality, as "curses solidify the perception of the enemy and maintain clear insistence that members of the community must stay away from the enemy, and guard against following the enemy's ways."[43] As I will argue in section 3, however, the inclusion of the grave in all three of the Second Temple Period ritual texts—whether individuals are saved from or consigned to it—should lead us to see all of these texts as creating boundaries of sorts.

In all three of the Late Second Temple Jewish liturgies discussed thus far, we have found elaborations on the basic structure found previously in Ps 148. God is to be blessed or praised for his creation of the various spheres or domains of existence, from the heavens down to the earth. The detailed lists created in the Song and 4QBerakhot[a] especially show remarkable similarities, though also stark differences. While 4QBerakhot[a] lacks the antiphonal refrain and narrative elements of the Song, it does add curses and clearer performative cues. Both are structured to include the same basic sites of creation that are called upon to bless God,

---

[41] E.g., 1QH[a] 9:24; 10:12; 13:28; 20:16, 32. See Krause, "Community," 232–3.

[42] Angela Kim Harkins, *Reading with an "I" to the Heavens: Looking at the Qumran Hodayot through the Lens of Visionary Traditions*, Ekstasis 3 (Berlin: de Gruyter, 2012). For Harkins, this is part of the general movement in 1QHodayot[a], which narrates a merging of spaces and a general vertical progression from col. IX onwards.

[43] Arnold, *Social Role of Liturgy*, 164; Arnold's argument is prefigured by the work of Jonathan Z. Smith who argues that all ritual transforms space through its sacralising effects. See Smith, *Take Place*, 47–73.

and both add the grave to the downward movement, as does the Words of the Luminaries. From these elaborations, though, we may adduce theological and rhetorical differences.

Rhetorical Development and Religio-Political Discourse in Creational Blessings

The growing, dynamic tradition of creational blessings thus evinces both consistency and adaptation. Much like the sorts of elaboration we find in legal traditions, these texts point back to a scriptural foundation, while making a claim regarding the fulfillment of the blessings promised in these sacred texts. Creational accounts are fundamentally political insofar as they describe the creation of the cosmos from the perspective of a specific nation or group, often characterizing this group and its land or worship as specially blessed. In this way, we find that Michael Swartz' comment on blessings lists from Late Antiquity—that the authors sought to objectify the creation that they recount—is truer of the Late Second Temple period than has been recognized previously.[44] In this final section, I will discuss the possible rhetorical objectives inherent in these texts and the implications for how we should read them. In terms of cosmological ordering and boundary-marking, I will argue that these texts lay claim to God's favor in both the initial creation and in the contexts in which they were written. I will contend that the ending of the Song of the Three Youths is far from the clumsy secondary addition that it is usually made out to be, but rather a carefully redacted text that is taking part in the larger discourse evident in creational blessings lists of the Second Temple Period.

First, the common elaboration of the grave or Abaddon, as these chthonic spaces are the final spaces listed, is also a place meant specifically to 'other'. This particular discussion is part of the larger discourse regarding the demarcation of transgressive/impure and elect/pure, especially in terms of the use of cursing as a rite of affliction in 4QBerakhot[a].[45] While the comprehensive blessings of 4QBerakhot give a sense of universalism that is absent in the covenant blessings and curses of 1QS cols. I–III, we must note that all humans who are in league with Belial (which

---

[44] Swartz, "Aesthetics," 191.
[45] See Krause, "Community," 217–37. Rites of Affliction are those rituals meant to expel or keep out unwanted powers, spirits, or 'evil' humans; see Victor Turner, *The Forest of Symbols: Aspects of Ndembu Ritual* (Ithaca: Cornell University Press, 1967), 9–11.

presumably is most of them) are already consigned to Sheol and Abad-don.[46] As is common in the so-called sectarian texts, promises and bless-ings that are pronounced with respect to the nation in Torah texts are claimed exclusively for themselves by members of the *Yaḥad* move-ment.[47] To this we might compare the seeming blessings declared from the grave or Abaddon in 4QDibHam[a] 1–2 VII, recto 8. Even here, we find that such inclusion makes a religio-political statement, as God has fashioned the grave, which is usually associated with the enemies of God in this period, and he has thus brought it under his control. This should be read as being analogous to the inclusion of sea monsters, the primor-dial enemies of creators and orderly creation in most ancient Near East-ern creation accounts, in Pr Azar 57. Thus, returning to the Song of the Three Youths, the declaration that God had saved the three youths from the grave and destruction (Pr Azar 66) is equally a statement that the God of the Jewish people has saved the three youths from death at the hand of their Babylonian oppressors. Unlike Daniel, who often stands apart from his Judean and Jewish compatriots in the book that bears his name, Shadrach, Meshach, and Abednego are Jewish every-men, which leads back to the sense that their blessings and curses are representative of the rest of their people. This should cause us to question Henze's assertion that, unlike the Prayer of Azariah, the Song does not presuppose some form of oppression.[48] This movement down to the furnace is also in line with the growing association of chthonic spaces with fire and annihilation in the Late Second Temple Period, as we find in 4QBer[a] 7 II, 5–10, 1QS 4:11–14, or the reference to Gehenna (γεέννα) as a place of destruction in the New Testament (e.g., Matt 23:15; Mark 9:43; Luke 12:5). In this reading, then, God's salvific work in saving these three representative

---

[46] Krause, "Community," 230–6. For the standard work on the link between demons and political barriers in ancient religious discourse, see Jonathan Z. Smith, "Towards Inter-preting Demonic Powers in Hellenistic and Roman Antiquity," *ANRW* II.16.1 (1978): 425–39. Smith argues that demonic discourse always contains a locative function, as vague, shapeless ideas of evil are replaced with specific imagery and associations with the enemies of the writers and their communities.

[47] For examples, see Alison Schofield, "The Em-Bodied Desert and Other Sectarian Spaces in the Dead Sea Scrolls," in *Contested Spaces IV: Further Developments in Examining Ancient Israel's Social Space*, ed. Mark K. George (New York: Blooms-bury, 2013), 155–74; Andrew R. Krause, "They Shall Not be Admitted to the Assem-bly of the Lord: Community and Space in the Exegesis of Deuteronomy 23:1–8 in the Dead Sea Scrolls," in *Recent Perspectives on the Qumran Community: From the Ess-enes to the Yahad, and Beyond,* ed. Jörg Frey, WUNT II (Tübingen: Mohr Siebeck), forthcoming.

[48] Cf. Henze, "Additions," 132.

Jews from the fire is politically meaningful insofar as it presents the God who is eulogized for creation as also saving his people, who are set apart through the boundaries created by their separate blessing in vv. 61–65. Thus, in all three cases, the grave and destruction become meaningful as they and their inhabitants are 'othered' from the good, ordered creation that has been objectified in the preceding blessings, or they have been tamed as part of it.

Second, the intended and actual performative communities are rhetorically relevant in each of these three texts. Unlike in the priestly and Levitical blessings and curses of 1QS cols. I–III, the ritual performance of 4QBerakhot is based on the authority and actions of the "Council of the Community" (4QBer^a 7 II, 1), which represents the *Yaḥad* movement as a whole. In terms of Jokiranta's model for blessing and cursing, these blessings and curses combine 'action-based' and 'agent-based' agencies, as the ritual itself would create boundaries and the council itself possesses authority as a congregation of the divinely elect.[49] Likewise, in the Words of the Luminaries, the unnamed—or at least non-extant—ritual performers are meant to identify with those in the Babylonian exile, as well as with those chosen by the Creator God.[50] This latter notion, in many ways, matches what we find in the Song. Here, three Jewish heroes are saved from the hands of the paradigmatic oppressors, the Babylonians. Thus, not only does this remove the praise of God from the lips of the oppressors (Dan 3:28 MT), it places these blessings into the mouths of those God has saved, who will eventually comprise the nation as a whole. This sense of national praise is buttressed by the listing not only of priests, but also of servants, the spirits and souls of all the righteous, and all those holy and humble in heart from Israel who should bless God (Pr Azar 60–65). This depiction of exilic Jews singing these praises is only heightened by the fact that the statement in Tob 8:5, a text which is universally viewed as connected to the Song, is uttered by Tobias and Sarah after they exorcise Asmodeus in the Median city of Ecbatana.

Conclusion

As with other instances of creational blessings lists from this period, the Song of the Three Youths exhibits both a careful, detailed consistency and a creative adaptability. Utilizing the complex ritual concept of

---

[49] Jokiranta, "Towards," 37–45.
[50] Penner, "Words of the Luminaries," 16.

blessing or praising, all of the compositions discussed in this chapter make the entire cosmos a ritual site. All three of the Second Temple Period lists have shown an elaboration on the basic structure of Ps 148, though bringing a wider scriptural repertoire to bear on this tradition as they seek to order God's creation in way that matches their particular worldview. In the cases of both the Song and the extant text of 4QBerakhot[a] cols. I–IV, we find sections of heavenly and earthly spaces, which are followed by brief mentions of God's elect, including ritual markers of those who are meant to perform the full set of blessings. These spatial and ontological categories, as well as the ritual choreography, give a sense of lived experience and habitus to the texts beyond mere literary flourish. Likewise, the addition of discussion of the grave in all three texts adds a new category of alterity. Whether the grave is the place from which the elect are saved, to which Belial and other transgressors are adjured, or simply another place brought under the auspices of God's power and the ritual's imperatives to praise, this expansion adds to the social and political objectification and rhetorical authority. In each case, the elect of God not only reproduce God's creative works as they understand them, but they are able to place themselves above the rest of creation, both as counterparts to those who utter praise and as those with sufficient authority to call the rest of creation to praise God.

Bibliography

Aitken, James K. *The Semantics of Blessing and Cursing in Ancient Hebrew.* ANESSup 23. Leuven: Peeters, 2007.

Alt, Albrecht. "Die Weisheit Salomos." *TLZ* 76 (1951): 139–44.

Anderson, Jeff S. "Curses and Blessings: Social Control and Self Definition in the Dead Sea Scrolls." Pages 47–60 in vol. 1 of *The Dead Sea Scrolls in Context: Integrating the Dead Sea Scrolls in the Study of Ancient Texts Languages, and Cultures.* Edited by Armin Lange, Emmanuel Tov, and Matthias Weigold. VTSup 140.1. Leiden: Brill, 2011.

Angel, Joseph L. "The Material Reconstruction of 4QSongs of the Sage[b] (4Q511)." *RevQ* 27 (2015): 25–82.

Arnold, Russell C. D. *The Social Role of Liturgy in the Religion of the Qumran Community.* STDJ 60. Leiden: Brill, 2006.

Chazon, Esther G. "Is Divrei ha-me'orot a Sectarian Prayer?" Pages 3–17 in *The Dead Sea Scrolls: Forty Years of Research.* Edited by Devorah Dimant and Uriel Rappaport. STDJ 10. Leiden: Brill, 1992.

Chazon, Esther G. "Prayer and Identity in Varying Contexts: The Case of the *Words of the Luminaries.*" *JSJ* 46 (2015): 484–511.

Collins, John J. *Daniel: A Commentary on the Book of Daniel.* Hermeneia. Minneapolis: Fortress Press, 1993.

Daise, Michael A. "The Temporal Relation between the Covenant Renewal Rite and the Initiation Process in 1QS." Pages 150–60 in *Qumran Studies: New Approaches, New Questions*. Edited by Michael Thomas Davis and Brent A. Strawn. Grand Rapids: Eerdmans, 2007.

Davila, James R. *Liturgical Works*. ECDSS 6. Grand Rapids: Eerdmans, 2000.

Falk, Daniel K. *Daily, Sabbath, and Festival Prayers in the Dead Sea Scrolls*. STDJ 27. Leiden: Brill, 1998.

Frechette, Christopher G. "Blessing and Cursing." Pages 59–63 in *The Oxford Encyclopedia of the Bible and Law*. Edited by Brent A. Strawn. Oxford: Oxford University Press, 2015.

Gösta, Gabriel. *enūma eliš – Weg zu einer globalen Weltordnung*. ORA 12. Tübingen: Mohr Siebeck, 2014.

Gaster, Moses. "The Unknown Aramaic Original of Theodotion's Additions to the Book of Daniel." *PSBA* 16 (1894): 280–317.

Harkins, Angela Kim. "Another Look at the Cave 1 Hodayot: Was CH I Materially Part of the Scroll 1QHodayot[a]?" *Dead Sea Discoveries* 25.2 (2018): 185–216.

Harkins, Angela Kim. *Reading with an "I" to the Heavens: Looking at the Qumran Hodayot through the Lens of Visionary Traditions*. Ekstasis 3. Berlin: de Gruyter, 2012.

Henze, Matthias. "Additions to Daniel." Pages 122–39 in *Outside the Bible: Ancient Jewish Writings Related to Scripture*. Edited by Louis H. Feldman, James L. Kugel, and Lawrence H. Schiffman. Lincoln: University of Nebraska Press, 2013.

Hilgert, Markus. "Von ‚Listenwissenschaft' und ‚epistemischen Dingen'. Konzeptuelle Annäherungen an altorientalische Wissenspraktiken." *Zeitschrift für allgemeine Wissenschaftstheorie* 40.2 (2009): 277–309.

Jaffee, Martin S. "Deciphering Mishnaic Lists: A Form Critical Approach." Pages 19–34 in *Text as Context in Early Rabbinic Literature*. Edited by William Scott Green. Vol. 3 of *Approaches to Ancient Judaism*. BJS 11. Chico: Scholars Press, 1981.

Jokiranta, Jutta. "Ritualization and the Power of Listing in 4QBerakhot[a] (4Q286)." Pages 438–58 in *Is There a Text in this Cave? Studies in the Textuality of the Dead Sea Scrolls in Honour of George J. Brooke*. Edited by Ariel Feldman, Maria Ciotă, and Charlotte Hempel. STDJ 119. Leiden: Brill, 2017.

Jokiranta, Jutta. "Towards a Cognitive Theory of Blessing: The Dead Sea Scrolls as a Test Case." Pages 27–47 in *Functions of Psalms and Prayers in the Late Second Temple Period*. Edited by Mika S. Pajunen and Jeremy Penner. BZAW 486. Berlin: de Gruyter, 2017.

Kitz, Anne Marie. *Cursed are You: The Phenomenology of Cursing in Cuneiform and Hebrew Texts*. Winona Lake: Eisenbrauns, 2013.

Krause, Andrew R. "Community, Alterity, and Space in the Qumran Covenant Curses." *DSD* 25 (2018): 217–37.

Krause, Andrew R. "They Shall Not be Admitted to the Assembly of the Lord: Community and Space in the Exegesis of Deuteronomy 23:1–8 in the Dead Sea Scrolls." In *Recent Perspectives on the Qumran Community: From the*

Essenes to the Yahad, and Beyond. Edited by Jörg Frey. WUNT II. Tübingen: Mohr Siebeck, forthcoming.

Kuhl, Curt. *Die drei Männer im Feuer.* BZAW 55. Giessen: Töpelmann, 1930.

Milik, J.T. "Milkî-ṣedeq et Milkî-reša' dans les anciens écrits juifs et chrétiens." *JJS* 23 (1972): 95–144.

Moore, Carey A. *Daniel, Esther, and Jeremiah: The Additions.* AB 44. New York: Doubleday, 1977.

Newsom, Carol A. *The Self as Symbolic Space: Constructing Identity and Community at Qumran.* STDJ 52. Leiden: Brill, 2004.

Nitzan, Bilhah. "4QBerakhot A-e (4Q286-290): A Covenantal Ceremony in the Light of Related Texts." *RevQ* 16.4 (1995): 487–506.

Nitzan, Bilhah. "Harmonic and Mystical Characteristics in Poetic and Liturgical Writings from Qumran." *JQR* 85 (1994): 163–83.

Nitzan, Bilhah. "Berakhot." Pages 1–74 in *Qumran Cave 4, VI: Poetical and Liturgical Texts.* Edited by Esther Eshel, Hanan Eshel, Carol Newsom, Bilhah Nitzan, Eileen Schuller, and Ada Yardeni. DJD 11. Oxford: Clarendon, 1998.

Nitzan, Bilhah. "Textual, Literary, and Religious Character of *4QBerakhot* (4Q286–290)." Pages 636–56 in *The Provo International Conference on the Dead Sea Scrolls.* Edited by Donald W. Parry and Eugene Ulrich. STDJ 30. Leiden: Brill, 1999.

Pajunen, Mika S. "Creation as the Liturgical Nexus of the Blessings and Cursings in 4QBerakhot." Pages 27–39 in *Ancient Readers and their Scriptures: Engaging the Hebrew Bible in Early Judaism and Christianity.* Edited by John Anthony Dunne and Garrick V. Allen. AJEC 107. Leiden: Brill, 2018.

Penner, Jeremy. "Mapping Fixed Prayers from the Dead Sea Scrolls onto Second Temple Period Judaism." *DSD* 21 (2014): 39–63.

Penner, Jeremy. "The *Words of the Luminaries* as a Meditation on the Exile." *RevQ* 28.2 (2016): 175–90.

Pfann, Stephen J. "The Essene Yearly Renewal Ceremony and the Baptism of Repentance." Pages 337–52 in *The Provo International Conference on the Dead Sea Scrolls.* Edited by Donald W. Parry and Eugene Ulrich. STDJ 3. Leiden: Brill, 1999.

Rad, Gerhard von. "Hiob 38 und die altägyptische Weisheit." Pages 293–301 in *Wisdom in Israel and the Ancient Near East.* Edited by Martin Noth and Winston Thomas. VTSup 3. Leiden: Brill, 1955.

Schofield, Alison. "The Em-Bodied Desert and Other Sectarian Spaces in the Dead Sea Scrolls." Pages 155–74 in *Contested Spaces IV: Further Developments in Examining Ancient Israel's Social Space.* Edited by Mark K. George. New York: Bloomsbury, 2013.

Seri, Andrea. "Some notes on *enūma eliš.*" *JAOS* 137 (2017): 833–8.

Smith, Jonathan Z. *To Take Place: Toward Theory in Ritual.* Chicago: University of Chicago Press, 1987.

Smith, Jonathan Z. "Towards Interpreting Demonic Powers in Hellenistic and Roman Antiquity." *ANRW* II.16.1 (1978): 425–39.

Soden, Wolfram von. "Leistung und Grenze sumerischer und babylonischer Wissenschaft: Die Welt als Geschichte." *Zeitschrift für universalgeschichtliche Forschung* 2 (1936): 411–64, 509–57.

Sollamo, Raija. "The Creation of Angels and Natural Phenomena Intertwined in the *Book of Jubilees* (4QJubᵃ)." Pages 273–90 in *Biblical Traditions in Transmission: Essays in Honour of Michael A. Knibb*. Edited by Charlotte Hempel and Judith M. Lieu. JSJSup 111. Leiden: Brill, 2006.

Sørensen, Jesper. *A Cognitive Theory of Magic*. Plymouth: Altamira Press, 2007.

Sparks, Kenton L. "'Enūma Elish' and Priestly Mimesis: Elite Emulation in Nascent Judaism." *JBL* 126 (2007): 625–48.

Stegemann, Hartmut. "The Material Reconstruction of the *Hodayot*." Pages 272–84 in *The Dead Sea Scrolls: Fifty Years after their Discovery*. Edited by Lawrence H. Schiffman, Emmanuel Tov, and James C. VanderKam. Jerusalem: Israel Exploration Society, 2000.

Stegemann, Hartmut. "Methods for the Reconstruction of Scrolls from Scattered Fragments." Pages 189–220 in *Archaeology and History in the Dead Sea Scrolls*. Edited by Lawrence H. Schiffman. JSPSup 8. Sheffield: JSOT Press, 1990.

Stegemann, Hartmut, Eileen Schuller, and Carol Newsom. *Qumran Cave 1, III: 1QHodayotᵃ: With Incorporation of 1QHodayotᵇ and 4QHodayotᵃ⁻ᶠ*. DJD XL. Oxford: Clarendon, 2009.

Stone, Michael E. "Lists of Revealed Things in Apocalyptic Literature." Pages 414–52 in *Magnalia Dei: The Mighty Acts of God*. Edited by Frank Moore Cross, Werner E. Lemke, and Patrick D. Miller, Jr. New York: Doubleday, 1976.

Swartz, Michael D. "The Aesthetics of Blessing and Cursing: Literary and Iconographic Dimensions of Hebrew and Aramaic Blessing and Curse Texts." *JANER* 5 (2006): 187–211.

Turner, Victor. *The Forest of Symbols: Aspects of Ndembu Ritual*. Ithaca: Cornell University Press, 1967.

Tzoref, Shani. "4Q252: *Listenwissenschaft* and Covenantal Patriarchal Blessings." Pages 337–57 in *Go Out and Study the Land (Judges 18:2): Archaeological, Historical, and Textual Studies in Honor of Hanan Eshel*. Edited by Aren M. Maier, Jodi Magness, and Lawrence H. Schiffman. JSJSup 148. Leiden: Brill, 2011.

PRAYER IN NARRATIVE

PRAYER AS MNEMONIC
FOR THE BOOK OF DANIEL

Jennie Grillo

By late antiquity, the book of Daniel had come to exist as a sort of meme: a single, simple image of a praying figure in a place of peril. We meet this image first in the catacomb frescoes: standing figures holding up outspread hands, with fire lapping around their Persian boots or lions crouched at Daniel's naked feet.[1] As a compressed kernel of the book of Daniel, this image becomes common coin across many visual cultures, so that the nutshell of the whole Daniel-book can be present simply as this spare pictogram, prayer in the place of danger. An example is the author illumination for the book of Daniel in the Paris Syriac Bible: here, the skilled seer of the biblical book is reduced iconographically to a praying figure in a tight space.[2] The lions' den is so stylized it is really just a round hole; it occupies a slot in the story which could easily be swapped for a furnace or a garden, and Daniel exchanged for Azariah or Susanna.[3] And the basic template is replicated across time and across media: in the silver of the Nea Herakleia reliquary, in ivory on the Murano diptych; on processional crosses, amulets, sarcophagus reliefs, gold-glass bowls, textiles, clasps and combs.[4]

---

[1] See, e.g., James Stevenson, *The Catacombs: Rediscovered Monuments of Early Christianity*, Ancient Peoples and Places 91 (London: Thames and Hudson, 1978), 75–81.

[2] BN.Syriac MS 341, f.186r (late 6th c. or early 7th c.). https://gallica.bnf.fr/ark:/12148/btv1b10527102b/f377.item.

[3] See Reiner Sörries, Die Syrische Bibel von Paris: Paris, Bibliothèque Nationale, syr 341: Eine frühchristliche Bilderhandschrift aus dem 6. Jahrhundert (Wiesbaden: Reichert, 1991), 44; it is his suggestion that the large square pedestal with a central circular hole is a reminder of the lions' den.

[4] For images of a number of these, see Kurt Weitzmann, *Age of Spirituality: Late Antique and Early Christian Art, Third to Seventh Century: Catalogue of the Exhibition at the Metropolitan Museum of Art, November 19, 1977, through February 12, 1978* (New York: Metropolitan Museum of Art in association with Princeton University Press, 1979), 400, 403, 413, 417, 421, 425, 428, 430–1, 485, 597. See the discussion of several examples in Robin M. Jensen, *Understanding Early Christian Art* (London: Routledge, 2000), 77–84, 171–8. For a comprehensive summary, see Henri Leclerq, "Daniel," *Dictionnaire d'archéologie chrétienne et de liturgie* 4:221–48; idem, "Hébreux (Les

When the stories in the book of Daniel are reduced to a template in this way, the contours of the individual tales are fused together, and they can be mapped onto one another: the lions' den story takes the impress of the furnace story, with its central motif of prayer. A Byzantine pyxis at Dumbarton Oaks illustrates this slippage: Daniel stands at the center of the composition, praying like his friends in the flames; on either side of him, an angel shuts a lion's mouth, reflecting the lions' den story of ch. 6; at the same time, a snake wraps around a statue of an idol, taking us into the second lions' den story of ch. 14.[5] Two stories are compressed into one praying figure. The subsequent memory of Daniel and the three youths takes this stamp so completely that they can be recognized in the scarcest traces of feet and flames on a broken fresco, or in the faintest outline of a pair of hands and a pair of lions on a stone cross worn almost to smoothness. André Grabar suggestively called abbreviated representations like these in early Christian art "image-signs"; Thomas Mathews calls them "staccato images"; Ruth Clements "'freeze-frame,' single-moment representations."[6] In each case, though, it is especially telling to observe *what* content or *which* motifs of any given longer story belongs indispensably to the compressed visual kernel. Prayer in the moment of danger pushes to the center of the Daniel stories; but this process of 'natural selection' rests on a textual basis which is often later obscured.

The image of a praying Daniel is already more of a product of hindsight than first sight. In the apocalypse known as the *Questions of Ezra*, the angel who is exhorting Ezra to pray says to him, "For if your prayer were such as Moses wept for forty days and spoke with God mouth to mouth, likewise also Elijah was taken up to heaven in a fiery chariot, likewise Daniel also prayed in the lions' den..."[7] At first glance it makes intuitive sense to include Daniel like this in a list of prophets who prayed

trois jeunes)," *Dictionnaire d'archéologie chrétienne et de liturgie* 6:2107–26, idem, "Suzanne," *Dictionnaire d'archéologie chrétienne et de liturgie* 15:1742–52.
[5] Weitzmann, *Age of Spirituality*, 469–70.
[6] André Grabar, *Christian Iconography: A Study of Its Origins* (Princeton: Princeton University Press, 1980), 9–10; Thomas F. Mathews, *The Clash of Gods: A Reinterpretation of Early Christian Art* (Princeton: Princeton University Press, 1993), 12–6; Ruth A. Clements, "The Parallel Lives of Early Jewish and Christian Texts and Art: The Case of Isaac the Martyr," in *New Approaches to the Study of Biblical Interpretation in Judaism of the Second Temple Period and in Early Christianity*, ed. Florentino García Martínez, STDJ 106 (Leiden: Brill, 2013), 218, 226.
[7] Recension A, 39–40 in the translation from the Armenian of M.E. Stone in James H. Charlesworth, *The Old Testament Pseudepigrapha* (London: Darton, Longman & Todd, 1983), 1:591–9.

Byzantine pyxis (BZ.1936.22); copyright Dumbarton Oaks,
Byzantine Collection, Washington, DC.

great prayers: Daniel's voice is, after all, the one behind the long penitential prayer of Daniel 9. But in the lions' den Daniel did not, in fact,
pray like the angel in *Questions of Ezra* says he did. Praying in his upper
room was the act which got him thrown into the lions' den, but the Masoretic Text does not represent Daniel praying *in* the lions' den. The Aramaic text does not actually represent him in the lions' den at all, but cuts
straight from the moment Daniel is thrown into the den to the moment
Darius summons him out; for the duration of time that Daniel is in the
den, the narrative focus is on the king. Where, then, does the idea of
Daniel praying in the lions' den come from? It is true that in the lions'
den of ch. 14 Daniel does have a brief interjection, poised between prayer
and testimony: in Theodotion, "For you have remembered me, O God,
and have not forsaken those who love you" (Dan 14:38).[8] In the Old
Greek, this is directed away from direct address to God: "And Daniel
said, 'For the Lord God who does not forsake those who love him has

---

[8] All quotations from both Greek versions are taken from Albert Pietersma and Benjamin
G. Wright III, eds., *A New English Translation of the Septuagint* (New York: Oxford
University Press, 2007).

remembered me'.'" The Peshitta too has third-person testimony with
a brief glance upwards, "God has remembered me, his compassion has
not gone from me—indeed I know that you do not forsake those who
love you."[9] But there is another, weightier textual pressure that turns
Daniel in the lions' den into a man of prayer like Moses or Jonah: the
source of this pressure is the expanded text of Greek Dan 3, reoriented
around the prayer of the three youths facing death.

The longer versions of Dan 3 bring prayer into the heart of the furnace.
The massive expansion of the Greek texts, with their magnificent liturgical offerings of penitence and praise, turns the three youths into proto-
types of martyrs who go to their deaths praying. V. 24, "And they were
walking around in the middle of the flames, singing hymns to God and
blessing the Lord," acts as a caption for the entire expansion, casting the
whole episode as a story of prayer. The Old Greek takes this process even
further than Theodotion in chapter 3: OG seems to put the prayer of
Azariah in the mouths of all three youths together, when Azariah
"acknowledged the Lord together with his companions in the middle of
the fire" (3:25). The text there is awkwardly repetitive and probably
composite,[10] but it was followed by the Vetus Latina, and the effect on
the history of reading has been to make the words that follow into the
prayer of all three youths, and even Daniel. All three in the furnace pray
Azariah's prayer with him, just as all sing the canticle that follows, and
in much of the later reception Daniel's voice is assimilated to the chorus
in the furnace too.

When we see Daniel praying in the lions' den, as he begins to do in
the versions of Dan 14 and as a text like *Questions of Ezra* simply
assumes he does, the lions' den story is being read on the pattern of the
furnace story. As the set of Daniel stories is retold and redrawn across
different times and different media, the separate contours of the individual tales merge, and shared outlines pull spreading narrative loops into
a common shape. This process happens with several features of the text.
To take a parallel example, we might think of the angel of chapter 3: the
angel briefly mentioned by Nebuchadnezzar in the Masoretic Text (3:28;
cf. v. 25) is developed into a more crucial role in the Additions to chapter 3, coming down into the furnace to be with the Three, shaking out the

---

[9] Translation of the Peshitta from George Anton Kiraz et al., *The Syriac Peshiṭta Bible
with English Translation. Daniel*, Antioch Bible (Piscataway, NJ: Gorgias Press, 2015).
[10] Carey A. Moore, *Daniel, Esther, and Jeremiah: The Additions*, AB 44 (Garden City,
NY: Doubleday, 1977), 56–7.

flame and bringing a cooling dew (3:49–50). This development spreads to the lions' den story: there, the angel we never meet but only hear about in chapter 6 (sent by God to shut the lions' mouths, v. 23), becomes a full on-stage character in the lions' den story of chapter 14, summoning—and then bringing—Habakkuk from Judea, and descending into the pit to be with Daniel. We could call this process a kind of motif-creep, or motif-spread; and the 'creep' which happens with the motif of the angel has happened also with the motif of prayer. But without the Additions to ch. 3, there would be no prayer here.

The process of re-reading Dan 6 on the basis of the Additions in this way is nicely illustrated by Aphrahat. In a homily "On Prayer," he—like the author of the *Questions of Ezra*—has a list of praying figures leading up through Jonah and the three youths to Daniel, sealed in the pit of Dan 6.[11] But in Aphrahat's telling, the angel who closes the lions' mouths in Dan 6 is summoned by the *prayers* of Daniel, and the lions even stretch out their paws in supplication, in imitation of him. The lions' den comes to resemble the furnace, full of light and prayer, and an explicit comparison is made with the sparser tradition of prayer which actually belongs to ch. 6: Aphrahat writes, "The den was illuminated more than an upper room with many windows, since there he multiplied his prayers more than in his upper room, where he only prayed three times a day."[12] All of this underlines the fact that the broad stream of reception of the tales of Daniel is really, of course, reception of the version *with Additions*. When the three youths or Daniel are pictured in their most characteristic pose—the *orans* in the place of danger—the textual basis for this framing of their stories is the longer version of Dan 3, where they first open their mouths to pray. The Additions take the first step towards the coalescing of the whole book of Daniel around the single image of a praying figure in a place of peril. Images like the early Christian 'freeze-frame' *orant* figures are later points on a trajectory which begins *within* the Additions. The exegetical work done by the Additions, re-ordering the furnace around the motif of prayer, is what eventually generates this kind of synopsis of the book of Daniel.

It is worth noting that this re-ordering of Daniel around the memory of the prayer of the three youths happens not only in the Christian

---

[11] *Demonstrations* 4.9 in Adam Lehto, trans., *The Demonstrations of Aphrahat, the Persian Sage*, Gorgias Eastern Christianity Studies 27 (Piscataway, NJ: Gorgias Press, 2010), 135–6.

[12] Lehto, *The Demonstrations of Aphrahat, the Persian Sage*, 135–6.

tradition but also in Jewish circles, even though the main stream of rabbinic tradition lacks the Additions, in the Masoretic text. From Roman Palestine, a broken mosaic in the Naʿaran synagogue preserves the paws of two lions either side of the raised arms of a praying figure, below an inscription that reads "Danie[l]. Shalom"; the posture and position of the figure echo the place of the prayer leader in the synagogue service.[13] Even more fragmentary is the mosaic at Susiyya, where a large tufted feline tail waves alongside a single outstretched palm and the letters ʾl—the broken-off end of "Daniel"?[14] Pictured in a Jewish catacomb at Beit Sheʿarim, a man stands with upraised hands, a lion crouching to spring at him: Mazar identifies this as a praying Daniel in the lions' den.[15] In the Sardis synagogue, three fragments of a fifth-century marble relief show four snarling lions, claws out, facing a standing figure: only a long tunic, a foot, and an upraised left arm carrying a scroll remain.[16] And all of these images find an echo in the praying hands and upraised eyes of both Daniel and his lions in a northern French Hebrew miscellany in the British Library, one of the most lavishly illustrated surviving Jewish manuscripts from medieval northern Europe.[17] All of these attest to the ongoing intelligibility of the motif of prayer in the place of danger as a shorthand for Daniel in the Jewish tradition. It is unlikely that all of these are simply the result of Christian influence.[18] Jewish texts continue to refer to the longer Daniel, from 1 Maccabees around the turn of the 1st century BCE to Yannai in perhaps the 6th century, and beyond.[19]

---

[13] See the drawing in Lee I. Levine, ed., *Ancient Synagogues Revealed* (Jerusalem: Israel Exploration Society, 1981), 136.

[14] See Rachel Hachlili, *Ancient Synagogues – Archaeology and Art: New Discoveries and Current Research*, Handbook of Oriental Studies. Section 1, Ancient Near East 105 (Leiden: Brill, 2013), 420.

[15] Benjamin Mazar, *Beth Sheʿarim: Report on the Excavations during 1936–1940* (New Brunswick, NJ: Rutgers University Press on behalf of the Israel Exploration Society and the Institute of Archaeology, Hebrew University, 1973), 1:77–8.

[16] Marcus Rautman, "Daniel at Sardis," *BASOR* 358 (2010): 47–60.

[17] British Library Add. Ms. 11639, f.260r, dated 1277–1324; in this case the imagery was strongly influenced by French Gothic manuscripts made for Christian use (I am grateful to Pamela Patton for explaining this to me).

[18] Cf. Géza G. Xeravits, "A Possible Greek Bible Source for Late Antique Synagogue Art," in *Construction, Coherence and Connotations: Studies on the Septuagint, Apocryphal and Cognate Literature*, ed. Pierre J. Jordaan and Nicholas P.L. Allen, DCLS 34 (Berlin: de Gruyter, 2016), 233–48, who suggests that the motif is borrowed into Jewish sources from Christian representations of Dan 14.

[19] 1 Macc 2:60 recalls Daniel's innocence (ἁπλότης) from OG Susanna v. 62; Yannai includes that 'Bel and his pedestal fell in the middle of night' within a list of God's nocturnal miracles for Israel, in a *qedushta* on Exod 12:29; translation in Richard S. Sarason, "Midrash in Liturgy," in *Encyclopaedia of Midrash: Biblical Interpretation*

Nicholas de Lange reminds us that the Greek Bible remained in circulation among Jews spread across the Byzantine world, and not only in those versions abbreviated to reflect the proto-MT in Daniel. He draws attention to a probably Jewish early 4th c. parchment roll, P.Lit.Lond.211, which reproduces the text of Daniel 1 in Theodotion's version.[20] Memories of Daniel in Jewish as well as Christian circles, then, sometimes clustered around the organizing principle of prayer derived from the longer versions of the stories.

We can observe the same crystallizing of narrative around the motif of prayer taking place in representations of Susanna. She is also very often represented as an *orant*, hands raised and fully facing the viewer, this time poised between the two elders rather than lions or flames. One example is the early 5th-century catacomb fresco from Thessaloniki, where a tall, dignified matron raises her sleeved arms to heaven between the two elders under their two trees.[21] A very full treatment is preserved on the fourth-century Brescia casket from northern Italy: on the front face of this finely-worked ivory box, she spreads out her hands in prayer beneath the trees as the elders approach.[22] But in all of these, the story has been condensed to create a visual center in Susanna's praying figure: in both Greek versions, Susanna actually prays not in the garden but right at the end of the narrative, in the trial scene which takes place the following day (OG 35a, Th 42–43). So time here has been folded around the motif of prayer, conforming Susanna's story to the pattern of prayer in a place of peril—in her case the garden where, as she says, "things are narrow for me" (Sus 22). The plot has been harmonized to the bare elements of prayer in danger. What is represented here, then, is not

---

in *Formative Judaism*, ed. Jacob Neusner and Alan J. Avery-Peck (Leiden: Brill, 2005), 1:490.

[20] Nicholas. R. M. de Lange, *Japheth in the Tents of Shem: Greek Bible Translations in Byzantine Judaism*, Texts and Studies in Medieval and Early Modern Judaism 30 (Tübingen: Mohr Siebeck, 2015), 58, 72–3. For evidence of continuing knowledge of the longer Daniel, see the large number of proposals for allusions to the Additions in rabbinic texts amassed by C.J. Ball in the Speaker's Commentary: C.J. Ball, "Additions to Daniel," in *The Holy Bible, According to the Authorized Version (A. D. 1611), with an Explanatory and Critical Commentary and a Revision of the Translation: Apocrypha*, ed. Henry Wace (London: John Murray, 1888), 2:305–60, 2:305–7, 326–30, 344–9.

[21] Anastasia Drandaki, Dēmētra Papanikola-Bakirtzē, and Anastasia Tourta, *Heaven & Earth: Art of Byzantium from Greek Collections* (Athens: Hellenic Ministry of Culture and Sports; Benaki Museum, 2013), 71.

[22] See the photographs and treatment in Catherine Brown Tkacz, *The Key to the Brescia Casket: Typology and the Early Christian Imagination*, Collection Des Études Augustiniennes. Série Antiquité 165 (Notre Dame: University of Notre Dame Press, 2001).

'freeze-frame'; not a frozen single moment but multiple moments gathered to a single focus of prayer in mortal danger.

All of these early readers of the book of Daniel, in their textual and
visual modes of interpretation, attest to the way that the Additions have
centered the book of Daniel on chapter 3, and on the place of danger as
a place of prayer. In closing, I will examine one further way in which the
reception of the prayers in the Additions to Daniel amplifies and perhaps
clarifies for us some of the moves which the Additions themselves are
making as they adapt and expand their underlying base text of Daniel:
I want to consider the penitential orientation of some of the scribal work
in the Additions to Dan 3.

The prayer of Azariah in Dan 3:26–34 is of course most cogently
understood within a particular genre of Second Temple prayer, where
disaster is confessed as the just punishment of a righteous God upon
a sinful nation.[23] Azariah's prayer is an unhoped-for fulfilment of
Solomon's prayer at the dedication of the Jerusalem temple: in the experience of Daniel and his friends, Israel has indeed now been carried away
captive to the land of the enemy, and now pleads with heart and soul
saying, essentially, "We have sinned, and have done wrong; we have
acted wickedly" (Solomon's words in 1 Kgs 8:47). The prayer in Dan 3
shares a literary and spiritual milieu with prayers such as those at Ezra
9:6–15, Neh 1:5–11 and 9:6–37, Dan 9:4–19, Tob 3:11–15, 3 Macc
2:2–19 and 6:2–15, Jdt 9:2–14, Addition C 2(13)–10(17) in Greek
Esther, Bar 1:15–3:8, 1 Esd 8:71–87, and the Qumran texts Words of
the Heavenly Luminaries (4Q504), the communal confession 4Q393,
and the abbreviated penitential prayer embedded in the Damascus Document at CD 20:28–30. Usually, it is assumed that Azariah's prayer is an
existing liturgical composition borrowed into the book of Daniel, and
perhaps adapted to reflect the redactors' Maccabean atmosphere of stress
under "an unjust king and the most wicked in the world" (Dan 3:32).[24]
A closer interpretive relationship to the Daniel tradition is also possible:

---

[23] The classic recognition of these late penitential prayers as a genre is that of Claus
Westermann, in a 1954 article translated into English in Claus Westermann, *Praise and
Lament in the Psalms*, trans. Keith R. Crim and Richard N. Soulen (Atlanta; Richmond,
VA: John Knox, 1981), 165–213, esp. 201–13. For an overview of recent work see
Eileen Schuller, "Penitential Prayer in Second Temple Judaism: A Research Survey,"
in *The Development of Penitential Prayer in Second Temple Judaism*, (vol. 2 of *Seeking
the Favor of God*, ed. Mark J. Boda, Daniel K. Falk, and Rodney A. Werline, EJL 22
(Atlanta: SBL Press, 2007), 1–15.

[24] John J. Collins, *Daniel: A Commentary on the Book of Daniel*, Hermeneia (Minneapolis: Fortress Press, 1993), 198–200; Moore, *Daniel, Esther, and Jeremiah*, 41; Klaus
Koch, *Deuterokanonische Zusätze zum Danielbuch: Entstehung und Textgeschichte*,

rather than a borrowed, finished piece, Azariah's prayer may reflect scribal exegesis in Hebrew or even in Greek.[25]

Azariah's prayer in Greek Dan 3 thus already belongs within a penitential genre. But in its early reception, that penitential emphasis flourishes, and in the light of that penitential reading the prayer itself comes to seem more integrally embedded in its narrative surroundings. When later readers elaborate on the prayer's setting within the narrative context created by the chapter, the prayer itself comes to blend with the purgative power of the elements in the furnace, as the dewy breeze drops down tears of remorse and the flames of the fire scourge away sin. Cyril of Jerusalem imagines his audience within the fiery furnace, in a catechetical lecture on repentance probably given in Lent of 349 CE. In Cyril's use of Dan 3 it is penance—rather than a rescuing angel—which quenches the flames of the furnace, and the prescribed form of that penance is the recitation of the prayer of Azariah itself:

> For confession has the power to quench even fire; it can tame lions. If you doubt it, consider what happened to Anania and his companions. What streams did they pour out? How many measures of water were needed to quench a flame forty-nine cubits high? But wherever the fire threatened to overwhelm them, there their faith gushed rivers, as they repeated the words that worked like a charm: 'You are just in all you have done to us: for we have sinned and committed iniquity.' And their penitence subdued the flames.[26]

That is, the words of the prayer are now the supernatural agent able to cool the fire: penitential prayer, not an angel, has the divine power to work 'like a charm.' This ordering of the chapter—narrative and all—towards penitence is nowhere clearer than in a supplication which is still appointed to be read after the canticles of Dan 3 in the Armenian liturgy, and was once even woven in between verses of the Prayer of Azariah:

AOAT 38 (Kevelaer: Butzon & Bercker; Neukirchen-Vluyn: Neukirchener Verlag, 1987), 2:80.

[25] In Hebrew or Aramaic: Ulrike Mittmann-Richert, "Why Has Daniel's Prophecy Not Been Fulfilled? The Question of Political Peace and Independence in the Additions to Daniel," in *Reading the Present in the Qumran Library: The Perception of the Contemporary by Means of Scriptural Interpretations*, ed. Kristin De Troyer and Armin Lange, SBLSymS 30 (Atlanta: SBL Press, 2005), 103-23. In Greek: Jan Joosten, "The Prayer of Azariah (Dan LXX 3): Sources and Origin," in *Septuagint and Reception: Essays Prepared for the Association for the Study of the Septuagint in South Africa*, ed. Johann Cook, VTSup 127 (Leiden: Brill, 2009), 5–16.

[26] Catechesis 2.15-16 in Leo P. McCauley, trans., *The Works of Saint Cyril of Jerusalem. Volume 1*, FC 61 (Washington, DC: Catholic University of America Press, 2005), 105–6.

Make fall, O Lord, the dew of thy beneficent mercy upon our sinful souls. Quench the flame of the furnace of our transgressions and deliver us from the everlasting fire. Make us worthy, together with the three holy children and with the blessed holy martyrs, to bless and to praise thee, saying: O God, be gracious unto me, a sinner; O God, be gracious unto me, a sinner; O God, be gracious unto me, a sinner, and expiate me of my sins and save me.[27]

In a complete assimilation of the prayer to penitential archetypes, Azariah's words can now be paraphrased as the words of the tax collector in Luke 18:13. The fire itself is no longer the persecution of a tyrant, but due punishment: "the furnace of *our transgressions*." Offering commentary on the place of the Prayer of Azariah in the Armenian liturgy, the eighth-century catholicos Yovhannes Ojneci recognizes its penitential archetype in 1 Kgs 8, and shows how that model structures the sequence of different kinds of prayer in Dan 3: repentance comes before blessing in Solomon's prayer of dedication, and likewise the remorseful Prayer of Azariah must come before the blessings in the Song of the Three. "It is necessary for the sinner first to be justified through penance, and then to have authority and to give orders to creatures. First of all to say, 'We have sinned, we have transgressed;' and then to say, 'Bless the Lord, all works of the Lord'."[28] And the furnace itself as well as the dew inside it will become part of this penitential formation: Azariah's prayer teaches anyone who recites it "to melt himself in a fire of contrition, and as if in heavenly dew, to shower and be purified in the distillation of tears."[29] The dew is no longer a deliverance from flames, but from sin, and the fiery dissolution of self inside the furnace is now a longed-for mortification. These penitential readings press further on an emphasis which began when the Additions drew Dan 3 to a focus around prayer, first specified as penitential prayer: reception, here, is part of the imprint of the text's own processes of growth.

---

[27] *The Book of Hours, or The Order of Common Prayers of the Armenian Apostolic Orthodox Church: Matins, Prime, Vespers and Occasional Offices* (Evanston, IL: Ouzoonian House, 1964), 8. Cf. Michael D. Findikyan, ed., *The Commentary on the Armenian Daily Office by Bishop Step'anos Siwnec'i: Critical Edition and Translation with Textual and Liturgical Analysis*, OrChrAn 270 (Roma: Pontificio istituto orientale, 2004), 354. For an interlinear placing of this refrain within v. 35 of Pr Azar, see Athanase Renoux, ed., *Le codex arménien Jérusalem 121*, PO 35 (Turnhout: Brepols, 1969), 62.

[28] *Oratio synodalis* 14 in Findikyan, *The Commentary on the Armenian Daily Office by Bishop Step'anos Siwnec'i ([Died] 735)*, 346–7.

[29] Findikyan, *The Commentary on the Armenian Daily Office by Bishop Step'anos Siwnec'i ([Died] 735)*, 354.

Bibliography

The Book of Hours, or The Order of Common Prayers of the Armenian Apostolic Orthodox Church: Matins, Prime, Vespers and Occasional Offices. Evanston, IL: Ouzoonian House, 1964.

Ball, C.J. "Additions to Daniel." Pages 305–60 in vol. 2 *The Speaker's Commentary: The Holy Bible, According to the Authorized Version (A.D. 1611), with an Explanatory and Critical Commentary and a Revision of the Translation: Apocrypha.* Edited by Henry Wace. London: John Murray, 1888.

Cabrol, Fernand, and Henri Leclercq. *Dictionnaire d'archéologie chrétienne et de liturgie.* 15 vols. Paris: Letouzey et Ané, 1907.

Charlesworth, James H. *The Old Testament Pseudepigrapha.* London: Darton, Longman & Todd, 1983.

Clements, Ruth A. "The Parallel Lives of Early Jewish and Christian Texts and Art: The Case of Isaac the Martyr." Pages 207–40 in *New Approaches to the Study of Biblical Interpretation in Judaism of the Second Temple Period and in Early Christianity.* Edited by Florentino García Martínez. STDJ 106. Leiden: Brill, 2013.

Collins, John J. *Daniel: A Commentary on the Book of Daniel.* Hermeneia. Minneapolis: Fortress Press, 1993.

de Lange, Nicholas R. M. *Japheth in the Tents of Shem: Greek Bible Translations in Byzantine Judaism.* Texts and Studies in Medieval and Early Modern Judaism 30. Tübingen: Mohr Siebeck, 2015.

Drandaki, Anastasia, Dēmētra Papanikola-Bakirtzē, and Anastasia Tourta. *Heaven & Earth: Art of Byzantium from Greek Collections.* Athens: Hellenic Ministry of Culture and Sports; Benaki Museum, 2013.

Findikyan, Michael Daniel, ed. *The Commentary on the Armenian Daily Office by Bishop Step'anos Siwnec'i: Critical Edition and Translation with Textual and Liturgical Analysis.* OrChrAn 270. Roma: Pontificio istituto orientale, 2004.

Grabar, André. *Christian Iconography: A Study of Its Origins.* Princeton: Princeton University Press, 1980.

Hachlili, Rachel. *Ancient Synagogues – Archaeology and Art: New Discoveries and Current Research.* Handbook of Oriental Studies. Section 1, Ancient Near East 105. Leiden: Brill, 2013.

Jensen, Robin M. *Understanding Early Christian Art.* London: Routledge, 2000.

Joosten, Jan. "The Prayer of Azariah (Dan LXX 3): Sources and Origin." Pages 5–16 in *Septuagint and Reception: Essays Prepared for the Association for the Study of the Septuagint in South Africa.* Edited by Johann Cook. VTSup 127. Leiden: Brill, 2009.

Kiraz, George Anton, Joseph Bali, Donald M. Walter, and Gillian Greenberg. *The Syriac Peshiṭta Bible with English Translation. Daniel.* Antioch Bible. Piscataway, NJ: Gorgias Press, 2015.

Koch, Klaus. *Deuterokanonische Zusätze zum Danielbuch: Entstehung und Textgeschichte.* AOAT 38. Kevelaer: Butzon & Bercker; Neukirchen-Vluyn: Neukirchener Verlag, 1987.

Lehto, Adam, trans. *The Demonstrations of Aphrahat, the Persian Sage.* Gorgias Eastern Christianity Studies 27. Piscataway, NJ: Gorgias Press, 2010.

Levine, Lee I., ed. *Ancient Synagogues Revealed*. Jerusalem: Israel Exploration Society, 1981.

Mathews, Thomas F. *The Clash of Gods: A Reinterpretation of Early Christian Art*. Princeton: Princeton University Press, 1993.

Mazar, Benjamin. *Beth She'arim: Report on the Excavations during 1936–1940*. 3 vols. New Brunswick, NJ: Rutgers University Press on behalf of the Israel Exploration Society and the Institute of Archaeology, Hebrew University, 1973.

McCauley, Leo P., trans. *The Works of Saint Cyril of Jerusalem. Volume 1*. FC 61. Washington, DC: Catholic University of America Press, 2005.

Mittmann-Richert, Ulrike. "Why Has Daniel's Prophecy Not Been Fulfilled? The Question of Political Peace and Independence in the Additions to Daniel." Pages 103–23 in *Reading the Present in the Qumran Library: The Perception of the Contemporary by Means of Scriptural Interpretations*. Edited by Kristin De Troyer and Armin Lange. SBLSymS 30. Atlanta: SBL Press, 2005.

Moore, Carey A. *Daniel, Esther, and Jeremiah: The Additions*. AB 44. Garden City, NY: Doubleday, 1977.

Pietersma, Albert, and Benjamin G. Wright III. *A New English Translation of the Septuagint*. New York: Oxford University Press, 2007.

Rautman, Marcus. "Daniel at Sardis." *BASOR* 358 (2010): 47–60.

Renoux, Athanase, ed. *Le codex arménien Jérusalem 121*. PO 35. Turnhout: Brepols, 1969.

Sarason, Richard S. "Midrash in Liturgy." Pages 463–92 in vol. 1 of *Encyclopaedia of Midrash: Biblical Interpretation in Formative Judaism*. Edited by Jacob Neusner and Alan J. Avery-Peck. Leiden: Brill, 2005.

Schuller, Eileen. "Penitential Prayer in Second Temple Judaism: A Research Survey." Pages 1–15 in *The Development of Penitential Prayer in Second Temple Judaism*. Vol. 2 of *Seeking the Favor of God*. Edited by Mark J. Boda, Daniel K. Falk, and Rodney A. Werline. EJL 22. Atlanta: SBL Press, 2007.

Sörries, Reiner. *Die Syrische Bibel von Paris: Paris, Bibliothèque Nationale, syr 341: Eine frühchristliche Bilderhandschrift aus dem 6. Jahrhundert*. Wiesbaden: Reichert, 1991.

Stevenson, James. *The Catacombs: Rediscovered Monuments of Early Christianity*. Ancient Peoples and Places 91. London: Thames and Hudson, 1978.

Tkacz, Catherine Brown. *The Key to the Brescia Casket: Typology and the Early Christian Imagination*. Collection Des Études Augustiniennes. Série Antiquité 165. Notre Dame: University of Notre Dame Press, 2001.

Weitzmann, Kurt. *Age of Spirituality: Late Antique and Early Christian Art, Third to Seventh Century: Catalogue of the Exhibition at the Metropolitan Museum of Art, November 19, 1977, through February 12, 1978*. New York: Metropolitan Museum of Art in association with Princeton University Press, 1979.

Westermann, Claus. *Praise and Lament in the Psalms*. Translated by Keith R. Crim and Richard N. Soulen. Atlanta; Richmond, VA: John Knox, 1981.

Xeravits, Géza G. "A Possible Greek Bible Source for Late Antique Synagogue Art." Pages 233–48 in *Construction, Coherence and Connotations: Studies on the Septuagint, Apocryphal and Cognate Literature*. Edited by Pierre J. Jordaan and Nicholas P.L. Allen. DCLS 34. Berlin: de Gruyter, 2016.

ESTHER'S PRAYER (ADDITION C) AS A THEOLOGICAL REINTERPRETATION OF THE HEBREW ESTHER STORY

Beate Ego

In an article published in 2003, the well-known Septuagint researcher Johannes Marböck referred to Esther's Prayer in the Esther Septuagint[1] narration as "a sum of the Greek reinterpretation of the Hebrew Book":

> The prayer of Esther derives its relevance not merely from its key position in the chain of events along Esther's walk to the King, but also from its length. With the motifs outlined therein (e.g. the praise of the one God, the mention of Israel as the inheritance of the Lord and the abidance by the Jewish law–B.E.), the prayer could (in conjunction with Mordecai's Prayer) be referred to as a sum of the Greek reinterpretations of the Hebrew Book, in which the actions of the human protagonists open up through prayer to God's plan of saving His people, which had been mysteriously hinted at in the dream.[2]

---

[1] For the literary genre of this text as a Greek romantic novel see Cameron Boyd-Taylor, "Esther's Great Adventure: Reading the LXX Version of the Book of Esther in Light of its Assimilation to the Conventions of the Greek Romantic Novel," *BIOSCS* 30 (1997): 81–113; Lawrence M. Wills, "Jewish Novellas in a Greek and Roman Age: Fiction and Identity," *JSJ* 42 (2011): 141–65. All texts from the Greek Esther are quoted according to the translation by Carey A. Moore, *Daniel, Esther, and Jeremiah: The Additions*, AB 44 (Garden City, NY: Doubleday, 1977).

[2] See Johannes Marböck, "Das Gebet der Ester: Zur Bedeutung des Gebetes im griechischen Esterbuch," in *Prayer from Tobit to Qumran: Inaugural Conference of the ISDCL at Salzburg, Austria, 5-9 July 2003*, ed. Renate Egger-Wenzel and Jeremy Corley, Deuterocanonical and Cognate Literature Yearbook 2004 (Berlin: de Gruyter, 2004), 73–94, here: 91; quotation translated from German. For Esther's prayer see also Linda M. Day, *Three Faces of a Queen: Characterization in the Books of Esther*, JSOTSup 186 (Sheffield: Sheffield Academic, 1995), 63–84; Markus H. McDowell, *Prayers of Jewish Women: Studies of Patterns of Prayer in the Second Temple Period*, WUNT II/211 (Tübingen: Mohr Siebeck, 2006), 37–41 (with a brief overview of the text); Moore, *Daniel, Esther, and Jeremiah*, 208–15; Ingo Kottsieper, "Zusätze zu Ester," in *Das Buch Baruch; Der Brief des Jeremia: Zu Ester und Daniel*, ed. Odil Hannes Steck, Reinhard G. Kratz and Ingo Kottsieper, ATD Apokryphen 5 (Göttingen: Vandenhoeck & Ruprecht, 1998), 109–207, here: 166–78; Stefan Schorch, "Genderising Piety: The Prayers of Mordecai and Esther in Comparison," in *Deuterocanonical Additions of the Old Testament Books: Selected Studies*, ed. Géza G. Xeravits and József Zsengellér, DCLS 5 (Berlin: de Gruyter, 2010), 30–42, here: 32–9; Marie-Theres Wacker, "Innensichten und Außensichten des Judentums im septuagintagriechischen Estherbuch

Moreover, Johannes Marböck emphasises that the incorporation of this text leads to a shift in the balance from Mordecai towards Esther in the Greek Esther narration. Despite several ambivalences, Esther is presented as an exemplary Israelite: she had been brought up to be one by Mordecai, according to Esth 2:20 LXX. In the Septuagint, Esther is not only the intercessor before the King and the saviour of her people; through her prayer, she first and foremost becomes the intercessor before God and the King of Israel, a paragon and a witness of Jewish piety in heathen surroundings. To describe the development of Esther's character from the Hebrew Esther text to the Septuagint, Marböck uses the term "heroization."[3]

Since Marböck's thesis constitutes one of the fundamental insights of Esther studies, it seems important to address and re-evaluate it in the context of a volume dedicated to the topic "Prayer in Deuterocanonical Literature." In order to throw light on the question how the overall understanding of the narrative has changed following the insertion of Esther's Prayer, it is necessary to first take stock of the characteristics of the prayer and its specific role within the Septuagint text of Esther. Subsequently, I will turn my attention to the function that Esther's Prayer fulfils in the interpretation of the Hebrew Esther text.

Esther's Prayer as Part of the Greek Esther: Structure, Motifs and Context

As has already been shown in research literature, Esther's Prayer seems likely to be made up of a pre-existing, poetic folk lament with a "we" narrator, supplemented with prosaic "I" statements and adapted to match Esther's specific situation.[4] Esther initially invokes God as the only king (C 14); in her loneliness, which is most likely an allusion to her isolated, risky position at court, he is the only one who can help her

---

(Est[LXX])," in *Gesellschaft und Religion in der spätbiblischen und deuterokanonischen Literatur*, ed. Friedrich V. Reiterer, Renate Egger-Wenzel and Thomas R. Elßner, DCLS 20 (Berlin: de Gruyter, 2014), 55–88.

[3] Marböck, "Das Gebet," 92: "Durch das Gebet geschieht auch eine Verschiebung der Balance von Mardochai ... zugunsten Esters ... Die Zusätze tragen ... noch zu ihrer größeren Individualisierung und Heroisierung bei. Ja, es scheint, dass in diesen griechischen Texten der Spätzeit die Rolle der Frauen als Vorbilder und Lehrerinnen des Glaubens überhaupt stärker hervortritt als in der hebräischen Bibel".

[4] This aspect was clearly demonstrated by Kottsieper, "Zusätze zu Ester," 169; see also the brief remarks in Marböck, "Das Gebet," 79; Moore, *Daniel, Esther, and Jeremiah*, 213.

(C 14).[5] As to Marie-Theres Wacker, we can find here a pun: The only King and God should come to her aid, since she is alone and has no human being beside her in this situation, but also: The only God and King should come to the aid of the only one who can provide human help in this distressed situation. Esther's monotheism is, on the one hand, from the outset a declaration of war on all others who call themselves kings, and on the other hand it is inseparably linked to the hope of help and salvation that can only come from this one God.[6]

When Esther expounds in C 16 that she has heard all her life in her family tribe that God "chose Israel from all the nations" and her fathers "from all their predecessors" as an "eternal inheritance" (εἰς κληρονομίαν αἰώνιον) the remarkable thing is that she places herself explicitly in the community of her tribe in which the knowledge of God's saving acts has been passed on from generation to generation.[7] Moreover, Esther makes use of a common pattern of the psalm prayer that aims at inciting God to act by reminding him of his covenant with his people and of his former saving acts.[8] God has chosen Israel from among all nations, and the inviolable nature of the relationship between God and his people is illustrated by the term *eternal inheritance*.

On the level of pragmatics, this statement of Esther—as well as the fact that she makes use of traditional material in her prayer—is highly significant as it shows that she identifies herself strongly with her people and its prayer tradition. According to Kottsieper:

> By linking her own distress with the folk lament, which is also reflected in the emphasis of the fact that Esther prays explicitly to the God of Israel (C 14), the narrator moreover stresses that Esther wishes to be the saviour of her entire people and does not make recourse to private prayers. Thus, Esther makes the distress of her people her own in the truest sense of the word, and she places herself at the centre of events.[9]

This is followed by a confession of sins, where Esther admits that her people has extolled foreign gods; this is the reason why God has handed

---

[5] Marböck, "Das Gebet," 82. Cf. Moore, *Daniel, Esther, and Jeremiah,* 213, who summarizes the different epithets for God used in Esther's prayer; see also McDowell, *Prayers*, 38.

[6] Wacker, "Innensichten und Außensichten des Judentums," 81–2.

[7] See Marböck, "Das Gebet," 83, who refers to Deut 6:20–23 and Ps 78:3–6 as examples. See also Wacker, "Innensichten und Außensichten des Judentums," 82, who uses the term "Erzählgemeinschaft."

[8] For the motif of the covenant see Kottsieper, "Zusätze zu Ester," 174.

[9] So Kottsieper, "Zusätze zu Ester," 169 (translation from German); cf. Schorch, "Genderising Piety," 39, who stresses Esther's distance to her people.

Israel over to its enemies, and Esther concludes at the end of this section that God is just (C 17, 18).[10] This confession of Israel's sins and God's justice assume the structure of penitential prayers from the post-exilic era, such as e.g. Ezra 9:7–15 and Dan 9:5–19.[11] Like Ezra and Daniel, Esther includes herself among the group of sinners even though she herself has not engaged in any actual personal sin of idolatry.[12] Thus it becomes obvious, that the figure of Esther serves as representative figure for her people. Moreover, the fact that this type of prayer has a prominent leader highlights Esther's importance in the Septuagint narrative.

According to C 19, the text then turns to the enemies of the people who oppress it. Here, Esther accuses her pursuers of wishing to destroy the people of Israel and its temple with the aid of their gods. A key word in this section is the term "mouth": The nations want to nullify the promise that came from the mouth of God, i.e. they want to erase God's pledge that Israel was his chosen people—an idea, which is coined here with the term "κληρονομία." Thus, it is obvious that again Israel is referred to as the inheritance. They want to silence the lips of those who praise God, and in so doing they intend to "open the mouths of the pagans" in order to "idolise forever a mere mortal king" (C 21). This illustrates that the nations oppose God's plan for history as their intention is the annihilation of Israel.[13] With the motif of Israel's song of praise, the lament, moreover, picks up an argumentation typical of psalms, according to which God himself is affected by the enemies' victory, since he would thus lose the praise of his people that is rightly due to Him. Moreover, the enemy's plans here do not target only the allegedly subversive lifestyle of the Jewish people and their laws in general (Esth 3:8; cf. B 4–5); rather, they are directed at the cult of Israel (C 19–21).[14] This

[10] Marböck, "Das Gebet," 80, gives only a short reference to the motif of Esther's sin. Moore, *Daniel, Esther, and Jeremiah,* 214, references to the parallels with Daniel's prayer in Dan 9:4–5.
[11] Marböck, "Das Gebet," 86; cf. Ulrike Mittmann-Richert, *Historische und legendarische Erzählungen,* JSHRZ VI/1 (Gütersloh: Gütersloher Verlagshaus, 2000), 105.
[12] For this aspect see Angela Kim Harkins, "Penitential Elements and Their Strategic Arousal of Emotion in the Qumran Hodayot (1QH cols.1[?]–8)," in *Ancient Jewish Prayers and Emotions,* ed. Stefan C. Reif and Renate Egger-Wenzel, DCLS 26, Berlin: de Gruyter, 2015), 297–316, here 303. For the literary genre in general see Mark J. Boda, Daniel K. Falk and Rodney A. Werline, eds., *Seeking the Favor of God,* 3 vols., SBLEJL 21–23 (Atlanta: Society of Biblical Literature, 2006–2008).
[13] Cf. Kottsieper, "Zusätze zu Ester," 173.
[14] In this context, Marböck, "Das Gebet," 80, sees the background of Esther's statement generally "in processes concerning the sanctuary in Jerusalem in connection with the Hellenization".

reference to the threat to the temple may be regarded as a reflection of the religious persecution under Antiochus IV (175–164).[15]

Finally, Esther's lament implicitly includes a reflection of the pagan ruler cult when she speaks of the eternal idolisation of a mortal king. This lament, which is supposed to implicitly incite God to intervene and to act, is followed by Esther's intercession, starting in C 22 with the entreaty to God to turn the enemies' plot against them (C 23)—a motif that can be frequently found in numerous Imprecatory Psalms (Ps 7:13–17; 9:16–17; 35:4–8; 40:15; Neh 3:36).[16] The image of enemies laughing at Israel evokes the horror that would result from defeat expresses a traditional motif found in the psalms (e.g., Ps 25:2; 44:14).[17] Since with the annihilation of Israel the rule of the one and only God would ultimately be at stake, Esther places the threat to the people in a power struggle between God and the gods and makes it a matter for God himself.[18] Esther thus entreats God to remember his people's distress (C 23a) and to rescue it (C 25). In using the first person plural in this passage, Esther thus complies with the style of the prayer as a whole, and explicitly integrates herself within the larger history and fate of her people.

Inserted into this collective speech pattern is the individual section, adapted to the concrete context of action. Esther initially asks for courage and for the ability to find the right words when faced with the "lion," i.e. the overwhelming and dangerous king, so that she can persuade the king to fight against her enemies and their allies (C 23b, 24). After stressing the fact that she is alone and that she has no-one but God to turn to for help (C 25b), Esther launches a self-justification in C 26, addressing the problematic nature of her marriage as a Jewish woman to a non-Jew. She loathes her crown to such an extent that she describes it as a "menstruous rag."[19] In this context, Ingo Kottsieper has stated:

> Hardly unbeatable, this prayer describes her inner disgust for her royal dignity (v. 27): the robes, the ornaments and everything else that distinguishes her as a queen and can thus expose her to the reproach of pride, of arrogance, have nothing proud or distinguishing for her, but

---

[15] Marböck, "Das Gebet," 86, who speaks of "the culpable entanglement of Jewish representatives in the Maccabean period" ("die schuldhafte Verstrickung jüdischer Repräsentanten in der Makkabäerzeit"); cf. Mittmann-Richert, *Erzählungen*, 105.

[16] Kottsieper, "Zusätze zu Ester," 174.

[17] Kottsieper, "Zusätze zu Ester," 174.

[18] Wacker, "Innensichten und Außensichten des Judentums," 81–2.

[19] McDowell, *Prayers*, 39, hints at the fact that here "feminine imagery" is used, while "most of this prayer by Esther could be put in the mouth of any Israelite/Jew, male or female, in any similar situation."

are dirty for her like a sanitary napkin. Thus, it becomes clear that for
her being queen corresponds to a defilement in which, according to
Jewish consciousness, a woman is considered impure … [This comparison is suitable], because it implies an argument that can clarify
Esther's situation: Just as the period pollutes a woman without this
being the woman's fault and she is nevertheless considered a pious
Jewess, so the situation of Esther is presented as a kind of pollution
for which she cannot be held responsible. It is just an inevitable predicament in which she finds herself. Therefore, the accusation that she
became queen out of arrogance is refuted.[20]

Moreover, she renounces sexual intercourse with the uncircumcised. In
this section, the term βδελύσσομαι—loathe—is used three times. The
question to what extent Esther has committed a sin by her intercourse
with the King remains open; since she does in fact wear the royal crown,
she is indeed depicted as a tragic figure, torn between what she aspires
to within her heart and how she is forced to behave to meet expectations.
She is, however, able to emphasise her blamelessness by pointing out that
she adheres to the Jewish food laws even at the foreign king's court.
In this context, it is to be noted in particular that in her praying Esther
uses a terminology that plays an important role in the overall context of
the Hellenistic crisis. Her statement that she despises (cf. the term βδελύσσομαι)[21] her matrimonial bed and royal crown (C 26, 27) also alludes
to the abomination of desolation (cf. 1 Macc 1:57; 6:7) that was installed
on the altar of the Temple in Jerusalem during the Hellenistic Reform.

Esther's Prayer concludes with yet another invocation of God, who is
now referred to as "the God of Abraham" (C 29). Here, Esther once
again references the folk lament and summarises it: God, whose might
prevails over all, is entreated to hear the voice of the despairing and to
save them from the hands of the wicked (C 29–30).

Esther's Prayer in Context

Formally, Esther's Prayer, along with Mordecai's Prayer, constitutes the
centrepiece of the Greek Book of Esther. Whereas the Book of
Tobit, the Book of Judith, and 2 Maccabees contain several prayers each,
the Book of Esther contains only two, which, notably, make up 30% of

---

[20] See Kottsieper, "Zusätze zu Ester," 176.
[21] For this term see Werner Foerster, "βδελύσσομαι, βδέλυγμα, βδελυκτός," *TWNT*
1:598–600.

the 105 verses of the so-called "Additions".[22] The prayers appear at strategic points in the narrative, namely, the greatest moment of distress, prior to the turning point that follows Esther's appearance as the intercessor before the King.

Esther's Prayer carries a greater significance than Mordecai's Prayer. The first aspect is a formal one. Esther's prayer has 337 words and 15 verses, and is much longer than Mordecai's Prayer, which consists of 178 words and 11 verses. Whereas Mordecai's Prayer is not connected by narrative elements to the wider context of the narrative, Esther's Prayer is largely set up through the context of the narrative. In Esth 4:8 LXX, Mordecai had sent a message to Esther, advising her to call upon God and intercede with the King on behalf of her people. The significance of the prayer as an integral element of the rescue is, moreover, implied by the entire framework of Mordecai's dream (cf. A 9) and its interpretation (cf. F 6).[23] Finally, the narrative framework of Esther's Prayer is more extensive than that of Mordecai's Prayer. Whereas Mordecai's Prayer is framed by two short and prosaic sentences, Esther's Prayer is embedded in a dramatic and highly emotional framework.[24] In C 12, it is the narrator who speaks, aware that Esther is "terrified" (C 12) and seeking refuge in the Lord. It becomes obvious, that the prayer is accompanied by practices of self-abasement, as Esther puts on "clothes appropriate for distress and mourning" and neglects her appearance by foregoing any adornments and headdress (C 13). Even though the narrator does not speak explicitly about the protagonist's feelings at this point, the description of her garments as "clothes appropriate for distress and mourning" and the mention of terrifying agonies illustrate the emotional state of Esther's mind. The fact that Esther is mortally terrified and finds herself in a situation of extreme distress does not require any further elaboration.

Following Esther's Prayer, we immediately hear the narrator's voice again, describing how Esther goes to the King together with her maids, in order to make her plea before him. This paragraph is highly dramatic, too: Esther's extreme distress is expressed by the details that she is being physically supported by her maids. She collapses the moment she beholds

---

[22] Marböck, "Das Gebet," 73. For the additions in general see David A. DeSilva, *Introducing the Apocrypha: Message, Context, and Significance* (Grand Rapids: Baker Academic, 2002).

[23] Marböck, "Das Gebet," 82.

[24] Cf. the beginning of C 1a "Then remembering all the deeds of the Lord, Mordecai prayed to the Lord, saying ..."; after the prayer the narrator states in C 11: "And all Israel cried out as loud as they could because their end was near."

the King's fearsome face. In contrast to the description of Esther's grace
and beauty at the beginning, where we see a discrepancy between her
appearance on the one hand and her state of mind on the other, here,
Esther's faintness makes her fear and distress transparent. Eventually,
Esther collapses once again when she talks to the King and tells him that
she sees him as an angel of God. Interestingly enough, after this section
Esther's intercession is no longer required; rather, it is God who renders
the King merciful, even before Esther has the chance to address him
(D 1–13).

In his article, Johannes Marböck emphasized the fact that Esther's
Prayer incorporates various key motifs from the Esther Septuagint and
that the prayer appears to be an intertextual knot in which many threads
are tied. In fact, no section in the Greek tradition is so densely packed
with theological statements as this one. More specifically, the following
elements should be noted. First of all, Esther's prayer stresses God's
uniqueness. It opens with the words "My Lord, our King, you are the
only one (translation B.E.)" (Κύριέ μου ὁ βασιλεὺς ἡμῶν, σὺ εἶ μόνος)
and thus, it obviously indicates a closed relationship to the beginning of
the *"Sh^ema' Isra'el"* in Deut 6:5 (cf. Deut 6,4 LXX: κύριος ὁ θεὸς
ἡμῶν κύριος εἷς ἐστιν).[25] In the context of the narration, this motif is
connected to the reference to Mordecai's refusal to perform προσκύνη-
σις before Haman in C 5–7, which he justifies by saying that it does not
befit a human to prostrate themselves before another human because
of God's glory—an argument that implicitly reinforces the uniqueness of
God.[26]

Secondly, Esther refers to the election of her people as "God's inheritance (κληρονομία)" when she states in her prayer: "All my life I have
heard in my family's tribe that you, Lord, chose Israel from all the
nations, and our fathers from all their predecessors, for a perpetual inheritance" (C 16). Furthermore, in C 20 she accuses Israel's enemies of
wanting to destroy God's inheritance. This theologumenon can be regarded
as a *Leitmotiv* in the Greek Esther story. It also occurs in Mordecai's
prayer (C 8), namely when Mordecai says that the enemy wants to
destroy God's inheritance, and the term is then prominently displayed at
the end of the narrative, when Purim commences. Here, the text provides
an explicitly theological interpretation of Purim, as Mordecai is able to

---

[25] Marböck, "Das Gebet," 82–3.
[26] Marböck, "Das Gebet," 88–9. A further connection between Esther's and Mordecai's
prayer consists in the invocation of God as the God of Abraham; cf. C 29 and C 8.

conclude in F 7–10 that God had created two fates (δύο κλῆροι): one for his people and one for the nations. When these two fates come up before God at the time of judgement, God remembers his people and grants justice to his inheritance (κληρονομία). Consequently, the day of Purim is one in which God reaffirms his commitment to his people, who deserve judgment in the same way all other nations do. Purim can thus be considered as a "realisation of the inheritance relationship."[27]

Finally, regarding the connection of Esther's prayer to the narrative as a whole, the motif of obedience to the Jewish law should be mentioned. When Esther abides by the Jewish dietary laws by dissociating herself from the table of the nations, she refers to her uncle's request who had instructed her to observe God's commandments at the royal court (Esth 2:20 LXX).[28]

Esther's Prayer in the Greek Text as a Rewriting of the Hebrew Version

As already mentioned above, Johannes Marböck described the interpretative function of Esther's Prayer as a means of stressing human actions in the context of God's plan for rescuing his people and to strengthen the entire cult of Israel (C 19–21).[29]

Against this background, it strikes me as important to integrate the motifs of guilt as well as the implicit references to the Temple and its abomination into the interpretation as a whole.[30] Esther's statement that God is just and that it was Israel's sin that made him hand them over to the enemy (C 17) illustrates the deep theological dimension of the narrative, which is not found in the Hebrew text. This opens up a new horizon for understanding the desperate situation in which the nation has found itself, which puts a strain on the people and entails a justification for divine action. The motif of sin also plays a vital role for understanding the rescue as a whole, since Esther has brought some degree of guilt upon herself by marrying a non-Jew. But by dissociating herself from that guilt

---

[27] Mittmann-Richert, *Erzählungen*, 107; s.a. Marböck, "Das Gebet," 83–6.

[28] See also Marböck, "Das Gebet," 89. For Esther's obedience to the Torah see also Day, *Three Faces*, 43.

[29] Cf. Moore, *Daniel, Esther, and Jeremiah,* 213: "Queen Esther voices her strong feelings on two matters not even alluded to in the MT: the temple at Jerusalem [...] and *kašrût* [...]. So devout a Jewess is Esther and so strong are her religious scruples that her role as queen and its social obligations are very distasteful to her (cf. vss. 26–9); yet in the MT there is no hint of any reluctance or reservation on her part."

[30] Marböck, "Das Gebet," 86, mentions this aspect only in passing.

and by demonstrating that she acts in accordance with the Torah in other respects, she shows a way out of her entrapment; all this accomplished, she can take up her intercession (Esth 5:1–2 LXX). Accordingly, Esther is not merely an exemplary supplicant, but she also embodies the ideal of penance. Therefore, Marböck's term "heroisation" has to be considered in its different nuances in this context. In the Septuagint, Esther is not an innocent, "pure" heroine; rather, she is a complex character who has undergone serious challenges and who emerges transformed. In this regard, the greater attention to Esther's emotional struggles highlights the broader theological themes that distinguish the Greek from the Hebrew Esther. Esther's confession of sin puts the entire chain of events into a coherent sequence: because Israel had sinned, persecution came upon them in the era of King Ahashverosh; eventually, their willingness to entrust themselves to God through prayer and to confess their sins, in combination with their adherence to the Torah, moved God to intervene and to help His people. In historical terms, these statements can be linked to the events under Antiochus IV and the desecration of the temple. The motif of the people's sin can provide an explanation for the suffering and persecution of the devout. Furthermore, as it is clearly shown in Judas' supplicatory prayer in 2 Macc 8:2–4 and in the larger work as a whole, prayer plays a prominent role in bringing about God's help and salvation for a sinful people. Nevertheless, no confession of sin is mentioned in this context (cf. 2 Macc 10:4; 13:10–12).

It is, moreover, apparent that Esther's Prayer leads to the result that the reader of the Septuagint version gets a deeper insight into Esther's character that it is provided by the Hebrew text. It should be noted that prayer can generally be regarded as a medium that facilitates introspection. In Esther's Prayer specifically, personal statements play a key role, voiced in the first person singular and interwoven with traditional prayer elements. The narrative framework, which describes Esther's appearance and her emotions in much greater detail than the Hebrew source, likewise contributes to a significant development of character's interiority. However—and this cannot be stressed enough—this development is connected with a tendency that can be best described with the term 'collectivisation.' Even in the Hebrew Esther story, the words of Mordecai in Esth 4:13–14 directly links Esther's fate to that of her people. In Esther's Prayer, this element is yet again reinforced, as the prayer not only has individual features, but also uses the traditional prayer language of Israel. By speaking in the first person plural, Esther thus integrates herself explicitly in the history of her people. This aspect is also reflected in her words when she says that she has heard of God's saving acts "all her life in her family's tribe" and when she addresses God as the "God of Abraham." Through her knowledge of God's power to save, and also through both her distress and her guilt, Esther appears as the representative of her people. Like Tobit and Sarah, Esther is not merely an individual character, she also stands for the people as a collective figure in whom the history of God's salvation has been realized.

Conclusion

Esther's Prayer was characterised by Johannes Marböck's words as "a sum of the Greek reinterpretation of the Hebrew Book."[31] In this context, the figure of Esther serves as a role model for her people who stand guilty, yet are still able to pray an efficacious prayer to God. The reference to the threat to the temple as well as the motif of contamination and guilt seems to point to time of the religious persecution under Antiochus IV (175–164 BC).

Bibliography

Boda, Mark J., Daniel K. Falk, and Rodney A. Werline, eds. *Seeking the Favor of God*. 3 vols. EJL 21–23. Atlanta: Society of Biblical Literature, 2006–2008.

Boyd-Taylor, Cameron. "Esther's Great Adventure: Reading the LXX Version of the Book of Esther in Light of its Assimilation to the Conventions of the Greek Romantic Novel." *BIOSCS* 30 (1997): 81–113.

Day, Linda M. *Three Faces of a Queen: Characterization in the Books of Esther*. JSOTSup 186. Sheffield: Sheffield Academic, 1995.

DeSilva, David A. *Introducing the Apocrypha: Message, Context, and Significance*. Grand Rapids: Baker Academic, 2002.

Foerster, Werner. "βδελύσσομαι, βδέλυγμα, βδελυκτός." *TWNT* 1:598–600.

Harkins, Angela Kim. "Penitential Elements and Their Strategic Arousal of Emotion in the Qumran Hodayot (1QH cols. 1[?]–8)." Pages 297–316 in *Ancient Jewish Prayers and Emotions*. Edited by Stefan C. Reif and Renate Egger-Wenzel. DCLS 26. Berlin: De Gruyter, 2015.

Kottsieper, Ingo. "Zusätze zu Ester." Pages 109–207 in *Das Buch Baruch: Der Brief des Jeremia: Zu Ester und Daniel*. Edited by Odil Hannes Steck, Reinhard G. Kratz, and Ingo Kottsieper. ATD Apokryphen 5. Göttingen: Vandenhoeck & Ruprecht, 1998.

Marböck, Johannes. "Das Gebet der Ester: Zur Bedeutung des Gebetes im griechischen Esterbuch." Pages 73–94 in *Prayer from Tobit to Qumran: Inaugural Conference of the ISDCL at Salzburg, Austria, 5-9 July 2003*. Edited

---

[31] Marböck, "Das Gebet," 90.

by Renate Egger-Wenzel and Jeremy Corley. Deuterocanonical and Cognate Literature Yearbook 2004. Berlin: de Gruyter, 2004.

McDowell, Markus H. *Prayers of Jewish Women: Studies of Patterns of Prayer in the Second Temple Period.* WUNT II/211. Tübingen: Mohr Siebeck, 2006.

Mittmann-Richert, Ulrike. *Historische und legendarische Erzählungen. JSHRZ* VI/1. Gütersloh: Gütersloher Verlagshaus, 2000.

Moore, Carey A. *Daniel, Esther, and Jeremiah: The Additions.* AB 44. Garden City, NY: Doubleday, 1977.

Schorch, Stefan. "Genderising Piety: The Prayers of Mordecai and Esther in Comparison." Pages 30–42 in *Deuterocanonical Additions of the Old Testament Books: Selected Studies.* Edited by Géza G. Xeravits and József Zsengellér. DCLS 5. Berlin / New York: de Gruyter, 2010.

Wacker, Marie-Theres. "Innensichten und Außensichten des Judentums im septuagintagriechischen Estherbuch (Est^{LXX})." Pages 55–88 in *Gesellschaft und Religion in der spätbiblischen und deuterokanonischen Literatur.* Edited by Friedrich V. Reiterer, Renate Egger-Wenzel, and Thomas R. Elßner. DCLS 20. Berlin: de Gruyter, 2014.

Wills, Lawrence M. "Jewish Novellas in a Greek and Roman Age: Fiction and Identity." *JSJ* 42 (2011): 141–65.

Zsengellér, József. "Addition or Edition? Deconstructing the Concept of Additions." Pages 1–15 in *Deuterocanonical Additions of the Old Testament Books: Selected Studies.* Edited by Géza G. Xeravits and József Zsengellér. DCLS 5. Berlin: de Gruyter, 2010.

JUDITH 9: A PRAYER
AND MORE THAN A PRAYER

Lawrence M. Wills

It is probably the case that all ancient prayers are complex, but this is certainly true of Judith 9. It is not clear, for instance, whether the prayer is an earnest expression of the author's theology, or the speech-in-character (*prosōpopoiia* in Greek rhetoric) of a transgressive character. We can also raise the question as to whether the prayers and speeches, on one hand, and the narrative actions on the other create two different arcs that negotiate with each other, or even contradict each other. If I may adopt a metaphor from music: in opera, the libretto, or words sung, often present a plot-line of events or emotions, while the music may ironically communicate moods *different from* or *counter to* the libretto. This distinction between libretto and music creates a dialogue of levels, and the irony of different views *at work simultaneously*. Judith's prayer can be analyzed, then, in a way to uncover the interplay between her words—the "libretto"—and her actions—the "music." In addition, I will suggest that there is a "biblicist" code in the text—the intertextual resonances of past biblical texts—as well as a "contextualist" code—the intertextual resonances of non-biblical or contemporary story traditions. What we will find is that, while the prayer in Judith 9 lies at the physical and theological center of the text, the negotiation between multiple resonances throughout the novella affects this passage also. Multiple meanings can be discerned here, in dialogue with each other. It will be left as an open question whether the content of the prayer "controls" the understanding of the story, or the irony of the narrative dictates that we understand her prayer as an ironic comment.

Past Treatments of Judith's Prayer

The prayer in Judith 9 has been viewed in various ways. Carey A. Moore's commentary, still a major resource, saw it as theologically questionable: "If most, or at least many, of the important ideas of Judaism exist in Judith, that is all they really do, that is, they do not seem alive and vibrant."[1] Yet Barbara Schmitz argued that if one investigates the prayers and speeches in Judith *taken together,* there is a structure of the whole that is actually different from the structure of the narrative.[2] Before her work, the scholars of the narrative arc, including myself, had minimized the speech arc.[3] Schmitz also argues that the prayers and speeches provide a theological anchor to the narrative components, and provide a meaning to the narrative arc that contrasts with the misogyny of a western art tradition that foregrounds the beheading scene and often "demoralizes" Judith.

Basing her analysis on all the prayers and speeches, then, Schmitz points to 9:9–10 as the theological center of the text:[4]

> Give to me, a widow, the strong hand to do what I plan. By the deceit of my lips strike down the slave with the prince and the prince with his servant; crush their arrogance by the hand of a woman.

Deborah Levine Gera has also discerned a difference in style between the prayers and speeches on one hand and the narrative sections on the other.[5] The narrative betrays a strong Semitic style, borrowing in a general way from Judges, while the direct speech contains Greek syntax, and often plays on more specific, identifiable biblical passages. The prayer in chapter 9, Gera notes, utilizes chiastic poetic constructions, internal rhyme, and varying order of genitive and nominative.

Multiple Transitions in Judith

Yet there are further questions. This center calls upon biblical motifs of hand, put to death by a woman, and reversal to celebrate deliverance.[6]

---

[1] Carey A. Moore, *Judith: A New Translation with Introduction and Commentary*, AB 40B (Garden City, NY: Doubleday, 1985), 195.

[2] Barbara Schmitz, *Gedeutete Geschichte: Die Funktion der Reden und Gebete im Buch Judit*, HBS 40 (Freiburg im Breisgau: Herder, 2004), passim.

[3] See Lawrence M. Wills, *The Jewish Novel in the Ancient World* (Ithaca, NY: Cornell University Press, 1995), 132–56, but my commentary, Lawrence M. Wills, *Judith*, Hermeneia (Minneapolis: Fortress Press, 2019), incorporates the insights of Schmitz.

[4] In addition to her work just cited, see also Barbara Schmitz and Helmut Engel, *Judit*, HThKAT 20 (Freiburg im Breisgau: Herder, 2014), 106–8, 296–7, and Géza G. Xeravits, "The Supplication of Judith (Judith 9:2–14)," in *A Pious Seductress: Studies in the Book of Judith*, ed. idem (Berlin: de Gruyter, 2012), 161–78, here at 170.

[5] Deborah Levine Gera, "Speech in Judith," in *XIV Congress of the IOSCS, Helsinki, 2010*, ed. Melvin K. H. Peters (Atlanta: SBL Press, 2013), 413–23, here at 413, 417–8; see also eadem, *Judith* (Berlin: de Gruyter, 2014), 296.

[6] See especially Patrick W. Skehan, "The Hand of Judith," *CBQ* 25 (1963): 94–110.

By emphasizing the specific biblical references here, there is a tendency to harmonize Judith's persona and even normalize it within biblical tradition. Contrary to the European artists who problematized Judith's deed, this approach then serves to redeem her. I will refer to this as the biblicist approach, as opposed to a narrative or contextual approach. I emphasize that I do not reject the biblicist analysis, but I do believe there are other levels in the text, *all* of which have to be integrated for a full analysis. I may offer as two twentieth-century comparison points the science-fiction classic *Forbidden Planet,* based on Shakespeare's *The Tempest,* and John Sayles's *Brother from Another Planet,* a satiric retelling of the gospel story of Jesus. In each case there is an older source that can be identified—by the academic, at least!—and an entertaining popular narrative that does not mention the source, in both cases in the genre of science fiction. The background narrative in these two cases influences the film without totally controlling the themes.

We may then also complicate the question of the "theological center" of the text. I have already mentioned two centers, the beheading scene featured in European art and the prayer utterance of 9:9–10, but I would also argue that there is a third, a "narrativist" center of release and reversal, found in Bagoas's excited utterance at 14:18:

> These slaves have deceived us! One woman of the Hebrews has shamed the house of King Nebuchadnezzar! Just look: Holofernes is lying on the ground, and his head is missing!

How different are these three centers! But multiple centers—or at least transitions—are not so unusual. One may compare several transitions in the roughly contemporary Book of Esther: Esther's instructions to the Jews of Persia in chapter 4 (where she finds strength to act), the king's discovery of the deeds of Mordecai in chapter 6 (the plot's first turning point), and the collapse of Haman on Esther's settee at 7:8 (the second turning point). In Greek Esther, one may also consider the prayers of Esther and Mordecai as transitions. Yet there is even one further transitional point in Esther, similar to Bagoas's declaration. The reversal in Esther is actually *announced* when Haman's wife Zeresh states, "If Mordecai, before whom your fall has begun, is of the Jewish people, you will not prevail against him, but will surely fall before him" (6:13). In both Esther and Judith, a non-Jewish, secondary character defines the Jews' triumph with a sort of unconscious prophecy.

The Ritual Context of the Prayer in Judith 9

With these broader considerations in mind, we return to the setting of the prayer in Judith 9. We should avoid what may be called the photographic fallacy, the notion that narratives provide a photograph of real or even typical actions in the world. To be sure, we must often *begin* with the question of the relationship of actions in the text to actions in the real world, but we often quickly conclude that a text constructs an unreal story-world that is not precisely related to actions in the real world. Judith's prayer is not a prayer that is actually prayed, it is a literary device at the center of a most outrageous narrative. There are, for instance, a series of ritual markers of mourning, related also to stricken prayer and penitential prayer. Disrobing or changing clothing is often a part, as is washing or other purification rituals:

> Falling upon her face, Judith placed ashes on her head and uncovered the sackcloth she was wearing. At precisely the time that the evening's incense was being offered in the house of God in Jerusalem, Judith uttered a loud cry to the Lord. (9:1)

Greek Esther and *Joseph and Aseneth* also present a similar undressing and redressing scene. The type scenes in Judith, Greek Esther, and *Joseph and Aseneth* exhibit a balanced V-pattern, with a prayer at the center:

protagonist rends self *	* emerges for mission
takes off beautiful garments *	* puts on beautiful garments
puts on mourning garments *	* takes off mourning garments
puts ashes on head *	* bathes
*prays	

The woman's prayer scene in all three novellas can be analyzed as a rite of passage, divisible into three stages: separation from society, a liminal period of being "betwixt and between"—when the prayer is uttered—and incorporation back into society in a new status.[7] The person enters the liminal stage, in which former status markers of social order, class, gender, and so on either disappear or are reversed; the person is

---

[7] On liminal states in rites of passage, see Arnold Van Gennep, *The Rites of Passage* (Chicago: University of Chicago Press, 1960); Victor Turner, "Betwixt and Between: The Liminal Period in *Rites de Passage*," in *The Forest of Symbols: Aspects of Ndembu Ritual*, ed. idem (Ithaca, NY: Cornell University Press, 1970), 93–111; Wills, *Jewish Novel*, 224–32.

temporarily isolated from society as a whole. In this liminal stage, space and time are not regulated by mundane markers, and there may be an element of danger and exposure to cosmic forces. Communication with the divine is direct, unmediated, even prophetic, mystical, or shamanic. Judith's scene, the earliest of these women's prayer scenes, may have established a model for the others.[8]

Yet, in each of the three women's scenes, there is a question of what the woman's new, "truer" identity is. In Greek Esther, the protagonist states that her beautified self is a *false* identity. In *Joseph and Aseneth,* Aseneth's new identity is a conversion or even mystical identity.[9] But what is the "true" identity for Judith, the vamp who deceives? Is it to emerge as a courtesan? We think here of Tamar (Gen 38:14–15). The three women thus go through similar ritual processes but emerge with very different identities. Judith also expresses a sinlessness in her prayers and speeches, even a sense of self-righteousness in relation to the imperfect townspeople. This is very different from the similar scenes in Esther and *Aseneth.* Yet Angela Kim Harkins reminds us that in the penitential tradition, the man who prays for Israel does not confess *his own sins.*[10]

---

[8] It is, incidentally, very similar to Wayne Meeks's V-shaped diagram of the process of early Christian baptism; see Wayne Meeks, *First Urban Christians: The Social World of the Apostle Paul* (New Haven: Yale University Press, 1983), 156. Some of the relations here are plumbed in Lawrence M. Wills, "Ascetic Theology Before Asceticism? Jewish Narratives and the Decentering of the Self," *JAAR* 74 (2006): 902–25.

[9] The mystical identity and themes that have suggested conversion occur throughout *Joseph and Aseneth,* but note esp. 10:9–17, 14:14–15, and the transformations of Aseneth that follow in chaps. 15–21. See Wills, *Jewish Novel,* 170–84, 224–32; Randall D. Chesnutt, *From Death to Life: Conversion in Joseph and Aseneth,* JSPSup 16 (Sheffield: Sheffield Academic Press, 1995); Jill Hicks-Keeton, *Arguing with Aseneth: Gentile Access to Israel's Living God in Jewish Antiquity* (New York: Oxford University Press, 2018), esp. 1–40, 118–39.

[10] Angela Kim Harkins, "A Phenomenological Study of Penitential Elements and Their Strategic Arousal of Emotion in the Qumran Hodayot (1QH cols. 1[?]–8)," in *Ancient Jewish Prayers and Emotions,* ed. Renate Egger-Wenzel and Stefan Reif (Berlin: de Gruyter, 2015), 297–316, here at 303. Judith's sinlessness is therefore not unusual in this tradition, except for three aspects: first, she is a woman; second, she is not sympathetic to the Bethulians' weakness; third, she certifies that Israel as a whole has been virtually sinless regarding idolatry (8:18). Cf. also Eve Levavi Feinstein, *Sexual Pollution in the Hebrew Bible* (Oxford: Oxford University Press, 2014), 68. In Wills, "Ascetic Theology," a distinction is made between the stricken penitent—Esther, Aseneth, Qumran *Hodayot,* and most Christian asceticism—and the confident ascetic—Judith and *Testament of Job.* This distinction plays out in an interesting way in Paul, where it was formerly assumed, based on Romans 7, that he was a stricken penitent, although Krister Stendahl, *Paul Among Jews and Gentiles* (Philadelphia: Fortress, 1976), 78–96, demonstrated that he exhibited a "robust" rather than an "introspective" conscience.

The elevated male mediator—Moses in Exodus 34, Ezra in Ezra 9, Nehemiah in Nehemiah 9, Daniel in Daniel 9—confesses the *community's* sins, not his own.

The Content and Structure of Judith's Prayer: vv. 2–4

These observations provide some of the narrative context for the prayer; we look now more closely at the content. Judith 9 contains the elements of psalms of lament, albeit in a slightly altered order.

— address (9:2a)
— introductory petition (9:4b)
— God's mighty acts in the past (9:2b–4a)
— confession of trust (9:5–6)
— lament (9:7)
— petition (9:8–10)
— vow of praise (9:14)

A structural division of the prayer also highlights a number of biblical phrases and motifs, the most important of which are:

1) 9:2–4   Simeon's revenge for the rape of Dinah (Genesis 34)
2) 9:5–6   God as lord of past, present, and future (related to Second Isaiah)
3) 9:7–11   Song of the Sea (Exodus 15)
4) 9:12–14 Prayer of the national leader as intermediator (various biblical parallels)[11]

I focus here on sections 1 and 3. Schmitz, Claudia Rakel, and others perceive intricate rhetorical patterns here, and Géza Xeravits "an artfully

---

[11] Xeravits, "The Supplication of Judith," 171–4; Schmitz and Engel, *Judit,* 272, collapse parts two and three together. They also place v. 4e with section two. See also Barbara Schmitz, "The Function of the Speeches and Prayers in the Book of Judith," in *A Feminist Companion to Tobit and Judith,* ed. Athalya Brenner-Idan and Helen Efthimiadis-Keith, FCB 20 (London: Bloomsbury, 2015), 164–74, here 167–8. For other notes on structure, see Claudia Rakel, *Judit – über Schönheit, Macht, und Widerstand im Krieg: Eine feministisch-intertextuelle Lektüre* (Berlin: de Gruyter, 2003), 84–92; Adolfo D. Roitman, "Achior in the Book of Judith: His Role and Significance," in *No One Spoke Ill of Her: Essays on Judith,* ed. James C. VanderKam, EJL 2 (Atlanta: Scholars Press, 1992), 31–45; Ernst Haag, *Das Buch Judit,* Geistliche Schriftlesung – Altes Testament 15 (Düsseldorf: Patmos, 1995), vii–viii; Jan Willem van Henten, "Judith as an Alternative Leader: A Rereading of Judith 7–13," in *A Feminist Companion to Esther, Judith and Susanna,* ed. Athalya Brenner, FCB 7 (Sheffield: Sheffield Academic Press, 1995), 224–52, esp. 225–32.

arranged prayer,"[12] but I would add, following Gera, that Judith 9 is bombastic and aggressive, often out of rhythm, with violent images. This can partly be seen in an interesting pattern in vs 2: aorist verbs (here underlined) are used, followed by objects that produce an assonance (μήτραν/μηρὸν/μήτραν), each followed by εἰς + a strong negative term (μίασμα/αἰσχύνην/ὄνειδος). This section is then concluded with an insistent summary statement:

> God of my ancestor Simeon,
>> in whose hand you <u>placed</u> a sword
>>> for (εἰς) revenge on the foreigners,
>> who <u>loosened</u> the μήτραν (womb) of a virgin
>>> as (εἰς) a μίασμα (pollution),
>> and <u>uncovered</u> her μηρὸν (thigh)
>>> as (εἰς) an αἰσχύνην (shame),
>> and <u>defiled</u> her μήτραν (womb)
>>> as (εἰς) a disgrace.
> For you said: It shall not be done—yet they did!

> Κύριε ὁ θεὸς τοῦ πατρός μου Συμεών,
>> ᾧ <u>ἔδωκας</u> ἐν χειρὶ ῥομφαίαν
>>> εἰς ἐκδίκησιν ἀλλογενῶν,
>> οἳ ἔλυσαν μήτραν παρθένου
>>> εἰς μίασμα
>> καὶ ἐγύμνωσαν μηρὸν
>>> εἰς αἰσχύνην
>> καὶ ἐβεβήλωσαν μήτραν
>>> εἰς ὄνειδος.
> Εἶπας γάρ Οὐχ οὕτως ἔσται, καὶ ἐποίησαν.

This section emphasizes Simeon positively, and often affirms a collusion across the centuries between Judith and the violent Simeon rather than an appeal for God to act. Simeon's masculine, "family redeemer" (גואל) revenge is highlighted. Yet, whereas in Genesis Simeon's revenge is condemned by Jacob (Gen 49:5–7), according to Judith, Simeon not only acted heroically, but God was behind the revenge and shared the

---

[12] Schmitz, *Gedeutete Geschichte*; and Schmitz and Engel, *Judit,* 272; Rakel, *Judit,* 33–5; Xeravits, "Supplication of Judith," 161; Gera, *Judith,* 274, 296, 299; eadem, "Speech in Judith"; Pancratius C. Beentjes, "Bethulia Crying, Judith Praying: Context and Content of Prayers in the Book of Judith," in *Prayer from Tobit to Qumran,* ed. Renate Egger-Wenzel and Jeremy Corley, DCLY 2004 (Berlin: de Gruyter, 2004), 231–54; Sabine M. L. van den Eynde, "Crying to God: Prayer and Plot in the Book of Judith," *Bib* 85 (2004): 217–31.

brothers' outrage.[13] Judith's prayer also has a male-gendered perspective; there is blood and defilement, a championing of Simeon's revenge, and slaughter of those who raped Dinah, but no sympathy or identification with Dinah as the person who was raped—this is also true for Genesis 34. Still, Judith identifies the earlier profanation of Dinah's body with the threat to her own body, and the threat of profanation of the temple as well; the profanation of Dinah, Judith, and temple merge. Judith's prayer may also be more comparable to Mordecai's prayer in Greek Esther than Esther's: if Esther's prayer is gendered "female" and Mordecai's "male," then Judith's prayer is more "male."[14]

In 9:3–4, the prayer continues with rough parallelism:

> So you gave over
>> their rulers to be killed,
>>> and their bed—ashamed of the deceit they had practiced—
>>>> was stained with blood,
> and you struck down
>> slaves along with princes,
>> and princes on their thrones.
> You gave over
>> their wives   to (εἰς) booty,
>> and their daughters   to (εἰς) captivity,
>> and all their booty   to (εἰς) a division among your beloved children
>>> who burned with zeal for you
>>> and abhorred the pollution (μίασμα) of their blood
>>> and called on you for help.
> O God, my God, hear me also, a widow!

> ἔδωκας
>> ἄρχοντας αὐτῶν εἰς φόνον
>> καὶ τὴν στρωμνὴν αὐτῶν, ἣ ᾐδέσατο τὴν ἀπάτην αὐτῶν, ἀπατηθεῖσαν εἰς αἷμα
> καὶ ἐπάταξας
>> δούλους ἐπὶ δυνάσταις,
>> καὶ δυνάστας ἐπὶ θρόνους αὐτῶν.
> καὶ ἔδωκας
>> γυναῖκας αὐτῶν εἰς προνομὴν
>> καὶ θυγατέρας αὐτῶν εἰς αἰχμαλωσίαν
>> καὶ πάντα τὰ σκῦλα αὐτῶν εἰς διαίρεσιν υἱῶν ἠγαπημένων ὑπὸ σοῦ,

[13] Judith was not the only ancient source to valorize this deed. *Jubilees* 30 and *Testament of Levi* 2–6 betray no ambivalence about the revenge, and *Joseph and Aseneth* 23:13 mentions Simeon's violent nature without condemning it.

[14] These aspects are also treated in my commentary, *Judith*, 279–80.

οἳ καὶ ἐζήλωσαν τὸν ζῆλόν σου
καὶ ἐβδελύξαντο μίασμα αἵματος αὐτῶν
καὶ ἐπεκαλέσαντό σε εἰς βοηθόν.
ὁ θεὸς ὁ θεὸς ὁ ἐμός, καὶ εἰσάκουσον ἐμοῦ τῆς χήρας

The themes of μίασμα and αἰσχύνην from vs 2 continue here. The outrage committed against Dinah is interpreted in language of pollution—as
in Esther's prayer.

The Content and Structure of Judith's Prayer: vv. 7–11

Next we turn to the third section of the prayer, verses 7–11. Schmitz's
argument that verses 9c–10 constitute the theological center of the book
will find support in the structure adopted here. Seven imperative petitions, here underlined, are found in the verses before verse 9:

> Break their strength with your might …
> And bring down their power with your anger!
> Look at their arrogance,
> Send your wrath upon their heads,
> Place in my hand—that of a widow!—the strong act
>   that *I have conceived.*
> Strike the slave—*by the deceit of my lips*—with the prince
>   and the prince with his servant!
> Crush their arrogance with a female hand! (emphasis added)

Within this overall pattern, there is also an explanatory aside inserted at
the point of the ellipsis:

> for they intend to defile your sanctuary,
> and to pollute the tabernacle
>   where your glorious name resides,
> and to break off the horns of your altar with the sword.

The combined effect of these lines is to lead to 9c–10, Schmitz's theological center, as a climax. Judith 9:7–11 thus constitute the central petition of her prayer: God is to intervene, but by means of *Judith's deed* to
destroy the enemy. Judith has indeed already conceived her plan. Does
she pray for God to save the people through her, or does she pray for
God to stay out of her way and allow her to carry out *her* plan? There is
perhaps intentional irony here. Her many references to hand call to mind
God and Moses, and these references rhetorically overpower the one
mention of Nebuchadnezzar's hand. The emphasis on hand throughout
could be taken as emphasizing either God's hand or Judith's. To be sure,
Judith invokes her humble status as servant of God's mission—"Give to

me, a widow, a strong hand"—but she continues, *"to do the strong act that I have conceived."* Is this the same plan that God conceived at 9:5? Whose plan is it? Judith's own initiative is emphasized at 9:9, 15:10; her role as God's instrument at 8:33, 12:4, 13:14–15, 16:5. This is in contrast to the Song of the Sea which consistently specifies God's hand (Exod 15:6, 12, 17, 19; cf. Jdt 9:11, 13:4). Scholars have thus drawn varied conclusions about Judith's agency.[15]

This so-called "double causation" is also found in regard to male biblical heroes: both God and the male leader are responsible for the completion of a heroic action.[16] But Judith pushes the limits by maintaining more ownership of her deed. Deborah F. Sawyer emphasizes that Judith carefully uses language to skirt God's agency and even relegate God to the status of witness: *"Look* this hour on the work of *my* hands…Now indeed is the time to help *your inheritance* and to carry out *my design"* (13:4–5).[17] Matthew Thiessen even suggests that Judith "appears to *provoke* the very scenario that will force God's hand to rescue her."[18] Judith's act forces God's hand in re-playing Simeon's vengeance. Yet I would not criticize this aspect of the narrative, as some have, but place it in a context of popular novellas and the transgressive nature of our heroine. Cross-culturally, she is like the women warriors in the mold of Fa Mulan, Semiramis, and Arabic stories: she makes her own luck.[19]

[15] Pamela J. Milne, "What Shall We Do with Judith? A Feminist Reassessment of a Biblical 'Heroine'," *Semeia* 62 (1993): 37–58, here at 48–55. See also Gera, *Judith,* 7, 99; Jan Willem van Henten, "Judith as a Female Moses: Judith 7–13 in Light of Exodus 17, Numbers 20, and Deuteronomy 33:8–11," in *Reflections on Theology and Gender,* ed. Fokkelien van Dijk-Hemmes and Athalya Brenner (Kampen: Kok Pharos, 1994), 33–48; and Toni Craven, "Judith Prays for Help: Judith 9.1–14," in *Prayer from Alexander to Constantine: A Critical Anthology,* ed. Mark Kiley (London: Routledge, 1997), 59–64.

[16] A tension can be perceived between God as agent and Moses as agent in the Exodus narrative; see Howard Jacobson, *The Exagoge of Ezekiel* (Cambridge: Cambridge University Press, 1983), 142–4 (cf. also Judg 3:9, 15; 4:14–15; 1 Sam 19:5; 2 Sam 23:10, 12, and regarding Judah Maccabee: 1 Macc 2:66, 3:3–9, 9:21; cf. 4:11, 16:3), and two originally separate traditions about Gideon have now been joined in Judges: a brash, heroic, self-made agent, and an instrument of God's miraculous interventions (Judg 7:24–8:28 and 6:1–7:23 respectively).

[17] Deborah F. Sawyer, "Dressing Up/Dressing Down: Power, Performance, and Identity in the Book of Judith," *Theology and Sexuality* 8 (2001): 23–31; eadem, "Gender Strategies in Antiquity: Judith's Performance," *Feminist Theology* 28 (2001): 9–26.

[18] Matthew Thiessen, "Protecting the Holy Race and Holy Space: Judith's Reenactment of the Slaughter of Shechem," *JSJ* 49 (2018): 165–88, here at 183.

[19] Deborah Levine Gera, *Warrior Women: The Anonymous Tractatus de Mulieribus* (Leiden: Brill, 1997), 82; also 93, 120. Johan Weststeijn, "Wine, Women, and Revenge in Near Eastern Historiography: The Tales of Tomyris, Judith, Zenobia, and Jalila," *JNES*

Indeed, while Claude Levi-Strauss and Northrop Frye had maintained that the rise of novels killed off the elegance of poetry, Mikhail Bakhtin welcomed the multiplicity of voices and styles in the novel, and found value in precisely this sort of excess.[20]

Conclusion

There are many levels, then, to Judith's prayer. I have mentioned a biblicist versus a contextual approach, or a vertical reading that highlights the earlier tradition, and a horizontal reading that introduces comparisons to contemporary Israelite and non-Israelite literature. Both approaches, the biblicist and the contextualist—and others!—would seem to be necessary for a full analysis. In addition, there is a negotiation between what Judith *says*—the "libretto"—and what she *does*—the "music." This gives rise to a fuller discussion of the narrative role of her prayer: should the prayers and speeches "control" the understanding of the story, or does the irony of the narrative dictate that we understand her prayer as an ironic comment?

Bibliography

Bakhtin, Mikhail. *The Dialogic Imagination: Four Essays by M. M. Bakhtin.* Austin: University of Texas Press, 1981.

Bakhtin, Mikhail. *Problems of Dostoevsky's Poetics.* Minneapolis: University of Minnesota Press, 1984.

Beentjes, Pancratius C. "Bethulia Crying, Judith Praying: Context and Content of Prayers in the Book of Judith." Pages 231–54 in *Prayer from Tobit to Qumran.* Edited by Renate Egger-Wenzel and Jeremy Corley. DCLY 2004. Berlin: de Gruyter, 2004.

Chen, Fan Pen Li. "Female Warriors, Magic and the Supernatural in Traditional Chinese Novels." Pages 91–109 in *The Annual Review of Women in World*

75 (2016): 91–107; idem, "Zenobia of Palmyra and the Book of Judith: Common Motifs in Greek, Jewish, and Arabic Historiography," *JSP* 22 (2013): 295–320. On Chinese examples, see Fan Pen Li Chen, "Female Warriors, Magic and the Supernatural in Traditional Chinese Novels," in *Heroic Women*, vol. 2 of The *Annual Review of Women in World Religions*, ed. Arvind Sharma and Katherine K. Young (Albany, NY: State University of New York Press, 1992), 91–109.

[20] Claude Lévi-Strauss, *The Origin of Table Manners: Introduction to a Science of Mythology: 3* (London: Jonathan Cape, 1978), 129–31; Northrop Frye, *Anatomy of Criticism*, 250, 304–6; idem, *The Secular Scripture: A Study of the Structure of Romance* (Cambridge: Harvard University Press, 1976); Bakhtin, *The Dialogic Imagination: Four Essays by M. M. Bakhtin* (Austin: University of Texas Press, 1981), esp. 89, 375; idem, *Problems of Dostoevsky's Poetics* (Minneapolis: University of Minnesota Press, 1984).

Religions vol. 2: Heroic Women. Edited by Arvind Sharma and Katherine K. Young. Albany, NY: State University of New York Press, 1992.

Chesnutt, Randall D. *From Death to Life: Conversion in Joseph and Aseneth*. JSPSup 16. Sheffield: Sheffield Academic Press, 1995.

Craven, Toni. "Judith Prays for Help: Judith 9.1–14." Pages 59–64 in *Prayer from Alexander to Constantine: A Critical Anthology*. Edited by Mark Kiley. London: Routledge, 1997.

Feinstein, Eve Levavi. *Sexual Pollution in the Hebrew Bible*. Oxford: Oxford University Press, 2014.

Frye, Northrop. *The Secular Scripture: A Study of the Structure of Romance*. Cambridge: Harvard University Press, 1976.

Frye, Northrop. *Anatomy of Criticism*. Princeton: Princeton University Press, 1957.

Gera, Deborah Levine. *Warrior Women: The Anonymous Tractatus de Mulieribus*. Leiden: Brill, 1997.

Gera, Deborah Levine. "Speech in the Book of Judith." Pages 413–23 in *XIV Congress of the IOSCS, Helsinki, 2010*. Edited by Melvin K. H. Peters. Atlanta: SBL Press, 2013.

Gera, Deborah Levine. *Judith*. Boston: de Gruyter, 2014.

Haag, Ernst. *Das Buch Judit*. Geistliche Schriftlesung – Altes Testament 15. Düsseldorf: Patmos, 1995,

Harkins, Angela Kim. "A Phenomenological Study of Penitential Elements and Their Strategic Arousal of Emotion in the Qumran Hodayot (1QH cols. 1[?]–8)." Pages 297–316 in *Ancient Jewish Prayers and Emotions*. Edited by Renate Egger-Wenzel and Stefan Reif. Berlin: de Gruyter, 2015.

Hicks-Keeton, Jill. *Arguing with Aseneth: Gentile Access to Israel's Living God in Jewish Antiquity*. New York: Oxford University Press, 2018.

Jacobson, Howard. *The Exagoge of Ezekiel*. Cambridge: Cambridge University Press, 1983.

Lévi-Strauss, Claude. *The Origin of Table Manners: Introduction to a Science of Mythology: 3*. London: Jonathan Cape, 1978.

Meeks, Wayne. *First Urban Christians: The Social World of the Apostle Paul*. New Haven: Yale University Press, 1983.

Milne, Pamela J. "What Shall We Do with Judith? A Feminist Reassessment of a Biblical 'Heroine'." *Semeia* 62 (1993): 37–58.

Moore, Carey A. *Judith: A New Translation with Introduction and Commentary*. AB 40B. Garden City, NY: Doubleday, 1985.

Rakel, Claudia. *Judit – über Schönheit, Macht, und Widerstand im Krieg: Eine feministisch-intertextuelle Lektüre*. Berlin: de Gruyter, 2003.

Roitman, Adolfo D. "Achior in the Book of Judith: His Role and Significance." Pages 31–45 in *No One Spoke Ill of Her: Essays on Judith*. Edited by James C. VanderKam. EJL 2. Atlanta: Scholars Press, 1992.

Sawyer, Deborah F. "Dressing Up/Dressing Down: Power, Performance, and Identity in the Book of Judith." *Theology and Sexuality* 8 (2001): 23–31.

Sawyer, Deborah F. "Gender Strategies in Antiquity: Judith's Performance." *Feminist Theology* 28 (2001): 9–26.

Schmitz, Barbara. *Gedeutete Geschichte: Die Funktion der Reden und Gebete im Buch Judit*. HBS 40. Freiburg im Breisgau: Herder, 2004.

Schmitz, Barbara, and Engel, Helmut. *Judit*. HThKAT 20. Freiburg im Breisgau: Herder, 2014.

Schmitz, Barbara. "The Function of the Speeches and Prayers in the Book of Judith." Pages 164–74 in *A Feminist Companion to Tobit and Judith*. Edited by Athalya Brenner-Idan and Helen Efthimiadis-Keith. FCB 20. London: Bloomsbury, 2015.

Skehan, Patrick W. "The Hand of Judith." *CBQ* 25 (1963): 94–110.

Stendahl, Krister. *Paul Among Jews and Gentiles*. Philadelphia: Fortress, 1976.

Thiessen, Matthew. "Protecting the Holy Race and Holy Space: Judith's Reenactment of the Slaughter of Shechem." *JSJ* 49 (2018): 165–88.

Turner, Victor "Betwixt and Between: The Liminal Period in *Rites de Passage*." Pages 93–111 in *The Forest of Symbols: Aspects of Ndembu Ritual*. Edited by Victor Turner. Ithaca, NY: Cornell University Press, 1970.

van den Eynde, Sabine M. L. "Crying to God: Prayer and Plot in the Book of Judith." *Bib* 85 (2004): 217–31.

van Gennep, Arnold. *The Rites of Passage*. Chicago: University of Chicago Press, 1960.

van Henten, Jan Willem. "Judith as an Alternative Leader: A Rereading of Judith 7–13." Pages 224–52 in *A Feminist Companion to Esther, Judith and Susanna*. Edited by Athalya Brenner. FCB 7. Sheffield: Sheffield Academic Press, 1995.

van Henten, Jan Willem. "Judith as a Female Moses: Judith 7–13 in Light of Exodus 17, Numbers 20, and Deuteronomy 33:8–11." Pages 33–48 in *Reflections on Theology and Gender*. Edited by Fokkelien van Dijk-Hemmes and Athalya Brenner. Kampen: Kok Pharos, 1994.

Weststeijn, Johan. "Zenobia of Palmyra and the Book of Judith: Common Motifs in Greek, Jewish, and Arabic Historiography." *JSP* 22 (2013): 295–320.

Weststeijn, Johan. "Wine, Women, and Revenge in Near Eastern Historiography: The Tales of Tomyris, Judith, Zenobia, and Jalila." *JNES* 75 (2016): 91–107.

Wills, Lawrence M. *The Jewish Novel in the Ancient World*. Ithaca, NY: Cornell University Press, 1995.

Wills, Lawrence M. "Ascetic Theology Before Asceticism? Jewish Narratives and the Decentering of the Self." *JAAR* 74 (2006): 902–25.

Wills, Lawrence M. *Judith*. Hermeneia. Minneapolis: Fortress Press, 2019.

Xeravits, Géza G. "The Supplication of Judith (Judith 9:2–14)." Pages 161–78 in *A Pious Seductress: Studies in the Book of Judith*. Edited by Géza Xervatis. Berlin: de Gruyter, 2012.

"LORD, GOD OF ALL MIGHT" (JDT 13:4 LXX). A COMPARISON BETWEEN THE GREEK VERSION (JDT 13:4–5, 7 LXX) AND THE VULGATE (IDT 13:6–7, 9 VULG.)

Barbara Schmitz

The book of Judith, as is well known, exists today in two different versions: in the Greek version found in the Septuagint and in the Latin version found in the Vulgate. No evidence has yet come to light that a Hebrew version existed in antiquity.[1]

The question concerning the original version is often discussed: Jerome, in his *praefatio* to the book of Judith, mentions that he had access to a "Chaldean version" (*chaldeo tamen sermone conscriptus*). Jerome's comment has led some to conclude that the Greek version is a translation of a lost Hebrew original.[2] This conclusion is based above all on the observation that the Greek of the LXX version sounds very Semitic.[3] For a long time, therefore, there was consensus that the Greek version was the translation of a Hebrew original,[4] which was the same as or similar to the version that Jerome had in front of him when he translated the Judith narrative some time between 398 and 407 CE.[5]

---

[1] Cf. Stephen D. Ryan, "The Ancient Versions of Judith and the Place of the Septuagint in the Catholic Church," in *A Pious Seductress: Studies in the Book of Judith*, ed. Géza G. Xeravits, DCLS 14 (Berlin: de Gruyter, 2012), 1–21; Deborah Levine Gera, *Judith*, CEJL (Berlin: de Gruyter, 2014), 14–5.

[2] For the arguments for this position see Erich Zenger, *Das Buch Judit*, JSHRZ I/6 (Gütersloh: Gütersloher Verlagshaus Gerd Mohn, 1981), 430–1.

[3] See the list in Carey A. Moore, *Judith*, AB 40 (Garden City, NY: Doubleday, 1985), 66–7 in the appendix to Robert H. Pfeiffer, "The Book of Judith," in *History of New Testament Times: With an Introduction to the Apocrypha*, ed. Robert H. Pfeiffer (London: Black, 1949), 298–9.

[4] Because of this consensus it is not surprising that a retranslation into Hebrew was published: Yehoshua M. Grintz, *Sefer Jehudît: A Reconstruction of the Original Hebrew Text with Introduction, Commentary, Appendices and Indices* [Hebrew] (Jerusalem: Bialik Institute, 1957).

[5] Cf. Alfons Fürst, *Hieronymus: Askese und Wissenschaft in der Spätantike* (Freiburg: Herder, 2003), 87; Heinrich Schlange-Schöningen, *Hieronymus: Eine historische Biografie* (Darmstadt: Wissenschaftliche Buchgesellschaft, 2018).

In the past few years, however, the state of research on the book of Judith has changed decisively. Hans Yohanan Priebatsch had already pointed out that there was a number of very Hellenistic words, motifs and themes in the Greek Judith narrative,[6] and in 1992 Helmut Engel was able to show that the existing Greek narrative was originally composed in Greek.[7] One of the arguments for this conclusion is the fact that passages from the Judith narrative are quotations from the LXX and that these passages in the Old Greek differ significantly from the Hebrew text (Jdt 8:16 cf. Num 23:19 LXX; Jdt 9:2 cf. Gen 34:7 LXX; Jdt 9:7; 16:2 cf. Exod 15:3 LXX; cf. Jdt 7:28). Another argument is the wordplays, some of which are in fact constitutive of the structure of the book. These wordplays cannot be retroverted into Hebrew. One example of this phenomenon is the lexeme -οικ-, with its various compounds (οἰκέω, κατοικέω, παροικέω, κατοικίζω). The lexeme and its compounds are constitutive of the structure of Achior's speech but cannot be retroverted into one and the same lexeme in Hebrew. Engel concludes, therefore, that the existing Greek text of the book of Judith is a narrative written originally in Greek, whose author used the LXX and employed a Semitic style.

In 2007 Jan Joosten offered his own proof for Greek as the original language.[8] Providing a string of examples, he was able to show that the Greek narrative was marked by a Greek with elevated choice of vocabulary and syntax for which there is no simple Hebrew equivalent. The Judith narrative is marked, furthermore, by good, at times elevated, specifically Greek sentence construction (cf. Jdt 5:3, 8, 12, 23; 7:30; 9:2 etc.). Joosten also concludes, therefore, that the Judith narrative was composed in Greek.

The linguistic idiosyncrasies of the Greek text of Judith that sound Semitic were then investigated by Jeremy Corley in 2008.[9] Carey

---

[6] Hans Yohanan Priebatsch, "Das Buch Judit und seine hellenistischen Quellen," *ZDPV* 90 (1974): 50–60.

[7] Helmut Engel, "Der HERR ist ein Gott, der Kriege zerschlägt: Zur Frage der griechischen Originalsprache und der Struktur des Buches Judith," in *Goldene Äpfel in silbernen Schalen*, ed. Klaus-Dietrich Schunck and Matthias Augustin, BEATAJ 20 (Frankfurt: Lang, 1992), 155–68.

[8] Jan Joosten, "The Original Language and Historical Milieu of the Book of Judith," in *Meghillot: Studies in the Dead Sea Scrolls V–VI: A Festschrift for Devorah Dimant*, ed. Moshe Bar-Asher and Emanuel Tov (Haifa: University of Haifa, The Publication Project of the Qumran Scrolls; Jerusalem: The Bialik Institute, 2007), 159–76.

[9] Jeremy Corley, "Septuagintalisms, Semitic interference, and the Original Language of the Book of Judith," in *Studies in the Greek Bible: Essays in Honor of Francis T. Gignac*, ed. Jeremy Corley, CBQMS 44 (Washington, DC: The Catholic Biblical Association of America, 2008), 65–96.

A. Moore had listed more than 30 examples of evidence for a Hebrew text in his commentary from 1985; Corley reviewed this list item by item and came to the conclusion "that the proposed instances of Hebraic phraseology and style in the Greek text of Judith do not necessarily indicate a Hebrew origin of the book, since they can easily be evidence of either mimetic appreciation of Septuagintal style or Semitic interference. [… A] Hebrew Vorlage cannot be presumed, while a Greek origin can be suggested as very possible."[10]

If Greek can legitimately be regarded as the original language of the Judith narrative in the Septuagint, then a presupposition for research on the book of Judith has also changed significantly, since the point of reference for the Greek version of Judith is no longer the Hebrew Bible but rather the Greek Bible. The new commentaries by Gera and Schmitz/ Engel are the first to be written on this new foundation.[11]

The changed state of research on the Greek Judith narrative prompts the question: what is the relationship of this version to the Vulgate version? That the Vulgate version has a completely different shape from the Greek text is readily apparent: the Vulgate version is 20 percent shorter than the Greek version, and, because the Vulgate version also includes extensive expansions and reworked passages,[12] Judith LXX and Iudith Vulg. share only approximately half of the same text.

Unfortunately, the textual history of the Vulgate version of Iudith[13] has not yet been adequately investigated. There are hardly any exegetical studies of the Vulgate Iudith. In 2016 Lydia Lange investigated the figure of Iudith in the Vulgate version in a monograph.[14] In her study she compared the Vulgate text not only to the Greek text but also to the Old Latin text. She was able to show that there were numerous formulations, motifs and theological topoi in the Vulgate that were specific to the Vulgate version; these were found neither in the Greek version nor in the Vetus

---

[10] Corley, "Septuagintalisms," 96.

[11] Gera, *Judith*; Barbara Schmitz and Helmut Engel, *Judit*, HThKAT (Freiburg: Herder, 2014). The older position is now hardly ever found in the more recent literature; see, however, Lisa M. Wolfe, *Ruth, Esther, Song of Songs and Judith* (Eugene, OR: Cascade Books, 2011), 203.

[12] Pierre-Maurice Bogaert, "Jérôme hagiographe et conteur: La conversion d'Achior dans le livre de Judith," in *La surprise dans la Bible: Hommage à Camille Focant*, ed. Geert van Oyen and André Wénin, BETL 247 (Leuven: Peeters, 2012), 111–23.

[13] For ease of reference, Iudith and the abbreviation "Idt" always refers to the Vulgate text; when the Greek text is intended, "Judith" and "Jdt" are used.

[14] Lydia Lange, *Die Juditfigur in der Vulgata: Eine theologische Studie zur lateinischen Bibel*, DCLS 36 (Berlin: De Gruyter, 2016). See Edmon L. Gallagher, "Why Did Jerome Translate Tobit and Judith?" *HTR* 108 (2015): 356–75.

Latina, but they did appear in Jerome's *praefatio* with its clear interpretative tendencies, and in his other writings, especially in his letters. These
formulations, motifs and topoi are typical of the theological discourse of
the 4th and 5th centuries CE.

The extensive studies of Pierre-Maurice Bogaert on the various Vetus
Latina manuscripts of Judith have shown that ms 151 (according to the
Beuron numbering) is one of the oldest manuscripts of the Vetus Latina
tradition. This manuscript, also referred to as Corbeiensis 7 or Sanger-
manensis 7,[15] has been edited by Bogaert[16] and may have been—according to Bogaert—one of Jerome's source texts.[17] Because ms 151 preserves the oldest pre-Jerome versions of the text of Iudith in Old Latin,
it has been consulted regularly in this essay for comparative purposes.[18]

A more thorough scholarly investigation of the text of Vulgate Iudith
is a desideratum, so that the textual history of the entire Judith tradition
can be reconstructed more accurately, and the distinctive profile of the
Vulgate narrative can be seen. This is even more important, as the Vulgate text is the one that was read in the Catholic and Protestant[19] traditions and therefore was the text of the western (and largely Christian)
reception of Judith in art, music, and literature.

The goal of this essay is to examine Judith's two short prayers immediately before her act, focusing on the differences between the Greek
version (Jdt 13:4–5 and Jdt 13:7)[20] and the Latin version of the Vulgate
(Idt 13:7 and Idt 13:9),[21] and in each case to inquire as to the function
and intention of these prayers in the two versions.[22]

---

[15] Paris, Bibliothèque nationale lat. 11549.

[16] Pierre-Maurice Bogaert, "Recensions de la vieille version latine de Judith: I. Aux origines de la Vulgate hiéronymienne: Le 'Corbeiensis'," *RBén* 85 (1975): 7–37. Cf.
Pierre-Maurice Bogaert, *Judith: Einleitung*, VL 7/2, Faszikel 1 (Freiburg: Herder,
2001).

[17] Cf. Roger Gryson, *Die altlateinischen Handschriften* (Freiburg: Herder, 1999), 227.
See also Bogaert, "Recensions," 9, 35.

[18] Unfortunately, the volume containing a critical edition of the Vetus Latina version of
the Book of Judith has not yet appeared in the edition being prepared by the Beuron
Vetus Latina Institute.

[19] Martin Luther translated the Vulgate text, not the Greek version.

[20] Cf. Robert Hanhart, *Iudith*, Septuaginta: Vetus Testamentum Graecum VIII/4 (Göttingen: Vandenhoeck & Ruprecht, 1979); Robert Hanhart, *Text und Textgeschichte des
Buches Judith*, MSU 14 (Göttingen: Vandenhoeck & Ruprecht, 1979).

[21] Robert Weber and Roger Gryson, *Biblia Sacra iuxta Vulgatam Versionem*, 5th ed.
(Stuttgart: Deutsche Bibelgesellschaft, 2007).

[22] The English translation of the Greek text follows Gera, *Judith*; that of the Vulgate version is based on Edgar Swift, *The Vulgate Bible: Volume 11B: The Historical Books.
Douay-Rheims Translation* (Cambridge: Harvard University Press, 2011).

Prayers in the Book of Judith LXX

The book of Judith is known above all for its key plot element, which is
regarded with ambivalence and is sometimes even seen as scandalous:
the killing of the Assyrian general Holofernes at the hand of the beautiful
Judith. Indeed, the plot of the book of Judith can be outlined in such
a way that everything hinges on this act: Nabouchodonosor, the king of
the Assyrians who lives in Nineveh, wants to rule as king over the entire
oikumene and to be worshipped as (the only) God. He sends his general,
Holofernes, on a mission to bring the west into submission. One people
after another submits to him on his awe-inspiring triumphal march.
Only the people of Israel are willing to resist this military superpower.
Bethulia, the paradigmatic but fictitious village, is besieged and starved,
and is ready to capitulate after 34 days. The beautiful, rich widow Judith
appears for the first time and takes advantage of the five-day window in
order to go herself to the Assyrian camp to win the trust of Holofernes.
At the end of a private feast Judith kills the completely drunk Holofernes
with his own sword and manages to leave the Assyrian camp without
being noticed. The now headless—in the truest sense of the word—
Assyrians are put to flight and in the end a great feast of thanksgiving
for liberation can be celebrated in Jerusalem.

Even if the course of action of the book of Judith is accurately presented in the summary above, much of the Biblical narrative is missing
in such a brief paraphrase. In the summary above it is precisely the
speeches and prayers that are omitted, even though they make up almost
one-third of the narrative. But the speeches and prayers are significant
not only because of the amount of text that they comprise in the narrative
composition, but also because of the function they have: in Jdt 2; 5; 8;
9; 11 and 16 the speeches and prayers are distributed equally across the
narrative and function as occasions for reflection.

Before the western world is conquered by the Assyrians, Nabouchodonosor proclaims his lengthy, programmatic *speech* (*Jdt 2:5–13*), in
which he announces the fate that will fall on all of the peoples who do
not submit to him. Before Holofernes takes the field against Israel, he
summons a council and is given (unwelcome) *speech* of advice by Achior
(*Jdt 5:5–21*). Before Judith becomes active and goes to the camp of the
Assyrians, she gives a lengthy *speech* to the elders in which she grounds
her future action theologically (*Jdt 8:11–27*); she also prepares for this
action in her long *prayer* to God (*Jdt 9:2–14*). Before Judith begins to
live in the camp of the Assyrians, she explains her new role in the camp

of the Assyrians in an ambiguous and deeply ironic *speech* before Holofernes (*Jdt 11:5–19*). Only the final *hymn* does not reflect on future events but rather looks back on the whole event, sums it up, and interprets it retrospectively (*Jdt 16:1–17*).

It is clear, therefore, that the speeches and prayers are an integral part of the narrative, functioning as occasions for reflection. Their function becomes apparent only on a second reading: they explain and interpret the action to come so that these do not appear to be spontaneous and unreflective but rather are embedded in a coherent framework that has previously been explicated.

In this way, then, the book of Judith is structured by two different storylines:[23] on the one hand by the narrative action and on the other by the speeches and prayers, in which the action is laid out proleptically and grounded. Each storyline has its own peak: in the narrative storyline the peak is the killing scene (Jdt 13), whereas in the storyline of the speeches and prayers the peak is reached in the two speech units placed in the middle of the book, the speech before the elders (Jdt 8:11–27) and Judith's comprehensive prayer to God (Jdt 9:2–14). This double storyline, each of which follows its own logic, gives the book of Judith significant narrative as well as a theological tension. Therefore, it is not only the story of violent seduction,[24] but it is also a story of deep theological reflections and prayers.

Two of the six speech units are prayers. One of these is placed in the storyline of the speeches and prayers in the middle of the narrative: Judith's long prayer before she goes to the camp (Jdt 9:2–14). The second is the long prayer at the end of the narrative that looks back at the action and retrospectively interprets it (Jdt 16:1–7).

It is noteworthy that these are not the only prayers in the narrative, although they are the longest. There are additional prayers, which can be divided into two groups. The first group consists of those prayers that are mentioned and occasionally given in indirect speech (cf. Jdt 4:9–12; 4:14–15; 7:19; 7:29; 10:9; 12:8; 16:18); the second group is comprised

---

[23] Barbara Schmitz, *Gedeutete Geschichte: Die Funktion der Reden und Gebete im Buch Judit*, HBS 40 (Freiburg: Herder, 2004), 433–52; Barbara Schmitz, "The Function of the Speeches and Prayers in the Book of Judith," in *Tobit and Judith*, ed. Athalya Brenner-Idan and Helen Efthimiadis-Keith, FCB Second Series 20 (London: Bloomsbury T&T Clark, 2015), 164–74.

[24] See, on the ambiguous, polysemantic use of the lexeme -ἀπατ-, Schmitz and Engel, *Judit*, 278–9.

of short prayers in direct speech. There are five short prayers in direct speech in total:

— The prayer of the people in Bethulia after Achior's report about what has happened in the camp (6:19) (the people at the culmination of the reception of Achior in Bethulia)
— Judith's first short prayer before her deed (13:4–5)
— Judith's second short prayer before her deed (13:7)
— Judith's short prayer following her return to Bethulia (13:14)
— The people's response to Judith's report (13:17)

In the following, Judith's first two short prayers will be the focus. These two prayers are inserted in a significant location in the narrative, namely, at the peak of the storyline composed of the narrative action, the killing scene of Holofernes.

The Prayers of Judith in Jdt 13:4–5, 7 LXX

The two short prayers are embedded in a scene that is described at length, after Judith and her maid have been in the Assyrian camp for four days. On the fourth day, Holofernes organizes a private banquet (Jdt 12:10–12). He wants to put to rest any doubts about his virility (Jdt 12:12). Judith comes to Holofernes's tent, beautifully groomed and dressed in fine clothing and jewelry. The effect is immediate: "Holofernes' heart (καρδία) was distraught because of her, his soul was shaken, and he had an overwhelming desire to sleep with her, for he had looked for an opportunity to seduce her from the day he saw her"[25] (Jdt 12:16).

Holofernes's state of mind is clear, his intentions are revealed to readers in the baldest way possible. His urging that Judith drink (Jdt 12:17) is intended to bring him closer to his goal, but the opposite happens: in anticipation of the night he has planned with Judith, Holofernes consumes so much alcohol that, before he is able to realize his intentions, he gets drunk and simply falls asleep (Jdt 13:1–2). The decisive moment arrives: Judith and Holofernes are, as planned, unobserved and alone, but the mighty Holofernes has fallen asleep, stupefied, and is therefore defenseless. But before Judith can realize her intention to kill Holofernes (Jdt 13:8), a series of events intervene that delay the action while at the same time increase the suspense. First it is made clear that Judith really

---

[25] Jdt 12:16: καὶ ἐξέστη ἡ καρδία Ολοφέρνου ἐπ᾽ αὐτήν, καὶ ἐσαλεύθη ἡ ψυχὴ αὐτοῦ, καὶ ἦν κατεπίθυμος σφόδρα τοῦ συγγενέσθαι μετ᾽ αὐτῆς· καὶ ἐτήρει καιρὸν τοῦ ἀπατῆσαι αὐτὴν ἀφ᾽ ἧς ἡμέρας εἶδεν αὐτήν.

is alone: she has instructed her maid to wait outside because she intends
to go out to pray later. She has also told this to Bagoas (Jdt 13:3–4a).
This explanatory interjection interrupts and delays the action. At the same
time, the mention of the usual evening prayer (cf. Jdt 12:7–8) serves to
make the deed appear to be thought-out and planned. But Judith does not
straightaway do the deed; rather, the action is interrupted again by the
two prayers (Jdt 13:4b–7).

Judith is first portrayed standing by the bed (καὶ στᾶσα Ιουδιθ παρὰ
τὴν κλίνην αὐτοῦ); it is made clear that Judith prays the following
prayer "in her heart," that is, inwardly and not audibly (εἶπεν ἐν τῇ
καρδίᾳ αὐτῆς).[26] It is the readers and not the figures in the narrative who
hear Judith's prayer. With the word "heart" the two protagonists are
contrasted in this scene. While Judith's heart is clear and reflective,
Holofernes's heart is so ravished (cf. Jdt 12:16) that he has made himself
incapable of action because of his consumption of alcohol.

Judith's first prayer is as follows:

[4]καὶ στᾶσα Ιουδιθ παρὰ τὴν κλίνην αὐτοῦ εἶπεν ἐν τῇ καρδίᾳ αὐτῆς Κύριε ὁ θεὸς πάσης δυνάμεως, ἐπίβλεψον ἐν τῇ ὥρᾳ ταύτῃ ἐπὶ τὰ ἔργα τῶν χειρῶν μου εἰς ὕψωμα Ιερουσαλημ·	[4]Judith stood near his bed and said in her heart, "Lord, God of all might, look this hour upon the work of my hands for the exaltation of Jerusalem.
[5]ὅτι νῦν καιρὸς ἀντιλαβέσθαι τῆς κληρονομίας σου καὶ ποιῆσαι τὸ ἐπιτήδευμά μου εἰς θραῦσμα ἐχθρῶν, οἳ ἐπανέστησαν ἡμῖν.	[5]For now is the time to lay claim to your heritage and to carry out my plan to shatter the enemies who have risen against us."

This prayer, in a narrative context of great agitation and tension, reveals
itself to be a precisely composed prayer, which incorporates lexemes and
motifs that are of great importance in the narrative and are key words
within it.[27]

The first element forming the intertextual network of this prayer is the
word "lord," κύριος. The address to God with which Judith begins her
prayer ("Lord, God of all might," Κύριε ὁ θεὸς πάσης δυνάμεως),
recalls the end of her first great prayer in Jdt 9:14, where she praises God
as the "God of all might and strength" (θεὸς πάσης δυνάμεως καὶ
κράτους). Judith calls her Lord the "God of all might" (ὁ θεὸς πάσης
δυνάμεως) in the midst of the great Assyrian army (δύναμις); moreover,

---

[26] See below for more on the trope "to speak in one's heart."
[27] Zenger, *Judit*, 433–4.

Judith repeats the word "might" (δύναμις) that is an important motif in
the narrative and especially in her prayer in Jdt 9 (cf. Jdt 9:7, 8, 14). In
addition, addressing God as "lord," κύριος, expresses an extremely
important motif in the narrative. In the book of Judith the lexeme κύριος
is used on the one hand for Nabouchodonosor (Jdt 2:5, 13, 14, 15; 6:4,
etc.) and Holofernes (Jdt 5:5, 20, 21, etc.), and on the other hand also for
the God of Israel (Jdt 4:2, 11, 13, 14, 15; 6:19; 7:19; 8:13, 14; 9:1, 2,
7, 8, etc.). The word is polysemantic, inasmuch as it refers at first glance
to the mighty ruler and his general, but on second glance it applies to the
God of Israel, who alone is mighty. Judith's speech in Jdt 11 plays precisely with this lexeme (cf. Jdt 11:5, 6, 10, 11, 17, 22). In her prayer in
Jdt 13:4–5, however, the lexeme is exclusive: κύριος, "lord," refers only
to the God of Israel, the God of all might (Jdt 13:4).

Judith's petition to God "in this hour" (ἐν τῇ ὥρᾳ ταύτῃ) asks that
God look on "the work of my hands" (ἐπὶ τὰ ἔργα τῶν χειρῶν μου).[28]
'Hand' is another important motif in the book of Judith that is developed
in multifaceted ways.[29] It is highlighted here in Jdt 13:4 as this is not
only the actual moment of her deed but also because Judith understands
herself as the agent, as the work "of *my* hands" (τῶν χειρῶν *μου*).
Judith herself takes the responsibility for her deed and does not pass
along the responsibility at the decisive moment. She consciously takes it
upon herself, since *she* is the one who acts and who must accept responsibility.[30] This contrasts with her other *interpretations* of her deed—either
prospective (Jdt 8:33; 9:9, 10 in connection to Jdt 9:2; 12:4) or retrospective (Jdt 13:14, 15; 16:5)—in which she places her deed in the context of *God's* acts. In her prayer in Jdt 13:4, however, Judith speaks of
her own agency and thus of her own responsibility for the deed. In the
narrative, this assessment of her deed is later interpreted similarly by
the High Priest Joakim and the Israelite elders (Jdt 15:10).

The goal of her act is "the exaltation of Jerusalem" (εἰς ὕψωμα Ιερουσαλημ). Judith lifts her deed out of the binary narrative framework
(Holofernes—Judith) and places it in a collective framework (Jerusalem),
which both points back to the desire of the elders of Bethulia that Judith
find a good reception in the Assyrian camp in order that Jerusalem be
"exalted" (Jdt 10:8), as well as forward to the thanks of the high priest

---

[28] The formulation ἐπὶ τὰ ἔργα τῶν χειρῶν μου "the work of my hands" is found only
here in the Judith narrative; Judith otherwise refers to her future action using the word
πρᾶγμα (Jdt 8:32; 11:6, 16) or ἐπιτήδευμα (Jdt 10:8; 11:6; 13:5).
[29] Schmitz and Engel, *Judit*, 296–7.
[30] So also Gera, *Judith*, 393.

and the elders of Jerusalem, who praise Judith as the personified "glory of Jerusalem" (Jdt 15:9).

Next in Judith's prayer she gives a reason why God should be motivated to do the act she has outlined—now is the decisive moment (καιρός) for God to embrace his own "heritage" (Jdt 13:5, κληρονομία). The word κληρονομία, "heritage," picks up on an important motif in the Judith narrative (κληρονομ, cf. Jdt 4:12; 5:15; 8:22; 9:12; 16:21). The term designates the special relationship of God to Israel, or, more precisely, to the land inhabited by Israel.[31] The lawful possession of the hill country inhabited by Israel, which in the narrative is now threatened by Nabouchodonosor and Holofernes, had been stressed by Achior in his speech before Holofernes. His speech, structured via the lexeme -οικ-,[32] is an idiosyncratic historical overview of the episodes of dwelling in the land and the lawful possession of this land. When, therefore, Judith pleads with God to embrace his κληρονομία, "heritage," she is referring back to Achior's account, in which he recounts the labor and time it took Israel to come into possession of the land as κληρονομία, "heritage," as "ethnic homeland."[33] Readers do not need to be told that, as a result, there is a special responsibility.

How God should embrace his κληρονομία, "heritage," Judith's prayer goes on to explain: the following καί is a καί *epexegeticum*, in other words, an 'and' that introduces an explanation. God should embrace his κληρονομία, "heritage," by carrying out (ποιῆσαι "to do, to carry out") Judith's plan (ἐπιτήδευμα) for annihilating the enemy.

The goal, "to shatter the enemies" (εἰς θραῦσμα ἐχθρῶν cf. Jdt 7:9) points to the verb θραύω, "to shatter," which is used also in Jdt 9:10; 13:14 for Judith's act. With this repetition, Judith's agency and responsibility is again stressed.

When Judith's first prayer has ended she takes Holofernes's sword from the bed post and approaches his bed a second time (cf. Jdt 13:4). Now, however, she seizes his hair and prays a second time (Jdt 13:6–7). While Judith is speaking her second, shorter prayer immediately before her deed, she is in physical contact with Holofernes via the hair she has grasped, and prays:

---

[31] Cf. Anssi Voitila, "Judith and Deuteronomistic Heritage," in *Changes in Scripture*, ed. Hanne von Weisenberg, Juha Pakkala, and Marko Marttila (Berlin: De Gruyter, 2011), 369–88; Schmitz and Engel, *Judit*, 188–9.

[32] Engel, "Herr," 158; Schmitz and Engel, *Judit*, 169, 170.

[33] Anne-Mareike Wetter, *On Her Account: Reconfiguring Israel in Ruth, Esther, and Judith* (London: Bloomsbury, 2015), 207–10.

⁷Κραταίωσόν με, κύριε ὁ θεὸς   ⁷Make me strong, Lord, God of
Ισραηλ, ἐν τῇ ἡμέρᾳ ταύτῃ.   Israel, on this very day.

In this second prayer two central motifs or lexemes reappear that connect this short prayer to the narrative and also refer back to the first prayer in Jdt 13:4–5. The request that God make Judith strong ("strengthen me," Jdt 13:7, κραταίωσόν με) uses, with the verb κραταιόω, the second word of the triad ἰσχύς, "power,"³⁴ κράτος, "strength,"³⁵ and δύναμις, "(military) might"³⁶ (δύναμις also appears in Jdt 13:4). This triad marks the whole Judith narrative, especially Judith's prayer in Jdt 9, where the three words appear together in Jdt 9:8.³⁷ The keyword κραταιόω recalls earlier requests by Judith that God give his power (Jdt 9:9) and also stresses at the decisive moment that God is the source of this power (cf. Jdt 9:14, and also Jdt 13:11).

As she did already in her first prayer (Jdt 13:4), in her second prayer Judith also addresses God as κύριε ὁ θεὸς Ισραηλ, "Lord, God of Israel" (Jdt 13:7). As in the first, the polysemous word κύριος, "lord," is here unequivocally reserved for the God of Israel.

These two short prayers immediately before she kills Holofernes stand out among the group of short prayers. Because both are spoken in 'real time,' they delay the narrative action and therefore increase the narrative tension. The tension on the level of action peaks at this point: three times³⁸ it is stressed that the fate of Israel and the whole world depends on this moment as the *kairos* moment.

That the peak of the action is delayed by two short prayers serves not only to increase the tension, it also serves, on the level of action, to bring into play the storyline of the speeches and prayers as a level of reflection. The logic of the storyline of the speeches and prayers is incorporated into the course of the action. Again, before anything happens, there is a reflection on the action about to take place.

Both short prayers are shown to be deeply connected to the narrative. Key themes, motifs and lexemes in the narrative are taken up: for

---

³⁴ ἰσχ- in Jdt 2:5; 5:3, 15, 23; 9:8, 11; 11:7, 10; 13:8, 11, 19; 14:2, 16; 16:13.
³⁵ κράτ- in Jdt 1:13, 14; 2:12; 5:3, 18, 23; 6:2, 3, 12; 7:12, 22; 9:8, 9, 11, 14; 11:7, 22; 13:7, 11; 15:7.
³⁶ δύνα- in Jdt 1:4 *bis*, 13 *bis*, 16; 2:4, 7, 14 *bis*, 19, 22; 3:6, 10; 4:15; 5:1, 3, 23; 6:1; 7:2 *bis*, 9, 12, 26; 9:3 *bis*, 7, 8, 11, 14; 10:13, 19; 11:8, 18; 13:4, 15; 14:3, 19; 16:3, 6.
³⁷ Schmitz and Engel, *Judit*, 290–2.
³⁸ Jdt 13:4, ἐν τῇ ὥρᾳ ταύτῃ, "in this hour"; Jdt 13:5, καιρός "today"; Jdt 13:7, ἐν τῇ ἡμέρᾳ ταύτῃ, "on this very day."

example, the polysemantic motif κύριος (in both prayers), δύναμις and κράτος, Judith's hand, the "exaltation of Jerusalem," the land as κληρονομία, and the desire that the enemy be annihilated. These key words are used more systematically in other parts of the narrative; in the midst of this *kairos* they are only briefly mentioned and thrown together in a crucible as it were. This highlights another central function of the two prayers in the LXX version: at the peak of the action all of the important elements are on display that are otherwise found in the first place in the storyline of the speeches and prayers.

Besides the function of the prayers in Jdt 13, their theological valence also needs to be stressed. Judith's explicit use of the motif κύριος is a response, even before she acts, to what Nabouchodonosor, the mightiest ruler, has put into question (cf. Jdt 3:8; 6:2): namely, that Nabbouchodonosor is not the "Lord," (κύριος), i.e., the true God, only the God of Israel is. As the narrative function of the prayers has already made clear, here, too, in these two prayers, the decisive theme of the Judith narrative finds its key expression.

This God does not, however, act as a savior god in the sense of a *deus ex machina*. Rather, it is up to humans like Judith to act; they can do no more than pray to God for support. God—according to Judith—must embrace his inheritance, but this happens only inasmuch as he allows her project to succeed (cf. Jdt 13:5).

Against the background of this anthropological view the two prayers leave no room for doubt about the ethical stance: Judith is the agent, and—as much as she might refer her act to God in prayer and reflection—she alone is responsible for her act.

A tentative conclusion to the discussion of the prayers in Jdt 13:4–5 and 13:7 in the Greek version might run as follows: the two short prayers offer in concentrated form a summary of the theology, anthropology, and ethics of the entire narrative, and are placed at the point of peak tension in the storyline of narrative action.[39]

Prayers in the Iudith Narrative of the Vulgate Version

The storyline of the Greek version is structured around the speeches and prayers; the speeches and prayers, however, differ considerably in the Vulgate version. First, some of the texts are markedly shorter compared with the Greek version; for example, the long speech of

---

[39] So also Zenger, *Judit*, 508.

Nabouchodonosor to Holofernes (Jdt 2:5–13), which is programmatic in the Greek version, is only two verses long in the Vulgate version (Idt 2:5–6). Second, there are texts with extensive expansions, as for example in Achior's speech to Holofernes (Idt 5:5–25) in which the verses Idt 5:11b–19 are plus texts. Third, there are texts that are approximately the same length but the content of which differ greatly compared with the Greek version, as in Iudith's speech to the elders (Idt 8:10–27) in verses Idt 8:12, 14, 16, 17, 23–27. For the prayers the observation about the speeches holds true: there are clear changes, consisting of both abbreviations and expansions. It appears that the prayers are the favored place in the Vulgate version to present a distinctly different theology from that of the Greek version.[40]

That the prayers in the Vulgate version have their own, different function is apparent also from the words that are used for "prayer." In the Greek version the most common verb used to identify or to introduce a prayer is the verb (ἀνα)βοάω "cry out, call," (Jdt 4:9, 12, 15; 5:12; 6:18; 7:19, 29; 9:1), followed by the simple indication of direct speech λέγω "to say."[41] These openings of the prayers are in the tradition of the openings of the prayers in the Hebrew Bible, that is, the Hebraic style of the LXX tradition. The verb δέομαι, "plead, pray," which is on the face of it the most likely terminus technicus for "prayer," is used for prayer only in Jdt 8:31 and Jdt 12:8 (cf. also δέησις in Jdt 9:12) and προσεύχομαι in Jdt 11:17, εὐχή in Jdt 4:17 and προσευχή in Jdt 12:6; 13:3, 10.

In ms 151, the lexemes δεο- and ευχ- both are translated as *(ad)ora-* (δέομαι in Jdt 8:31, 12:8 and προσευχή in Jdt 12:6; 13:10).[42] Furthermore, ms 151 uses the lexeme *(ad)ora-* another five times,[43] because ms 151 also translates the verb προσκυνέω as *(ad)orare* (Jdt 5:8; 6:18; 8:18; 10:8/9;[44] 10:23; 11:17; 13:17, 14:7; 16:8). The Greek verb προσκυνέω has a broad meaning, as it can refer to the reverence towards a king as well as to the devotion for God.[45] The Latin lexeme *ora-* has

---

[40] See Idt 4:8–10, 15–17; 7:4, 18–21; 10:10; 12:5, 6, 8; 13:7, 9, 22–25, or in Idt 6:15–16.

[41] Jdt 6:18 (ἐβόησαν λέγοντες); 13:4 (εἶπεν ἐν τῇ καρδίᾳ αὐτῆς), 7, 14 (εἶπεν πρὸς αὐτοὺς φωνῇ μεγάλῃ), 17 (εἶπαν ὁμοθυμαδόν); 16:1.

[42] Idt 13:3 in ms 151 differs compared to the Greek version.

[43] Idt 5:8; 6:18; 8:18, 31; 10:9, 23; 11:17; 12:6, 8; 13:10, 17; 14:7; 16:18; see changes in Jdt 4:14 ms 151 (*precantes dominum*).

[44] Cf. Hanhart, *Iudith*, 111; Hanhart, *Text und Textgeschichte*, 93–4.

[45] προσκυν- in the Greek version see, Schmitz and Engel, *Judit*, 178–9.

also broad semantics.[46] But as the verb *(ad)orare* is a translation for three different verbs in ms 151, ms 151 emphasizes the verb *(ad)orare* particularly. Therefore, the Latin verb *(ad)orare* is a new *Leitwort* in ms 151 and strengthens the importance of prayer and praying in ms 151.

This change from the Greek version to ms 151 is even more obvious in the Vulgate. In the Vulgate version, the verbs for prayer are used more often than in the Greek version or in ms 151: the verb *orare*, "to pray," appears 11 times (Idt 4:13, 17; 6:21; 7:4; 8:29, 31; 10:10; 11:14; 12:6, 8; 13:6), the noun *oratio*, "prayer," five times (Idt 4:12; 6:16; 8:33; 12:5; 13:12), the noun *prex*, "prayer," three times (Idt 4:12 *bis*; 6:14) and the verb *colere* five times (Idt 5:9, 18; 8:21; 11:14; 16:31). In addition, the praying scenes in the Vulgate are often changed by adding plus texts or changes in the text (see, e.g., the prayer of the High Priest *Heliachim* in Idt 4:11–17 or *orare* in Idt 4:13, 17, *oratio* in Idt 4:12 and *prex* in Idt 4:12; another example is Idt 6:14–21 or Idt 7:4, etc.).

There are not only changes in the wording, but also in the concept of praying: in the Vulgate, the prayers seem, for example, to be a prerequisite for God's action (e.g., the huge differences between Jdt 4:13–14.15 and Idt 4:11–17). These shifts concern also the character Judith: In the Greek version in Jdt 8:31, Judith urges the elders to take action in her theological speeches (Jdt 8:11–27), but the elders fail to understand her concerns. Therefore, they ask her 'only' to pray as a God-fearing woman (Jdt 8:31, καὶ νῦν δεήθητι περὶ ἡμῶν, ὅτι γυνὴ εὐσεβὴς εἶ). That Judith could act salvifically is not within their understanding, only that she can pray. Judith's response is not that she will pray (even though she does so repeatedly in what follows) but rather that she will *act* (Jdt 8:32–34). In the Vulgate version too the elders urge Iudith, as a holy and God-fearing woman, to pray (Idt 8:29, *nunc ergo ora pro nobis quoniam mulier sancta es et timens Dominum*), but Iudith's reaction is to urge the elders three times to pray for the success of her undertaking (Idt 8:31, 32, 33).

An interesting plus text concerning prayers in the Vulgate version is at the end of the story: the last verse of the Vulgate version is completely new. It notes that the triumph of Iudith has been added as a feast among the holy days, and that since that time it is celebrated among Jews (Idt 16:31).

---

[46] Cf. Peter G.W. Glare, *Oxford Latin Dictionary*, Vol. I + II. 2nd ed. (Oxford: Oxford University Press, 2012), 59. 1399–1400.

More striking, however, is the plus text in Idt 9:1 in the Vulgate version compared with the Greek version and ms 151: Judith does not pray, as in the Greek version and ms 151, in the tent (σκηνή / *tabernaculum*) on the roof of her house. This is Judith's preferred location, publicly visible, where she also receives the elders of Bethulia (Jdt 8:5; 10:2).[47] The Iudith of the Vulgate version, however, goes daily with her maids into a *secretum cubiculum*, an enclosed room in the top story of her house (Idt 8:5), a typical feature of houses in Roman times.[48] It is not explicitly stated whether she has also received the elders of Bethulia there. The prayer portrayed in Idt 9 takes place in the *oratorium* (Idt 9:1), which either refers to a room in her house intended exclusively for prayer or is another term for the *secretum cubiculum*.[49] In quite a number of letters[50] Jerome recommends that widows should follow the example of Mary and retire to a *cubiculum*. The question arises, therefore, whether the Vulgate version of Judith reflects the (Christian) world of the 4th or 5th century CE or whether the variants and plus texts in the Vulgate go back to a Hebrew original. The *praefatio* that Jerome attached to the Judith narrative makes clear that Jerome has himself played a large role in shaping the Judith narrative in his translation into Latin. As I have shown elsewhere, in the *praefatio* he describes his practice of translation and notes that he undertook the translation somewhat grudgingly; more importantly, he also prefaces the narrative with an interpretation of the story that follows.[51] In his interpretation he highlights the chastity (*castitas*) of the widow Judith, which is not a feature of either the Greek version nor ms 151. The recommendation that widows (at least those of the wealthy Roman upper class) live in chastity and seclusion is, however, a well-known theme in the writings and letters of Jerome.

The impression that the Vulgate version has its own theological point of view and that this point of view is reflected also in the prayers, needs thorough investigation. In the remainder of this essay, I will use the two short prayers of Judith immediately before her act as a case study to highlight some of the tendencies of the Vulgate version.

---

[47] Schmitz and Engel, *Judit*, 243.

[48] Idt 8:5: *et in superioribus domus suae fecit sibi secretum cubiculum in quo cum puellis suis clausa morabatur.*

[49] The word *oratorium* (Idt 9:1) is a *hapax legomenon* in the Vulgate.

[50] For examples see: Lange, *Juditfigur*, 139–42.

[51] Barbara Schmitz, "Ιουδιθ und Iudith: Überlegungen zum Verhältnis der Judit-Erzählung in der LXX und der Vulgata," in *Text-critical and Hermeneutical Studies in the Septuagint*, ed. Johann Cook and Hermann-Josef Stipp, VTSup 157 (Leiden: Brill, 2012), 359–79; cf. Lange, *Juditfigur*, 124–8.

The Prayer of Iudith in Idt 13:6–7, 9 Vulg.

If one compares the Greek text ms 151 as the exemplary text that Jerome presumably used with the Vulgate texts, three observations jump out. The phrases that are shared by ms 151 and the Vulgate are underlined; the text in the Vulgate that has no parallel in ms 151 or the Greek text is set in italics.

Jdt 13:4–5 LXX	Jdt 13:4–5 ms 151	Idt 13:6–7 Vulg.
⁴καὶ στᾶσα Ιουδιθ παρὰ τὴν κλίνην αὐτοῦ εἶπεν ἐν τῇ καρδίᾳ αὐτῆς	⁴et stetit ad caput holofernis et dixit in corde suo:	⁶stetitque Iudith ante lectum *orans cum lacrimis et labiorum motu in silentio* ⁷dicens
Κύριε ὁ θεὸς πάσης δυνάμεως, ἐπίβλεψον ἐν τῇ ὥρᾳ ταύτῃ ἐπὶ τὰ ἔργα τῶν χειρῶν μου εἰς ὕψωμα Ιερουσαλημ· ⁵ὅτι νῦν καιρὸς ἀντιλαβέσθαι τῆς κληρονομίας σου καὶ ποιῆσαι τὸ ἐπιτήδευμά μου εἰς θραῦσμα ἐχθρῶν, οἳ ἐπανέστησαν ἡμῖν.	<u>Confirma me domine deus israhel</u> et respice in hodierna die ad opera manuum mearum ut exaltetur hierusalem. ⁵Et fiat cogitatio mea aduersus inimicos qui insurrexerunt super nos.	<u>confirma me Domine Deus Israhel</u> et respice in hac hora ad opera manuum mearum *ut sicut promisisti Hierusalem civitatem tuam erigas et hoc quod credens per te posse fieri cogitavi perficiam*

First, there is clear agreement between the Greek text and ms 151: *et respice in hodierna die ad opera manuum mearum ut exaltetur hierusalem*, "look this hour upon the work of my hands for the exaltation of Jerusalem." This is a faithful translation of the Greek text (ἐπίβλεψον ἐν τῇ ὥρᾳ ταύτῃ ἐπὶ τὰ ἔργα τῶν χειρῶν μου εἰς ὕψωμα Ιερουσαλημ), and shows how closely the Latin translation of ms 151 stays to the Greek text.

Second, there are agreements between ms 151 and the Vulgate, but the text they have in common is different from the Greek text: for example, the address Κύριε ὁ θεὸς πάσης δυνάμεως, "Lord, God of all might," is given as *Domine Deus* in ms 151 and the Vulgate with the addition of *Israhel* ("O Lord, God of Israel"). Likewise, the demand, *confirma me*, "strengthen me," in both is an expansion over the Greek text. This agreement strengthens the thesis that Jerome must have had ms 151 (or a similar text) in front of him as he translated.

What accounts for those instances where ms 151 (and the Vulgate text that follows it) departs from the Greek text? Viewed from the perspective of the whole translation, such instances are considerably less common. The reason may be found in Judith's second prayer:

Jdt 13:7 LXX	Jdt 13:7 ms 151	Idt 13:9 Vulg.
⁷Κραταίωσόν με, κύριε ὁ θεὸς Ἰσραηλ, ἐν τῇ ἡμέρᾳ ταύτῃ.	⁷Confirma me domine deus israhel in hodierna die.	⁹confirma me Domine Deus Israhel in hac hora

Ms 151 translates the Greek very closely: Κραταίωσόν με, "make me strong," as *confirma me*, "strengthen me"; κύριε ὁ θεὸς Ἰσραηλ, "Lord, God of Israel," as *Domine Deus Israhel*, "O Lord, God of Israel"; and ἐν τῇ ἡμέρᾳ ταύτῃ, "on this very day," as *in hodierna die*, "on this day." This translation is also found (with the exception of *in hac hora*) in the Vulgate. The translation in ms 151 (and the Vulgate) of Jdt 13:7 LXX is repeated word for word in Jdt 13:4 ms 151 (with the parallel in Idt 13:7 Vulg., see table below). From this we can conclude that in ms 151 the text of Jdt 13:7 ms 151 was taken over in Jdt 13:4 ms 151 and so a parallelism is established between the two prayers, which is then taken over by the Vulgate.

Third, there are distinct deviations in the Vulgate compared to ms 151 and the Greek text. These—in italics below—are found both in the introduction to Judith's words and in the second half of the prayer:

Idt 13:6–7 Vulg.	Idt 13:6–7 Vulg.
⁶stetitque Iudith ante lectum *orans cum lacrimis et labiorum motu in silentio*	⁶And Judith stood before the bed *praying with tears and moving her lips in silence*
⁷dicens confirma me Domine Deus Israhel et respice in hac hora ad opera manuum mearum	⁷saying, "Strengthen me, O Lord, God of Israel, and in this hour look on the work of my hands
ut sicut promisisti Hierusalem civitatem tuam erigas et hoc quod credens per te posse fieri cogitavi perficiam	*that as you have promised may you raise up Jerusalem, your city, and that I may bring about what I have proposed, believing that it might be done by you"*

The formulation *orans cum lacrimis et labiorum motu in silentio* is a plus text over ms 151 and the Greek text.[52] In the first place, the verb

---

[52] Cf. on what follows also Lange, *Juditfigur*, 295–9.

orare, "to pray," gives greater specificity to Judith's words, in contrast to the Greek which uses the more neutral εἶπεν, "she said." It was already noted above that words from the semantic field "to pray" and "prayer" (including the instances in Jdt 8:32 and 12:8) occur in plus texts and appear frequently in the Vulgate of Judith.

The prayer here is portrayed as a prayer with tears (*cum lacrimis*). In the Vulgate text the word *lacrima*, "tears," is found in Idt 7:23; 8:14, 13:6, yet in all three instances, neither the Greek text nor ms 151 refer to tears. The increased use of words like *lacrima*, "tears," and *flere*, "to weep,"[53] in the plus texts means that the characters in the Vulgate are presented in a much more emotional way.[54] It is not only Iudith who weeps, but also Ozias, the people of Bethulia and Bagoas. While the combination of prayer and weeping is known already in the Hebrew Bible (Joel 1:8, 13; 2:17; Jer 3:21; cf. 2 Sam 12:21), it does appear that prayer, especially silent prayer with tears, is specific to Jerome. Vincent Skemp points out that this is also the case in the plus text of the Vulgate version of the Book of Tobit (Tob 3:11; 7:13; 12:12 Vulg.).[55] Praying silently under tears, however, is not an invention by Jerome, but is very important in the ascetic circles of the 4th and 5th century CE, especially among the desert fathers in Egypt.[56] In his letters as well Jerome writes of how he himself prayed with tears (e.g., *Epist.* 22.7, 18).[57]

Iudith's prayer is portrayed as *et labiorum motu in silentio* ("and the moving of her lips in silence," Idt 13:6). The Greek version and ms 151 describe the prayer as taking place ἐν τῇ καρδίᾳ αὐτῆς, "in her heart" (*in corde suo*). This formulation is found in the Hebrew Bible (cf. Gen 8:21; 17:17; 27:41; 1 Sam 27:1; 1 Kgs 12:26; Isa 47:10; Ps 10:6, see

[53] It is true that weeping is found in the Greek version three times (Jdt 7:29; 14:16; 16:17), twice in ms 151 (Jdt 7:29; 14:16), but the verb *flere* "to weep" is used six times in total in the Vulgate version (Idt 6:14, 16; 7:18, 22; 8:17; 14:14).
[54] The LXX avoids almost completely portraying characters as having emotions; see Barbara Schmitz, "Judith and Holofernes: An Analysis of the Killing Scene (Jdt 12:10–13:9)," in *Emotions in Prayer during the Second Temple Period*, ed. Renate Egger-Wenzel, Jonathan Ben-Dov, and Stefan Reif, DCLY 2011 (Berlin: De Gruyter, 2015), 177–92.
[55] Vincent T.M. Skemp, *The Vulgate of Tobit Compared with Other Ancient Witnesses* (Atlanta: SBL Press, 2000), 113, 252, 368–9.
[56] Barbara Müller, *Der Weg des Weinens: Die Tradition des „Penthos" in den Apophthegmata Patrum*, Forschungen zur Kirchen- und Dogmengeschichte 77 (Göttingen: Vandenhoeck & Ruprecht, 2000); see also Franz Dodel, *Das Sitzen der Wüstenväter: Eine Untersuchung anhand der Apophtegmata Patrum*, Paradosis 42 (Fribourg: Universitäts-Verlag, 1997), 91–3.
[57] Cf. on this point Lange, *Juditfigur*, 163–5.

also 1 Sam 1:13), but there it is a stylistic device for presenting the secret thoughts and inner reasoning of the characters.[58] The use of the two-part formula *labiorum motu* ("the moving of her lips") and *in silentio* ("in silence") serves to foreground not the character of the thought but whether or not it was audible.

Whereas the first part of the prayer in the Vulgate text is very close to the version in ms 151 and the Greek text, the second half differs considerably.[59] The request, in this hour to look on the work of Iudith's hands, is expanded with two additions: first that God, as he has promised, will restore his city Jerusalem, and, second, that Iudith will be able to carry out what she has proposed to do, believing that it will be done through God (Idt 13:7 Vulg.). That God has promised something is conveyed occasionally in the Vulgate by means of the verb *promittere* (cf. Deut 10:9; Jos 9:24 Vulg.; Heb 6:13 Vulg.), but also in a plus text in the Vulgate of Iudith (Idt 13:18).[60] So, too, the verb *erigere* appears in the Vulgate of Iudith in plus texts (cf. Idt 8:21; 9:11; 13:7). Furthermore, it is especially noteworthy that Iudith refers to her action as *credens*, "believing." In Vulgate Iudith, the verb *credere*, "believe," is used three times: Idt 8:27 and 13:7 are plus texts; for the use of *credere* in Vulgate Iudith, Idt 14:6 is instructive:

Jdt 14:10 LXX	Jdt 14:10 ms 151	Idt 14:6 Vulg.
ἰδὼν δὲ Αχιωρ πάντα,	Videns autem achior	tunc Achior videns
ὅσα ἐποίησεν ὁ θεὸς	omnia que fecit dominus	virtutem quam fecit
τοῦ Ισραηλ,	in israhel	Deus Israhel
ἐπίστευσεν τῷ θεῷ		*relicto gentilitatis ritu*
σφόδρα καὶ	credidit deo et	credidit Deo et
περιετέμετο τὴν σάρκα	circumcidit carnem	circumcidit carnem
τῆς ἀκροβυστίας αὐτοῦ	prepucii sui	praeputii sui

The verb πιστεύω appears only once in the Judith narrative, precisely here in Jdt 14:10; in ms 151 and in the Vulgate it is translated as *credere*. But only the Vulgate has the plus text *relicto gentilitatis ritu*, "leaving the religion of the Gentiles."[61] In Idt 14:6 the plus text specifies the meaning of *credere*: Achior's conversion is portrayed as an act of

[58] Cf. Gera, *Judith*, 392.
[59] Here too ms 151 has a shorter text compared with the Greek text.
[60] Cf. Idt 8:9; 9:11; 11:21.
[61] The word *caerimonia* appears in similar formulation in a plus text in the Vulgate in Achior's speech. Achior reports that the ancestors of Israel abandoned the rites of their fathers, which included the worship of many gods (*deserentes itaque* caerimonias *patrum suorum quae in multitudine deorum erant* Idt 5:8).

faith and confession and involves a change of religion. A conversion understood in this way corresponds much more closely to the model of Christian conversion in the 4th and 5th centuries CE.[62] Robert Markus was able to show in this connection how, in the 4th century CE, the understanding of belonging to a religion changed and the concept of the secular arose.[63] This differs considerably from the model of a shared and much more comprehensive ethnic identity that can be identified in the Judaism of pre-Roman times.[64]

This exploration into the two prayers in Idt 13:7 and 13:9 has highlighted the connection between the Vulgate version of the Iudith narrative and its relationship to ms 151 and the Greek text. The plus texts in the Vulgate stand out above all and can be explicated by a comparison with ms 151 and the Greek text. The distinctive features of the Vulgate can be accounted for as reflecting Jerome's writings, thought, and theology, and they bear the clear traces of the Christian world of the 4th and 5th centuries CE. The question remains, however, whether the characteristics specific to the Vulgate are more accurately described as characteristics specific to Jerome.

Conclusion

The short prayers that are placed as Judith's speech immediately before her deed (Jdt 13:4–5, 7 LXX and Idt 13:7, 9 Vulg.) function in both narratives to delay the deed, to pause as the tension grows, and thus heighten the narrative tension. At the same time, they incorporate speeches and prayers into the storyline which influence how a reader might reflect on the overall story. Both the Greek and the Latin Judith narratives share these features. The two short prayers were shown to be deeply embedded in the narrative: they take up central themes, motifs and keywords of the narrative, nevertheless, the two versions differ considerably in how these are expressed. It is clear that the two narratives are conceptually different; each with its own understanding of the

---

[62] Cf. Lange, *Juditfigur*, 318.

[63] Robert A. Markus, *Christianity and the Secular* (Notre Dame: University of Notre Dame Press, 2006).

[64] Cf. Steve Mason, "Jews, Judaeans, Judaizing, Judaism: Problems of Categorization in Ancient History," *JSJ* 38 (2007): 457–512; Steve Mason, *Josephus, Judea, and Christian Origins: Methods and Categories* (Peabody, MA: Hendrickson, 2009); Benedikt Eckhardt, *Jewish Identity and Politics between the Maccabees and Bar Kokhba: Groups, Normativity, and Rituals*, JSJSup 155 (Leiden: Brill, 2012). See for Judith: Wetter, *On Her Account*, 195–221.

function of the narrative. The Greek version of the Judith narrative is a witness to the theological and cultural history of the Hellenistic period. The Vulgate version is, however, much more than a mere translation—it can be understood as a glimpse of the theological and cultural transition from the 4th to the 5th centuries CE.

Bibliography

Bogaert, Pierre-Maurice. "Recensions de la vieille version latine de Judith: I. Aux origines de la Vulgate hiéronymienne: Le 'Corbeiensis'." *RBén* 85 (1975): 7–37.

Bogaert, Pierre-Maurice. *Judith: Einleitung*. VL 7/2, Faszikel 1. Freiburg: Herder, 2001.

Bogaert, Pierre-Maurice. "Jérôme hagiographe et conteur: La conversion d'Achior dans le livre de Judith." Pages 111–23 in *La surprise dans la Bible: Hommage à Camille Focant*. Edited by Geert van Oyen and André Wénin. BETL 247. Leuven: Peeters, 2012.

Corley, Jeremy. "Septuagintalisms, Semitic interference, and the Original Language of the Book of Judith." Pages 65–96 in *Studies in the Greek Bible: Essays in Honor of Francis T. Gignac*. Edited by Jeremy Corley. CBQMS 44. Washington, DC: The Catholic Biblical Association of America, 2008.

Dodel, Franz. *Das Sitzen der Wüstenväter: Eine Untersuchung anhand der Apophtegmata Patrum*. Paradosis 42. Fribourg: Universitäts-Verlag, 1997.

Eckhardt, Benedikt. *Jewish Identity and Politics between the Maccabees and Bar Kokhba: Groups, Normativity, and Rituals*. JSJSup 155. Leiden: Brill, 2012.

Engel, Helmut. "Der HERR ist ein Gott, der Kriege zerschlägt: Zur Frage der griechischen Originalsprache und der Struktur des Buches Judith." Pages 155–68 in *Goldene Äpfel in silbernen Schalen*. Edited by Klaus-Dietrich Schunck and Matthias Augustin. BEATAJ 20. Frankfurt: Lang, 1992.

Fürst, Alfons. *Hieronymus: Askese und Wissenschaft in der Spätantike*. Freiburg: Herder, 2003.

Gallagher, Edmon L. "Why Did Jerome Translate Tobit and Judith?" *HTR* 108 (2015): 356–75.

Gera, Deborah Levine. *Judith*. CEJL. Berlin: de Gruyter, 2014.

Glare, Peter G.W. *Oxford Latin Dictionary*. Vol. I + II. 2nd ed. Oxford: Oxford University Press, 2012.

Grintz, Yehoshua M. *Sefer Jehudît: A Reconstruction of the Original Hebrew Text with Introduction, Commentary, Appendices and Indices* (hebr.). Jerusalem: Bialik Institute, 1957.

Gryson, Roger. *Die altlateinischen Handschriften*. Freiburg: Herder, 1999.

Hanhart, Robert. *Iudith*. Septuaginta: Vetus Testamentum Graecum VIII/4. Göttingen: Vandenhoeck & Ruprecht, 1979.

Hanhart, Robert. *Text und Textgeschichte des Buches Judith*. MSU 14. Göttingen: Vandenhoeck & Ruprecht, 1979.

Joosten, Jan. "The Original Language and Historical Milieu of the Book of Judith." Pages 159–76 in *Meghillot: Studies in the Dead Sea Scrolls V–VI:*

A Festschrift for Devorah Dimant. Edited by Moshe Bar-Asher and Emanuel Tov. Haifa: University of Haifa, The Publication Project of the Qumran Scrolls; Jerusalem: The Bialik Institute, 2007.

Lange, Lydia. *Die Juditfigur in der Vulgata: Eine theologische Studie zur lateinischen Bibel*. DCLS 36. Berlin: de Gruyter, 2016.

Markus, Robert A. *Christianity and the Secular*. Notre Dame: University of Notre Dame Press, 2006.

Mason, Steve. "Jews, Judaeans, Judaizing, Judaism: Problems of Categorization in Ancient History." *JSJ* 38 (2007): 457–512.

Mason, Steve. *Josephus, Judea, and Christian Origins: Methods and Categories*. Peabody, MA: Hendrickson, 2009.

Moore, Carey A. *Judith*. AB 40. Garden City, NY: Doubleday, 1985.

Müller, Barbara. *Der Weg des Weinens: Die Tradition des „Penthos" in den Apophthegmata Patrum*. Forschungen zur Kirchen- und Dogmengeschichte 77. Göttingen: Vandenhoeck & Ruprecht, 2000.

Pfeiffer, Robert H. "The Book of Judith." Pages 285–303 in *History of New Testament Times: With an Introduction to the Apocrypha*. Edited by Robert H. Pfeiffer. London: Black, 1949.

Priebatsch, Hans Yohanan. "Das Buch Judit und seine hellenistischen Quellen." *ZDPV* 90 (1974): 50–60.

Ryan, Stephen D. "The Ancient Versions of Judith and the Place of the Septuagint in the Catholic Church." Pages 1–21 in *A Pious Seductress: Studies in the Book of Judith*. Edited by Géza G. Xeravits. DCLS 14. Berlin: de Gruyter, 2012.

Schlange-Schöningen, Heinrich. *Hieronymus: Eine historische Biografie*. Darmstadt: Wissenschaftliche Buchgesellschaft, 2018.

Schmitz, Barbara. *Gedeutete Geschichte: Die Funktion der Reden und Gebete im Buch Judit*. HBS 40. Freiburg: Herder, 2004.

Schmitz, Barbara. "Ιουδιθ und *Iudith*: Überlegungen zum Verhältnis der Judit-Erzählung in der LXX und der Vulgata." Pages 359–79 in *Text-critical and Hermeneutical Studies in the Septuagint*. Edited by Johann Cook and Hermann-Josef Stipp. VTSup 157. Leiden: Brill, 2012.

Schmitz, Barbara, and Helmut Engel. *Judit*. HThKAT. Freiburg: Herder, 2014.

Schmitz, Barbara. "The Function of the Speeches and Prayers in the Book of Judith." Pages 164–74 in *Tobit and Judith*. Edited by Athalya Brenner-Idan and Helen Efthimiadis-Keith. FCB Second Series 20. London: Bloomsbury T&T Clark, 2015.

Schmitz, Barbara. "Judith and Holofernes: An Analysis of the Killing Scene (Jdt 12:10–13:9)." Pages 177–92 in *Emotions in Prayer during the Second Temple Period*. Edited by Renate Egger-Wenzel, Jonathan Ben-Dov and Stefan Reif. DCLY 2011. Berlin: de Gruyter, 2015.

Skemp, Vincent T.M. *The Vulgate of Tobit Compared with Other Ancient Witnesses*. Atlanta: SBL Press, 2000.

Swift, Edgar. *The Vulgate Bible: Volume 11B: The Historical Books. Douay-Rheims Translation*. Cambridge: Harvard University Press, 2011.

Voitila, Anssi. "Judith and Deuteronomistic Heritage." Pages 369–88 in *Changes in Scripture*. Edited by Hanne von Weisenberg and Juha Pakkala and Marko Marttila. Berlin: de Gruyter, 2011.

Weber, Robert, and Roger Gryson. *Biblia Sacra iuxta Vulgatam Versionem*. 5th ed. Stuttgart: Deutsche Bibelgesellschaft, 2007.

Wetter, Anne-Mareike. *On Her Account: Reconfiguring Israel in Ruth, Esther, and Judith*. London: Bloomsbury, 2015.

Wolfe, Lisa M. *Ruth, Esther, Song of Songs and Judith*. Eugene, OR: Cascade Books, 2011.

Zenger, Erich. *Das Buch Judit*. JSHRZ I/6. Gütersloh: Gütersloher Verlagshaus Gerd Mohn, 1981.

"I DID NOT DESPISE THEM": ELEAZAR'S PRAYER IN 3 MACCABEES (6:2–15)

Noah HACHAM

The verse "I did not despise them" (Lev 26:44) embodies God's promise not to reject His people, but rather to accompany them even outside their land and divested of political independence. According to 3 Maccabees (6:15), at the last moment before the Jews' annihilation, Eleazar the priest who prays in the Hippodrome, concludes his supplication by asking God to fulfill this promise. The verse appears also in Mordechai's prayer according to Midrash Esther Rabbah and in numerous rabbinic homilies concerning various Diasporas.[1] Mordechai's prayer in Greek Esther also possibly alludes to this verse.[2] This, apparently, is the natural and standard use of the verse that bespeaks God's promise to protect Israel.

Moreover, Eleazar's prayer (3 Macc 6:2–15) initially appears generic—recalling many prayers of the Second Temple period. Like these prayers, it relies on Scripture, incorporates biblical precedents, and conveys a specific request. Nevertheless, the citing of the "I did not despise them" verse here is not standard and formulaic: rather it is deliberate and uniquely suited to this prayer. In fact, the entire prayer deviates from the mold: it faithfully mirrors the plot line of 3 Maccabees and, at the same time, articulates the unique views of the book's author. This paper is devoted to analyzing the various aspects of Eleazar's prayer.

Structure

Eleazar's prayer encompasses fourteen verses. As with Simon's prayer in chapter 2 (2–20), it contains an introduction and two main sections. Verses 2–3 introduce the prayer; they address God with a variety of epithets illustrating his power (2) and beseech God to look upon his nation who is in distress (3). Verses 4–8 contain a list of historical

---

[1] Esth. Rab. 8.7; Esth. Rab. Petihta 4; cf. b. Meg. 11a.
[2] Add Esth C7. The verb ὑπεροράω used here appears also in Lev 26:44.

precedents that is bookended by the vocative πάτερ (end of vv. 3 and 8).
Except for the final verse, the list has a uniform structure. Each example
(vv. 4–7) begins with the word σύ (you), and the accusative, the key
character in the precedent, appears immediately afterwards. The topic of
verses 9–15 is the current threat and they present the request for God to
manifest himself and deliver his people.[3]

Historical Precedents

Unlike Simon's prayer, that enumerates precedents of Divine intervention
solely in cases of arrogance and sin (3 Macc 2:4–8), the historical precedents in Eleazar's prayer are not exclusively of this type. While Pharaoh
and Sennacherib (4–5) do belong to this category, the three other biblical
events mentioned in the prayer—the deliverance of the three companions,
Hananiah, Mishael and Azariah, from the fires of the furnace (6); the
deliverance of Daniel from the lion's den (7); and Jonah's return home
(8)—diverge from this mold.[4] The common denominator that links these
three events is the deliverance of people dwelling or existing outside of
the land of Israel, yet the first two precedents are not included under this
heading.[5] If we hypothesize that the focus of this list is Israel's rescue
from heathen gentiles who plot to annihilate them,[6] then Jonah's inclusion is unclear.[7] Moreover, it is unclear why the example of Jonah

---

[3] For a similar view on the structure of the prayer see Micháļīs Z. Kopidákīs, *To III Makkabaion kai o Aischulos: Aischuleies mnemes sto lektiko kai ste thematografia III Makkabaion* (Herakleion Kretes: Bikelaia Bibliotheke, 1987), 53; Anna Passoni Dell'Acqua, "Le
preghiere del III libro dei Maccabei: genere letterario e tematica," *RivB* 43 (1995): 157;
Thomas Knöppler, *3. Makkabäerbuch*, JSHRZ 1,9 (Gütersloh: Mohn, 2017), 914–6.

[4] Therefore, the subject of this list cannot be the punishment of the arrogant. This seems to
be the view of Judith Newman, "God Condemns the Arrogance of Power: The Prayer in
3 Maccabees 6:2–15," in *Prayer from Alexander to Constantine: A Critical Anthology*, ed.
Mark Kiley et al. (London: Routledge, 1997), 48–52, based on the title of her article.

[5] Cf. Barbara Schmitz, "Pharao und Philopator: Exodusrezeption im Dritten Makkabäerbuch als Deutung des Lebens in der Diaspora," in *Exodus. Interpretation durch Rezeption*, ed. Matthias Ederer and Barbara Schmitz, SBB 74 (Stuttgart: Katholisches Bibelwerk, 2017), 171.

[6] See N. Clayton Croy, *3 Maccabees*, Septuagint Commentary Series (Leiden: Brill,
2006), 99, who defines the list as "prominent events in Israel's salvation history" (see
also André Paul, "Le Troisème livre des Macchabées," *ANRW* 20.1: 298-336). This still
does not explain why the first two precedents focus on the punishment of the evil nor
why these specific events were chosen.

[7] Newman, "God Condemns the Arrogance of Power," 49, suggests that Daniel and the
companions appear in the list in order to point out various instances of Jews delivered
from heathen nations, yet she does not explain or even mention the case of Jonah.

appears last and not in its chronological place ahead of Sennacherib. In short: What is the unifying principle of this list?

Ostensibly, the list is an outline of the entire plot of 3 Maccabees.[8] Verse 4 relates the historical precedent of the arrogant Pharaoh who was drowned with his chariots and army in the sea. The portrayal of Pharaoh as the ancient ruler of "this" Egypt (τὸν πρὶν Αἰγύπτου ταύτης δυνά-στην) connects the biblical Pharaoh with present-day Egypt. In doing so, the author establishes the relevance between the drowning of Pharaoh and his time. This relevance is expressed primarily by the fact that, like his predecessor, the present ruler of Egypt also deserves to be punished. Moreover, the Ptolemies identified themselves as Pharaohs, were also called Pharaoh,[9] and the author clearly alludes to this identification. These, however, are not the only links between Pharaoh and the author's days. Several expressions that describe Pharaoh in this verse also appear

---

[8] Passoni Dell'Acqua, "Le preghiere," 159–64, identified the close connection between the historical precedents in this prayer and the tribulations of the Egyptian Jews. Still her proposal in general, as well as its particulars, differs from ours. In general, our explanation maintains that the list of examples provides a synopsis of the entire book, while Passoni Dell'Acqua believes the list of examples relates only to the events in Egypt and corresponds to the predicament of the Jews in the hippodrome. Furthermore, she does not touch upon most of the lexical affinities. She claims (161) that the precedent of the Exodus and the splitting of the Red Sea corresponds to the prayer of the Jews imprisoned in the Hippodrome by the Ptolemaic/Egyptian king and their plea to be rescued from the king who wishes to kill them. I believe this precedent does indeed correspond to a conflict between Jews and an Egyptian king who wishes to kill them. Yet, according to my proposal, this precedent does not refer to the dilemma of the Jews in Egypt but rather, primarily to the first part of the story of 3 Maccabees, to the narrative of Philopator in Jerusalem. Indeed, Passoni Dell'Acqua herself notes (173–5, and nn. 97, 100) the incompatibility of the prayer's reference to Pharaoh and Sennacherib with her interpretation: Sennacherib's siege of Jerusalem is mentioned in Eleazar's prayer, although the Egyptian Jews are endangered and not the Jerusalemite Temple. The absence of any mention of the Israelites' Egyptian bondage in Eleazar's prayer is also problematic, since the Jews in the hippodrome were oppressed and tortured, recalling their forefathers' enslavement to Pharaoh in Egypt. Due to these difficulties, Passoni Dell'Acqua concludes that Pharaoh and Sennacherib are mentioned as examples of arrogant people who rely upon their might and deny God's power, a kind of *theomachos*, and she further explains the author's choice of these precedents (n. 97). According to our proposal, no difficulty exists. The Egyptian bondage is not mentioned in the precedent of Pharaoh since this precedent alludes to Philopator's attempt to enter the Holy of Holies in Jerusalem and not to any oppression of the Egyptian Jews. Sennacherib's siege of Jerusalem is mentioned since it parallels Philopator's attempt to damage the sanctity of the Temple in Jerusalem.

[9] See e.g. Günther Hölbl, *A History of the Ptolemaic Empire*, trans. T. Saavedra (London: Routledge, 2001), 77–90; Joseph Gilbert Manning, *The Last Pharaohs: Egypt under the Ptolemies, 305–30 BC* (Princeton: Princeton University Press, 2010), 81–82. Note that the meaning of the Demotic word pr-aA (Pharaoh) is king; see e.g. *CPJ* 597c (P.Berl. Dem. II, 3096), l. 1.

at the beginning of the book in the description of Philopator's deeds in Jerusalem. Pharaoh is described as "lifted high with his ... insolence" (ἐπαρθέντα ... θράσει)—the same words that are used to describe Philopator's visit to Jerusalem in 2:21 (θράσει ... ἐπηρμένον).[10] Philopator's insolence is described again in 1:26, and the verb θρασύνω is used there. Philopator's deed is termed "lawless and arrogant" (1:27, τὴν ἄνομον καὶ ὑπερήφανον πρᾶξιν). Pharaoh's insolence is also called lawless (ἄνομος) and his army is also called ὑπερήφανος (6:4). By creating linguistic resonance between the Jerusalem narrative and Eleazar's prayer the author evidently intended to portray Philopator like Pharaoh— a resemblance that carries through to their actions and behavior. Eleazar's prayer depicts Pharaoh's arrogance as inspired by his great army. Such a description suits Philopator's behavior too, when he arrives in Jerusalem following his army's victory at the battle of Raphia. Eleazar's prayer states that Pharaoh was "conceited in his lawless impudence and boasting tongue" (6:4). Philopator also spoke insolently by demanding to enter the Temple (1:12). Thus, the reference to Pharaoh in Eleazar's prayer can be interpreted as an allusion to the story at the beginning of 3 Maccabees concerning Philopator's attempt to forcibly enter into the Temple.

Verse 5 invokes the precedent of Sennacherib who arrived with his mighty army, threatened the holy city, and was smitten by God. It seems inappropriate to cite an attempt against Jerusalem when the relevant danger looms over the Egyptian Jews and not the Temple. What is the connection between Sennacherib's siege of Jerusalem and elephants trampling the Jews in Egypt? There is no need to seek an indirect and artificial link between the two events: Sennacherib's siege appears because it recalls Philopator's similar attempt to damage the sanctity of the Temple in Jerusalem—the first clash between Philopator and the Jews that 3 Maccabees relates. Besides the essential content-related parallel,[11] there are apparent linguistic and thematic parallels between this precedent and the story in 3 Maccabees. The word "spear" (δόρυ) mentioned here in the depiction of Sennacherib's deeds occurs twice beforehand—when describing Philopator's fair attitude towards the peoples of Coele-Syria and Phoenicia whom he conquered without resorting to the power of the spear (3:15, μὴ βίᾳ δόρατος) and in his threat to campaign against

---

[10] This idiomatic phrase is not uncommon. See for example Add Esth B2; Thucydides, *History*, I.120.4; Philo, *Virt.* 2.

[11] Note that this verse is the only occurrence in the second part of the book of a place being described as "holy" (ἅγιος: τὴν ἁγίαν σου πόλιν: "your holy city"), and it parallels several indications of the holiness of place and the Temple in the first part of the book (3 Macc 2:9, 14, 16, 18).

Judaea with "fire and sword" (4:43, πυρὶ καὶ δόρατι). Both times this word relates to Philopator's attitude towards the land of Israel and the neighboring regions, in similarity with its function in Eleazar's prayer. As in the previous verse, the dative form of the word θράσος recurs, this time describing Sennacherib's words. As just stated, the same word is used above in 1:26 (a verb in the *participium*), and in 2:21 (in the dative form), to describe Philopator's insolence.[12] As in the previous precedent concerning Pharaoh, here too we are told that Sennacherib's words express his insolence. Sennacherib, according to verse 5, "was speaking fiercely with boasting and insolence," and similarly, Philopator expressed his desire to enter the Sanctuary in an insolent manner (1:12). Probably, the insolent words attributed to Pharaoh and Sennacherib may also allude to Philopator's invectives against God and his praise of idols (4:16). The two verses share some of the same vocabulary. The verb λάλω occurs there (4:16) twice and here it describes Sennacherib's deeds. One can detect additional identical terminology that is used for both Sennacherib and Philopator. 6:5 states that Sennacherib was "puffed up" (γαυρωθέ-ντα) by his immeasurable army, and before his first letter, Philopator is described (3:11) as elated (γεγαυρωμένος) by his success. This verb occurs only twice more in the Septuagint, thus its use in 3 Maccabees in these two incidents is significant.

It seems therefore that the two negative personages mentioned in Eleazar's prayer allude to Philopator and his deeds, particularly those transpiring in Jerusalem.

Persons threatened with various dangers who are subsequently saved represent the theme of the other three examples. The first example (3 Macc 6:6) mentions the three companions in Babylon, Hannaniah, Mishael, and Azariah, who refused to worship idols on pain of death by fire. However, they were delivered from this peril unscathed, and the strong soldiers who threw them into the fiery furnace were burnt alive instead. This story is quite similar to the persecution of the Egyptian Jews described in 3 Maccabees. The decree to worship Dionysus (3 Macc 2:28–30) and the refusal on the part of most Jews to obey this decree (2:32) marked the beginning of the persecution.[13] As a result of this refusal, the king finally ordered that the Jews were to be killed in the hippodrome in Alexandria by drunken elephants (3:25; 4:14; 5:2). Like

---

[12] The word appears several more times in Simon's prayer (2:2, 4, 6, 14); perhaps this also underlines the connection between Pharaoh and Sennacherib in Eleazar's prayer and the events in Jerusalem.

[13] Passoni Dell'Acqua, "Le preghiere," 162, notes this parallel.

king Nebuchadnezzar who spoke arrogantly and disrespectfully against the god of the three companions (Dan 3:15), Philopator also "with a mind led far astray from the truth and a vile mouth... praised that which is deaf and unable to speak or to assist itself, while uttering improprieties to the supreme God" (3 Macc 4:16). The three companions were thrown into the fire, and the Egyptian Jews were threatened with fire (3 Macc 2:29; 5:43).[14] Like the three companions, the Egyptian Jews were also rescued and not injured. The elephants turned around and trampled the soldiers marching behind them (3 Macc 6:21), just as the soldiers who threw the three companions into the fire were killed by the very same fire (Dan 3:22). The motif of being chained is presumably also common to both stories. The three companions were thrown to the furnace in chains (Dan 3:20); in 3 Maccabees the Jews in the hippodrome were bound (5:5; 6:27), and the angels bound the enemies of the Jews with shackles (6:19). In both stories some other figures were involved in the rescue: angels in 3 Maccabees (6:18–20) and someone "looks like a divine being" (Dan 3:25, בר אלהין) or "a divine angel" (Dan 3:49 LXX, ἀγγέλου θεοῦ) in the story of the companions. In both cases non-Jewish people beheld the divine figure(s) (Dan 3:25; 3 Macc 6:18), and in both "Hades" (ᾅδης) is mentioned as the place where the victims were supposed to be if the king had fulfilled his plot (3 Macc 5:51; Dan 3:88 LXX).

There is also a certain linguistic similarity between this verse and the account of the deliverance of the Egyptian Jews. The verb ῥύομαι ("to deliver") that is employed to describe the deliverance of the three companions also appears in the account of the deliverance of the Egyptian Jews (6:39).[15] The word ὑπεναντίοι ("the adversaries") in the description of the punishment of the enemies of the three companions (6:6) appears again in 6:19, which relates how the enemies of the Jews were filled with terror due to the revelation of the angels. This word does not appear again in 3 Maccabees.

The second example tells of Daniel's deliverance from the lion's den. Here as well, the protagonist is saved and escapes unscathed by the wild animal to whom he was fed. Several similarities are discernible between this description and the situation of the Jews in 3 Maccabees. Daniel, like

---

[14] In 5:43 it was a threat to seek revenge against the Egyptian Jews by burning Judaea and the Temple to the ground.

[15] However, this verb appears twice more in Eleazar's prayer (10, 11) and hence the importance of this linguistic affinity should not be overstated.

the Jews in 3 Maccabees, was to be executed by animals for being faithful to his religion, but was delivered unharmed. Daniel was the victim of envious slander (Dan 6:12–4), and the Jews were also victims of slander and defamation.[16] An angel was reportedly involved in Daniel's deliverance (Dan 6:23) and two were involved in the case of the Jews in the Hippodrome (3 Macc 6:18). Daniel's enemies were tossed into the lion's den and devoured in his stead (Dan 6:25); in 3 Maccabees, the king's soldiers were trampled by the elephants. Finally, just as Daniel was innocent of harming the king (Dan 6:23), so the Jews in Egypt were utterly loyal to the king (6:25–26; 7:7). There is also a linguistic affinity between Daniel and the Jews' salvation from the elephants. The word ἀσινής ("unhurt") is used to describe both Daniel and the Jews who returned home (7:20). This word does not appear elsewhere in the Septuagint. Furthermore, although Daniel was to be fed to lions while the Egyptian Jews were to be trampled by elephants, the lions here are also termed θήρ ("beast"), which brings to mind the similar designation θηρίον ("beast"; also "elephant") that relates several times to the elephants in 3 Maccabees (5:23, 29, 42, 45, 47; 6:16, 19).[17] The precedent of Daniel thus affords new allusions to the story of 3 Maccabees and again emphasizes the Jews' anticipated deliverance unharmed.

The deliverance of Jonah is the last precedent mentioned in Eleazar's prayer (6:8). This precedent also alludes to the persecution of the Jews. However, it does not refer to the threat that loomed over them but to the story's outcome.[18] Jonah returned home safe and sound[19] and the Egyptian Jews' safe return home is emphasized several times in the course of the story. In 6:27 the king decrees that the Jews are to be sent back to their homes in peace. Following a seven-day celebration, the Jews ask the king for permission to return home (6:37). The king does indeed write a decree (7:8) and the Jews return home under the king's protection (7:18, 19, 20). The Jews' safe return home is therefore an important clue

---

[16] See 3 Macc 2:26, 27; 3:2, 7, 22; 6:25–26; 7:3–4. Passoni Dell'Acqua, "Le preghiere," 163, comments on this affinity.

[17] Perhaps noting that Daniel was "below the earth" (κατὰ γῆς) and was brought up "to light" (εἰς φῶς) hints at the shipping of Jews "with solid planking fixed above, they were in total darkness" (4:10).

[18] Perhaps just as a dangerous animal threatened Jonah, dangerous animals were also the means employed to threaten the Egyptian Jews in 3 Maccabees.

[19] The narrator does not refer to the circumstances that precipitated Jonah's sojourn in the belly of the monster but rather to the detail—unmentioned in the Bible—that he returned home safe and sound. This demonstrates the author's main interest in this biblical figure.

in the story's conclusion and it seems that Jonah's safe return home alludes to the happy ending of 3 Maccabees. Although the account of the Jews' return home and the precedent of Jonah in Eleazar's prayer do not contain any common terminology, the thematic connection is quite strong. This is the only reasonable explanation for incorporating the precedent of Jonah in Eleazar's prayer, and placing it at the end of the list.[20]

In light of this analysis, the unifying principle of the list of examples in Eleazar's prayer is evidently not a particular theological idea of the destruction of arrogant people or the deliverance of those who suffer, but rather a specific story—the story of 3 Maccabees. The list's structure parallels the account of the clashes between the king and the Jews in 3 Maccabees. It alludes to the entire story from the initial stages of the conflict in Jerusalem until its happy resolution with the safe return of the Jews to their homes throughout Egypt. This prayer is consequently neither an unplanned random prayer nor a citation from another place; rather it is planned and tailored to fit the story of 3 Maccabees. Clearly, it is a product of an author who utilizes the medium of prayer in a meticulous and sophisticated manner in order to express his ideas. A prayer that anticipates the upcoming deliverance endeavors to underscore the religious importance of prayer, particularly one formulated to reflect the unique circumstances of the predicament at hand. The reader of the story is expected to understand that because Eleazar the priest addressed God in an appropriate way—through prayer—and uttered the correct words, the entire prayer was accepted.

[20] Passoni Dell'Acqua, "Le preghiere," 163, suggests that Jonah is cited as an example of Divine deliverance in the exilic period. However, Diaspora is not mentioned at all in the Jonah precedent and it is implausible that the main affinity between Jonah and 3 Maccabees would be absent. Moreover, Jonah is an improbable paradigm of deliverance in the exilic period, since the mortal danger threatening Jonah did not derive from an exilic situation or foreign rulers but rather from other factors. Philip S. Alexander, "3 Maccabees, Hanukkah and Purim," in *Biblical Hebrews, Biblical Texts: Essays in Memory of Michael P. Weitzman*, ed. Ada Rapoport-Albert and Gillian Greenberg, JSOTSup 333 (Sheffield: Sheffield Academic Press, 2001), 335, views Jonah as a symbol of the Jewish people; in the same way that Jonah could not escape the Divine presence and his prayer was heard by God even from deep within the whale, so the Jewish people, while in the land of their enemies, are not abandoned by God. However, although 3 Maccabees certainly asserts God's presence amongst His people in exile, the precedent of Jonah does not serve this end, since this topic is not even alluded to in this verse.

Theology and Ideology

The centrality of Eleazar's prayer in 3 Maccabees derives not only from its position as the turning point of the plot after which the Jews are rescued from annihilation, nor from the fact that it is a miniaturized reproduction of the entire plot. Rather, the prayer clearly and succinctly expresses the author's diasporan theological views that are also evinced elsewhere in the book. In the following section, I will examine the various principles expressed in the prayer by analyzing its constituent parts.

Divine Epithets

Eleazar's prayer opens, as one would expect from a prayer, with an appeal to God that includes a list of Divine epithets: "O king, dread sovereign, most high, almighty God, who govern all creation with compassion" (3 Macc 6:2, Βασιλεῦ μεγαλοκράτωρ ὕψιστε παντοκράτωρ θεὲ τὴν πᾶσαν διακυβερνῶν ἐν οἰκτιρμοῖς κτίσιν). It also contains some additional epithets incorporated in the prayer itself: "father" (vv. 3 and 8, πατήρ); "hater of insolence, all-merciful, protector of all" (9: μίσυβρις, πολυέλεος, ὁ ὅλων σκεπαστής); "Master" (vv. 5 and 10, δεσπότης); "eternal" (v. 12, αἰώνιος); "honored one" (v. 13, ἔντι-μος).[21] These are standard and conventional appellations, which emphasize God's power and rule. For example, "Almighty God" (6:2) expresses the vastness of God's rule and sovereignty over all, and "hater of insolence" (6:9), demonstrates that there is no place before God's for arrogance or insolence. These themes also appear in Simon's prayer (3 Macc 2:2–20) and these, in fact, are the appropriate emphases suitable to a situation in which an arrogant king insolently attempts to profane the Temple in Jerusalem. However, in contrast to the Divine epithets and attributes mentioned in the narrative of events in Jerusalem (3 Macc 1–2:24), the account of events in Egypt incorporates a different variety of epithets. The term "father" (πατήρ) does not appear in the Jerusalem narrative but does occur twice in Eleazar's prayer (3, 8). This kind of relationship, which appears several times in the story of the persecution of the Egyptian Jews (5:7; 6:28; 7:6), signifies the closeness of the supplicant and his community to God, and expresses the obligation and intimacy involved in the father-son-like relationship between God and his

---

[21] One may add the descriptions "possess all might and all sovereignty" (v. 12, ὁ πᾶσαν ἀλκὴν καὶ δυναστείαν ἔχων ἅπασαν) and "have power to save the nation of Jacob" (v. 13, δύναμιν ἔχων ἐπὶ σωτηρίᾳ Ιακωβ γένους).

people.[22] Moreover, God's attributes of mercy and lovingkindness are characterized in several different ways in the description of the events in Egypt. God is described as "merciful" (5:7, ἐλεήμων), "readily appeased" (5:13, εὐκατάλλακτος), "rich in mercy" (6:9, πολυέλεος), one who "governs all creation with compassion" (6:2, ἐν οἰκτιρμοῖς) and the "Protector of all" (6:9, ὁ ὅλων σκεπαστής). In the first two cases, the epithets focus upon God's relationship with the people of Israel and thereby augment the story's emphasis on the special relationship between God and his people. The other attributes mentioned do not actually involve the people of Israel. However, since Eleazar depicts the heathens as arrogant and worthy of hatred (9), God's mercy and protection clearly refer to those who are not arrogant, namely the people of Israel. Such Divine epithets are absent from the Jerusalem narrative.[23] Consequently, in contrast to the Jerusalem narrative, the epithets used to describe God in Eleazar's prayer and in the second part of 3 Maccabees create the impression that God's mercy and closeness to those who call upon him are more potent and manifest in Egypt than in Jerusalem. This conclusion is consistent with and supports my thesis presented elsewhere, regarding 3 Maccabees author's view about the superiority of Egyptian Jewry over the Jerusalemites.[24]

The Main Request

1. Gentiles

The prayer's second section (6:9–15) sets aside the historical precedents and focuses on the actual problem now confronting the Jews: their deliverance from death. Indeed, Eleazar pleads "rescue us" (v. 10, ῥυσάμενος ἡμᾶς) and "show mercy on us" (v. 12, ἐλέησον ἡμᾶς). However, the formulation of the plea and its reasoning appear in these seven verses in

[22] For a detailed discussion (and also for the meaning of the epithet πρόπατωρ in 3 Macc 2:21) see Noah Hacham, "Sanctity and the Attitude towards the Temple in Hellenistic Judaism," in *Was 70 C.E. a Watershed in Jewish History? On Jews and Judaism before and after the Destruction of the Second Temple*, ed. Daniel R. Schwartz and Zeev Weiss, AJEC 78 (Leiden: Brill, 2012), 162–3.

[23] The words "mercy" (ἔλεος) and "compassion" (οἰκτιρμοί) do appear in Simon's prayer (2:19, 20) not as descriptions of God but as a request for the manifestation of these Divine traits. Namely, what Eleazar perceives as factual in Egypt, is perceived by Simon, praying in Jerusalem, as a wish and a supplication.

[24] Hacham, "Sanctity and the Attitude towards the Temple in Hellenistic Judaism," 155–79; for a comparison between the two prayers see idem, 165–71.

a way that focuses on the gentiles, arrayed against the people of Israel and God's honor.

The gentiles are mentioned in this section in almost every verse. The word ἔθνη ("nations") appears three times (9, 13, 15); twice the gentiles are called "enemies" (vv. 10 and 15, ἐχθροί); and they are designated "vain-minded" (v. 11, ματαιόφρονες), "detestable" (v. 9, ἐβδελυγμένοι) and lawless (vv. 9 and 12, ἄνομοι). The gentiles are arrogant and boastful (vv. 9, 12), they humiliate the beloved of God and if their plot to annihilate Israel is successful, God's name will be mocked as the gentiles defy him (v. 11). Therefore, even if Israel is deserving of death, Eleazar pleas for their salvation from the gentiles and asks that God punish them himself (v. 10). For the gentiles to recognize that God did not turn away from his people, He must reveal himself (v. 15) and demonstrate his strength before the gentiles (v. 13). This would also vindicate the Jews and establish that they are not traitors, as the gentiles had thought to treat them (v. 12).

As we have seen, Eleazar's prayer is not a generic work but rather a unique creation of the author of 3 Maccabees, intended specifically for this book. Utterly unrelated to the historicity of the book's attestations of persecution against the Jews, Eleazar's prayer is clearly what would have been appropriate for such a prayer to contain under such circumstances, rather than an exact quote of any actual prayer. Thucydides famously stated that the speeches he includes in his *History* are not the exact words that each speaker actually said, but rather "what was called for in each situation" (History 1.22.1) or what the historian believed should have been said. This statement is relevant not only to ancient historiography but also to prayers in Jewish compositions. 3 Maccabees' prayers should be similarly regarded, as should those that appear in many other ancient Jewish literary and historical works.[25]

Eleazar's prayer thus expresses the diasporan views of the diasporan author of 3 Maccabees. The supplicant's words establish the gentiles as Israel's adversaries: they are loathsome, arrogant and lawless and the dwelling place of the supplicant and his people is termed "the land of their enemies." The king is also included among these "enemies" and evil people, since Pharaoh, "the former ruler of this Egypt" (v. 4)—like the "gentiles" (ἔθνοι) in verse 9—is described as "lawless" (v. 4), and he is the king of "the land of their enemies" (v. 15). In stark contrast to

[25] See: Iehoshua Gutman, "The Historical Value of Hashmonain 3," *Eshkolot* 3:53 [Hebrew]; Paul, "Le Troisème livre des Macchabées," 308.

the Letter of Aristeas—a contemporaneous Jewish work from the same locale, that depicts harmony between the Jews and the Ptolemaic king and the gentiles—Eleazar's prayer evokes an opposite picture. Other Jewish diasporan works that depict Jewish-gentile crises and a persecution of Jews portray it as an unfortunate accident, misunderstanding or exception to the rule and, at the same time, describe the gentiles' regard and positive feelings towards the Jews.[26] The fact that Eleazar's prayer includes a request that the gentiles fear God's might, reveals that gentile goodwill towards the Jews was unfamiliar to the author. Thus, according to Eleazar's prayer, the gentiles are hostile to the Jews and to their God and the two populations are disconnected and separated from each other.

This conclusion is the result of an independent analysis of the intensely negative attitude towards the gentiles manifest in the second part of Eleazar's prayer. Elsewhere I discussed the Jewish-gentile relationship in 3 Maccabees as a whole and reached a similar conclusion.[27] When an experiment conducted along two independent routes achieves consistent results, the veracity of the conclusion is corroborated. Apparently then, despite the common conception of the Jews' beneficent situation in Ptolemaic era Egypt, there were certain times, places and circumstances that caused the Jewish-gentile relationship to suffer, even in the Ptolemaic state.[28]

2. *Apoikia, Strange Land, the Enemies' Land*

The supplicant defines his location at three different occasions in the prayer. The negative characteristics provide a framework for the prayer: at the outset, Eleazar determines that the people of Israel are "strangers in a strange land" (6:3, ἐν ξένῃ γῇ ξένον) and he concludes the prayer

---

[26] For 2 Maccabees as such a composition see e.g. Daniel R. Schwartz, *The Second Book of Maccabees*, CEJL (Berlin: de Gruyter, 2008), 48–50; for general discussion see Sara R. Johnson, *Historical Fictions and Hellenistic Jewish Identity: Third Maccabees in Its Cultural Context*, HCS 43 (Berkeley: University of California Press, 2004), 151–69.

[27] Noah Hacham, "Hidden and Public Transcript: Jews and Non-Jews in 3 Maccabees," in *Israel in Egypt: The Land of Egypt as Concept and Reality for Jews in Antiquity and the Early Medieval Period*, ed. Alison Salvesen et al. (Leiden: Brill, 2020), 178-95.

[28] On the general situation of the Jews under the Ptolemaic regime see e.g. Joseph Mélèze-Modrzejewski, *The Jews of Egypt: From Rameses II to Emperor Hadrian*, trans. Robert Corman (Philadelphia: Jewish Publication Society, 1995), 45–157. He defines the period as "the Zenith" (45) and is decisive about "the generally sunny and peaceful atmosphere of the period" (157). He is aware, however, of the "wellspring of pagan antisemitism" that began to emerge at this period (135–57).

with the promise, cited from Leviticus (26:44), that God will not despise his people when they will be in "the land of their enemies" (ἐν τῇ γῇ τῶν ἐχθρῶν αὐτῶν). It is clear then, that he does not feel at home in Egypt.

However, in the middle of the prayer Eleazar describes the situation of the people as "apoikia" (v. 10, ἀποικία). This term means "settlement far from home" and its use in the Septuagint to translate golah (גולה) negates the pejorative aspects of golah.[29] The presence in Egypt is thus portrayed not as a punishment but rather as a migration and a colony— parallel to Greek colonization throughout the world—and neither foreign- ness nor enmity is implied. What then is the nature of the place inhabited by the supplicant according to this prayer?

It could be presumed that the author made perfunctory use of the term apoikia: he plucked the frozen term from the Septuagint, without regard for its inherent positive significance. However, there is, arguably, a dif- ferent explanation to this apparent contradiction. Possibly, the author harbors both sentiments simultaneously. On the one hand, as a diasporan Jew, he finds it difficult to view his situation as a punishment and dis- tancing from God. On the other hand, the reality with which he contends demonstrates that this Jewish "colony" (apoikia) is situated in a foreign, enemy land. He aspires to feel at home, to be part of the local social fabric: to belong, despite the surrounding dangers. Thus, the phenome- non of the Egyptian Diaspora is at once a "colony" but yet foreign and in "an enemy land". Indeed, one of the greatest outrages felt by the sup- plicant is that his coreligionists are treated as "traitors" (v. 12, ἐπίβου- λος), while it is clear to him—as the king himself will later unequivo- cally determine (6:25–26; 7:7)—that there are none more faithful to the kingdom than his own people. The supplicant's loyalty to his locale— Ptolemaic Egypt—expresses his deep belonging to his dwelling place, even if it does not respond in kind.[30]

---

[29] See e.g. Joseph Mélèze-Modrzejewski, "How to be a Jew in Hellenistic Egypt?" in Diasporas in Antiquity, ed. Shaye J. D. Cohen and Ernest S. Frerichs, BJS 288 (Atlanta: Scholars Press, 1993), 67–70; Isaiah M. Gafni, Land Center and Diaspora: Jewish Constructions in Late Antiquity, JSPSup 21 (Sheffield; Sheffield Academic Press, 1997), 28–9; see further: Noah Hacham, "Between mĕšûbâ and môšābâ: On the Status of Diaspora Jews in the Period of Redemption According to the Septuagint and Hel- lenistic Judaism," in XIV Congress of the IOSCS, Helsinki, 2010, ed. Melvin K.H. Peters, SCS 59 (Atlanta: Society of Biblical Literature, 2013), 127–42.

[30] As in the preceding discussion on the gentiles, here too, through analyzing other sec- tions of 3 Maccabees I reached a similar conclusion; see: Noah Hacham, "Is Judaism the εὐσέβεια of Alexandria? 3 Maccabees 2:31a Revisited," CP 109 (2014): 72–9.

3. Epiphany

The manifestation of God in order to deliver his people is a central request in Eleazar's prayer. It reappears in several different expressions in the prayer. Its appearance frames the second section of the prayer—the supplication. In the first verse of this section, Eleazar beseeches God to "swiftly manifest yourself" (6:9, τὸ τάχος ἐπιφάνηθι), and the last verse contains the supplication "let it be shown to all nations that you are with us" (6:15, δειχθήτω πᾶσιν ἔθνεσιν ὅτι μεθ' ἡμῶν εἶ).

Divine epiphany and the promulgation of God's might also appear in the list of precedents. In the deliverance of Israel from Pharaoh at the Red Sea God "manifested the light of your mercy on the race of Israel" (6:4, φέγγος ἐπιφάνας ἐλέους Ισραελ γένει). And while Sennacherib besieged Jerusalem God broke him "showing your might to many nations" (6:5, δεικνὺς ἔθνεσιν πολλοῖς τὸ σὸν κράτος). It is clear that by mentioning these epiphanies Eleazar asks that God similarly reveal himself in the current circumstances. Note that an epiphany was requested not only by Eleazar but also twice by the Jews in their spontaneous prayers in the hippodrome (5:8, 51). Eleazar's prayer and the supplications of the Jews that God reveal himself at the hippodrome in Egypt attest that the author assumes no impediment to Divine epiphany outside of the Temple of Jerusalem and even outside of the Land of Israel. The purpose of the epiphany is the determining factor: for deliverance of the people, and public confirmation that God has not forsaken his people, God reveals himself anywhere.

Comparing Eleazar's and Simon's prayers reveals that God's manifestation is much less central in Simon's prayer.[31] Viewed through the prism of the prayers' epiphany motif—as through the prism of their Divine epithets—it becomes clear that Egyptian Jewry enjoys precedence over the Jerusalem Temple. It also demonstrates that Divine epiphany—which ostensibly should be vigorously and unequivocally solicited on behalf of God's abode, namely the Jerusalem Temple—is actually pursued in these ways on behalf of the persecuted people in the Alexandrian hippodrome. Although he is in the Diaspora, the author of 3 Maccabees is assured of his closeness to God and the protection of Divine Providence that exceeds the closeness to God and the protection of Divine Providence enjoyed by

---

[31] In Simon's prayer, God glorified his place with a manifestation (2:9, ἐπιφάνεια) and Simon asks God to manifest (ἐπίφανον) his mercy (ἔλεος) (v. 19). In contrast to Eleazar's prayer, there is no explicit request for the heathen nations to acknowledge God's power and might, or for God to reveal himself.

his brethren in the Land of Israel and by the Temple in Jerusalem. The final salvation occurred in the hippodrome in Egypt, not in the Temple in Jerusalem.

Conclusion

Returning to the concluding verse of the prayer with which I began this paper, Eleazar requests: "Let it be shown to all nations that you are with us, Lord, and that you have not turned your face away from us, but as you said, 'Not even when they were in the land of their enemies did I despise them;' thus make it so, O Lord." The supplicant's material request also includes a plea to God to fulfill the continuation of the verse from Leviticus (26:44), "I did not despise them...so as to destroy them," which is a request regarding the exact situation of the Jews. At the same time, the verse also expresses the theological tenets of 3 Maccabees discussed above: even in the Diaspora God does not forsake his people but rather acts on their behalf; moreover, he even manifests on their behalf outside of his abode, although—or maybe because—the place where his people reside is the land of their enemies.

Eleazar's prayer thus transpires as a judicious, meticulously plotted work that encapsulates the worldview of its author, and which conveys a miniaturized version of 3 Maccabees' story of the Jews' salvations. Rather than a solitary case, this prayer is generally instructive of the nature of Second Temple Jewish literature's prayers, which should be viewed as historical and theological documents that merit close inspection to elicit their encoded secrets.

Bibliography

Alexander, Philip S. "3 Maccabees, Hanukkah and Purim." Pages 321–340 in *Biblical Hebrews, Biblical Texts: Essays in Memory of Michael P. Weitzman.* Edited by Ada Rapoport-Albert and Gillian Greenberg. JSOTSup 333. Sheffield: Sheffield Academic Press, 2001.

Croy, N. Clayton. *3 Maccabees.* Septuagint Commentary Series. Leiden: Brill, 2006.

Gafni, Isaiah. M. *Land Center and Diaspora: Jewish Constructions in Late Antiquity.* JSPSup 21. Sheffield: Sheffield Academic Press, 1997.

Gutman, Iehoshua. "The Historical Value of Hashmonain 3." *Eshkolot* 3 (1959): 49-62 [Hebrew].

Hacham, Noah. "Sanctity and the Attitude towards the Temple in Hellenistic Judaism." Pages 155–181 in *Was 70 C.E. a Watershed in Jewish History? On Jews and Judaism before and after the Destruction of the Second*

Temple. Edited by Daniel R. Schwartz and Zeev Weiss. AJEC 78. Leiden: Brill, 2012.

Hacham, Noah. "Between *měšûbâ* and *môšābâ*: On the Status of Diaspora Jews in the Period of Redemption According to the Septuagint and Hellenistic Judaism." Pages 127–42 in *XIV Congress of the IOSCS, Helsinki, 2010*. Edited by Melvin K.H. Peters. SCS 59. Atlanta: Society of Biblical Literature, 2013.

Hacham, Noah. "Is Judaism the εὐσέβεια of Alexandria? 3 Maccabees 2:31a Revisited." *CP* 109 (2014): 72–9.

Hacham, Noah. "Hidden and Public Transcript: Jews and Non-Jews in 3 Maccabees." Pages 178-195 in *Israel in Egypt: The Land of Egypt as Concept and Reality for Jews in Antiquity and the Early Medieval Period*. Edited by Alison Salvesen, Sarah Pearce, and Miriam Frenkel with the assistance of Daniel J. Crowther. Leiden: Brill, 2020.

Hölbl, Günther. *A History of the Ptolemaic Empire*. Translated by T. Saavedra. London: Routledge, 2001.

Johnson, Sara R. *Historical Fictions and Hellenistic Jewish Identity: Third Maccabees in Its Cultural Context*. HCS 43. Berkeley: University of California Press, 2004.

Knöppler, Thomas. *3. Makkabäerbuch*. JSHRZ 1,9. Gütersloh: Mohn, 2017.

Kopidákīs, Michálīs Z. *To III Makkabaion kai o Aischulos: Aischuleies mnemes sto lektiko kai ste thematografia III Makkabaion*. Herakleion Kretes: Bikelaia Bibliotheke, 1987.

Manning, Joseph Gilbert. *The Last Pharaohs: Egypt under the Ptolemies, 305–30 BC*. Princeton: Princeton University Press, 2010.

Mélèze-Modrzejewski, Joseph. "How to be a Jew in Hellenistic Egypt?" Pages 67–70 in *Diasporas in Antiquity*. Edited by Shaye J. D. Cohen and Ernest S. Frerichs. BJS 288. Atlanta: Scholars Press, 1993.

Mélèze-Modrzejewski, Joseph. *The Jews of Egypt: From Rameses II to Emperor Hadrian*. Translated by Robert Corman. Philadelphia: Jewish Publication Society, 1995.

Newman, Judith. "God Condemns the Arrogance of Power: The Prayer in 3 Maccabees 6:2–15." Pages 48–52 in *Prayer from Alexander to Constantine: A Critical Anthology*. Edited by Mark Kiley et al. London: Routledge, 1997.

Passoni Dell'Acqua, Anna. "Le preghiere del III libro dei Maccabei: genere letterario e tematica." *RivB* 43 (1995): 135–79.

Paul, André. "Le Troisème livre des Macchabées." *ANRW* 20.1: 298-336.

Schmitz, Barbara. "Pharao und Philopator: Exodusrezeption im Dritten Makkabäerbuch als Deutung des Lebens in der Diaspora." Pages 162–180 in *Exodus. Interpretation durch Rezeption*. Edited by Matthias Ederer and Barbara Schmitz. Stuttgart: Katholisches Bibelwerk, 2017.

Schwartz, Daniel R. *The Second Book of Maccabees*. CEJL. Berlin: de Gruyter, 2008.

LONG LIVE ZION:
THE MEANING OF ΣΚΗΝΗ
IN TOB 13:10 (G^{II}, VL)

Joseph P. RIORDAN

The psalm in chapter 13 of the book of Tobit, which the eponymous hero recites in the aftermath of his remarkable healing and reversal of fortune, marks a shift in perspective. Like the diverse prayers and *berakoth* that structure and punctuate pivotal moments in the plot of the core narrative, the hymn of praise in Tob 13 harks back to Tobit's experience. On the other hand, and in contrast to the earlier prayers, the psalm correlates his restoration with the eschatological fate of Jerusalem, even if this oscillation is not quite as obtrusive as some scholars insist.[1] There is a certain asymmetry between the plight of Tobit and that of the exiled nation, insofar as Tobit enjoys the fullness of God's mercy and blessings at the end of the book, while Zion still waits in hope for the ultimate fulfillment of the divine promises (Tob 14).[2] This paper aims to clarify one aspect

---

[1] The claim that the hymn in chapter 13 resonates or coheres with Tobit's experience is controversial. Some source critics overstate the contrast between core and frame, see Lawrence M. Wills, *The Jewish Novel in the Ancient World* (Ithaca: Cornell University Press, 1995), 83–8. Collins also proposes a basic source division between the core story and the frame, which includes the hymn in chapter 13 that is usually segmented into two units, a "Deuteronomistic" song in praise of the Lord's kingship (Tob 13:1–8) and the latter Zion psalm (Tob 13:9–18). John J. Collins, "The Judaism of the Book of Tobit," in *The Book of Tobit: Text, Tradition, Theology: Papers of the First International Conference on the Deuterocanonical Books, Pápa, Hungary, 20–21 May, 2004*, ed. Géza G. Xeravits and József Zsengellér, JSJSup 98 (Leiden: Brill, 2005), 23–9. While this division is valid, I hasten to add that the core narrative also trades off the tight correlation between the fate of the individual and that of the nation (e.g., the prayer of Tobit in Tob 3:1–6), albeit without the same focus on Jerusalem. For an eloquent articulation of this linkage, see Gary A. Anderson, "Tobit as Righteous Sufferer," in *A Teacher for All Generations: Essays in Honor of James C. VanderKam*, ed. Eric Farrel Mason, JSJSup 153 (Leiden: Brill, 2012), 493–507.

[2] As Nickelsburg points out, Tobit serves as a paradigm and proffers his own story of deliverance to console the people in exile: "Parallel to the story of Tobit is the uncompleted story of Israel. Tobit's situation is paradigmatic for the exiled nation. As God has chastised Tobit, so Israel, suffering in exile, is being chastised. But God's mercy on Tobit and his family guarantees that this mercy will bring the Israelites back to their land. Since this event, described only in predictions, awaits fulfillment, one level of the

of the eschatological profile in Tob 13 that fails to register in many recent debates. More specifically, my claim is that the striking turn of phrase in Tob 13:10 (G[II],VL) about Zion's σκηνή, i.e., her "dwelling" or "tent" that is to be rebuilt, refers primarily to the city and its repopulation rather than to the Temple or Tabernacle.

Like the manuscript transmission of the Book of Tobit itself, the textual situation of Tob 13:10 is rather convoluted, which makes it incumbent to draw on various versions and editions to piece together the verse in its entirety. It is worthwhile to recall that only the ancient translations preserve the complete text of Tobit. Among these ancient versions, the Greek and Latin traditions enjoy pride of place.[3] The Old Greek is extant in two recensions, a shorter edition known as G[I] and its more expansive and semitizing counterpart, G[II].[4] The Latin tradition is comprised of the hasty and idiosyncratic translation of Jerome in the Vulgate (Vulg.) and the longer Vetus Latina (VL), which bears an affinity to G[II]. Cave 4 at Qumran yielded five scrolls with fragments of Tobit that date roughly from the Hasmonean to Herodian era, one in Hebrew and four in Aramaic (4Q196–200), which laid to rest the debate over its Semitic provenance, if not that over its language of composition.[5]

---

double story is incomplete." George W. E. Nickelsburg, "Tobit," in *Harper's Bible Commentary*, ed. James Luther Mays (San Francisco: Harper & Row, 1988), 791.

[3] There are also translations of Tobit in Arabic, Armenian, Coptic, Ethiopic, Syriac, as well as several medieval Aramaic and Hebrew versions. On the whole, these seem to be either later elaborations or heavily dependent on the Greek recensions, and thus only sporadically of any text-critical consequence. There is, however, one important exception in this case, the Hebrew Tobit of Fagius. For details, see Robert Hanhart, *Tobit*, Septuaginta VIII/5 (Göttingen: Vandenhoeck & Ruprecht, 1983). Unless otherwise noted, I follow the verse numbering and divisions of Hanhart.

[4] There is also a third Greek edition referred to as G[III], which covers roughly half of the book, including part of chapter 13, though not 13:10. It is usually described as a composite text or compromise between the other two recensions, though Auwers points out that G[III] involves scribal innovation: "La recension moyenne n'est pas simplement un compromis entre les deux autres formes textuelles. Elle est une réécriture." Jean-Marie Auwers, "Tobit," *AVL* 49 (2017): 17–8, here 17.

[5] For a helpful summary of these debates, which make a strong case for Aramaic on linguistic grounds, see Joseph A. Fitzmyer, *Tobit*, CEJL (Berlin: de Gruyter, 2003), 18–27. If anything, the pendulum has swung even further toward Aramaic in recent research, as studies of Tobit against the backdrop of the Qumran Aramaic corpus have brought to the fore some striking family resemblances, e.g., George W. E. Nickelsburg, "Tobit and Enoch: Distant Cousins with a Recognizable Resemblance," in *George W.E. Nickelsburg in Perspective: An Ongoing Dialogue of Learning*, ed. Jacob Neusner and Alan Avery-Peck, JSJSup 80 (Leiden: Brill, 2003), 217–39; Daniel A. Machiela and Andrew B. Perrin, "Tobit and the Genesis Apocryphon: Toward a Family Portrait," *JBL* 133 (2014): 111–32; Andrew B. Perrin, "Tobit's Context and Contacts in the Qumran Aramaic Anthology," *JSP* 25 (2015): 23–51.

From a text-critical perspective, it is of capital significance that the Qumran scrolls on the whole vindicate the longer Greek and Latin texts (G[II], VL), which flies in the face of the critical bias in favor of the *lectio brevior*.[6] Unfortunately, in this case, only one of the Aramaic scrolls (4Q196) contains any part of the verse, consisting of four partial words that require some reconstruction. To further muddle the picture, the sole witness to G[II] for this chapter of Tobit is Codex Sinaiticus (א), which is marred by a lacuna in 13:6i–10b that omits the first part of the verse. Finally, the VL manuscripts display an impressive diversity of text type. There is as yet no critical edition for the VL of Tobit, though many of the principal witnesses have been helpfully gathered between the covers of a single book, which at least provides an interim solution.[7]

With these caveats in view, I reproduce below the chief textual witnesses to Tob 13:10 first from Qumran, i.e., the Aramaic scroll 4Q196,[8] and then from the Greek and Latin versions,[9] along with translations into English:

---

[6] This vindication, however, does not mean that the Qumran scrolls preserve the *Vorlage* of G[II] or the VL, since they are, as Fitzmyer notes, "at times even fuller than the so-called long recension, and ... they agree at times more with the long recension of VL than of Greek MS S." Fitzmyer, *Tobit*, 10. There are also instances where the scrolls support G[I] against G[II], including within chapter 13, though at least within the psalm, these cases are concentrated around the areas where א seems to be defective and shorter because of scribal error, e.g., 13:1, 6i–10b.

[7] Auwers began to work on a critical edition under the auspices of the Vetus Latina Institut of Beuron more than twenty years ago, but as of 2019, none of the Tobit fascicles have appeared. See Jean-Marie Auwers, "La tradition vieille latine du livre de Tobie: Un état de la question," in *The Book of Tobit: Text, Tradition, Theology: Papers of the First International Conference on the Deuterocanonical Books, Pápa, Hungary, 20–21 May, 2004*, ed. Géza G. Xeravits and József Zsengellér, JSJSup 98 (Leiden: Brill, 2005), 2. For the various readings of the VL, see Stuart Weeks, Simon Gathercole, and Loren Stuckenbruck, ed. *The Book of Tobit: Texts from the Principal Ancient and Medieval Traditions*, FSBP 3 (Berlin: de Gruyter, 2004). I follow the sigla for these manuscripts that Simon Gathercole proposes in his article, "Tobit in Spain: Some Preliminary Comments on the Relation between the Old Latin Witnesses," in *Studies in the Book of Tobit: A Multidisciplinary Approach*, ed. Mark Bredin, LSTS 55 (New York: T&T Clark, 2006), 6.

[8] The text and translation of 4Q196 are from Joseph A. Fitzmyer, *Qumran Cave 4. XIV*, ed. Emanuel Tov, DJD XIX (Oxford: Clarendon, 1996).

[9] The Old Greek texts (G[I], G[II]) and the Vulg. are from the respective critical editions of Hanhart and Weber and Gryson, while the VL reflects the Codex Regius (*r*) drawn from Weeks, Gathercole, and Stuckenbruck, which Sabatier and the editors of the Cambridge Septuagint adopted as the base text for their earlier editions. The rather literal English translations are my own. Hanhart, *Tobit*; Robert Weber and Roger Gryson, ed. *Biblia Sacra Iuxta Vulgatam Versionem*, 4th ed. (Stuttgart: Deutsche Bibelgesellschaft, 1994); Weeks, Gathercole, and Stuckenbruck, ed. *The Book of Tobit*.

(4Q196)

with righ]teousness acknowle[dge]

[shall be bui]lt for yo[u.]

[בקו]שטא הוד[י]

[יתבנ]ה לכ[י]

(G^I)	(G^{II} = א)	(VL = r)	(Vulg.)
ἐξομολογοῦ τῷ κυρίῳ ἀγαθῶς καὶ εὐλόγει τὸν βασιλέα τῶν αἰώνων, ἵνα πάλιν ἡ σκηνή αὐτοῦ οἰκοδομηθῇ ἐν[10] σοὶ μετὰ χαρᾶς. καὶ εὐφράναι ἐν σοὶ τοὺς αἰχμαλώτους καὶ ἀγαπήσαι ἐν σοὶ πάντας τοὺς ταλαιπώρους εἰς πάσας τὰς γενεὰς τοῦ αἰῶνος.	καὶ πάλιν ἡ σκηνή σου οἰκοδομηθήσεταί σοι μετὰ χαρᾶς. καὶ εὐφράναι ἐν σοὶ πάντας τοὺς αἰχμαλώτους καὶ ἀγαπήσαι ἐν σοὶ πάντας τοὺς ταλαιπώρους εἰς πάσας τὰς γενεὰς τοῦ αἰῶνος.	Confitere domino in bono et benedic domino saeculorum ut iterum tabernaculum tuum aedificetur in te cum gaudio, et laetos faciat in te omnes captiuos, et diligat omnes miseros in omnia saecula saeculorum.[11]	Confitere Domino in bonis et benedic Deum saeculorum ut reaedificet in te tabernaculam suum et revocet ad te omnes captivos et gaudeas in omnia saecula saeculorum.
Acknowledge the Lord worthily, and bless the king of the ages so that again his tent may be built in you with joy. And may he cheer within you those who are	And again your tent will be built for you with joy. And may he cheer within you all those who are captives and love within you all those who are wretched, for all	Acknowledge the Lord for [his] goodness, and bless the Lord of the ages so that your tent again may be built for you with joy. And may he make happy	Acknowledge the Lord in good things, and bless the God of the ages so that he may rebuild in you his tent, and may he call back to you all the captives, and may

[10] The 4th century Codex Vaticanus, which is the oldest witness to the short recension, lacks the preposition ἐν between the verb οἰκοδομηθῇ and σοι, as in א.

[11] Among the VL manuscripts, there are several variants in this verse, though they do not impinge on the issue at hand. For the sake of brevity, I only include below the first part of verse 10 from the texts that are available. Bibbia di Alcalá (x): "Confitere domino in die malorum et memorare bonorum tuorum et cognoscens peccatum tuum. benedicite deum saeculorum ut iterum tauernaculam tuum reedificetur in te." Codex Monacensis (M): "Confitemini domino in bono opere et benedicite deum regem saeculorum ut iterum tabernaculam tuum reaedificetur in te cum gaudio." Codex Bobbiensis (b): "Confetere domino deo saeculorum ut iterum tabernaculum tuum aedificetur cum gaudio." Bibbia di Roda (R): "Confitere ergo deo et benedic dominum seculorum ut iterum haedificetur tabernaculum tuum cum gaudio."

captives and love within you those who are wretched, for all the generations of the world.	the generations of the world.	within you all the captives and love all the wretched in every generation forever.	you rejoice in every generation forever.

To be sure, these witnesses provide a glimpse into the array of text-critical challenges that the Book of Tobit poses, which however fall beyond the scope of this essay to address in detail, let alone resolve. As with biblical books like Jeremiah, textual critics of Tobit recognize the presence of "multiple literary editions" that go back to an early stage in the story's development, even as they bemoan the serious questions and lacunae that remain.[12] It is to the good that recent commentaries eschew the quest to recover the singular *Urtext* of Tobit and attend more carefully to the Qumran evidence and the various recensions and versions.

On the other hand, some of these commentators, including those that train their sights on Codex Sinaiticus, seem to elide the nuance of σκηνή in 13:10 (G^{II}). Along these lines, Littman fills in the lacuna in א with Codex Vaticanus (= G^{I}, in italics below) and renders his eclectic text of verse 10 thus: "*Acknowledge the Lord in goodness and bless the King of the ages.* And again your Tabernacle will be erected in you with joy. And in you may he gladden all the captives, and in you may he love all the wretched for all the generations of eternity." He goes on to elaborate: "The 'tent' is the 'Tent of Meeting,' used by the Israelites in the desert as their central religious sanctuary (Exod 25–30) and which contained the Ark of the Covenant. It was incorporated into the Temple of Solomon

---

[12] Eugene C. Ulrich offers a concise definition: "By multiple literary editions I mean a literary unit—a story, pericope, narrative, poem, book, etc.—appearing in two or more parallel forms ... which one author, major redactor, or major editor completed and which a subsequent redactor or editor intentionally changed to a sufficient extent that the resultant form should be called a revised edition of that text," in "The Canonical Process, Textual Criticism, and Latter Stages in the Composition of the Bible," in Eugene C. Ulrich, *The Dead Sea Scrolls and the Origins of the Bible*, Studies in the Dead Sea Scrolls and Related Literature (Grand Rapids: Eerdmans, 1999), 63. For more on this *Tendenz* in textual criticism, which Hanhart had already intimated in his seminal monograph, see Christian Wagner and Tobias Nicklas, "Thesen zur textlichen Vielfalt im Tobitbuch," *JSJ* 34 (2003): 141–59. Michaela Hallermayer, *Text und Überlieferung des Buches Tobit* (Berlin: de Gruyter, 2008). Naomi Jacobs, "Scribal Innovation and the Book of Tobit: A Long Overdue Discussion," in *Sibyls, Scriptures, and Scrolls: John Collins at Seventy*, ed. Joel S. Baden, Hindy Najman, and Eibert J. C. Tigchelaar, JSJSup 175 (Leiden: Brill, 2016), 579–610. Robert Hanhart, *Text und Textgeschichte des Buches Tobit*, MSU 17 (Göttingen: Vandenhoeck & Ruprecht, 1984).

(1 Kgs 8:6)."[13] Zappella hews closely to the same line and additionally calls attention to the structural parallel with the ostensibly more perspicuous Temple allusion in 13:16 (G[II]):

> Gerusalemme assurge al polo di convergenza poiché in essa si trova la dimora del divin sovrano («la sua casa», *oikos autoû*: Tb 13,17) grazie al tempio, designato al v.11 con un termine (*skēnē'* «tenda»), che evoca la tenda dell'incontro, nella quale era possible incontrare YHWH durante la peregrinazione nel deserto (Es 33,7–11) e che conteneva l'arca dell'aleanza (Es 40,2–3.20–21), in seguito custodita nel santuario di Salomone (1Re 8,6).[14]

In other words, σκηνή is an archaic epithet that evokes the Tent of Meeting (ἡ σκηνὴ τοῦ μαρτυρίου) from Exodus, which serves as a "continuity theme" to connect the future Temple with the Tabernacle and its Solomonic successor (cf. 1 Kgs 8:4).[15]

It is vital to acknowledge off the bat that this interpretation captures the nuance of σκηνή in Tob 13:10, albeit more accurately for the text of G[I] than G[II]. The former recension has Tobit address Zion explicitly in 13:9 ("O Hierosolyma, holy city"), redirecting his voice from the Israelites (2nd person plural) in the first part of the hymn to the personified city of Jerusalem (2nd person singular). He urges her to acknowledge the Lord worthily and to bless the "king of the ages"[16] so that "his tent"

---

[13] Robert J. Littman, *Tobit: The Book of Tobit in Codex Sinaiticus* (Leiden: Brill, 2008), 152. Unless otherwise noted, all translations of Tobit G[II] are from Littman, while for G[I] I follow NETS.

[14] Marco Zappella, *Tobit: Introduzione, traduzione e commento*, Nuova versione della Bibbia dai testi antichi 30 (Cinisello Balsamo: San Paolo, 2010), 130.

[15] Ackroyd focuses on the vessels as a "continuity theme," probing how the tradition sought to minimize any hint of rupture within the praxis and spiritual life of the community, though he also comments incisively on the Chronicler's interest in the continuity between the Tabernacle and Temple. Peter R. Ackroyd, "The Temple Vessels – A Continuity Theme," in *Studies in the Religion of Ancient Israel*, ed. Helmer Ringgren, VTSup 23 (Leiden: Brill, 1972), 168. In his analysis of Tob 13:10, Griffin channels this language: "Referring to the temple as a tent serves to capture the spiritual and historical sense of the Lord's closeness to his people in the desert. Continuity is implied." Patrick Griffin, "The Theology and Function of Prayer in the Book of Tobit" (PhD diss., Catholic University of America, 1984), 306.

[16] The usage of divine titles is rightly beginning to gain a foothold in the source-critical debates, though these questions must be bracketed in this study. I would note in passing that the epithet "king of the ages," which would take on an outsize importance in later Judaism, surfaces almost exclusively within the hymn (Tob 13:6, 11, 15, 16; cf. 10:12 G[II]). On the other hand, it is unique in either Greek edition of chapter 13 for the Lord (ὁ κύριος) to be addressed baldly rather than as part of a compound or descriptive phrase ("Lord of Righteousness," etc.), as in this verse, though it mirrors the usual practice in the prayers of the core narrative.

(ἡ σκηνή αὐτοῦ) may be rebuilt "in you" (ἐν σοὶ). Contextually, the divine king is the clear antecedent of the masculine pronoun αὐτοῦ, and "his tent" correlates with the rhetoric of divine indwelling in the Tabernacle narrative in Exodus, which 1 Kgs 8:4 seems to project into the Temple, as Littman and Zappella note. In the wake of Zion's resounding praise, Tobit prophesies that the Temple will rise within the city of Jerusalem. The word σκηνή is hapax in the Book of Tobit, though the parallel between the divine king's tent in 13:10 and the house of the "great King" in 13:16 (οἶκος αὐτοῦ, i.e., "his house"; G^{II}) is suggestive, particularly since the latter is a more straightforward designation of the Temple (cf. Tob 14:4–5). Within the redactional frame, Tobit earlier describes Solomon's building with the cognate compound form κατασκήνωσις, again qualified by a possessive genitive with a divine antecedent, which further shores up this line of interpretation: "And in this place the Temple of the dwelling place of God (ὁ ναὸς τῆς κατασκηνώσεως τοῦ θεοῦ) was sanctified and founded (ᾠκοδομήθη ἐν αὐτῇ) for all future generations" (Tob 1:4 G^{II}).[17] Thus, it is clear that God's house/dwelling/tent flags the Temple in Tobit (13:16 G^{II}; 14:4–5; 1:4; 13:10 G^{I}, Vulg.), though it remains to be seen if Zion's dwelling is "interchangeable" in the same way.[18]

The VL (r) and G^{II} (א), in contrast, take a different slant on the σκηνή in 13:10, which warrants further consideration. From a textual standpoint, it is reasonable to fill in the first part of the verse with the VL (r), which in any case reflects a text close to G^{I}. It is probable that א's *Vorlage* contained the divine title "the king of the ages" of G^{I} rather than "the Lord of the ages" (r), as the repetition of this phrase in 13:6 and 13:10 seems to account for the parablepsis. The lacuna also explains the presence of καί (versus ἵνα/ut) and the indicative mood of the verb in א, since the basis of the purpose clause in 13:10a is lost but should be restored. All the VL manuscripts and G^{II} concur that the σκηνή belongs to the personified city of Zion ("your tent" 2nd person fem. sg.) rather

---

[17] G^{I} preserves a similar reading: "The dwelling place of the Most High, the Temple (ὁ ναὸς τῆς κατασκηνώσεως τοῦ ὑψίστου), had been built and consecrated for all the generations to come."

[18] Gregory notes that the wording of G^{I} and G^{II} differs slightly in 13:10, but presumes that they point to the same reality, i.e., the rebuilding of the Temple: "In discussing Tob 13–14 I use 'temple' and 'tabernacle' interchangeably since the claims are set in the context of Jerusalem and thus the two carry much the same force. In the LXX σκηνή is regularly used to translate both אהל and משכן." Bradley Gregory, "The Rebuilding of the Temple in the Text of Tobit 13 and Its Implications for Second Temple Hermeneutics," *Textus* 24 (2009): 153–78, here 161.

than to the divine king ("his tent" 3rd person masc. sg.), which is a crucial distinction.[19] There is genuine ambiguity about whether the tent is to be built for Zion or within her, which goes back to the Aramaic stratum and endures in the versions. As Cook points out, the preposition ל (+ pronominal suffix) casts a wide semantic net in Qumran Aramaic, including locative and datival aspects.[20] The bare Greek dative pronoun (2nd person singular) σοι primarily means "for you," though there is a rare locative meaning found in some poetry, which cannot be entirely excluded in the context of a psalm like Tob 13.[21] By the same token, the Latin phrase *in te* carries over the same duality, since the preposition can take both an accusative and ablative object, and the form of the 2nd person singular personal pronoun is identical in those oblique cases. The former case reflects a meaning in line with σοι/[י]לכ "for you," as in the VL (*r*) translation above,[22] while the tenor of the Vulgate seems to be locative, though context weighs as heavily in these judgements as morphology. To recapitulate, I propose that the reconstructed text of the GII edition of Tob 13:10 would run something like this:

ἐξομολογοῦ τῷ κυρίῳ ἀγαθῶς καὶ
εὐλόγει τὸν βασιλέα τῶν αἰώνων, ἵνα
πάλιν ἡ σκηνή σου **οἰκοδομηθῇ** σοι
μετὰ χαρᾶς. καὶ εὐφράναι ἐν σοὶ
πάντας τοὺς αἰχμαλώτους καὶ
ἀγαπήσαι ἐν σοὶ πάντας τοὺς
ταλαιπώρους εἰς πάσας τὰς γενεὰς
τοῦ αἰῶνος.

Acknowledge the Lord worthily,
and bless the king of the ages so
that again your tent **may** be built for
you with joy. And may he cheer
within you all those who are captives
and love within you all those who are
wretched, for all the generations of the
world.

---

[19] For examples of the interchange between σκηνή and its cognate σκήνωμα and *tabernaculum* in Jerome's Vulgate, see Vincent T. M. Skemp, *The Vulgate of Tobit Compared with Other Ancient Witnesses*, SBLDS 180 (Atlanta, GA: Scholars Press, 2000), 403.

[20] See the examples from Tobit and the *Genesis Apocryphon* in Edward C. Cook, ed. *Dictionary of Qumran Aramaic* (Winona Lake, IN: Eisenbrauns, 2015), 123–4. The fact that Fitzmyer translates the phrase in 4Q196 as "for you" in his DJD volume yet also claims Qumran support (indicated with italics) for his translation of GII "within you" in his commentary vividly illustrates the ambiguity. Note that just below in the same scroll (4Q196, Tob 13:11), the locative nuance is expressed with the preposition ב: "[from ge]nerations to generations they will present in you (בכי)."

[21] See the explanation and examples under the rubric "dative of place" in Herbert Weir Smyth, *Greek Grammar* (Cambridge, MA: Harvard University Press, 1956), 351–2.

[22] The preposition *in* + accusative sometimes carries a negative connotation, though not necessarily, as for example: *amor in patriam* i.e., love for one's country.

The words in boldface signal some deviation or correction to א. To be clear, my view is that the *lectio difficilior* of G^{II} and VL (*r*) stands closer to the earliest recoverable form of this edition, which is however not to be equated with the *Urtext* of Tobit, though it will serve as the basis for the analysis below.

The verse begins with Tobit's twofold command to Zion that she acknowledge (ἐξομολογοῦ) and bless (εὐλόγει) the eternal king worthily. The former verb is limited to the later chapters of the tale, more specifically to the period after Tobit's healing (Tob 11:13ff.). Within the last chapters (Tob 11–14), it occurs eleven times in G^{II}, including three times in chapter 13. This concentration is unsurprising in light of its meaning, which is to acknowledge or bear witness to God's mercies publicly, as Tobit does, for example, outside the gates of Nineveh as soon as his eyes are opened (Tob 11:17). The verbal pair ἐξομολογέομαι/ εὐλογέω hooks back to the core narrative, since the angel opens his address to Tobit and Tobias in Tob 12:6–7 with the same injunction, albeit in reverse order, and repeats it for good measure: "Bless (εὐλογεῖτε) God, and acknowledge (ἐξομολογεῖσθε) before all living people the good things he has done for you. By blessing (εὐλογεῖν) and praising his name, make known to all mankind with honor the words of God and do not shirk to acknowledge (ἐξομολογεῖσθαι) him. It is good to conceal the secret of a king, but to unveil and to acknowledge (ἐξομολογεῖσθαι) the works of God." Raphael circles back to these core directives again before his ascension (Tob 12:18–20), forming a kind of *inclusio*, right before he charges Tobit to put pen to paper: "Bless (εὐλογεῖτε) him all your days; praise him with song ... Now bless (εὐλογεῖτε) the Lord on earth and acknowledge (ἐξομολογεῖσθε) God ... Write all these things that have happened to you."

The verb εὐλογέω in various guises enjoys a wider distribution across the tale, meaning to bless or praise, and figures prominently in the prayers and *berakoth* that the cast of Tobit voices so readily. The hymn in chapter 13 is no exception, particularly if one includes the related adjectival form εὐλογητός "blessed" in the count (four times for the verb, four for the adjective in Tob 13 G^{II}). Tobit pulls a page out of the angel's playbook and bookends his speech with praise. Tobit 13:1 opens in Tobit's own voice "Blessed (εὐλογητὸς) be the Living God forever and ever and his kingdom" and closes with the personified gates and streets of Jerusalem swelling in a chorus of praise in communion with the saints: "Hallelujah, blessed (εὐλογητὸς) be the God of Israel. And the blessed will bless (εὐλογητοὶ εὐλογήσουσιν) the holy name forever and ever." (Tob 13:18)

This testimony to divine providence and praise for the "king of the ages" is bound up with the composition of the book itself, though there is also another kind of edification in view, at least in the hymn, namely the rebuilding of Zion's dwelling: ἵνα πάλιν ἡ σκηνή σου οἰκοδομηθῇ σοι μετὰ χαρᾶς. (Tob 13:10) This is the only appearance of the word σκηνή in Tobit, which is rarely paired in the LXX with the verb "to build" (οἰκοδομέω).[23] Within the ambit of classical Greek, its primary meaning is likewise "tent" or "booth," though in theatrical contexts it also came to denote the stage or background for plays, and metaphorically the acting or entertainment performed on the stage. The noun itself is fairly common in the Old Greek, albeit heavily concentrated in the Pentateuch (283 of its 434 recurrences) to describe human dwellings like the tents of the patriarchs and more significantly the Tent of Meeting (אהל מועד) and the Tabernacle (משכן). The LXX translators opt for σκηνή to render several Hebrew words, chiefly אהל "tent" (245 times) and משכן "tabernacle, dwelling" (93 times) as in the contexts above, and more rarely סך/סכה "booth" (25 times) and חצר "court" (6 times), though they sometimes settle on cognates like σκήνωμα (80 times) and κατασκήνωσις (5 times, including Tob 1:4).[24]

There is a fair amount of lexical interchange between permanent and portable structures in biblical discourse around domiciles, which adds another wrinkle to the semantic picture of σκηνή.[25] Aside from the texts in the OT that set אהל "tent" and בית "house" in parallel (e.g., Judg 20:8; Ps 84:11; Job 21:28; Prov 14:11), words like אהל or משכן also recur in contexts that seem to require בית "house" or היכל "palace, temple." The dozen examples of the Hebrew idiom meaning "to go home" (literally, "to one's tent(s)" אהל/σκήνωμα) are contextually incongruous

---

[23] There is an ample vocabulary to describe the erection of tents in Hebrew and Greek, but οἰκοδομέω "to build," which tracks closely with the Hebrew verb בנה, is not in this company, with one exception outside of Tob 13:10 (ἀνοικοδομέω + σκηνή in Amos 9:11) that will be discussed below.

[24] These totals are for the entire OT corpus of the LXX, which includes works that are Greek compositions and chronologically posterior to Tobit (e.g., Wisdom of Solomon).

[25] The analysis in this paragraph relies heavily on Homan's exhaustive study of ancient Israel's tent-dwelling heritage, and in particular on his second chapter on terminology, which adduces and categorizes the examples of terminological interchange. Michael M. Homan, *To Your Tents, O Israel! The Terminology, Function, Form, and Symbolism of Tents in the Hebrew Bible and the Ancient Near East*, CHANE 12 (Leiden: Brill, 2002).

yet illuminating, since ten of the cases arise in military settings in the aftermath of battle, which precisely inverts the thrust of the journey from camp to home.[26] This is not merely an idiomatic relic or archaism, as the same interchange recurs in sundry settings, including biblical texts that trade off this fluidity to describe long-standing permanent structures or entities such as the fortified city of Jerusalem and the Temple. Isaiah even appeals to this metaphorical sense to emphasize, ironically enough, the city's solidity and security: "When you gaze upon Zion, our city of assembly, your eyes shall behold Jerusalem as a secure homestead, a tent (אהל/σκηναί = "tents") not to be transported, whose pegs shall never be pulled up, and none of whose ropes shall break" (Isa 33:20; cf. Jer 10:18–20).[27] As Homan points out, the positive connotations that attach to tents and tent-homes, or in this case to the city as tent, set Israel athwart the cultural discourse in the ANE. And while this imagery would be anachronistic for Iron Age Israel, it did not necessarily come across as foreign or nomadic to a relatively sophisticated urban public.[28] There is no need to rehearse the many examples that depict the Temple as the Lord's אהל (Ps 15:1; 27:4–6, etc.) or משכן (Ps 43:3; 74:7; etc.), let alone to attempt to sort out the ideological crosscurrents and complexity that mark this material. To be sure, the "continuity motif" or tradition that sought to locate the Tabernacle inside the Temple muddies the waters somewhat in this area (1 Kgs 8:4 // 2 Chr 5:5),[29] though it is striking that the tenting language perdures even in a literary context that explicitly highlights the discontinuity of the Second Temple in this respect, such as 2 Macc 14:35.[30]

---

[26] Homan comments: "As the majority of troops were house-dwellers, it remains peculiar that they should return *to* their tents. Rather they should be going home *from* their tents." Homan, *To Your Tents*, 19.

[27] Unless otherwise noted, all translations of the MT are from the JPS version, while for the LXX, I follow NETS.

[28] Commenting on Tob 13:10 G[II], Rautenberg writes: "In the context of urban images used with regard to Jerusalem, the 'tent' as the place of God's presence comes across as a foreign element from the world of the nomads." Johanna Rautenberg, "The Meaning of the City of Jerusalem in the Book of Tobit: An Analysis of the Jerusalem Hymn in Tobit 13:8–18," in *Constructions of Space V: Place, Space and Identity in the Ancient Mediterranean World*, ed. Christl Maier and Gert Prinsloo (New York: Bloomsbury T&T Clark, 2013), 132. See Homan, *To Your Tents*, 35–8.

[29] To be clear, 1 Kgs 8:4 and 2 Chr 5:5 relate that the priests and Levites carried or brought up the Tent of Meeting, which hints that it may have landed in the Temple, though that is never stated outright, in contrast to the ark (1 Kgs 8:6 // 2 Chr 5:7).

[30] According to 2 Macc 2:4–8, the prophet Jeremiah led a delegation that brought the ark and tent from Jerusalem to Mt. Nebo, which he then hid in a cave whose location will remain unknown until God ingathers the people and shows mercy (2 Macc 4:7). Later

From a philological and exegetical perspective, there are some serious challenges that hinder the discernment of σκηνή's meaning in Tob 13:10, such as the tortuous textual history of the book, the lack of any ancient Semitic versions or scrolls that fully attest to this reading, the word's hapax status in Tobit and the rarity of this noun and verb conjunction within the corpus of the LXX, the terminological ambiguity in biblical discourse and poetry, and the like. On the other hand, to borrow from the folktale tradition that is so dear to the author of Tobit, there are some positive hints or "breadcrumbs" that dot the path through this dark forest, and it is to these clues or signs that our focus now turns.

Amid the copious references to Zion and Jerusalem in the OT, it is relatively rare to find mention of Zion's σκηνή. In addition to the metaphorical depiction of Zion as an immovable tent in Isa 33:20 cited above, the same book earlier (Isa 1:8) portrays Daughter Zion poignantly as left alone like a "booth" (סכה/σκηνή) in a vineyard, which underscores Jerusalem's plight as the lone survivor in the wake of Sennacherib's onslaught. This simile implies a close correlation between the personified city and the rather flimsy structure of the booth, though in contrast to a metaphor this type of comparison maintains a certain semantic distance or distinction between the two. There is a more direct metaphorical appeal to Daughter Zion's σκηνή in Lam 2:4, which is suggestive in light of the other resonances with the psalm in Tob 13 in that chapter (e.g., the personification of Zion and some of her architectural features): "He [the Lord] has killed all in whom we took pride in the tent of daughter Zion (באהל בת ציון/ἐν σκηνῇ θυγατρὸς Σιων); he has poured out his fury like fire." (NRSV) The text is beset with obscurities, and there is an ancient debate over its proper syntax, which has some bearing on the meaning of σκηνή, though in this context it seems to denote the city as the site of a massive slaughter.[31] Past question, the city includes the "House of the Lord" or Temple (Lam 2:7), but the structural features of the city (gates,

---

on after Nicanor threatens to level the Temple, in 2 Macc 14:35–36 the priests turn to the Lord in prayer: "O Lord of all, though you have need of nothing, you were pleased that there should be a shrine for your encamping (ναὸν τῆς σῆς σκηνώσεως) among us; so now, O holy One, Lord of all sanctification, keep undefiled forever this house that has so recently been purified."

[31] This is more clearly the drift of σκηνή in the LXX, as in the MT the Masoretic punctuation places the *athnaḥ* under עיר, hinting that perhaps the tent of Zion, i.e., the Temple, is instead the locus of divine wrath. Salters follows the Masoretic punctuation, yet still makes the case for the former option, which he deems the critical consensus. R. B. Salters, *Lamentations: A Critical and Exegetical Commentary*, ICC (London: Bloomsbury, 2010), 125–6.

walls, ramparts, bars, etc.) are ascribed to Daughter Zion in verses 8–9, which squares more easily with an urban profile.

To finish off this corner of the puzzle, Amos 9:11 provides an intriguing parallel, even though the oracle focuses on the fallen "booth" of David (סכת דויד/τὴν σκηνὴν Δαυιδ) rather than of Zion, since it is the only LXX text outside of Tob 13:10 that combines σκηνή with a form of the verb οἰκοδομέω.[32] The fallen booth of David may stand as a metaphor for the city of Jerusalem in its current "falling" or failing state in the period of Nehemiah if it is a late insertion, as Eidevall argues, though if it is from a pre-exilic redactional layer, then the fallen booth likely symbolizes the rupture of the United Kingdom or Davidic "house."[33] In the latter schema, its rebuilding intimates the hope for a return to the former glory and borders of the Davidic dynasty, though in either case the image is primarily "political" in the root sense rather than cultic.

Looking beyond the confines of the canon, there is an intriguing line from the *Apocryphon of Joseph* (4Q372), which is a non-Qumranic work that seems to reflect a polemical divide between the Jerusalemites and the community at Mt. Gerizim that would trace its lineage back to Joseph. The scroll of 4Q372 recounts the trials that Jacob's sons endured, and how their opponents terrified them "with the words of their mouth to revile against the tent of Zion (1:13) "...(אהל ציון).[34] It is difficult to discern the nuance of Zion's tent in the context of a fragmentary scroll, though as the DJD editors observe, the city and Temple are both viable options that enjoy a biblical pedigree: "Although the 'tent of Zion' might refer to the city of Jerusalem (cf. Isa 33:20), 'tent' can also be equivalent to 'temple' (2 Kgs 2:38; 29:30; Ezek 41:1; Ps 15:1; 27:5; 61:5; CD VII 15; *Tg. Lam* 2:4)."[35] On the other hand, the case for the latter interpretation is not as persuasive as they imply, since these texts refer to the Lord's tent rather than that of Zion, apart from Lam 2:4, which is

---

[32] Amos 9:11 "ἐν τῇ ἡμέρᾳ ἐκείνῃ ἀναστήσω τὴν σκηνὴν Δαυιδ τὴν πεπτωκυῖαν καὶ ἀνοικοδομήσω τὰ πεπτωκότα αὐτῆς καὶ τὰ κατεσκαμμένα αὐτῆς ἀναστήσω καὶ ἀνοικοδομήσω αὐτὴν καθὼς αἱ ἡμέραι τοῦ αἰῶνος."

[33] "The ensuing references to repair and rebuilding projects (in v. 11b) would rather seem to support an alternative interpretation of David's 'hut' (*sukkâ*), as (primarily) a metaphor for the city of Jerusalem." Göran Eidevall, *Amos: A New Translation with Introduction and Commentary*, AB 24G (New Haven: Yale University Press, 2017), 240.

[34] The text and translation of the scroll are from Moshe Bernstein and Eileen Schuller, "4QNarrative and Poetic Composition[b]," in *Qumran Cave 4, Miscellanea, Part 2*, ed. Douglas M. Gropp, James VanderKam, and Monica Brady, DJD XXVIII (Oxford: Clarendon, 2002), 165–97.

[35] Ibid., 175.

ambiguous at best. The Targum to that verse, which they also enlist in support, actually points in the opposite direction, since it fills out the meaning of the phrase in a collective or congregational sense, which ill suits the Temple: "In the tent of the Congregation of Zion (במשכן כנישתא דציון) he poured out his anger like burning fire."[36]

There is a final example of Zion's σκηνή in Isa 54:1–3 that deserves special consideration, as it comes from a chapter in Deutero-Isaiah whose imprint on Tob 13 is routinely acknowledged in the secondary literature:

> Shout, O barren one, you who bore no child! Shout aloud for joy, you who did not travail! For the children of the wife forlorn shall outnumber those of the espoused—said the Lord. Enlarge the site of your tent (מקום אהלך/τὸν τόπον τῆς σκηνῆς σου), extend the size of your dwelling (ויריעות משכנותיך/τῶν αὐλαιῶν σου),[37] do not stint! Lengthen the ropes, drive the pegs firm. For you shall spread out to the right and the left; your offspring shall dispossess nations and shall people the desolate towns.

The prophet addresses the personified figure of Zion directly and urges her to break out in joyful praise. This charge is incongruous with her appellation as a barren woman whose path to motherhood seems barred, like the matriarch Sarah or her namesake in Tobit, the accursed daughter of Raguel. Zion's misfortune is to be miraculously reversed, and the dejected wife will find herself inundated with new life, outpacing even the former stature of the "espoused" Davidic capital and repopulating her abandoned daughter towns. As a result, she is told to enlarge the footprint of her tent, which here stands for the city of Jerusalem, as in Isa 33:20.[38]

The σκηνή of Zion in Tob 13:10 channels and alludes to the tenting metaphor for the city in Isa 54:1–3, which is the only biblical occurrence

---

[36] The translation is from Philip Alexander, *The Targum of Lamentations*, ArBib 17B (Collegeville, MN: Liturgical Press, 2008). The primary meaning of כנישתא is "assembly" or "gathering" of the people, which in the context means the population or city of Jerusalem. And while the word sometimes applies to a building like a synagogue or school-house, the Temple is not a congregational or public building in the same sense. As the private domain of the deity (or as the dwelling of the divine name), access is restricted to the clergy and the public is generally barred.

[37] The LXX preserves a shorter or condensed text: "Enlarge the site of your tent and of your curtains."

[38] As Whybray observes in his commentary on this pericope: "It should be noted that Deutero-Isaiah here makes no mention of a rebuilt Temple: his thought is entirely concentrated on the renewed community itself." R. N. Whybray, *Isaiah 40-66*, New Century Bible Commentary (Grand Rapids: Eerdmans, 1975), 188.

of any form of this word with a 2ⁿᵈ personal singular personal pronoun
that refers to the personified figure of Zion rather than the Lord. The
command to break out in joyful praise finds an echo in the imperative in
Tob 13:10 (εὐλόγει), and the impetus to acknowledge (ἐξομολογοῦ)
divine providence likewise looms large in Isa 54:1–3, though its expression is complicated somewhat by the rhetorical setting (as in the core
narrative of Tobit), which projects these graces into the future. The primary difference is that the praise and acknowledgment in Tob 13:10
causes the tent to be erected, while in Isa 54:1–2 the accent falls on the
Lord's promise as the grounds for its expansion.[39] Isa 54 and Tob 13
appeal to the same topos to account for Zion's fortunes, namely the hid-
ing of God's face (Isa 54:8; Tob 13:6) and the turn from divine anger to
mercy (Isa 54:7–9; Tob 13:2, 5, 9), and they share a panoptic view of
Israel's history from the storied past and downfall ahead to her eschatological glory (Isa 54:1–3, 11–14; Tob 13:9–11). Zion is emphatically
a metropolis or mother city (cf. Isa 54:3; Tob 13:9 Gᴵ "O Hierosolyma,
holy city, he will afflict you for the works of your sons") and the Lord's
chosen or beloved wife (Isa 54:5 MT "For he who made you will espouse
you"; Tob 13:11 Gᴵᴵ "The name of the chosen (ἐκλεκτῆς)
will be for the generations of eternity"), in contrast to the portrayal of
Daughter Zion in Lam 2:4 and Isa 1:8, which seems to stress her vulnerability and isolation.

These correspondences are by no means exhaustive, as the imprint of
Isa 54 (or for that matter Deutero-Isaiah more generally) on the psalm in
Tobit requires further elucidation, but the strong affinity and resonances
between these texts suggest a deliberate appropriation or allusion to this
imagery in 13:10, which is all the more credible in light of the critical
consensus that Tob 13:16–17 lifts from Isa 54:11–12.[40] In addition to the

---

[39] Oswalt maintains that the difficult verbal form in the MT of Isa 54:13 (יְשׁוּ "let them
extend"), which BHS wants to emend to the passive יֻשׁע, is an indefinite 3ʳᵈ person
plural that functions as a passive. John N. Oswalt, *The Book of Isaiah, Chapters 40–66*,
NICOT (Grand Rapids: Eerdmans, 1998), 411. The passive sense in any case finds
some support in the Greek tradition. The implication seems to be that Zion's "sons" or
"builders" (cf. Isa 54:13 MT versus 1QIsaᵃ; Isa 49:17) are to stretch out the tent for
her, which the passive voice of the verb + dative in Tob 13:10 (οἰκοδομηθῇ σοι)
reflects. On the wordplay between sons and builders in Isaiah, which Tobit seems to
channel, see Christopher R. North, *The Second Isaiah: Introduction, Translation, and
Commentary to Chapters XL–LV* (Oxford: Clarendon, 1964), 251.

[40] To my knowledge, the monograph of Henderson is the only study that strives to discern
in any detail the Isaianic allusions in Tob 13. She registers the affinity between Isa
54:1–3 and Tob 13:10, though does not connect all of the dots. Ruth Henderson, *Second Temple Songs of Zion: A Literary and Generic Analysis of the Apostrophe to Zion*

textual and philological evidence surveyed thus far, this allusion to Isa 54 supports the conclusion that the σκηνή of Zion in Tob 13:10 foregrounds the rebuilding and repopulation of the city, which is not dissimilar to the fate of Tobit's own tent or "house" that is brought back from the brink and miraculously restored. This view does not imply any polemical opposition to the Temple or its exclusion from the picture (cf. Acts 7:39–53; Rev 21:22–23), but it is rather simply one element or feature in the vast panorama of the city skyline. The contrast with the attention that the priestly writer in Exodus lavishes on every inch and stitch of the Tabernacle, which is moreover "superfluously" revisited and held up for contemplation, could not be starker.[41]

Turning back to the context in Tob 13 G^{II}, there are several features in the Zion hymn that come into sharper focus in light of this nuance. Some brief reflections will have to suffice, leaving the door open to further research, as it is unfeasible to delve into its exegetical dynamics and structure in too much detail at this point. First of all, the difference between the σκηνή in G^{I} and G^{II} is not merely an isolated variant, but forms part of a redactional *Tendenz* in the short recension to shift the spotlight away from the city as mediator and spouse and to direct attention to the Temple or God directly, which seems to be achieved either via textual emendation or omission, though the role of scribal error and other factors should not be discounted.

Along these lines, in 13:10 G^{II} praise and acknowledgment spur the tent or city to be rebuilt, leading to the edification and consolation of the exiles ("And in you may he gladden all the captives"). After Zion is made whole, the city shines with a brilliant light, and the nations wend their way on pilgrimage to Jerusalem and to her holy name (13:11 "to you ... to your holy name"). The light of Zion is extinguished or absent in G^{I}, as is the spousal imagery at the end of the verse ("the name of the chosen will be for the generations of eternity"), and the Gentiles make their way instead "to the name of the Lord God." As is clear from 13:10, Tobit heralds the creative power of the word, though he also elaborates on the inverse dynamic and applies it at length to the personified city and

---

(11QPsa XXII 1–15), Tobit 13:9–18 and 1 Baruch 4:30–5:9, DCLS 17 (Berlin: de Gruyter, 2014).

[41] It is superfluous in the sense that the priestly writer is capable of brevity or shorthand, but consciously chooses to pause and savor every detail of its construction for theological reasons. See Gary A. Anderson, "Towards a Theology of the Tabernacle and Its Furniture," in *Text, Thought, and Practice in Qumran and Early Christianity*, ed. Ruth Clements and Daniel R. Schwartz, STDJ 84 (Leiden: Brill, 2009), 161–94.

her architectural features in the curses of 13:12 G^{II}: "Cursed will be all who will say a harsh word, cursed will be all who destroy you and those who pull down your walls and all those who overturn your towers and set on fire your dwellings. And blessed for eternity will be all who fear you." The laconic parallel in G^I, in contrast, downplays the power of language and its link to the features of the city: "Cursed are all who hate you; blessed forever will be all who love you."

The text of 13:16 G^{II} poses some difficulties, particularly if it is emended and massaged so as to mirror the cultic view of 13:10 G^I as it sometimes is, though the final form of 13:10 (א) confirms the primacy of Jerusalem qua city, which is a genuine parallel to 13:10 G^{II}, with the further proviso that God's house stands in its midst:

ὅτι Ἰερουσαλὴμ οἰκοδομηθήσεται, τῇ πόλει οἶκος αὐτοῦ εἰς πάντας τοὺς αἰῶνας.	For Jerusalem shall be rebuilt, in the city his house [shall be rebuilt] for all ages.[42]

This picture also matches the eschatological sequence laid out in Tob 14:5, which envisions the return from exile and the rebuilding of Jerusalem honorably, followed by the construction of the glorious Temple at the appointed time. The mention of the Lord's house may be a later gloss in this vein, as the equivalent in the Old Latin is gender-ambiguous, and the parallel with 13:10 actually favors the construal of *illius* as feminine (= αὐτῆς) with Jerusalem as its antecedent, which suggests a tight correlation between the city and the house/tent of Zion.[43] Finally, the holy name of Zion closes out the psalm in 13:18 G^{II}, coming full circle with the psalm's opening invocation in 13:9 ("Jerusalem, holy city"): "And all her houses will say, 'Hallelujah, blessed be the God of Israel.' And the blessed will bless the holy name forever and ever." This ending

---

[42] The translation is my own. Cf. Rabenau's German ("Denn Jerusalem wird aufgebaut sein, in der Stadt sein Haus in alle Ewigkeiten") and Zappella's Italian ("perché Gerusalemme sarà riconstruita; nella città la sua casa per sempre"). Merten Rabenau, *Studien zum Buch Tobit* (Berlin: de Gruyter, 1994), 87. Zappella, *Tobit*, 133.

[43] VL (*r*) reads: "Quia liberauit Hierusalem, et aedificabit iterum domus illius in omnia saecula saeculorum," which is grammatically awkward. None of the manuscripts contain the accusative of "house" (*domum*) that an active verb would require, which suggests that the text should be slightly emended, turning the verb into the passive voice (i.e., *aedificabitur*), as in R, M, *x*, *b*, and the Gothic Breviary. I would render the corrected VL (*r*) thus: "Because he has freed Jerusalem; and her house [// to *tabernaculum tuum* in 13:10] will be built again for all the ages." Galdos put forward this view almost a century ago in his commentary, albeit under the strain of outmoded assumptions about historicity and genre. Romualdo Galdos, *Commentarius in librum Tobit*, Cursus Scripturae Sacrae 12/1 (Paris: Lethielleux, 1930), 280–3.

is curtailed in G^I, and the blessing reserved to God alone, as the lanes rather than houses of Jerusalem acclaim: "Blessed be God, who has exalted all the ages."

To sum up, my claim is that the *lectio difficilior* in the long recension of Tob 13:10 (G^{II}, *r*) preserves an older reading of this verse, which refers to the city of Jerusalem poetically as the σκηνή or tent of Zion, alluding to Isa 54. Within the literary context of the psalm, this tent imagery foregrounds the rebuilding of Jerusalem and her repopulation, which folds in the Temple though not as the focus or center of attention.[44] This understated approach matches the tenor of other "eschatological psalms" from the Second Temple period to which Tob 13 may be profitably compared, such as, Bar 4:30–5:9, Sir 36, *Pss. Sol.* 11, and the *Apostrophe to Zion*.[45] It remains to be seen how much this tack owes to the powerful ideological crosswinds that buffeted Hellenistic Judaism or reflects a certain ambivalence toward the Second Temple, though it is at least clear that Zion and her Temple provoked controversy and scribal innovation in Tobit, which are not without analogues in our own day.[46]

Bibliography

Ackroyd, Peter R. "The Temple Vessels – A Continuity Theme." Pages 166–81 in *Studies in the Religion of Ancient Israel*. Edited by Helmer Ringgren. VTSup 23. Leiden: Brill, 1972.

---

[44] There is an intriguing parallel in the Hebrew Tobit of Fagius, which first came to press during the Reformation period though reflects an older tradition that is preserved in fragments from the Cairo Genizah. The Fagius text nods to a kind of Name theology, which is a unique redactional feature of this edition, and elaborates on the rebuilding of the "ruined dwellings" or tent of Jerusalem, which explicitly designates the city and alludes to the ingathering of her exiled children: "O Jerusalem, bless and praise the King of eternal life, for continuously (he is) to turn to you and to make his name dwell in your midst. And your ruined dwellings will be rebuilt, and he will gather to you with joy all your exiles and will plant all your children in your midst forever and ever." For a helpful overview and the translation above, see Loren Stuckenbruck, "The 'Fagius' Hebrew Version of Tobit," in *The Book of Tobit: Text, Tradition, Theology: Papers of the First International Conference on the Deuterocanonical Books, Pápa, Hungary, 20–21 May, 2004*, ed. Géza G. Xeravits and József Zsengellér, JSJSup 98 (Leiden: Brill, 2005), 189–219.

[45] David Flusser, "Psalms, Hymns, and Prayers," in *Jewish Writings of the Second Temple Period: Apocrypha, Pseudepigrapha, Qumran, Sectarian Writings, Philo, Josephus*, ed. Michael E. Stone, CRINT 2 (Philadelphia: Fortress Press, 1984), 551–71. Henderson, *Second Temple Songs*.

[46] See Daniel Schwartz, "Temple or City: What Did Hellenistic Jews See in Jerusalem?," in *The Centrality of Jerusalem: Historical Perspectives*, ed. M. Poorthuis and C. Safrai (Kampen: Kok Pharos, 1996), 114–27.

Alexander, Philip. *The Targum of Lamentations*. ArBib 17B. Collegeville, MN: Liturgical Press, 2008.

Anderson, Gary A. "Tobit as Righteous Sufferer." Pages 493–507 in *A Teacher for All Generations: Essays in Honor of James C. VanderKam*. Edited by Eric Farrel Mason. JSJSup 154. Leiden: Brill, 2012.

Anderson, Gary A. "Towards a Theology of the Tabernacle and Its Furniture." Pages 161–94 in *Text, Thought, and Practice in Qumran and Early Christianity*. Edited by Ruth Clements and Daniel R. Schwartz. Leiden: Brill, 2009.

Auwers, Jean-Marie. "La tradition vieille latine du livre de Tobie: Un état de la question." Pages 1–21 in *The Book of Tobit: Text, Tradition, Theology: Papers of the First International Conference on the Deuterocanonical Books, Pápa, Hungary, 20-21 May, 2004*. Edited by Géza G. Xeravits and József Zsengellér. JSJSup 98. Leiden: Brill, 2005.

Auwers, Jean-Marie. "Tobit." *AVL* 49 (2017): 17–8.

Bernstein, Moshe, and Eileen Schuller. "4QNarrative and Poetic Composition[b]." Pages 165–97 in *Qumran Cave 4, Miscellanea, Part 2*. Edited by Douglas M. Gropp, James VanderKam, and Monica Brady. DJD XXVIII. Oxford: Clarendon, 2002.

Collins, John J. "The Judaism of the Book of Tobit." Pages 23–9 in *The Book of Tobit: Text, Tradition, Theology: Papers of the First International Conference on the Deuterocanonical Books, Pápa, Hungary, 20–21 May, 2004*. Edited by Géza G. Xeravits and József Zsengellér. JSJSup 98. Leiden: Brill, 2005.

Cook, Edward C., ed. *Dictionary of Qumran Aramaic: 123–4*. Winona Lake, IN: Eisenbrauns, 2015.

Eidevall, Göran. *Amos: A New Translation with Introduction and Commentary*. AB 24G. New Haven: Yale University Press, 2017.

Fitzmyer, Joseph A. *Qumran Cave 4. XIV*. Edited by Emanuel Tov. DJD XIX. Oxford: Clarendon, 1996.

Fitzmyer, Joseph A. *Tobit*. CEJL. Berlin: de Gruyter, 2003.

Flusser, David. "Psalms, Hymns, and Prayers." Pages 551–71 in *Jewish Writings of the Second Temple Period: Apocrypha, Pseudepigrapha, Qumran, Sectarian Writings, Philo, Josephus*. Edited by Michael E. Stone. CRINT 2. Philadelphia: Fortress Press, 1984.

Galdos, Romualdo. *Commentarius in librum Tobit*. Cursus Scripturae Sacrae 12/1. Paris: Lethielleux, 1930.

Gathercole, Simon. "Tobit in Spain: Some Preliminary Comments on the Relation between the Old Latin Witnesses." Page 5–11 in *Studies in the Book of Tobit: A Multidisciplinary Approach*. Edited by Mark Bredin. LSTS 55. New York: T&T Clark, 2006.

Gregory, Bradley. "The Rebuilding of the Temple in the Text of Tobit 13 and Its Implications for Second Temple Hermeneutics." *Textus* 24 (2009): 153–78.

Griffin, Patrick. "The Theology and Function of Prayer in the Book of Tobit." PhD diss., Catholic University of America, 1984.

Hallermayer, Michaela. *Text und Überlieferung des Buches Tobit*. Berlin: de Gruyter, 2008.

Hanhart, Robert. *Text und Textgeschichte des Buches Tobit*. MSU 17. Göttingen: Vandenhoeck & Ruprecht, 1984.

Hanhart, Robert. *Tobit*. Septuaginta VIII/5. Göttingen: Vandenhoeck & Ruprecht, 1983.

Henderson, Ruth. *Second Temple Songs of Zion: A Literary and Generic Analysis of the Apostrophe to Zion (11QPsa XXIII 1–15), Tobit 13:9–18 and 1 Baruch 4:30–5:9*. DCLS 17. Berlin: de Gruyter, 2014.

Homan, Michael M. *To Your Tents, O Israel! The Terminology, Function, Form, and Symbolism of Tents in the Hebrew Bible and the Ancient Near East*. CHANE 12. Leiden: Brill, 2002.

Jacobs, Naomi. "Scribal Innovation and the Book of Tobit: A Long Overdue Discussion." Pages 579–610 in *Sibyls, Scriptures, and Scrolls: John Collins at Seventy*. Edited by Joel S. Baden, Hindy Najman, and Eibert J. C. Tigchelaar. JSJSup 175. Leiden: Brill, 2016.

Littman, Robert J. *Tobit: The Book of Tobit in Codex Sinaiticus*. Leiden: Brill, 2008.

Machiela, Daniel A., and Andrew B. Perrin. "Tobit and the Genesis Apocryphon: Toward a Family Portrait." *JBL* 133 (2014): 111–32.

Nickelsburg, George W. E. "Tobit and Enoch: Distant Cousins with a Recognizable Resemblance." Pages 217–39 in *George W.E. Nickelsburg in Perspective: An Ongoing Dialogue of Learning*. Edited by Jacob Neusner and Alan Avery-Peck. JSJSup 80. Leiden: Brill, 2003.

Nickelsburg, George W.E. "Tobit." Page 791–803 in *Harpers's Bible Commentary*. Edited by James Luther Mays. San Francisco: Harper & Row, 1988.

North, Christopher R. *The Second Isaiah: Introduction, Translation, and Commentary to Chapters XL–LV*. Oxford: Clarendon, 1964.

Oswalt, John N. *The Book of Isaiah, Chapters 40–66*. NICOT. Grand Rapids: Eerdmans, 1998.

Perrin, Andrew B. "Tobit's Context and Contacts in the Qumran Aramaic Anthology." *JSP* 25 (2015): 23–51.

Rabenau, Merten. *Studien zum Buch Tobit*. Berlin: de Gruyter, 1994.

Rautenberg, Johanna. "The Meaning of the City of Jerusalem in the Book of Tobit: An Analysis of the Jerusalem Hymn in Tobit 13:8–18." Page 125–140 in *Constructions of Space V: Place, Space and Identity in the Ancient Mediterranean World*. Edited by Christl Maier and Gert Prinsloo. New York: Bloomsbury T&T Clark, 2013.

Salters, R.B. *Lamentations: A Critical and Exegetical Commentary*. ICC. London: Bloomsbury, 2010.

Schwartz, Daniel. "Temple or City: What Did Hellenistic Jews See in Jerusalem?" Pages 114–27 in *The Centrality of Jerusalem: Historical Perspectives*. Edited by M. Poorthuis and C. Safrai. Kampen: Kok Pharos, 1996.

Skemp, Vincent T. M. *The Vulgate of Tobit Compared with Other Ancient Witnesses*. SBLDS 180. Atlanta, GA: Scholars Press, 2000.

Smyth, Herbert Weir. *Greek Grammar*. Cambridge, MA: Harvard University Press, 1956.

Stuckenbruck, Loren. "The 'Fagius' Hebrew Version of Tobit." Pages 189–219 in *The Book of Tobit: Text, Tradition, Theology: Papers of the First Inter-*

national Conference on the Deuterocanonical Books, Pápa, Hungary, 20–21 May, 2004. Edited by Géza G. Xeravits and József Zsengellér. JSJSup 98. Leiden: Brill, 2005.

Ulrich, Eugene C. *The Dead Sea Scrolls and the Origins of the Bible*. Studies in the Dead Sea Scrolls and Related Literature. Grand Rapids: Eerdmans, 1999.

Wagner, Christian, and Tobias Nicklas. "Thesen zur textlichen Vielfalt im Tobitbuch." *JSJ* 34 (2003): 141–59.

Weber, Robert, and Roger Gryson, eds. *Biblia Sacra Iuxta Vulgatam Versionem*. 4th ed. Stuttgart: Deutsche Bibelgesellschaft, 1994.

Weeks, Stuart, Simon Gathercole, and Loren Stuckenbruck, eds. *The Book of Tobit: Texts from the Principal Ancient and Medieval Traditions*. FSBP 3. Berlin: de Gruyter, 2004.

Whybray, R. N. *Isaiah 40-66*. New Century Bible Commentary. Grand Rapids: Eerdmans, 1975.

Wills, Lawrence M. *The Jewish Novel in the Ancient World*. Ithaca: Cornell University Press, 1995.

Zappella, Marco. *Tobit: Introduzione, traduzione e commento*. Nuova versione della Bibbia dai testi antichi 30. Cinisello Balsamo: San Paolo, 2010.

PRAYER AND THE WISDOM BOOKS

PRAYER IN THE WISDOM
OF SOLOMON

Matthew E. GORDLEY

At first glance, Wisdom of Solomon does not appear to have a particularly heavy emphasis on prayer. Though prayer and related terms do occur in a number of passages, the first mention of prayer does not occur until Wis 7. Nevertheless, in the overall appeal to the reader to hold on to the traditional Jewish practices and beliefs in the face of pressure to turn away, the passages in which prayer occurs are significant. As a text purporting to be the wisdom "of Solomon," part of the strategy of pseudonymity is carried forward by references to Solomon's wisdom as a gracious gift of God in response to Solomon's prayer (Wis 7:7). Solomon's prayer itself is provided to the reader, in part, as a model prayer (Wis 9). In addition to promoting prayer by the model of Solomon, the text reveals the folly of prayer offered to idols. Some of the sharpest and most pointed rhetoric against idols is deployed in a section which vividly describes the absurdity of the act of praying to inanimate objects (Wis 13:17–14:1). Finally, lessons from Israel's history are drawn out from the Exodus narratives including the obligation to pray and give thanks to God at dawn (Wis 16:28) and the efficacy of Aaron's prayer (18:21). In the text as a whole, both positive and negative examples of prayer show the reader the desirable path in their current age.

Although a few studies on Wis have engaged the topic of prayer directly, the majority of them have focused on the prayer of Solomon in Wis 9.[1] The present study examines each of the references to prayer in Wis with particular attention to how the references function within the larger context of the composition. Attention both to the portrayal of

---

[1] Maurice Gilbert, "La Structure de la Prière de Salomon (Sg 9)," *Bib* 51 (1970): 301–31; Helmut Engel, "Gebet im Buch der Weisheit," in *Prayer from Tobit to Qumran: Inaugural Conference of the ISDCL at Salzburg, Austria, 5 - 9 July 2003*, ed. Renate Egger-Wenzel and Jeremy Corley, DCLY 2004 (Berlin: de Gruyter, 2004), 293–312; Markus Witte, "Emotions in the Prayers of the Wisdom of Solomon," in *Ancient Jewish Prayers and Emotions: Emotions Associated with Jewish Prayer in and around the Second Temple Period*, ed. Stefan C. Reif and Renate Egger-Wenzel, DCLS 26 (Berlin: de Gruyter, 2015), 161–76.

prayer and to the functions of Solomon's prayer in its wider contexts shows that references to prayer are an important part of the author's larger strategy to promote adherence to Jewish tradition in a Hellenistic context. Interestingly, we see that this prayer path differs in emphasis from the ways in which prayer is promoted within other instances of Solomonic discourse such as Psalms of Solomon: Prayer in Wis shows a minimal emphasis on the temple, a strong connection with language in praise of Isis, and inclusion of numerous philosophical and Hellenistic features.

Solomon's Act of Prayer (Wis 7:7; 8:21)

Descriptions of Solomon's act of prayer for wisdom mark the first and second direct mentions of prayer in Wis. The first explicit mention of prayer is found in 7:7 and the second in 8:21, both in the second major section of the book (chs. 7–10) where the author, in the voice of Solomon, describes wisdom in exalted terms and describes his own search for wisdom (7:1–8:21). Much has been made of the author's descriptions of wisdom in this section, particularly its connections to earlier Jewish texts as well as its engagement with Hellenistic philosophical thought and popular religion.[2] Wis 7:22–8:1, the central passage and thus the focal point of this section, certainly represents a high point in the Jewish wisdom tradition of praise of personified wisdom using philosophical terminology. Comparatively less attention has been given to the way in which prayer is portrayed in the verses which serve as a frame for the descriptions of wisdom in between. In this section, as we examine the way in which the author presents Solomon's act of prayer we will notice a distinct intensification compared to the earlier biblical texts, both in the language about the act of prayer and in the ways in which God's gift of wisdom is described.

In 7:7 the author explains:

> Therefore I prayed (εὐξάμην), and understanding (φρόνησις) was given me; I called on God (ἐπεκαλεσάμην), and the spirit of wisdom (πνεῦμα σοφίας) came to me.[3]

---

[2] See, for example, David Winston, "Wisdom in the Wisdom of Solomon," in *In Search of Wisdom: Essays in Memory of John G. Gammie*, ed. Leo G. Perdue, Bernard B. Scott, and William J. Wiseman (Louisville, KY: Westminster John Knox, 1993), 149–64.

[3] English translations are from the NRSV unless otherwise noted.

Related terminology about prayer is used in 8:21, the verse which introduces the text of the prayer itself:

> But I perceived that I would not possess wisdom unless God gave her to me—
> and it was a mark of insight to know whose gift she was—
> so I appealed (ἐνέτυχον) to the Lord and implored (ἐδεήθην) him,
> and with my whole heart I said (καὶ εἶπον ἐξ ὅλης τῆς καρδίας μου).

These verses about Solomon's asking for wisdom are closely connected to the biblical accounts of Solomon's request for wisdom as narrated in 1 Kgs 3:6–9 and 2 Chr 1:8–10. However, by comparison the biblical narratives which include Solomon's request for wisdom are fairly sparse. 1 Kgs 3:6 introduces the prayer simply with the straightforward, "And Solomon said," while 2 Chr 1:8 adds, "And Solomon said to God." The Hebrew of 1 Kings and 2 Chronicles is the common verb אמר ("to say"), reflected in the LXX by the common verb εἶπεν (aorist of λέγω). Interestingly, neither of these earlier passages refers to Solomon's request explicitly as a prayer. In 1 Kgs 3 the context is a conversation between God and Solomon which takes place in a dream. In 2 Chr 1 it is also a conversation, but without the dream context. So when we turn to Wis and find an extended description of Solomon's request using language associated with prayer, the fuller description is quite instructive.[4]

While the biblical accounts used one simple verb to describe Solomon's request, Wis uses five different verbs to describe Solomon's prayer. First, εὔχομαι (7:7) is used commonly in the LXX, early Jewish writings, and New Testament, as well as many Greek authors to describe praying or making a request to a god or gods.[5] Likewise, ἐπικαλέω (7:7) in the sense of calling upon a deity, is common in Jewish, Christian, and Greco-Roman writings.[6] In 8:21 the verb ἐντυγχάνω has the sense of appealing to someone, and is also used in the literature in appeal to God

---

[4] For a comparison of the biblical contexts and the context of the prayer in Wis, see Judith H. Newman, "The Democratization of Kingship in Wisdom of Solomon," in *The Idea of Biblical Interpretation: Essays in Honor of James L. Kugel*, ed. Hindy Najman and Judith H. Newman, JSJSup 83 (Leiden: Brill, 2004), 309–28, esp. 313–5; Gilbert, "Structure," 321–6.

[5] On the language of prayer in the ancient world, see David E. Aune, "Prayer in the Greco-Roman World," in *Into God's Presence: Prayer in the New Testament*, ed. Richard N. Longenecker, McMaster New Testament Studies (Grand Rapids, MI: Eerdmans, 2001), 23–42, esp. 28–9. Cf. Simon Pulleyn, *Prayer in Greek Religion*, OCM (Oxford: Clarendon Press, 1997), 59–63. For an outline of the Greek terms for prayer in Wis see Witte, "Emotions," 162.

[6] Note this verb is used to describe the Israelites calling up God when they were thirsty (11:4) and also to describe the act of praying to idols (13:17).

(note its use later in 16:28). Next, δέομαι "ask" or "beg", can also be used of asking something of a person or of a deity.[7] Finally, in the line before the prayer itself, we do see the verb εἶπον, "to say," which was the verb used in the LXX of 1 Kgs and 2 Chr. But here in Wis it is modified with ἐξ ὅλης τῆς καρδίας μου, "with my whole heart." Comparing these introductory lines with what we see in 1 Kgs 3:6 and 2 Chr 1:8, we can readily observe a significant degree of expansion on the biblical text. Where in the biblical text Solomon merely speaks in response to a request to God in a dream, here in Wis the impression is that Solomon enthusiastically sought wisdom from God specifically through prayer, calling upon God, appealing, asking, and doing so with his whole heart.

Given the larger purposes of the author of Wis, we can suggest that this intensification of the prayer aspect of Solomon's request for wisdom serves at least two purposes. First, it highlights the divine origins of wisdom as a gift from God. Wisdom is a gift that God alone gives. Solomon was not special or unique, nor was he able to find wisdom on his own. This is a theme that we will see is reinforced through the text of Solomon's prayer provided in Wis 9. Second, the enhanced language highlights the importance of the act of prayer, making it unmistakable that Solomon actually *prayed*, and what kind of prayer it was—namely, heartfelt prayer to a deity. This observation is reinforced by the way in which this description of Solomon's praying is repeated from 7:7 to 8:21. In Wis it is unmistakable that Solomon *prayed* for wisdom.

It is also noteworthy that Solomon prayed *for wisdom*. In 1 Kgs he asks simply for a "listening heart" (1 Kgs 3:9) which in 2 Chr becomes "wisdom and understanding" (2 Chr 1:10). Wisdom of Solomon picks up explicitly on the request for wisdom and expands on this greatly. The two verses under discussion here (7:7 and 8:21) frame a larger section which is structured in a chiastic form and which has as its focal point the beautiful poem about the nature of wisdom in 7:22b–8:1.[8] Leading up to the wisdom poem, the author elaborates on the virtues and value of wisdom. In vv. 17–22, for example, the author elaborates on the scope of the knowledge that was given to him including knowledge of the world, the seasons, the stars, animals, plants, roots, spirits, and human thoughts, extending from what is manifest to what is secret. In v. 22 he explains, "For wisdom, the fashioner of all things, taught me."

---

[7] It is used later in 16:25 in the sense of supplication of God, but in 18:2 it has the sense of asking something of a human as the Israelites' Egyptian captors beg their pardon.

[8] Engel, "Gebet," 295.

While it is beyond the scope of this study to explore the portrayal of wisdom in Wis, it is important to note here that the author draws together strands of several different ancient discourses to create his portrait of wisdom. While biblical wisdom traditions are clearly in view, the author uses a number of other elements to create a more universal picture of the role of wisdom in the world.[9] This portrayal resonates with Greek writers and their more philosophical treatment of the connection between wisdom and the divine.[10] For example, in his *De Iside et Osiride* Plutarch describes the necessity of humans' asking the deity for knowledge:

> All good things, my dear Clea, sensible men must ask from the gods; and especially do we pray that from those mighty gods we may, in our quest, gain a knowledge of themselves, so far as such a thing is attainable by men. For we believe that there is nothing more important for man to receive, or more ennobling for God of His grace to grant, than the truth. God gives to men the other things for which they express a desire, but of sense and intelligence He grants them only a share, inasmuch as these are His especial possessions and His sphere of activity. For the Deity is not blessed by reason of his possession of gold and silver, nor strong because of thunder and lightning, but through knowledge and intelligence. (*Is. Os.* 1.351cd; [Babbitt, LCL])[11]

While such philosophical connections are important, it is also significant that the author uses language and ideas that connect very strongly with the popular worship of the goddess Isis. This universalizing presentation of wisdom utilizes the language and themes associated with the rhetoric and praises of Isis. Reese makes the case that "Ps-Solomon borrowed vocabulary and presentation from the literature of the Hellenized Isis cult which started to flourish in Egypt and the Aegean area during the second century BC as a result of efforts by the priests of Isis to enlarge her worship among the cosmopolitan Greek populace."[12] In the extant praises of Isis which come to us from antiquity we see that the Isis aretalogies

---

[9] David Winston, *The Wisdom of Solomon: A New Translation with Introduction and Commentary*, AB 43 (Garden City, NY: Doubleday and Company, 1979), 33–58.

[10] Winston suggests that the philosophical orientation of Wis is Middle Platonism and notes the significant points of contact with Philo. Ibid., 34, 59–63. See also James M. Reese, *Hellenistic Influence on the Book of Wisdom and Its Consequences*, AnBib 41 (Rome: Biblical Institute Press, 1970). Reese explains, "Ps-Solomon avoids the more concrete personification found in the Hebrew wisdom hymns; instead, he adopts a more universalizing and mystical approach that identifies Wisdom intimately with the nature and activity of God in the world" (41).

[11] Cf. Karl-Wilhelm Niebuhr, ed., *Sapientia Salomonis (Weisheit Salomos)*, SAPERE 27 (Tübingen: Mohr Siebeck, 2015), 121.

[12] Reese, *Hellenistic Influence*, 42. See also John S. Kloppenborg, "Isis and Sophia in the Book of Wisdom," *HTR* 75 (1982): 57–84.

follow the pattern of the classical Greek hymn. The author of Wis adopts this same strategy by treating (1) the nature of wisdom (6:22; 7:22–8:1); (2) a description of wisdom's powers and deeds (8:2–18); and (3) wisdom's benefits for humanity throughout history (Wis 10).[13] These features align well with the kinds of descriptive praises offered to Isis in encomiastic style. Reese concludes, "The picture of divine Wisdom that emerges bears remarkable similarities to the universalized Isis to whom pious contemporary pagans were turning as the great architect of their culture and the watchful guardian of civilization."[14] With the broader cultural context in view it is not difficult to see that the author of Wis has gone to great lengths to adapt the biblical portrait of wisdom and present the wisdom of God in ways that reflect the traits and powers of Isis.[15]

However, the author has not merely imitated the praises of Isis. His composition includes other unique features which tie back directly to Jewish biblical tradition.[16] The author's autobiographical sketch of his own search for wisdom (7:1–22a) is an addition to this tradition as is the inclusion of a prayer for wisdom (9:1–18). These additions enable the author to "engraft new ideas into traditional Jewish piety" enabling him to link universal wisdom with the God of the Jews.[17] Just as Isis was lauded for her saving role, the prayer shows that the final goal of the activity of wisdom is salvation (cf. Wis 9:18). As for the Jewish connections with this material, these sections framed within the two references to Solomon's act of prayer reflect similarities to other descriptions of the search for wisdom in Jewish wisdom literature. Sirach 51:13–30 is also a first-person account by a sage of his search for wisdom, with extensive discussion of wisdom's benefits. This sage, Ben Sira, also describes his prayer for wisdom:

---

[13] Reese, *Hellenistic Influence*, 43.

[14] Ibid., 45.

[15] It is noteworthy that in taking this approach, the author of Wis uses a different strategy than the allegorizing approach of Philo. Reese explains, "Through his abstract method of presenting divine Wisdom Ps-Solomon has found a means of preserving the absolute transcendence of the unique God of revelation while at the same time offering in attractive imagery the possibility of intimate personal communion with him. And he does so within the framework of traditional piety, without resorting to the allegorizing of Scripture to which Philo would later have recourse," ibid., 42.

[16] See, for example, Matthew E. Gordley, *Teaching through Song in Antiquity: Didactic Hymnody among Greeks, Romans, Jews and Christians*, WUNT 2/331 (Tübingen: Mohr Siebeck, 2011), 206–8.

[17] Reese, *Hellenistic Influence*, 44.

> While I was still young, before I went on my travels,
> I sought wisdom openly in my prayer (ἐν προσευχῇ μου).
> Before the temple I asked (ἠξίουν) for her,
> and I will search for her until the end. (51:13–14)[18]

Certainly the notion that wisdom is a gift of God is an idea with deep roots in the wisdom tradition. Prov 2:1–11 makes it clear that it is the Lord who gives wisdom (2:6) and that one must search wholeheartedly and even "cry out" for it (2:1–3). Both Wis and Sir depict their authors as earnestly seeking wisdom through prayer to God. As ideal sages, they then set a model for those who also desire to find wisdom. With the help of the writings of these sages, explicit prayer for wisdom seems to come more to the fore in the writings of the Second Temple period than in earlier writings. By the era of the New Testament, two letters in the Pauline tradition indicate the practice of praying for wisdom (cf. Col 1:9 and Eph 1:7), as does the letter of James which explicitly exhorts readers to ask God for wisdom (Jas 1:5).

This lengthy section in Wis 7:1–8:21, with its descriptions of wisdom, of Solomon's desire for wisdom, and of his act of prayer for wisdom sets the stage for the actual prayer to God for wisdom that follows in Wis 9:1–18. It is to the prayer itself that we now turn.

Solomon's Prayer (Wis 9:1–18)

Arguably the centerpiece of Wis is the prayer of Solomon in Wis 9:1–18.[19] This prayer concludes a lengthy section of the book comprising chapters 7–9 which Winston identifies as Solomon's speech.[20] The prayer also sets the stage for what will come in Wis 10 which outlines wisdom's saving role in history from Adam through the Exodus. To understand how the prayer functions in the context of the book as a whole we will draw attention to the similarities and differences between the prayer as recorded in the earlier biblical narratives, noting what is retained, left out, added, and changed from the biblical accounts. We will then note key features of the strophic structure of the prayer and how these convey the author's primary emphases.

---

[18] V. 14 ἀξιόω meaning request, ask "with implication of evaluation of need and ability of the potential giver to meet it" (BAGD, 94).

[19] Engel calls it the high point of the book: "Höhepunkt des ganzen Buches der Weisheit." Engel, "Gebet," 296.

[20] Winston, *Wisdom of Solomon*, 158.

Just as the narrative introduction to the prayer in Wis differs markedly
from the accounts in 1 Kgs 3 and 2 Chr 1, so does the prayer itself.[21]
A comparison between Wis 9:1–18 and the texts of the prayer in 1 Kgs
3:6–9 and 2 Chr 1:8–10 reveals a complex set of similarities and differences.[22] The connections to the biblical text are clear. These include:
direct address to God; an explicit request related to wisdom; God's
appointment of Solomon as king; mention of Solomon's father; a recognition of the weakness of Solomon (in 1 Kgs but not 2 Chr); Solomon
as servant (in 1 Kgs but not 2 Chr); mention of a throne (in 1 Kgs but
not 2 Chr); necessity of wisdom to be able to judge justly (in 1 Kgs
but not 2 Chr).

Some elements in the earlier biblical texts are left out of the prayer in
Wis 9. For example, while Solomon's "father" is mentioned just once
in Wis 9:12, the biblical text places a strong emphasis on "my father
David," repeating it (1 Kgs 3:6 and 7 and 2 Chr 1:8 and 9). The name
of David is excluded in Wis following the author's style in avoiding
proper names throughout the whole book. This stylistic device lends
a note of universality to Wis and here also serves to de-emphasize the
Davidic connections.[23] The notion of Israel's being "chosen" is also left
out of the prayer in Wis 9.

Other elements are added that are not found in the biblical precedents.
For example, the command of God for Solomon to build the temple
(9:8), while drawn from the biblical text, is not from the request for

---

[21] For an extended analysis see Gilbert, "Structure," 321–6; Newman, "Democratization
of Kingship," 313–7.

[22] Note that the comparison between the two biblical accounts themselves (1 Kgs 3:6–9
and 2 Chr 1:8–10) is also instructive, shedding insight on the distinctive perspectives
and emphases of the two historians. On this, see Gilbert, "Structure," 321–3.

[23] Along those lines, there is some ambiguity that the father mentioned in Wis may not
be David at all but rather God. At the very least the reference to "my father" is ambiguous and capable of carrying a double meaning. The use of the image of the throne in
three places in the prayer (vv. 4, 10, and 12) also may support this. In 1 Kgs 3:6 the
throne is mentioned only once and it is the "throne of my father David." In Wis 9:4
and 10 the throne that is mentioned is the heavenly throne of God by which wisdom
sits. After those first two uses of throne, the third is in Wis 9:12, the ambiguous "throne
of my father." As the third of three throne references this could again be the divine
throne of God his father; or in allusion to 1 Kgs 3:6 it could be referring to the earthly
throne of David. In support of this as a reference to the throne of God his father, we
can note that the people of Israel are identified in the prayer as "your sons and daughters" (v. 7) which is an addition to the biblical text. This may be a way that Solomon
is identified with the people, or vice versa. Solomon, as with all people, is a son of God.
When he refers to being worthy of "the throne of my father" it could then very well
be to be worthy of God.

wisdom in 1 Kgs 3 but from Solomon's later prayer of dedication of the temple (1 Kgs 8:23–53). Along with that addition, the reference to the temple being a copy of the "holy tent prepared from the beginning" (Wis 9:8) is a further addition. Other additions include: praise of God for creating the world by wisdom, and the presence of wisdom during creation (9:1–3, 9); the expanded descriptors of wisdom (9:9, 11); the idea that wisdom sits by the throne, is in heaven, and is equated with the holy spirit from on high (9:4, 9, 10, 17); and the more general statements that *all* people need wisdom, even the most perfect, and that wisdom is necessary to learn the will of God (9:6, 13–18). Further, in 9:9, 10, and 18 we encounter the concept of what is pleasing in your sight (ἀρεστόν; εὐάρεστον) and are told that wisdom understands it and therefore is the key for Solomon and for humans to be able to learn it.

Some elements of the prayer reflect the earlier biblical prayers but modify them in significant ways. For example, in 9:7 the expression "your people" is used but also expanded through synonymous parallelism with the phrase "your sons and daughters." Importantly, in Wis 9 it is not only Solomon who rules but all humans have dominion, rule, and judgment (Wis 9:2–3). The verb κρίνω "to judge" which is assigned to humanity (not Solomon) in Wis 9:3 is the same action that was ascribed to Solomon alone in 1 Kgs 3:9 and 2 Chr 1:10.

Another example of expansion relates to the concept of the throne. "Throne" is mentioned three times in Wis 9 in vv. 4, 10, and 12. In 1 Kgs 3:6 it is the throne of David, while in Wis 9:4 and 10 it is God's throne ("your throne"). In Wis 9:12 it is "the throne of my father." While seemingly a reference to David's throne, as noted above there is some degree of ambiguity here. At the very least the three repetitions of the term "throne" move the focus away from the earthly throne (sole focus of 1 Kgs) to the heavenly throne where wisdom dwells (major focus of Wis 9). A similar dynamic seems to be at play with the reference to the temple, where Wis 9 mentions the earthly temple but immediately shifts the focus from the earthly temple to the heavenly one (v. 8).

A particularly significant change is that the request for wisdom is quite different. To begin with, in the LXX of 2 Chr 1:10 it is σοφία and σύνεσις while in 1 Kgs 3:9 it is for "a heart to hear and judge justly" without the explicit mention of wisdom. And even though in 2 Chr Solomon asks explicitly for wisdom, in Wis 9 we see that the nature of that wisdom is identified more specifically as "your wisdom" (see 9:2, 4, 6, 9, and 17).[24]

---

[24] Gilbert, "Structure," 325–6.

These additions, omissions, and expansions are enough for us to identify that the author of the prayer has more in mind than just re-presenting
the biblical text. A more explicit focus on divine wisdom, on all of
humanity rather than just on Solomon, and on the frailty of humanity
apart from wisdom are all apparent. Many of the additions and changes
have the composite effect of creating a correspondence between
the works of God by wisdom, the works of Solomon by wisdom, and the
works of humanity by wisdom—a correspondence that is not in view in
the original biblical prayers. The following survey of the contents of the
prayer in light of its strophic structure will help us to gain further clarity
on what the author's interests are.[25]

Here we can summarize key features of each strophe and then draw
conclusions about the overall message and function of the prayer. The
first strophe, vv. 1–6, begins with an appeal to God's formation of the
world by wisdom, and his granting royal dominion not to Solomon but
to all humanity. This appeal to God's creative work in the world has the
effect of serving as an invocation reflecting Greco-Roman prayer conventions. Within this first strophe, Solomon explicitly asks for God to "Give
me the wisdom that sits by your throne." Here we encounter the request
and can observe that it is not simply for an understanding heart (as in
Kings) or wisdom and intelligence (as in Chronicles) but God's wisdom.[26] The strophe continues with an emphasis on Solomon's weakness
(v. 5) and the inability of any human to attain any reputation without
God's wisdom. And in this we see themes that are repeated in the other
two strophes. Winston draws out the theme of this strophe as "without
wisdom no human enterprise can succeed."[27]

The second strophe, vv. 7–12, shifts from humans broadly speaking to
Solomon specifically. Following Winston the strophe can be summarized
as follows: without wisdom Solomon could not reign.[28] The strophe
begins with reference to God's choosing of Solomon to be king, to be
judge of the people, and to build the temple (vv. 7–8). These actions are
those that Solomon will refer to as "my works" in the corresponding
section at the end of this strophe (v. 12). The strophe moves next to comments about wisdom's being with God and present when God made the
world, as well as understanding what pleases God and what is right (v. 9).

---

[25] In his detailed and persuasive literary analysis of the prayer of Solomon in Wis 9,
Gilbert outlined a chiastic structure embedded within a three strophe prayer.
[26] Ibid.
[27] Winston, *Wisdom of Solomon*, 200.
[28] Ibid., 203.

As with the opening lines of the strophe, these lines also have their corresponding parallel in the second half of the strophe in vv. 10b–11. In those lines Solomon looks forward to wisdom laboring at his side, to learning what pleases God, as he asserts that she knows "all things" and will guide and guard him. Those observations frame the center of the strophe (and the center of the entire prayer) which is the request for God to:

> Send her forth from the holy heavens,
> And from the throne of your glory send her. (v. 10a)

This marks the second explicit request for wisdom in the prayer. From these parallel lines, the strophe moves to unfold the remainder of the chiasm, as noted above. Notably, wisdom "who knows your works" is the one who will enable "my works" to be acceptable (cf. v. 9 and v. 12). The structure of the strophe makes a clear parallel between God's works ("your works," v. 9) and Solomon's works ("my works," v.12). These parallels suggest that as God created the world by wisdom, so Solomon would build the temple by wisdom.[29]

The third strophe, vv. 13–18, reflects similar ideas, but this time through a series of rhetorical questions and more of a philosophical reflection on the weakness of humanity.[30] The strophe shows that it is divine wisdom that brought salvation to humanity.[31] As with the other strophes, chiastic elements can be observed within it.[32] The central lines of the strophe are framed with double questions related to learning the counsel of God (v. 13; vv. 16–17). Also in chiastic correspondence to one another the third strophe contains the only third-person plural pronouns in the prayer (v. 15: "our designs are likely to fail;" v. 16 "we can hardly guess at what is on earth"), thereby shifting the focus away from Solomon and again back to all humanity. The first-person plural pronouns sharpen that effect by joining Solomon, a frail human being, with all others. The strophe ends with a broad statement bringing all humanity back into focus and introducing the theme of salvation. Winston notes that here in v. 18 is the first mention of σώζω in the book, but that the saving power of God will now be a recurring theme of the remainder

---

[29] Gilbert, "Structure," 330.

[30] Winston, *Wisdom of Solomon*, 206–7. Central to the third strophe is the Platonic philosophical motif about a perishable body weighing down the soul and an earthly tent burdening the thoughtful mind. There are two references to a tent in the prayer. The first is a reference to the temple being a copy of the heavenly tent (v. 8b). The second is this reference to an earthly tent weighing down the thoughtful mind (v. 15).

[31] Ibid., 207.

[32] Gilbert, "Structure," 308–10.

of the book.[33] This concluding verse also corresponds neatly with 9:1–3. Based on that correspondence Gilbert points out two poles of creation and salvation, both of which depend on wisdom.[34] Furthermore, the tri-colon that ends strophe two (v. 12) refers to Solomon's work, while a similar tri-colon ends the third strophe (v. 18) and refers to all of the devout in history who were saved by wisdom. Again, the clear expansion of scope from Solomon to all is unmistakable.

As noted above, this three strophe concentric structure points to the first two lines of 9:10 as the central pivot of the prayer: "Send her forth from the holy heavens, and from the throne of your glory send her." This line captures in synonymous parallelism the key features of the prayer and constitutes its central theme: wisdom is inaccessible to humans but resides with God and must be given as a gift. This is reinforced and supported by the introduction to the prayer (8:21), and also by 9:4 (the first request for wisdom) and 9:17 (a restatement of the request by a negative rhetorical question about the hopelessness of learning God's ways if God has not sent his wisdom). The connections between these verses alone are intriguing, not to mention the numerous parallels and connections with each strophe and between the strophes.[35]

As we have seen, although ostensibly the prayer is Solomon's asking for wisdom, the development of the prayer outlines a much wider scope embracing a paradigm for all of humanity. Newman's analysis provides an intriguing understanding of the way this prayer works. She shows that Solomon's prayer demonstrates and emphasizes the accessibility of God outside of the temple.[36] The changes to the original prayers, the raising of the status of all humanity as rulers and not just Solomon, and the diminishment of the role of the earthly temple and the monarchy, show that the message of the prayer is that wisdom is available to all who ask for it.[37]

---

[33] Winston, *Wisdom of Solomon*, 209.

[34] Gilbert, "Structure," 330.

[35] In addition to some of the parallels noted above see the many connections illuminated in Gilbert, "Structure," 305–20.

[36] Newman writes, "Solomon models the most important vehicle for discerning the will of God and obtaining the spirit of Wisdom: communicating with God not through sacrificial offering in the temple but through praise and petition" (328). In addition, "Wisdom is available to those who live righteously by doing the will of God and the means for acquiring wisdom is through prayer." Newman, "Democratization of Kingship," 327–8.

[37] Others draw the same conclusion, approaching the question from different angles. See, for example, Michael Kolarcik, "Sapiential Values and Apocalyptic Imagery in the

Once one recognizes this point, one can observe a contrast with other texts in the Solomonic tradition. For example, the Psalms of Solomon, composed in Jerusalem in roughly the same time period, perhaps a little later, demonstrates a deep concern for the temple. In that text prayer is oriented around the temple.[38] Righteousness in terms of purity and correct treatment of the temple, as part of the covenant relationship, is the critical foundation for successful prayer. God will answer prayer at the temple because of his covenant faithfulness. That idea is not the focus in Wis. And this element of prayer to God apart from the temple is one that plays out in references to prayer in the remainder of the book as well. As we will see, the remaining references are all to prayers made apart from the temple.

As much as it is obvious that the author draws heavily on the earlier Jewish traditions, in the wider context of Greco-Roman prayer, the contents of the prayer are also instructive. Thematic connections with Isis aretalogies may be observed here in the way in which wisdom is praised. The culmination of the prayer—the recognition of the salvific function of wisdom (9:18)—is a major theme of the praises of Isis. The "Ode to Wisdom's Saving Role in History" which follows in Wis 10 illustrates what the prayer suggests: the salvific power of wisdom is available to the righteous and has saved them throughout history.

At this point we may note that the author of Wis has already used the figure of Solomon in some very interesting ways. First, the author has drawn on the figure of Solomon as a revered person from Israel's past and has focused primarily on the one attribute of wisdom, both Solomon's request for it and his wise rule. Though this wisdom dimension of Solomon's reputation is noted in the Second Temple period, it is not the primary feature of his portrayal.[39] Wis thus presents a unique portrait of

---

Wisdom of Solomon," in *Studies in the Book of Wisdom*, ed. Géza G. Xeravits and József Zsengellér, JSJSup 142 (Leiden: Brill, 2010), 23–36, esp. 32–3.

[38] See Brad Embry, "Prayer in Psalms of Solomon or The Temple, Covenantal Fidelity, and Hope," in *Studies in Jewish Prayer*, ed. Robert Hayward, JSSSup 17 (Oxford: Oxford University, 2005), 89–99. While the temple is more of a focus in Pss. Sol., there is also some prayer apart from the temple. See Stefan Schreiber, "Can Wisdom be Prayer? Form and Function of the Psalms of Solomon," in *Literature or Liturgy? Early Christian Hymns and Prayers in Their Literary and Liturgical Context in Antiquity*, ed. Clemens Leonhard and Hermut Löhr, WUNT 2/363 (Tübingen: Mohr Siebeck, 2014), 90–104, 100–1, who notes that the purity practices are apart from the temple (fasting, prayer) because the community is at some distance from the temple.

[39] See Pablo A. Torijano, *Solomon the Esoteric King: From King to Magus, Development of a Tradition*, JSJSup 73 (Leiden: Brill, 2002), 33–5. Ben Sira's praise of the ancestors includes a section on Solomon (Sir 47:12–22). Torijano suggests that the portrait of

Solomon when viewed in the wider context. In this way Solomon functions as an example. Second, the author has adapted the figure of Solomon as an ideal type, the sage, and thus someone who speaks to the
community in their present moment. Features of the presentation of wisdom and of Solomon's quest for wisdom, including the notion of praying
for wisdom, align closely to other early Jewish wisdom writings that
do not name Solomon. Third, and related, the negative dimensions of
Solomon's rule are not referenced in the prayer or in the introduction
leading up to the prayer. This aligns with some instances of Solomonic
discourse (e.g. Pss. Sol.) while differing from others (e.g. T. Sol.; cf. the
portrayal of Solomon in Sir).

If Solomon is both an example and a teacher in this text, he is not the
only example of prayer that the author of Wis puts forward. Both negative and positive examples of prayer feature in the third and final, lengthy
section of Wis (chs. 11–18). It is to the negative examples that we now
turn.

Prayer to Idols (Wis 13:17–14:1)

As good protreptic discourse Wis promotes adherence to one way of life
and discourages the reader from being led astray to other ways.[40] In the
portrayal of wisdom in the attractive flavors of Isis, readers are reminded
that God is the source of wisdom, and that it is wisdom that includes all
the saving powers that have been sought in other deities. Accordingly,
readers are urged to seek wisdom themselves, and to do so through
prayer. While the attributes and qualities associated with Isis are shown
to truly belong to the wisdom of God, specific practices of the worship
of Isis are not necessarily attacked directly. That being said, there are
some specific worship practices from other traditions that are attacked
directly in Wis, namely, the idol worship of the Egyptians. A striking
declamatory section is found in the third part of Wis in what has been
called an excursus on worship of idols (13:1–15:9).[41] Within the larger

---

Solomon in Ben Sira follows that of Kings in its main points: Youth/wisdom vs. old
age/folly. "Ben Sira insists, then, on a darker image of Solomon that goes against the
general post-exiled trend represented by Chronicles, Psalm 72, and Song of Songs,
which silence the negative traits and emphasize the positive ones" (35).

[40] On the genre of Wis as *logos protreptikos*, see the arguments in Winston, *Wisdom of
Solomon*, 18–20 and Reese, *Hellenistic Influence*, 117–21.

[41] Ibid., 11. For an analysis of the themes of chs. 13–15 as a whole, see Moyna McGlynn,
Divine Judgement and Divine Benevolence in the Book of Wisdom, WUNT 2/139
(Tübingen: Mohr Siebeck, 2001), 132–69.

context of these attacks, we find an additional and important reference to ancient practices of prayer: prayer to idols. As we will see, the issue appears not to be the act of prayer per se, but the one to whom a person prays. The passage reads:

> When he prays (προσευχόμενος) about possessions and his marriage and children,
> he is not ashamed to address (προσλαλῶν) a lifeless thing.
> For health he appeals (ἐπικαλεῖται) to a thing that is weak;
> for life he prays (ἀξιοῖ) to a thing that is dead;
> for aid he entreats (ἱκετεύει) a thing that is utterly inexperienced;
> for a prosperous journey, a thing that cannot take a step;
> for money-making and work and success with his hands
> he asks (αἰτεῖται) strength of a thing whose hands have no strength.
> Again, one preparing to sail and about to voyage over raging waves calls upon (ἐπιβοᾶται) a piece of wood more fragile than the ship that carries him.
> (Wis 13:17–14:1)

Here we can make note of both the verbs and what is prayed for. One verb used here in common with Solomon's description of his own act of prayer is ἐπικαλέω (used in 7:7 and here in 13:17) in the sense of calling upon a deity, which as noted above is common in Jewish, Christian, and Greco-Roman writings. A second verb, προσεύχομαι, shares the *euche* root which Solomon uses in 7:7 to describe his prayer. The verb αἰτέω is used in this section to describe asking an idol for strength (13:18) but it is also used to describe the Israelites' asking for meat in the wilderness (cf. 19:11). The other verbs here (προσλαλέω, ἀξιόω, ἱκετεύω, and ἐπιβοάω) are not used elsewhere in Wis.

The rich tapestry of verbs used for prayer do not appear to target specific types of prayer as problematic. Rather, the focus is on the nature of the one to whom one prays. In addition, McGlynn has noted a contrast between the specific personal benefits that are asked for in this passage as compared to Solomon's prayer for wisdom itself, which is the source of all such benefits. She explains, "Not only is his idol incapable of delivering that which he requests, as the irony of vv. 17–19 makes plain, but additionally, the form of his petition shows that he has misunderstood life's goals. He does not search for virtue alone, but wishes to acquire the benefits of virtue (goods)."[42] This image of the one who prays to idols is thus set in stark contrast to Solomon himself who preferred

[42] Ibid., 147.

wisdom over earthly benefits such as power, riches, and health (cf. 7:7–12).

Without a doubt the critique of idol worship has a strong foundation in biblical literature. Isa 45:20b offers a good early example:

> They have no knowledge – those who carry about their wooden idols, and keep on praying to a god that cannot save.

In early Jewish writings, the author of Wis is not alone in this critique, particularly of the worship practices of the Egyptians. Philo offers a particularly harsh denunciation of idol worship in *Decal.* 66–76.[43] But while the whole context is reflective of the broader Jewish critique of idol worship, this passage and its critique also fits well within a Hellenistic context.[44]

If the focal point of 13:17–14:1 is the folly of prayer to idols, several portions of the remainder of the book point to the importance of prayer, thanks, and praise to the one true God.

Prayer and Praise in the Exodus (Wis 10:20; 11:4; 16:27–29; 18:9, 21; 19:9)

The third major section of Wis (chs. 11–19) consists of a retelling of events of the Exodus through a series of seven antitheses, with two excurses.[45] If the elaborate section on prayer to idols included in the second excursus makes clear the utter folly of praying to idols, several other references in this third section of the book promote the importance of prayer and praise directed to God. The seven antitheses show God's punishment of the Egyptians in contrast to the deliverance of the Israelites, drawing out important lessons for the reader.[46] Though prayer is not the primary focus of this section, explicit references to prayer do occur throughout. In addition to brief references where the act of prayer is mentioned in passing (e.g., 11:4), the author includes several more

---

[43] Niebuhr, *Sapientia Salomonis*, 129.

[44] The Jewish prophets were not the only ones to criticize such practices. The philosophical critique of idol worship was one strand of ancient understanding. A prime example can be found in the writings of Lucian of Samosata. For how the critique fits as part of protreptic discourse, see Reese, *Hellenistic Influence*, 120–1.

[45] Winston, *Wisdom of Solomon*, 11–2.

[46] Reese identifies the author's didactic use of history as a major theme of the book as a whole. "This didactic use of history, making concrete historical acts of divine intervention in the past serve as types of man's eternal salvation, shifts the center of God's saving activity to the arena of the entire world" (Reese, *Hellenistic Influence*, 144–5).

elaborate sections on prayer and praise. The fourth antithesis, focusing on God's miraculous provision of manna (16:24–29), is interpreted symbolically to provide a lesson specifically about morning prayer. The sixth antithesis, focusing on the death of the Egyptians and the deliverance of the Israelites through the Red Sea, alludes to liturgical traditions including Passover and Aaron's intercession on behalf of the people. Taken together, these references to prayer make explicit what is modeled earlier in the text by "Solomon" in his own prayer: God is the true source of wisdom and praying to God for wisdom is an essential prerequisite to experiencing God's saving power (9:18).

The first explicit mention of prayer is a brief but telling one. As part of a series of descriptions of God's rescuing work on behalf of his people through elements of nature, the author recounts the provision of water from a rock in 11:4:

> When they were thirsty, they called upon you (ἐπεκαλέσαντό σε)
> and water was given them out of flinty rock,
> and from hard stone a remedy for their thirst.

The verb used here is one of the verbs used to describe Solomon's own act of prayer for wisdom (7:7). It is also used with reference to prayer to idols in 13:17 (appealing for health to a thing that is weak). The lesson is clear: the people were in need; they prayed; and God provided for their need. The provision of water from the rock aligns with the overarching point of the section that God punished their enemies through the same features of creation by which he provided for God's children. But the inclusion of this act of calling upon God, which is not necessary for the specific point that the author is making (i.e., the logic works without the mention of prayer), suggests that the act of praying is one that he wanted his readers to have in view.

In Wis 16 we encounter the most explicit and pointed reference to prayer as a practice in which the devout should participate. In the fourth of the seven antitheses, the Egyptians' being plagued by thunderstorms is set against the feeding of Israel by a rain of manna (16:15–29). A very distinctive cosmology lies behind this in which creation favors the righteous and adapts on their behalf.[47] However, the author uses this antithesis not only to make a point about how creation works, but also to point

---

[47] This cosmology can be seen in Wis 16:24–26: "For creation, serving you who made it, exerts itself to punish the unrighteous, and in kindness relaxes on behalf of those who trust in you. Therefore at that time also, changed into all forms, it served your all-nourishing bounty, according to the desire of those who had need."

readers to the importance of the word of the Lord (16:26) and to prayer
(16:28). According to 16:26 these changes in nature occurred:

> so that your children, whom you loved, O Lord, might learn
> that it is not the production of crops that feeds humankind
> but that your word (τὸ ῥῆμά σου) sustains those who trust in you.

Here we see the manna episode interpreted and given a clear didactic
slant: this happened to show the importance of the word of the Lord as
a source of sustenance for those who trust God. This certainly draws
upon biblical precedents, most clearly Deut 8:3, which already has
the didactic emphasis. But in one of several interesting adaptations of the
original, for the author of Wis it is not "bread" as in Deut 8:3 but rather
"the production of crops" (v. 26).[48] In this shift we may see again
a subtle but clear contrast to Isis who is associated, among many other
things, with the production of crops.[49] When one considers the numerous
qualities of Isis for which divine wisdom is praised above in chs. 7–10,
this implicit contrast stands out a little more clearly.[50]

Immediately following this lesson about the word of God is a short
section about giving thanks and prayer to God (Wis 16:27–29). As above,
we will see that the point of the occurrence was so that the people of God
might learn a lesson:[51]

> For what was not destroyed by fire
> was melted when simply warmed by a fleeting ray of the sun,
> to make it known that one must rise before the sun to give you thanks
> (ἐπ᾽ εὐχαριστίαν σου),
> and must pray to you (ἐντυγχάνειν σοι) at the dawning of the light;
> for the hope of an ungrateful person will melt like wintry frost,
> and flow away like waste water.

Here the author teaches the reader that it is necessary both to give thanks
and to pray, and to do so at the rising of the sun. The term for prayer here
is ἐντυγχάνειν (16:28), one of the terms the author used above in 8:21
to describe Solomon's act of praying for wisdom. The noun εὐχαριστίαν
is used for the first and only time here.[52] Sharpening the contrast between

---

[48] For analysis of the adaptations, see Engel, "Gebet," 302.

[49] Maroneia inscriptions: I. Aeg. Thrace E205, 36.

[50] Reese, *Hellenistic Influence*, 46–9.

[51] "Another example of our author's eagerness to uncover the symbolic meaning behind physical events whenever he is able to do so." Winston, *Wisdom of Solomon*, 301.

[52] The verb εὐχαριστέω is used in 18:2 but not in the sense of giving thanks to God, but rather the Egyptians' being thankful that the Israelites were not exacting revenge on them for their cruelty.

the devout who pray and give thanks and those who are ungrateful is a play on words between giving thanks (εὐχαριστίαν), an ungrateful person (ἀχαρίστου), and waste water (ὕδωρ ἄχρηστον).[53]

This notion of calling on the Lord in prayer in the morning is not unique to Wis, although connecting it to the manna narrative certainly seems to be.[54] Ben Sira describes the ideal sage along similar lines:

> He sets his heart to rise early to seek the Lord who made him,
> and to petition the Most High;
> he opens his mouth in prayer and asks pardon for his sins. (Sir 39:5)

This emphasis on prayer and giving thanks at dawn can be found in another instance of Solomonic discourse. Psalm of Solomon 6 describes the righteous person who calls on the Lord, including when he arises from his sleep.[55] Here we may note with interest that the initiates of Isis prayed to her as well at a set time, but in the evening, "at the rising of the stars" (P.Oxy. XI 1380 159–161).[56] It may well be again, as with the crops, a subtle contrast with the worship of Isis is implied.

The concluding lines of this section are important with their emphasis on the hope of an ungrateful person melting away, again reinforcing the importance of gratitude. With this connection the author returns to a theme that was introduced earlier in the first section of Wis.[57] Thus, with both a positive and negative example, gratitude and trusting are put forward as desired qualities with the actions of relying on the word of the Lord, praying, and giving thanks in the morning as their practical manifestation.

In the sixth antithesis (18:5–25) the firstborn sons of the Egyptians are destroyed but Israel is protected and glorified. This section includes an explicit reference to the prayer of Aaron on behalf of the Israelites when,

---

[53] Noted by Engel, "Gebet," 303.

[54] Philo interprets the manna along a different line. See ibid., 302.

[55] For a list of other references to morning prayer, see Niebuhr, *Sapientia Salomonis*, 132. He includes also Let. Aris. 304–305; T. Jos. 3:6; Philo, *Contempl.* 27; and Josephus, *B.J.* II 128, among others.

[56] Cited in Reese, *Hellenistic Influence*, 49. Josephus also speaks to this, but suggests the importance of giving thanks both at dawn and in the evening: "Twice every day, at the dawn thereof, and when the hour comes for turning to repose, let all acknowledge before God the bounties which he has bestowed on them through their deliverance from the land of Egypt: thanksgiving is a natural duty, and is rendered alike in gratitude for past mercies and to incline the giver to others yet to come." (*Ant.* 14.212) Cited in Jerome H. Neyrey, *Give God the Glory: Ancient Prayer and Worship in Cultural Perspective* (Grand Rapids: Eerdmans, 2007), 50.

[57] Engel, "Gebet," 303.

in the wilderness, they began to worship the golden calf (cf. Num 17:1–13). The author's primary point is, once more, that God rescued his chosen people, but it is significant for our purposes that it was accomplished through prayer (v. 21). The author writes:

> For a blameless man was quick to act as their champion;
> he brought forward the shield of his ministry,
> prayer (προσευχὴν) and propitiation by incense;
> he withstood the anger and put an end to the disaster,
> showing that he was your servant.

Here, προσευχή is the noun used to describe his prayer.[58] Unlike the interpretation of the manna in the wilderness which had symbolic meaning, the prayer of Aaron seems to be taken historically with no symbolic significance attached to it. This makes sense given the author's earlier emphases about the efficacy of prayer in crying out to God and receiving deliverance.[59] Presenting this episode without symbolic meaning suggests that Aaron may be seen as another exemplary model for the reader or at the very least an example of the importance of prayer. The qualities noted here are that he was blameless and a servant of God, qualities which the reader is thereby invited to value as well.[60]

In addition to the explicit references to prayer noted above, the sixth antithesis also includes a reference to other aspects of liturgical practice including sacrifices and the singing of praise. In 18:9 we read about the sacrifice and praise in the context of Passover (cf. Exod 12:1–28, 43–50):

> For in secret the holy children of good people offered sacrifices (ἐθυσίαζον),
> and with one accord agreed to the divine law,
> so that the saints would share alike the same things,
> both blessings and dangers;
> and already they were singing the praises of the ancestors (πατέρων ἤδη προαναμέλποντες αἴνους).

The phrase πατέρων ἤδη προαναμέλποντες αἴνους, "raising a chant of the praises of the fathers," in 18:9 is an interesting one.[61] Philo speaks

---

[58] Note that two other references to the *euch-* root are in 7:7, where Solomon describes his act of prayer using the verb προσεύχομαι, and in 13:17 in reference to the prayers of Egyptians to idols.

[59] For a detailed analysis of this episode, see Engel, "Gebet," 303–11.

[60] Interestingly, only three individuals in the LXX are called "blameless" using this term, and they all are described as interceding in prayer for others: Abraham, Job, and Esther. See discussion in ibid., 305.

[61] See Winston, *Wisdom of Solomon*, 316. Cf. 2 Chr 30:21; 35:15; Jub. 49:6.

in a similar manner about fulfilling "with prayers and hymns the custom handed down by their fathers" (*Spec.* 2.148).[62] Though the practice of praise is not the focus of this study, it is significant to note that this reference to praise (αἶνος) is not an isolated one in Wis but connects with a thread that runs through the book. The Ode to Wisdom's Saving Role in History (10:1–21), itself a narrative of praise with features of didactic hymnody, concludes with praise:[63]

> Therefore the righteous plundered the ungodly;
> they sang hymns (ὕμνησαν), O Lord, to your holy name,
> and praised with one accord (ἤνεσαν ὁμοθυμαδόν) your defending hand. (10:20)

The importance of this particular reference to praising God can be seen in that it is echoed again in the concluding verses of Wis 19:

> For they ranged like horses,
> and leaped like lambs,
> praising you (αἰνοῦντές σε), O Lord, who delivered them. (19:9)

Both verses mark the only other two uses of the verb αἰνέω in Wis and form an inclusion for the lengthy final section of the book. Praise for God's acts of deliverance thus provides a broader context for understanding the practices of prayer that we have examined.

In summary, in the second half of Wis we see clearly that prayer and praise both played a role in the Exodus: prayer, through Aaron's petition on behalf of the people, and praise as the people praised God for God's deliverance. The examples of righteous people in the Exodus thus provide a model for the righteous readers of Wis. In addition, events of the Exodus have symbolic meaning, teaching the people of Israel of the importance of trusting in God, relying on his word, giving thanks, and praying at dawn. Taken together, this set of explicit references to prayer and allusions to related liturgical activities provides reinforcement of the practice of morning prayer, giving thanks, celebration of Passover, reading of scripture, remembrance of Israel's past leaders, and communal praise.

---

[62] See also the references in Niebuhr, *Sapientia Salomonis*, 133.
[63] Gordley, *Teaching through Song in Antiquity*, 201–8.

Conclusion

Having surveyed the references to prayer found in Wis, we may now draw the following conclusions. First, from the rich treasury of Solomonic themes available, the author of Wis chose to emphasize Solomon as the ideal sage. As such, Solomon received his wisdom as a gracious gift of God not through any special merit of his own, but through fervent prayer (7:7; 8:21). This emphasis was made clear by the elaborate introduction to the prayer which uses five different terms to describe Solomon's prayer. In the biblical texts, the narrators report to us that Solomon simply asked for "a heart of understanding" or "wisdom and insight" in a conversation with God; but in Wis, Solomon himself tells us explicitly and emphatically that he prayed with his whole heart for the wisdom that is from God.

Second, the author crafted a prayer in Wis 9 that adapts aspects of Solomon's biblical prayer and adds to it in ways that reflect the conventions of Greco-Roman prayer and the emphases of the book as whole. Themes of the prayer support the author's focus on the universal availability of wisdom and of wisdom as the savior of the righteous. Notably, the prayer downplays the importance of the temple as well as the importance of the Davidic line. It instead shows the availability of wisdom and the need of wisdom for all humans.

Third, in a rhetorical flourish, the foolishness of prayer to idols is included in a large section critiquing Egyptian religious practices. Warnings like this are a standard feature of proptreptic discourse. The negative judgment of Egyptian practices serves to dissuade readers from abandoning their Jewish practices.

Fourth, it was increasingly popular to pray to Isis and praise Isis for her saving actions in peoples' lives in the first century BCE, yet Wis depicts the devout in biblical history praying to God, giving thanks to God, and praising God for the deliverance that comes through wisdom. This language that contests the place of Isis in Egyptian culture is seen most clearly in the introduction to the prayer (sections of Wis 7–8), the prayer itself (sections of Wis 9), and in the Ode to Wisdom's Saving Role in History (Wis 10). References in the second half of Wis also support this theme (cf. 16:26, 28).

Taken as a whole this set of themes point to the conclusion that Wis offers a unique combination of features of Solomonic discourse and prayer practices. Through the voice of Solomon the author uses examples from history, dissuasion, and exhortation to challenge readers to follow the model of Solomon, pray for wisdom, and continue the practices of the devout in history including prayer for wisdom and thankful praise for God's deliverance.

Bibliography

Aune, David E. "Prayer in the Greco-Roman World." Pages 23–42 in *Into God's Presence: Prayer in the New Testament*. Edited by Richard N. Longe-necker. McMaster New Testament Studies. Grand Rapids, MI: Eerdmans, 2001.

Embry, Brad. "Prayer in Psalms of Solomon or The Temple, Covenantal Fidel-ity, and Hope." Pages 89–99 in *Studies in Jewish Prayer*. Edited by Robert Hayward. JSJSup 17. Oxford: Oxford University, 2005.

Engel, Helmut. "Gebet im Buch der Weisheit." Pages 293–312 in *Prayer from Tobit to Qumran*: *Inaugural Conference of the ISDCL at Salzburg, Austria, 5 - 9 July 2003*. Edited by Renate Egger-Wenzel and Jeremy Corley. DCLY 2004. Berlin: de Gruyter, 2004.

Gilbert, Maurice. "La Structure de la Prière de Salomon (Sg 9)." *Bib* 51 (1970): 301–31.

Gordley, Matthew E. *Teaching through Song in Antiquity: Didactic Hymnody among Greeks, Romans, Jews and Christians*. WUNT 2/331. Tübingen: Mohr Siebeck, 2011.

Kloppenborg, John S. "Isis and Sophia in the Book of Wisdom." *HTR* 75 (1982): 57–84.

Kolarcik, Michael. "Sapiential Values and Apocalyptic Imagery in the Wisdom of Solomon." Pages 23–36 in *Studies in the Book of Wisdom*. Edited by Géza G. Xeravits and József Zsengellér. JSJSup 142. Leiden: Brill, 2010.

McGlynn, Moyna. *Divine Judgement and Divine Benevolence in the Book of Wisdom*. WUNT 2/139. Tübingen: Mohr Siebeck, 2001.

Newman, Judith H. "The Democratization of Kingship in Wisdom of Solomon." Pages 309–28 in *The Idea of Biblical Interpretation: Essays in Honor of James L. Kugel*. Edited by Hindy Najman and Judith H. Newman. JSJSup 83. Leiden: Brill, 2004.

Neyrey, Jerome H. *Give God the Glory: Ancient Prayer and Worship in Cultural Perspective*. Grand Rapids: Eerdmans, 2007.

Niebuhr, Karl-Wilhelm, ed. *Sapientia Salomonis (Weisheit Salomos)*. SAPERE 27. Tübingen: Mohr Siebeck, 2015.

Plutarch. *Moralia, Volume V*. Translated by Frank Cole Babbitt. LCL 306. Cam-bridge, MA: Harvard University Press, 1936.

Pulleyn, Simon. *Prayer in Greek Religion*. OCM. Oxford: Clarendon Press, 1997.

Reese, James M. *Hellenistic Influence on the Book of Wisdom and Its Conse-quences*. AnBib 41. Rome: Biblical Institute Press, 1970.

Schreiber, Stefan. "Can Wisdom be Prayer? Form and Function of the Psalms of Solomon." Pages 90–104 in *Literature or Liturgy? Early Christian Hymns and Prayers in Their Literary and Liturgical Context in Antiquity*.

Edited by Clemens Leonhard and Hermut Löhr. WUNT 2/363. Tübingen: Mohr Siebeck, 2014.

Torijano, Pablo A. *Solomon the Esoteric King: From King to Magus, Development of a Tradition*. JSJSup 73. Leiden: Brill, 2002.

Winston, David. *The Wisdom of Solomon: A New Translation with Introduction and Commentary*. AB 43. Garden City, NY: Doubleday and Company, 1979.

Winston, David. "Wisdom in the Wisdom of Solomon." Pages 149–64 in *In Search of Wisdom: Essays in Memory of John G. Gammie*. Edited by Leo G. Perdue, Bernard B. Scott, and William J. Wiseman. Louisville, KY: Westminster John Knox, 1993.

Witte, Markus. "Emotions in the Prayers of the Wisdom of Solomon." Pages 161–76 in *Ancient Jewish Prayers and Emotions: Emotions Associated with Jewish Prayer in and around the Second Temple Period*. Edited by Stefan C. Reif and Renate Egger-Wenzel. DCLS 26. Berlin: de Gruyter, 2015.

PRAYER AND SELF-MASTERY
IN SIRACH 22:27–23:6 LXX

Bradley C. Gregory

The presence of prayer in Ben Sira's book may be somewhat surprising given that the book is situated within traditional Jewish sapiential thought and its most prominent focus is on moral instruction. Yet, as several recent studies have shown, prayer plays an important role in Ben Sira's understanding of the sage.[1] In addition to various references to prayer as part of a life of wisdom throughout the book (e.g. 3:5; 7:10, 14; 17:25; 28:2; 34:29–31; 35:20–21; 37:15; 38:9; 39:5–6), Ben Sira also models this essential part of the sage's life by including three prayers in his book: 22:27–23:6; 36:1–22; and 51:1–12.[2] The first of these, a petition for God's help in achieving self-control, is particularly important for three reasons. First, not only is it the first prayer in the book, but it is also the only one that is an individual petition since 36:1–22 is a communal petition and 51:1–12 is a prayer of thanksgiving.[3] Whether

---

[1] For an overview, see Maurice Gilbert, "Prayer in the Book of Ben Sira: Function and Relevance," in *Prayer from Tobit to Qumran: Inaugural Conference of the ISDCL at Salzburg, Austria, 5–9 July 2003,* ed. Renate Egger-Wenzel and Jeremy Corley, DCLY 2004 (Berlin: de Gruyter, 2004), 117–34; and the full-length study of Werner Urbanz, *Gebet im Sirachbuch: Zur Terminologie von Klage und Lob in der griechischen Text-tradition,* Herders Biblische Studien 60 (Freiburg: Herder, 2009). Also valuable is Stefan Reif, "Prayer in Ben Sira, Qumran and Second Temple Judaism," in *Ben Sira's God: Proceedings of the International Ben Sira Conference, Durham—Ushaw College 2001,* ed. Renate Egger-Wenzel, BZAW 321 (Berlin: de Gruyter, 2002), 321–41.

[2] The authenticity of 36:1–22 has been doubted by some scholars, e.g. John J. Collins, *Jewish Wisdom in the Hellenistic Age,* OTL (Louisville: Westminster John Knox Press, 1997), 110–1; Samuel L. Adams, *Wisdom in Transition: Act and Consequence in Second Temple Instructions,* JSJSup 125 (Leiden: Brill, 2008), 164–9; and Burkard M. Zapff, *Jesus Sirach 25–51,* NEchtB 39 (Würzburg: Echter, 2010), 236. Others, however, argue that it was original, e.g. Maurice Gilbert, "Prayer in the Book of Ben Sira," 118; Johannes Marböck, "Das Gebet um die Rettung Zions Sir 36,1-22 (G: 33,1-13a; 36,16b-22) im Zusammenhang der Geschichtsschau Ben Siras," in *Memoria Jerusalem: Freundesgabe Franz Z. Sauer zum 70. Geburtstag,* ed. Johann Baptist Bauer and Johannes Marböck (Graz: Akademische Druck- und Verlagsanstalt, 1977), 93–115.

[3] Nuria Calduch-Benages, "Emotions in the Prayer of Sirach 22:27-23:6," in *Ancient Jewish Prayers and Emotions: Emotions Associated with Jewish Prayer in and around the Second Temple Period,* ed. Stefan C. Reif and Renate Egger-Wenzel (Berlin: de Gruyter, 2015), 149.

the individual petition in 22:27–23:6 should be taken as autobiographical (as 51:1–12 usually is) has been a matter of debate. While Sauer thinks it is a deeply personal prayer from Ben Sira's own experience, Gilbert believes it is not autobiographical and that the first-person form of the prayer is stylized.[4] A mediating position argues that the concern of the prayer may have been rooted in Ben Sira's own experience, but the prayer as we have it was crafted to be relevant to every person.[5] However one decides the issue of its autobiographical source, it seems safe to conclude that the inclusion of the prayer in Ben Sira's book suggests that he thought it broadly applicable and that it therefore reflects his understanding of anthropology and piety.

The second reason that the prayer in 22:27–23:6 is particularly significant is that, as Reiterer points out, its proximity to the center of the book suggests a heightened importance.[6] Given that the prayer's concern with sins of speech and passion introduces the following discussions of speech (23:7–15) and sexual sin (23:16–27), it is part of a structural complex that brings the first half of the book to completion.[7] If Corley is correct that the first edition of the book consisted of 1:1–23:27 + 51:13–30 then the focus of 22:27–23:27 on self-control in matters of speech and desire would have originally preceded the final exhortation to wisdom in 51:13–30.[8] In the latter passage Ben Sira notes that he sought wisdom through prayer (51:13–14), that his true desire and struggle was for her (51:15–21), and that his reward was a well-trained tongue (51:22). In other words, he describes himself as someone who achieved success in the struggle represented in 22:27–23:6. As the book was expanded, additional resonances would have been produced by contrasting the desolation that comes from a lack of self-control in 22:27–23:27 with the fruitfulness and life found in obedience to divine law and to Woman Wisdom in 24:1–34.[9] Thus, connections with both the central wisdom

---

[4] Georg Sauer, *Jesus Sirach/Ben Sira*, ATD Apokryphen 1 (Göttingen: Vandenhoeck & Ruprecht, 2000), 171; Gilbert, "Prayer in the Book of Ben Sira," 118.

[5] See Friedrich V. Reiterer, "Gott, Vater und Herr meines Lebens: Eine poetisch-stilistische Analyse von Sir 22,27–23,6 als Verständnisgrundlage des Gebetes," in Egger-Wenzel and Corley, *Prayer from Tobit to Qumran*, 137–70, 146.

[6] Friedrich V. Reiterer, "Gott, Vater und Herr meines Lebens," 137.

[7] Pancratius Beentjes, "Sir 22:27–23:6 in zijn Context," *Bijdr* 39 (1978): 144–51.

[8] Jeremy Corley, "Searching for structure and redaction in Ben Sira: An investigation of beginnings and endings," in *The Wisdom of Ben Sira: Studies on Tradition, Redaction, and Theology*, ed. Angelo Passaro and Giuseppe Bellia, DCLS 1 (Berlin: de Gruyter, 2008), 21–47, 41.

[9] See Nuria Calduch-Benages, "Ben Sira 23:27 – A Pivotal Verse," in *Wisdom for Life: Essays Offered to Honor Prof. Maurice Gilbert, SJ on the Occasion of His Eightieth*

poem in chapter 24 and the autobiographical conclusion of the book in chapter 51 imbue this prayer with special rhetorical importance.

The third reason the prayer in 22:27–23:6 is particularly significant for the overall teaching of Ben Sira is that it culminates a three-fold pattern in the first half of the book in which self-control in matters of speech and desire are juxtaposed. In Ben Sira's first major discussion of speech ethics he warns that the consequences for misuse of the tongue can be severe: disgrace, downfall, and condemnation (5:9–6:1). The stakes are so high that it is better to err on the side of silence than risk a misstep (5:12). Because this passage on speech ends with a reference to friends in 6:1, one might expect Ben Sira to move directly into the discussion of friendship in 6:5–17, especially since that passage begins by noting the importance of speech in friendship (6:5). Instead, however, Ben Sira includes a digression into the topic of unruly passion in 6:2–4 which parallels his worry about speech sins in three ways: both sins can lead to downfall, to disgrace, and to severe calamity. This tendency to place speech sins and the danger of passion in parallel continues in chapters 18–19. In 18:30–19:3 Ben Sira takes up the danger of desire, again noting the consequences of public disgrace (18:31) and destruction (19:3). He then pivots to discuss the destructive speech sins of gossip and slander (19:4–17) and even concedes that the tongue is so difficult to master that everyone fails at one time or another (19:16). The prayer in 22:27–23:6, especially insofar as it introduces the discussions of speech in 23:7–15 and sexual immorality in 23:16–27, then represents the third major instance in which Ben Sira places these topics in parallel. As we will see, the prayer in 22:27–23:6 is rhetorically structured to show that the dangers of the tongue and of improper desire are interconnected and so threatening that divine help is considered essential for mastering them.

In order to understand how prayer is related to this important theme of self-control in Ben Sira, we will first consider the description of the twin dangers of the tongue and desire in 22:27–23:6 and then turn to consider the role of prayer in overcoming them. This prayer, so important in the context of the book, is unfortunately not extant in the Hebrew. Because attempts to reconstruct the Hebrew on the basis of the Greek and Syriac are methodologically unsound, we will focus on the Greek version of this text while making reference to the Syriac and Latin versions where needed. Besides the fact that the Greek version of the book is completely

Birthday, ed. Nuria Calduch-Benages, BZAW 445 (Berlin: de Gruyter, 2014), 186–200.

extant (unlike the Hebrew) and is considered a very reliable version,[10] focusing on this version affords the opportunity to ask how the prayer in its Greek form would have been understood in its Hellenistic milieu where the topic of self-mastery was an important part of moral discourse.[11]

The Threats Addressed by the Prayer

The Greek text of the prayer, as found in Ziegler's critical edition,[12] and a translation read:[13]

22:27   τίς δώσει ἐπὶ στόμα μου φυλακὴν
        καὶ ἐπὶ τῶν χειλέων μου σφραγῖδα πανοῦργον
        ἵνα μὴ πέσω ἀπ' αὐτῶν
        καὶ ἡ γλῶσσά μου ἀπολέσῃ με
23:1   κύριε πάτερ καὶ δέσποτα ζωῆς μου
        μὴ ἐγκαταλίπῃς με ἐν βουλῇ αὐτῶν

---

[10] As is well known, the Greek translator concedes in his prologue that he took liberties with his Hebrew *Vorlage* (which itself was different from the Hebrew manuscripts that have survived and in all likelihood different from the *Vorlage* of those manuscripts); yet the Greek version is still of very high value and is considered by some to be the best version of the book *overall* since the extant Hebrew witnesses also reveal transmissional developments. See the discussion of the texts and text-forms of Ben Sira in Jan Liesen, *Full of Praise: An Exegetical Study of Sir 39,12–35,* JSJSup 64 (Leiden: Brill, 200), 5–25. Liesen concludes, "Although the Hebrew Vorlage of this Gk I can be shown to have been modified already, it (Hb I*) is still closer to the original than the Hebrew mss that represent Hb I. In short: 'despite...limitations, the Greek...constitutes, to this day, the major basis for study of Ben Sira'" (19, quoting Yigael Yadin, *The Ben Sira Scroll from Masada* [Jerusalem: Israel Exploration Society, 1965], 6). Similarly, Jeremy Corley concludes that, "since the Hebrew text is lacking for about one-third of the book (including most of Sir 16:27–30:10), and also has many corruptions where it has survived, the Greek version is generally viewed as the primary witness to the text of the book" (Jeremy Corley, "4.3 Greek of Ecclesiasticus/Ben Sira," in *The Textual History of the Bible vol. 2B: The Deuterocanonicals,* ed. Matthias Henze [Leiden: Brill, 2019], 214–31). In his introduction to Ben Sira in the same volume, Wright notes that "After more than a century of study of the Hebrew, scholars now largely agree that the extant Hebrew manuscripts *essentially* contain the Hebrew of the second-century book, even though all are also riddled to varying degrees with corruptions, scribal errors, and intentional scribal interventions, which often obscure earlier forms of the text, and that the Greek translation still preserves in many cases the best form of the text" (Benjamin G. Wright, "4.1 Textual History of Ben Sira," in Henze, *The Textual History of the Bible vol. 2B,* 187–98).

[11] For more on this kind of approach to the versions of Ben Sira and the reasons for it, see Pancratius Beentjes, "Some Major Topics in Ben Sira Research," in "*Happy the One who Meditates on Wisdom*" *(Sir. 14:20): Collected Essays on the Book of Ben Sira,* CBET 43 (Leuven: Peeters, 2006), 3–16, 3–6.

[12] Joseph Ziegler, *Sapientia Iesu Filii Sirach,* Septuaginta: Vetus Testamentum Graecum XII (Göttingen: Vandenhoek & Ruprecht, 1980), 230–1.

[13] Unless otherwise indicated, all translations are my own.

καὶ μὴ ἀφῇς με πεσεῖν ἐν αὐτοῖς
23:2   τίς ἐπιστήσει ἐπὶ τοῦ διανοήματός μου μάστιγας
        καὶ ἐπὶ τῆς καρδίας μου παιδείαν σοφίας
        ἵνα ἐπὶ τοῖς ἀγνοήμασίν μου μὴ φείσωνται
        καὶ οὐ μὴ παρῇ τὰ ἁμαρτήματα αὐτῶν[14]
23:3   ὅπως μὴ πληθυνθῶσιν αἱ ἄγνοιαί μου
        καὶ αἱ ἁμαρτίαι μου πλεονάσωσιν
        καὶ πεσοῦμαι ἔναντι τῶν ὑπεναντίων
        καὶ ἐπιχαρεῖταί μοι ὁ ἐχθρός μου
23:4   κύριε πάτερ καὶ θεὲ ζωῆς μου
        μετεωρισμὸν ὀφθαλμῶν μὴ δῷς μοι
23:5   καὶ ἐπιθυμίαν ἀπόστρεψον ἀπ' ἐμοῦ
23:6   κοιλίας ὄρεξις καὶ συνουσιασμὸς μὴ καταλαβέτωσάν με
        καὶ ψυχῇ ἀναιδεῖ μὴ παραδῷς με

22:27   Who will set a guard upon my mouth
                and on my lips a shrewd seal
        so that I may not fall because of them
                nor my tongue destroy me?
23:1   O Lord, Father and Master of my life,
        do not abandon me to their design;
                do not permit me to fall by them.
23:2   Who will apply whips on my thoughts
                and wise training on my heart
        so as not to spare (me) concerning my sins of ignorance
                nor overlook their sinful deeds,
23:3   lest my faults be multiplied
                and my sins may increase
        and I fall before my opponents
                and my enemy rejoice over me?
23:4   O Lord, Father and God of my life,
        do not give me haughty eyes
23:5   and turn away desire from me.
23:6   Let not the desire of the belly and sexual desire overcome me
                and do not hand me over to shameless appetite.

Careful studies by both Beentjes and Reiterer have shown that the prayer
is structured into two uneven, but parallel halves: 22:27–23:1 and

---

[14] While this is the reading of the Greek witnesses, it should probably be emended to
"my" (so also Calduch-Benages, "Emotions in the Prayer of Sirach 22:27-23:6," 148;
Patrick W. Skehan and Alexander Di Lella, *The Wisdom of Ben Sira: A New Translation with Notes by Patrick W. Skehan*, AB 39 [New York: Doubleday, 1987], 318).
Roger A. Bullard and Howard A. Hatton observe that for the Greek as it stands,
the antecedent of "their" would be the sins of ignorance in the previous line; thus, "the
sins of my ignorant errors" (*Sirach*, UBS Handbook Series [New York: United Bible
Societies, 2008], 464).

23:2–6.[15] Both portions begin with a rhetorical question (τίς) and a purpose clause (ἵνα μὴ), followed by an invocation of God (κύριε πάτερ) and prohibitions/imperatives, the first of which uses the emphatic form of μὴ + an aorist subjunctive verb. This paralleling of the stanzas suggests that the form of the prayer is a diptych which both introduces the following passages in 23:7–15 and 23:16–27 as well as implies that the threats addressed in each half share deep similarities.[16]

There is, however, a significant text-critical problem that affects the structure and interpretation of the passage. As the text stands in the Greek, the invocations of God in 23:1a and 23:4a disrupt the normal bicola structure. Notably, though, in the Syriac and Latin the line in 23:1b, "do not abandon me to their design," is found between 23:4a and 23:4b. Many commentators therefore move 23:1b to follow 23:4a, arguing that the agreement of the Syriac and Latin proves that was its original location and pointing out that this rearrangement also restores a normal bicola pattern to the prayer.[17] On the other hand, several scholars elect to retain the Greek sequence. Reiterer argues that little is gained by moving 23:1b and that doing so disrupts the poetic features of the passage. Further, he argues that the invocations of God deliberately disrupt the bicola structure in order to draw attention to God as the petitioner's only hope.[18] The issue is difficult to decide text-critically, but there are two interpretive consequences of following the present form of the Greek. First, the line "do not abandon me to their design" occurs in the first half of the prayer and therefore is to be related to the issue of speech rather than desire. Second, the invocations of God stand out structurally and as such also are enabled to function in a Janus-faced manner. They more easily can be heard both as the exclamatory answer to the rhetorical questions

---

[15] Beentjes, "Sir 22:27-23:6 in zijn Context," 145; Reiterer, "Gott, Vater und Herr meines Lebens," 139–59.

[16] Gilbert ("Prayer in the Book of Ben Sira," 117) suggests that technically 22:27–23:6 is a prayer that consists of two prayers, but it is better to lay the emphasis on the unitary nature of 22:27–23:6. The use of two rhetorical questions and invocations serves more to accent the similarities in how these threats are addressed than to distinguish two prayers.

[17] Examples include George H. Box and William O. E. Oesterley, "Sirach," in *The Apocrypha and Pseudepigrapha of the Old Testament*, ed. Robert H. Charles (Oxford: Clarendon Press, 1913), 1:268–517, 393; Norbert Peters, *Das Buch Jesus Sirach oder Ecclesiasticus*, EHAT 25 (Münster: Aschendorff, 1913), 184–5; and Skehan and Di Lella, *The Wisdom of Ben Sira*, 321.

[18] Reiterer, "Gott, Vater und Herr meines Lebens," 144, 155–7. Cf. James L. Crenshaw, "Sirach: Introduction, Commentary, and Reflections," *NIB* 5: 601–867, 749; and Johannes Marböck, *Jesus Sirach 1-23*, HThKAT (Freiburg: Herder, 2010), 265.

in 22:27 and 23:2–3 and as the personal address for the prohibitions/ imperatives which follow.[19] Both structurally and emotively these vocatives, therefore, serve as the anchors of the whole prayer.

In the first stanza of the prayer, 22:27–23:1, the threat concerns the loss of control of the tongue. Ben Sira expresses his worry with the generic mention of the terms "mouth," "lips," and "tongue". Elsewhere in his book he identifies specific speech acts that lead to a person's downfall: lying, slander, gossip, speaking rashly or carelessly, and the betrayal of secrets (cf. 5:9–6:1; 19:4–17; 20:1–8, 18–20, 24–26). In the most proximate passage, 23:7–15, he condemns improper use of the divine name and abusive, rash speech. In the Greek version of 23:13, lewd speech is also mentioned as unacceptable.[20] The general nature of the phrasing in 22:27 probably indicates that all of these speech sins are potentially in view as needing to be restrained. The meaning of 22:27c is unclear. Ziegler follows one uncial (V), one miniscule (46), the Latin, and the Syriac in reading ἀπ' αὐτῶν, "because of them."[21] The antecedent would then be "lips" and the sense would be that the lips are the means by which the person falls. However, all other Greek witnesses read ἀπ' αὐτῆς. On this reading, the pronoun could be anticipating "tongue" in the next line and would give largely the same sense: the tongue is the means by which the person falls.[22] On the other hand, the antecedent could be "guard" and give the sense that it is due to the guard that the person will *not* fall.[23] Either textual reading is possible, but in either case reading the line as indicating the lips or tongue as the instrument of falling would be more consistent with Ben Sira's rhetoric, as in 23:1c (cf. 5:13; 20:18; 28:18).[24] The consequences are expressed in terms of falling and destruction and these both refer to catastrophic personal ruin. Importantly, in this first half of the prayer the mouth and lips are imaged as a gate or portal such that they represent a liminal state between the

---

[19] Reiterer, "Gott, Vater und Herr meines Lebens," 147.

[20] The fact that neither the Syriac nor the Latin mentions lewd speech in this verse has suggested to some scholars that the Greek has introduced the idea, especially since it was a common concern in Greek discussions but not in Israelite/Jewish wisdom (see Jeremy Hultin, *Ethics of Obscene Speech*, NovTSup 128 (Leiden: Brill, 2008), 140–48).

[21] Ziegler, *Sirach*, 230.

[22] Marböck, *Jesus Sirach 1-23*, 264.

[23] Bullard and Hatton, *Sirach*, 462.

[24] Antonio Minissale, "The Metaphor of 'Falling': Hermeneutic Key to the Book of Sirach," in *The Wisdom of Ben Sira: Studies on Tradition, Redaction, and Theology*, ed. Angelo Passaro and Giuseppe Bellia, DCLS 1 (Berlin: de Gruyter, 2008), 235–75, 255–6.

interior life of a person and the external world.[25] As such they are metaphorically one step removed from the internal will and personified as
having an agency independent of and threatening to the speaker, an
important feature to which we will return below.

In the second stanza, 23:2–6, the threat concerns sinful desire, but the
description is more diversified in it specificity. In 23:2 Ben Sira identifies the interior life as what is in need of discipline, but the rhetorical
question includes mainly generic terms for wrongdoing. Yet, the rhetorical movement through 23:2–3 speaks to the tendency of these faults to
proliferate if undisciplined or unchecked, exactly the dynamic that is
characteristic of Ben Sira's description of desire (or sin more broadly)
elsewhere, including in the next passage (23:16) in which it is pictured
as a fire apt to blaze out of control (6:3–4; 9:8; cf. 3:30; 8:10; 16:6;
22:24; 28:10–11; 40:30). Moving to the petitionary portion of the second stanza (23:4–6), the terms for desire proliferate, rhetorically mirror-
ing the nature of sinful desire itself. In 23:4b–5 the terms μετεωρισμὸν
ὀφθαλμῶν and ἐπιθυμίαν are placed in parallel. While the latter is
a frequent term for desire (lexically neutral, but often used for improper
desire, as in 18:30–31), the meaning of the former is debated. Bullard
and Hatton, Crenshaw, and Schreiner all think that the phrase should be
taken in its most natural sense, "haughty eyes", i.e. pride.[26] The height
metaphor provides a natural counterpart to the consequence of "falling"
here and in other passages on the danger of pride (e.g. Isa 14; 1 Macc
1:1–7; 2 Macc 9:1–12; cf. Sir 10:6–18). However, others argue that the
sense is "brazen look" in the sense of a lustful stare. Calduch-Benages
points out that a similar phrase occurs in 26:9 as well as in Prov 6:5 and
4Q184 1:13–14 with this same sense and, further, the parallelism with
ἐπιθυμίαν in 23:5 suggests a sexual connotation here as well.[27] In addition, Skehan and Di Lella argue that this interpretation is strengthened
by the presence of a chiasm running across 23:4–6 in which "brazen
look" is paired with "shameless appetite."[28] Perhaps the ambiguity is
intentional since pride and sin/desire are closely aligned (10:12–13).
Further, as Balla observes, there is a close connection between sight and

---

[25] Noted by Sauer, *Jesus Sirach*, 171.

[26] Bullard and Hatton, *Sirach*, 465; Crenshaw, "Sirach," 749; Josef Schreiner, *Jesus
Sirach 1-24*, NEchtB 38 (Würzburg: Echter, 2002), 124.

[27] Calduch-Benages, "Emotions in the Prayer of Sirach 22:27-23:6," 151–2.

[28] Skehan and Di Lella, *The Wisdom of Ben Sira*, 322.

desire[29] and the use of this particular idiom allows the mention of such a stare to provide a wordplay with the theme of falling in the prayer (22:27 and 23:3).

The three terms in 23:6 are all conceptually connected. The first term, κοιλίας ὄρεξις, is literally "desire of the belly." Several scholars take this to refer to gluttony.[30] Others note that the Syriac has the sense of "fleshly lust" and take that to be the sense here as well.[31] In this regard it is worth noting that in Greco-Roman discourse, over-indulgence in the areas of food and drink and of sex, were often paired in discussions of self-control as two sides of the same coin. As Stowers explains, "in Greek thought, the stomach represents the bestial, wild, needy, and passionately desiring part of the human."[32] This was true in Hellenistic Judaism as well, where, for example, Philo identifies Sodom as replete with both gluttony and lust (*Abr.* 133–136).[33] Similarly, the Testaments of the Twelve Patriarchs warns that drunkenness and lust go hand-in-hand (T. Reu. 2–3; T. Jud. 14–16).[34] As Knust observes in relation to the pairing of these two in 1 Cor 6:12–13, "Gluttony and sexual excess often appear together as evidence of corruption and 'slavishness' in Greco-Roman sources. Allowing oneself to be mastered by either food or *porneia* was to fail in one's duties as a master of oneself and others. One cannot be a ruler of others if one cannot rule one's own belly and body."[35] Given that Ben Sira also treats gluttony and sexual temptation as interconnected in 9:1–9 and 19:2, the Greek translator may have intended the

---

[29] Ibolya Balla, *Ben Sira on Family, Gender, and Sexuality*, DCLS 8 (Berlin: de Gruyter, 2011), 52.

[30] For example, Balla, *Ben Sira on Family, Gender, and Sexuality*, 166; Bullard & Hatton, *Sirach*, 465; and Reiterer, "Gott, Vater und Herr meines Lebens," 152.

[31] So Box and Oesterley, "Sirach," 393; Calduch-Benages, "Emotions in the Prayer of Sirach 22:27-23:6," 152–3; Schreiner, *Jesus Sirach 1-24*, 124; Skehan and Di Lella, *The Wisdom of Ben Sira*, 318.

[32] Stanley K. Stowers, *A Rereading of Romans: Justice, Jews & Gentiles* (New Haven: Yale University Press, 1994), 49.

[33] From a time a little later than Philo, Knust quotes the Platonist Apuleius as describing an opponent as "a vile haunt and hideous habitation of lust and gluttony" (Jennifer Knust, *Abandoned to Lust: Sexual Slander and Ancient Christianity*, Gender, Theory and Religion Series [New York: Columbia University Press, 2006], 36).

[34] See Lewis J. Eron, "'That Women Have Mastery Over Both King and Beggar' (*TJud.* 15.5) — The Relationship of the Fear of Sexuality to the Status of Women in Apocrypha and Pseudepigrapha: 1 Esdras (*3 Ezra*) 3-4, Ben Sira, and the *Testament of Judah*," *JSP* 9 (1991): 43–66, 55–62.

[35] Knust, *Abandoned to Lust*, 78. Cf. "No wonder that Greco-Roman writers constantly link the appetite for food and sex with the weakening of men." Stowers, *A Rereading of Romans*, 50.

sense of κοιλίας ὄρεξις in 23:6 to be either gluttony or lust, or even as hinting at both. The important point is that the mention of "belly" in the context of illicit desire is quite natural as part of a Greek discourse on the need for self-mastery.

The second term, συνουσιασμός, is a *hapax*, but Balla and Calduch-Benages both make a compelling case that it is a euphemism for sexual intercourse, noting that its basic semantic meaning is "cohabitation" but it is used in 4 Macc 2:3 and the Greek translation of Aramaic Levi 6 to refer to sexual sin.[36] The final term of 23:6 is ψυχῇ ἀναιδεῖ, which means "unrestrained" or "shameless" in soul and Balla and Calduch-Benages likewise argue that because of its similar use in 26:11, ἀναιδεῖ here has a sexual connotation.[37]

In 23:2–6 the consequences for a lack of self-control mirror those of 22:27–23:1: falling and humiliation before one's enemies as well as internal subjection to one's base desires. As with the mouth in the first stanza, in the second stanza the power of desire metaphorically takes on a nearly independent agency that is pictured as conflicting with the will of the speaker. Importantly, he is worried about *both* the loss of social standing (23:3) *and* the loss of control over himself (23:5–6).[38] Or to put it another way, the consequentialist moral reasoning is both external and internal.[39]

How should Ben Sira's pairing of the dangers of the tongue and improper desire be understood? It seems clear by the parallel structuring of the prayer as well as the consistent pairing of these themes in his book (5:9–6:1 + 6:2–4; 18:30–19:3 + 19:4–17; and 23:7–15 + 23:16–27), that he perceived these threats as similar both in the severity of the threat and the catastrophic consequences for a lack of self-control in these are-as.[40] But further, these two areas also share a propensity to compound upon themselves and spiral out of control. While Jean Hadot has shown

---

[36] Balla, *Ben Sira on Family, Gender, and Sexuality*, 166; Calduch-Benages, "Emotions in the Prayer of Sirach 22:27-23:6," 153–4.

[37] Balla, *Ben Sira on Family, Gender, and Sexuality*, 166; Calduch-Benages, "Emotions in the Prayer of Sirach 22:27-23:6," 154.

[38] Noted by Balla, *Ben Sira on Family, Gender, and Sexuality*, 166.

[39] The combination of both of these in 22:27–23:6 is observed by Lawrence M. Wills, "Greek Philosophical Discourse in the Book of Judith?" *JBL* 135 (2015): 753–73, 764.

[40] It is perhaps also noteworthy, especially given the reference to the belly in the second stanza, that the mouth is the organ both of speaking and eating/drinking. See discussion of this link in the Hebrew Bible in Yael Avrahami, *The Senses of Scripture: Sensory Perception in the Hebrew Bible*, LHBOTS 525 (London: T&T Clark/Bloomsbury), 121–4.

convincingly that overall Ben Sira takes a view of free-will that is essentially voluntarist and that he does not espouse the rabbinic idea of an evil
יצר,[41] it is also true that some sins are understood by Ben Sira to pose
a particular danger because of their almost "magnetic" quality, both in
the tendency to commit them and in their propensity to take over the
person's will.[42] For speech, Ben Sira often exhorts his students to standard virtues like honesty, consistency, and gentleness, while condemning
standard vices like lying, gossip, and slander (e.g. 5:9–6:1; 19:4–17;
20:1–8; 27:16–21; 32:8). But at other times he shows an awareness that
people can "slip" with their tongues and fall into disaster (e.g. 20:18–20;
28:24–26), including within the passage immediately after this prayer
(23:13–15).[43] In one place Ben Sira laments that occasional slips of the
tongue are impossible to avoid, even for the wisest of people (19:13–17).
A similar anxiety that a person will lose control and succumb to the
power of sin is evident in his descriptions of desire. In 6:2–4 he warns
his students not to fall into the grip of desire because, like a fire, it will
consume a person and his productivity.[44] Likewise, in 18:30–19:3 Ben
Sira says that those who indulge their basest desires become (increasingly) subject to their control, leading to impoverishment and destruction.
And in 9:8–9 Ben Sira describes lust as a fire that once kindled by leer-
ing at a beautiful woman will lead the student's heart astray, plunging
him into destruction. Most germane to the prayer for self-control, in the
following passage about sexual immorality Ben Sira says that someone
with burning desire multiplies sins and the desire cannot be quenched
until it runs its course, which results in self-destruction (23:16). This
shared uncontrollable, "magnetic" quality of speech sins and improper

---

[41] Jean Hadot, *Penchant Mauvais et Volonté Libre dans la Sagesse de Ben Sira* (Brussels:
University of Brussels Press, 1970). For an overview of scholars who hold that Ben
Sira anticipates the rabbinic idea of the evil inclination, see Nicholas Ellis, *Hermeneutics of Divine Testing: Cosmic Trials and Biblical Interpretation in the Epistle of James
and Other Jewish Literature*, WUNT 396 (Tübingen: Mohr Siebeck, 2015), 81–2.

[42] So Marböck, *Jesus Sirach 1–23*, 268. Other examples of sins that have this dynamic of
increasing loss of control are anger (see 28:8–11) and greed (see 5:1–8 and 31:5–11).
On the latter, see the perceptive analysis by Gary A. Anderson, *Charity: The Place of
the Poor in the Biblical Tradition* (New Haven: Yale University Press, 2013), 56–60.

[43] Bradley C. Gregory, "Slips of the Tongue in the Speech Ethics of Ben Sira," *Bib* 93
(2012): 321–30. Interestingly, the idea of slipping with the tongue was heightened in
the Greek version in comparison to the Hebrew and Syriac (cf. 14:1; 21:7; and 25:8).

[44] Following the Hebrew in 6:2; the Greek has "do not lift yourself up in the counsel of
your soul" for 6:2a, which introduces the notion of pride. Nevertheless, in 6:4a
the Greek reads "evil desire will destroy the one who acquires it", which matches the
Hebrew.

desire is important for why Ben Sira finds prayer to be the most effective remedy for them.

But before examining that aspect, it is worth observing that his understanding of the tongue and desire as being related and even particularly dangerous was not in and of itself unique in the Greco-Roman world. At Qumran the Serek Hayaḥad places shameful lust and the blasphemous tongue side-by-side in a long list of heinous sins (1QS 3:9–11). A similar juxtaposition in a catalogue of vices occurs in Sib. Or. 2:254–264. Pseudo-Phocylides transitions from the sustained discussions of the control of the tongue to temperance and the control of desire (Ps.-Phoc. 48–69). And Paul juxtaposes slander and fornication in 1 Cor 5:11. The Testament of Judah 23:1–2 links sexual sin, deceit, and idolatry and this same triad of interconnected sins is condemned in Sib. Or. 3:36–45. A particularly good parallel with Ben Sira's prayer is found in Philo, who admonishes his Jewish contemporaries that people should show temperance "both in their language and in their appetites, both in and below the belly" (*Spec.* 2.195).[45] A key difference, however, is that elsewhere Philo presents reason and philosophical discourse as the antidote to these desires (*Decal.* 150; *Spec.* 4.95), though these are aligned with the Law (*Decal.* 142).[46] In fact, for Philo the law becomes a pathway to achieving self-mastery (*Virt.* 181–182).[47] And finally, Plutarch recounts the view of the legendary Anacharsis (6th century BCE), who was often idealized as the embodiment of self-mastery, that the tongue requires even greater self-control than sexual desire, a view which assumes that both were preeminent dangers (*Mor.* 505A).[48]

Prayer as the Source of Self-Mastery

The sense of anxiety and helplessness about the danger of the sins of the tongue and desire are amplified by both the rhetorical structure and the imagery of the prayer. In terms of structure, both halves of the prayer begin with a rhetorical question that functions like an exclamation of helplessness. As such 22:27 and 23:2–3 function somewhat analogously to the opening of Pss 2, 52, and 121 (none of which are petitionary

---

[45] Translation from Charles D. Yonge, *The Works of Philo* (Peabody, MA: Hendrickson, 1993), 586.

[46] Stowers, *A Rereading of Romans*, 59–61.

[47] Stowers, *A Rereading of Romans*, 64. Stowers memorably characterizes Philo's view of Judaism as "a school for self-mastery" (58).

[48] Cf. Stowers, *A Rereading of Romans*, 62.

prayers, however). But perhaps the closer parallel is Paul's exclamation in the Epistle to the Romans: "Miserable human that I am! Who will deliver me from this body of death?" (Rom 7:24). As Marböck notes, the use of this form to introduce Ben Sira's prayer highlights both the gravity of the threat of these sins and draws attention to the speaker's complete lack of confidence in controlling the tongue or his desire on his own.[49] This is even clearer through the content of these questions. In 22:27 the expressed need for a guard and a seal is telling. Virtually all commentators see this as an appropriation of Ps 141:3, "O LORD, set a guard on my mouth, keep watch over the door of my lips", and perhaps more remotely, Prov 21:23, "the one who guards his mouth and tongue guards himself from trouble." But the presence of similar terminology elsewhere demonstrates how common this kind of expression seems to have been. In the *Sayings of Ahiqar* we read, "My son, do not utter everything which comes into your mind, for there are eyes and ears everywhere. But keep watch over your mouth, lest it bring you to grief! Above all else, guard your mouth; and as for what you have heard, be discreet! For a word is a bird, and he who releases it is a fool!" (14b-15).[50] And in 4QSapiential-Didactic Work A, the sage advises, "Place a bond on your lips and on your tongue fortified doors" (4Q412 1,5).[51] Such imagery, while a common sapiential trope, bespeaks an urgent doubt that the mouth can be controlled unless it is monitored with vigilance. It also implies an anxiety on part of the speaker that he has any power within himself to control or effectively monitor this dangerous agent of his own destruction. The desperation of his rhetorical questions comes from the combined realities that the threat is so heightened and his ability to meet it so minimal.[52]

The same anxious urgency can be seen in the content of the second rhetorical question in 23:2–3, which parallels the form of 22:27. Instead of the mouth and lips, Ben Sira turns to the interior life, the thoughts and the heart. And in place of guards and seals, he begs for whips and either

---

[49] Marböck, *Jesus Sirach 1-23*, 266.

[50] This parallel is mentioned by Crenshaw, "Sirach," 748. The translation is from James M. Lindenberger, "Ahiqar," in *Old Testament Pseudepigrapha*, ed. James H. Charlesworth, ABRL (New York: Doubleday, 1983), 2:479–507, 500.

[51] This parallel is noted by Calduch-Benages, "Emotions in the Prayer of Sirach 22:27-23:6," 150.

[52] This is widely noted by commentators, e.g. Bullard and Hatton, *Sirach*, 465; Crenshaw, "Sirach," 748; Marböck, *Jesus Sirach 1-23*, 266; so also Balla, *Ben Sira on Family, Gender, and Sexuality*, 164; Reiterer, "Gott, Vater und Herr meines Leben," 140–1.

the rod of discipline (so the Syriac) or wise training[53] (so the Greek).[54]
These harsh implements of chastisement indicate that within this prayer
the speaker has placed himself in an educational context with God as the
implied pedagogue. Both whips and either the "rod of discipline" (Syriac) or *paideia* (Greek) suggest a pedagogy of corporal punishment, not
uncommon in the Hellenistic world. As Fox observes in relation to
Prov 13:24, "Ancient Wisdom commended child beating with some
zeal"; examples include Prov 13:24; 18:24; 22:15; 23:13–14 and Ben
Sira even has an entire instruction on it in 30:1–13.[55] The mention of
a whip is notable because in Proverbs it appears only as something
applied to livestock (Prov 26:3),[56] but Ben Sira mentions it in the context
of discipline here and in 30:1 in reference to children. In the Hebrew
Bible the whip appears as indicative of undue harshness from the king in
1 Kgs 12:11–14, but as an instrument of divine discipline in Isa 10:26;
28:18 (cf. Jer 49:3). As unsettling as these references to corporal punishment may be to modern readers, especially in Ben Sira's teaching in
30:1–13, it is striking that in the prayer of 22:27–23:6 Ben Sira asks for
these to be applied to himself as well. As Bullard and Hatton point out,
it is not so much that Ben Sira wants to be whipped as that he feels he
needs the threat of the harshest of punishments to deter him from these
sins.[57] The increased harshness expressed in moving from guards and
seals to whips and either discipline or the rod, combined with the more
elaborate descriptions in the second half of the prayer, suggest that while
the tongue is dangerous, improper desire is an even graver danger.[58]

The question then arises as to the nature and meaning of the divided
persona presented in the prayer of 22:27–23:6. What are we to make of
the fact that Ben Sira presents his own desires and faculties as incapable
of being mastered by himself and in need of outside divine help? One

---

[53] Here I am taking σοφίας as an attributive genitive; another possibility is to take it as
a subjective genitive, i.e. that he wants Wisdom to discipline his mind, but this seems
somewhat unlikely since in this passage God is clearly the desired agent of discipline
(cf. Bullard & Hatton, *Sirach*, 463).

[54] Because of the concreteness of the image in the Syriac, Box and Oesterley ("Sirach,"
393) and Skehan and Di Lella (*The Wisdom of Ben Sira*, 321) believe it is original and
the Greek is secondary. Alternatively, it could be argued that the Syriac represents an
adaptation of the verse to biblical phrasing (cf. Prov 22:15).

[55] Michael V. Fox, *Proverbs 10-31: A New Translation with Introduction and Commentary*, AB 18B (New Haven: Yale University Press, 2009), 571.

[56] However, the MT's "blows" is translated with "whips" with respect to fools in Prov
19:29 LXX.

[57] Bullard and Hatton, *Sirach*, 463.

[58] So Reiterer, "Gott, Vater und Herr meines Leben," 168.

way of explaining this has been suggested by Menachem Kister, who argues that Ben Sira ascribes traditional demonology language to the parts of his own body. It is not that Ben Sira sees himself as demon-possessed, but that he sees a personified evil resident in his own members. For this reason, Kister characterizes the prayer of 22:27–23:6 as "apotropaic." According to Ellis, Kister argues that Ben Sira views sin as interior to a person in order to oppose those who ascribed sin to external evil forces.[59] While Kister's observation that Ben Sira views the problem of sin as interior to a person rather than something done under the influence of evil spirits is surely correct, it seems much more likely in light of the rest of his teaching that the inner conflict described in places like 22:27–23:6 operates at the level of metaphor and rhetoric rather than representing an adaptation of demonology.

In fact, the inner struggle seen in this prayer can be better accounted for in light of contemporary discussions of self-mastery than by a contemporary Jewish debate over the role of evil spirits. So, for example, Balla follows Eron in arguing that "the detailed list of various human desires and their symptoms (23:4b–6) and the anxiety not to be controlled by them resemble the Cynic and Stoic ideal."[60] Similarly, Wills observes that while direct evidence for Stoic influence on Ben Sira is meager, there are conceptual parallels between a number of passages in Ben Sira and Greek ethical discussions, particularly on the topic of self-control.[61] Although the specific word ἐγκράτεια, "self-control," appears only in the Greek heading before 18:30 (and before 18:15 in Sinaiticus), the topic of self-control can be found throughout the book and is the theme of 22:27–23:6 in which pedagogical instruments are metaphorically internalized to express the struggle towards the ideal of self-mastery.[62]

---

[59] Menachem Kister, "The *Yetzer* of Man's Heart, the Body and Purification from Evil: Between Prayer Terminologies and World Views," *Meghillot* 8–9 (2010): 241–82. My description of Kister's argument is dependent on the summary of his position in Ellis, *Hermeneutics of Divine Testing*, 82–4.

[60] Balla, *Ben Sira on Family, Gender, and Sexuality*, 165; Eron, "That Women Have Mastery," 53.

[61] Wills, "Greek Philosophical Discourse," 762.

[62] Wills, "Greek Philosophical Discourse," 764. Interestingly, while Satlow also argues that Ben Sira reflects the ideal of self-mastery as a necessary requirement for pursuing wisdom, he does not list the prayer in 22:27–23:6 as an instance of this. Michael L. Satlow, "Try to Be A Man: The Rabbinic Construction of Masculinity," *HTR* 89 (1996): 19–40, 24.

This discourse of self-mastery in the classical world had several salient features. Beginning with Plato self-mastery is included as one of the cardinal virtues and he speaks of desire as having the power to imprison someone. Yet in yielding to that desire, the person becomes a collaborator in his imprisonment (*Phaedr.* 81e–83b).[63] Similarly, Xenophon contrasted the freedom found in self-mastery with the enslavement in succumbing to the power of desire (*Mem.* 1.5) and the same theme can be found throughout Greek novels.[64] For Plato, wisdom is the foundation of all virtue and once cultivated in the rational part of the soul, it enables the development of the virtues of the non-rational part of the soul, i.e. temperance, justice, and fortitude. However, most people are unable on their own to acquire virtue sufficient to attain self-mastery and need to be trained, or educated, by those who are virtuous, namely the philosophers.[65] Thus, in order to achieve self-mastery one needs prudence and the way to get prudence is through education. In terms of this progression, Aristotle draws a distinction between merely resisting temptation and self-mastery which involves the subduing and control of the desires (*Eth. nic.* 7.1150b).[66]

The Stoics, on the other hand, worked with a unitary conception of personality. From this perspective, the problem with describing the soul as a place of struggle between warring factions is that it fragments the self into multiple competing agencies and potentially allows one to evade moral responsibility by equating the "true self" with the "higher," nobler agent.[67] However, as Campbell notes, if the idea of warring factions is not taken literally, but is strictly a metaphorical expression of the appeal of competing goods within a person, then such rhetoric does have some explanatory power.[68] The Stoics, then, do not view desire as innately corrupt which is in need of subjugation by a "higher" part of the soul; instead, various desires are inclinations that can "distort" the reasoning process in weighing particular goods and thereby inhibit one's assent to virtue.[69] Moral growth, then, requires a proper understanding of

---

[63] Cited by Katy E. Valentine, "First Corinthians 10:1–13 in Light of the Rhetoric of Self-Control over the Desires," *Stone Campbell-Journal* 17 (2014): 47–61, 49.
[64] Discussed in Wills, "Greek Philosophical Discourse," 755–7.
[65] Raymond J. Devettere, *Introduction to Virtue Ethics: Insights of the Ancient Greeks* (Washington, DC: Georgetown University Press, 2002), 95.
[66] Cited in Stowers, *A Rereading of Romans*, 45.
[67] Keith Campbell, "Self-Mastery and Stoic Ethics," *Philosophy* 60 (1985): 327–40, 328–9.
[68] Campbell, "Self-Mastery and Stoic Ethics," 330.
[69] Campbell, "Self-Mastery and Stoic Ethics," 327, 330–1.

competing goods and the proper ordering of the reasoning process that weighs these. While Epictetus speaks of this as rather straight-forward, most people find this moral growth difficult and need guidance. Campbell helpfully uses the analogy of a golf swing. Doing it well requires many interconnected muscle mechanics which perform their tasks correctly and in sync with one another. Most people naturally have a bad golf swing and it takes a lot of work to train each part of the body to do the correct motion so that together they produce a good swing. It is so difficult to get all of these parts in order that virtually everyone needs a teacher to guide them.[70] Since the Stoics were more like Plato than Aristotle in viewing prudence as a skill, the sage is understood as an expert in living life well. Such a person has a virtuous disposition and understands all the factors in a given context correctly and so does not need the help of an instructor to act wisely. He does this naturally and with ease.[71] However, in this the early Stoics were unusual; most held that desire had a tendency to be unruly and could not be eliminated, merely subdued.[72]

How does Ben Sira's prayer in 22:27–23:6 compare with these Greek discussions of self-mastery? First, it should be noted that Ben Sira's relation to this discourse is of a general nature and the evidence for specific Stoic influence on Ben Sira is not very strong.[73] Therefore, Ben Sira is removed from the analysis of moral psychology that arises from the differing conceptions of the soul found in, e.g., Plato and the Stoics.[74] Nevertheless, the main features of this discourse can help to illuminate the rhetoric of the prayer in 22:27–23:6. First, the presentation of body parts and desires as having a certain nefarious agency which is opposed to the desire and will of the speaker is best understood as a metaphorical expression of competing desires, namely the desire for physical or social pleasure versus the desire for wisdom, rather than an internalized adaptation of demonology (at least understood in a literal sense). Leaving aside the specific psychologies that underlie the various rhetorical expressions of this struggle, Ben Sira's anxiety about the tongue and desire as uncontrollable and a threat towards enslavement (cf. also 3:23; 5:2; 6:4; 11:30;

---

[70] Campbell, "Self-Mastery and Stoic Ethics," 333–4.

[71] Devettere, *Introduction to Virtue Ethics*, 129–33.

[72] Stowers, *A Rereading of Romans*, 48. Stowers goes on to show how this psychology mirrored the external socio-political world of power struggles such that Greco-Roman thinkers typically saw an analogy between self-mastery and fitness to rule.

[73] See the review of the debate and the sober conclusion of Wills, "Greek Philosophical Discourse," 760–3.

[74] Cf. Wills, "Greek Philosophical Discourse," 762.

19:2–3) fits within the predominant view in the classical world. As Stowers summarizes it, "the dominant view in Greco-Roman culture held that desires in themselves were not bad but dangerous, powerful, and prone to act independently of rational control."[75]

Second, the consequences of self-control or lack thereof as being both internal and external finds its counterpart in Greek discourses around self-mastery as well. While Greek discussions often focus on the importance of the interior life, they also see self-mastery as embedded in social frameworks of honor, masculinity, and power.[76] A failure, therefore, to attain self-mastery was expected to lead not just to an internally disordered soul, but to defeat, a loss of power, and public disgrace (including emasculation),[77] largely the same consequences Ben Sira associates with moral failure in 22:27–23:6.

Finally, the educational context in which the need for discipline is placed within the prayer accords with other contemporary discussions of growth toward self-mastery. However, here an important difference emerges. While the Stoics generally portrayed the sage as one who had attained complete self-mastery, Ben Sira's prayer assumes otherwise. Although throughout his book he constructs himself as the ideal sage, in this prayer he concedes that he is in desperate need of discipline and places himself in the role of a student. This is a key point because it also implies that what characterizes the *idealized* sage is not the absence of moral struggle, but a piety expressed as dependence on God for moral success.[78] Importantly, this closely parallels his claim that the scribe is dependent on God for a spirit of understanding, wisdom, and discernment (39:6–7).[79] This parallel may explain why Ben Sira addresses God instead of Wisdom as the one to discipline him (cf. 6:18–31, where personified Wisdom educates through corporal discipline). The need for assistance in achieving self-mastery flows from a piety of "fear of the LORD", central to which was humble submission to God.[80]

---

[75] Stowers, *A Rereading of Romans*, 47.

[76] Satlow, "Try to Be A Man," 21–2; Eron, "That Women Have Mastery," 46.

[77] Valentine, "First Corinthians 10:1-13," 49.

[78] Benjamin G. Wright, "Ben Sira on the Sage as Exemplar," in *Praise Israel for Wisdom and Instruction: Essays on Ben Sira and Wisdom, the Letter of Aristeas and the Septuagint*, JSJSup 131 (Leiden: Brill, 2008), 165–82, 171.

[79] A point nicely made by Wright, "The Sage as Exemplar," 179–80.

[80] On this theme and its central importance for Ben Sira see the classic study of Josef Haspecker, *Gottesfurcht bei Jesus Sirach: Ihre religiöse Struktur und ihre literarische und doktrinäre Bedeutung*, AnBib 30 (Rome: Pontifical Biblical Institute, 1976). The

Both of the rhetorical questions in 22:27 and 23:2–3 set up the address to God in 23:1 and 4 as the only remedy for avoiding these temptations. In these addresses God is called both "Lord" and "Father". Some interpreters view these titles as intended to hold together both authority and intimate affection (cf. 51:10).[81] Yet, Skehan and Di Lella may be on the right track in noting that "the pious Jew can call God 'my Father'. Since God alone is the source of the moral life, only he can help one avoid the sins of the tongue."[82] In the wisdom tradition, the title of "father" is not simply one of filial affection, but of authoritative teacher and disciplinarian. This is why sages routinely address their students as "my son".[83] By extension, God can be imaged as a father precisely in his disciplinarian role, though this is not very common. As Prov 3:12 says, "The one whom the LORD loves he disciplines, as a father favors (his) son" (cf. 2 Bar. 13:9). Importantly, both Tob 13:4–5 and Wis 11:9–10 view discipline as an aspect of God's merciful fatherhood.[84] More common, however, is the general notion that God is the teacher of Israel, found especially in Deuteronomy (4:10; 5:31; cf. Exod 24:12) and Torah Psalms (e.g. Pss 1, 19, 25, 119; cf. 143).[85] From this angle, the prayer of 22:27–23:6 fits within the Hellenistic discourse of self-mastery, but the configuration of this moral struggle in the form of a prayer allows Ben Sira to connect a piety of ultimate dependence on God (i.e. "the fear of the Lord") with an understanding of God as the supreme pedagogue who applies the normal educational instruments of corporal discipline. The typical idea that humans require instruction to achieve self-mastery is reoriented along a vertical axis of the divine-human relationship and the

---

absence of the phrase "fear of the LORD" in the prayer itself is not surprising since it is a first person address to God; the prayer embodies the concept rather than talks about it.

[81] Crenshaw, "Sirach," 749; Marböck, *Jesus Sirach 1-23*, 266–7; so also Balla, *Ben Sira on Family, Gender, and Sexuality*, 164–5. Also note the discussion in Stefan C. Reif, "The Fathership of God in Early Rabbinic Liturgy," in *Family and Kinship in the Deuterocanonical and Cognate Literature*, ed. Angelo Passaro, DCLY 2012/13 (Berlin: de Gruyter, 2013), 505–25.

[82] Skehan and Di Lella, *The Wisdom of Ben Sira*, 322; similarly, Jeremy Corley, "God as Merciful Father in Ben Sira and the New Testament," in Egger-Wenzel, *Ben Sira's God*, 33–8, 36.

[83] See Wright, "From Generation to Generation: The Sage as Father in Early Jewish Literature," in *Praise Israel for Wisdom and Instruction*, 25–46.

[84] See Corley, "God as Merciful Father," 34–5.

[85] John Eaton, "Memory and Encounter: An Educational Ideal," in *Of Prophets' Visions and the Wisdom of Sages: Essays in Honour of R. Norman Whybray on his Seventieth Birthday*, ed. Heather A. McKay and David J. A. Clines, JSOTSup 162 (Sheffield: JSOT Press, 1993), 179–91, 187–9.

ideal sage is thereby cast as perpetually dependent on God's assistance to live morally.

This reorientation of moral pedagogy along a vertical axis results in the composition of a prayer in 22:27–23:6 that is quite unusual, though not completely unprecedented. Most Second Temple Jewish and Greek and Roman petitionary prayers sought divine help for "external" problems like health, daily needs, or deliverance and protection from enemies.[86] Much rarer were prayers that sought divine assistance for moral improvement. Within Judaism many scholars point to a precedent in Prov 30:7–9 which reads in part, "two things I ask from you…make lies and deception far from me…lest I be sated and fail and say, 'Who is the LORD?' or lest I be poor and steal and abuse the name of my God." Yet even here, commentators often add that Ben Sira's prayer goes well beyond this passage.[87] A partial parallel can be found in the "Prayer of Levi" which implores God to "Make far from me, O Lord, the unrighteous spirit, and evil thought and fornication, and turn pride away from me. Let there be shown to me, O Lord, the holy spirit, and counsel, and wisdom and knowledge and grant me strength in order to do that which is pleasing to you and find favor before you" (4Q213[a] [4QTLevi[a]] I,12–14).[88] While this prayer shares with Sir 22:27–23:6 the request for divine assistance in moral improvement and the belief that only God can grant wisdom, it differs from Ben Sira in understanding moral struggle as occurring under the influence of evil and righteous spirits.[89]

In extant literature from the Greek and Roman world, prayers for moral progress are also less common. As Mikalson observes, despite the concern for justice in Plato and other philosophers, they never pray for help in becoming just because for them justice comes from philosophy rather than as a divine gift.[90] In contrast to this, there is a prayer in the fragments of Xenophanes of Colophon (died ca. 478 BCE) which asks

---

[86] Cf. "Pagans generally prayed for health and beauty, for relief and protection, for safety and rescue, and for the needs of the household, in addition, of course, to mastery of one's enemies." Larry J. Alderink and Luther H. Martin, "Prayer in Greco-Roman Religions," in *Prayer from Alexander to Constantine: A Critical Anthology*, ed. Mark Kiley (London: Routledge, 1997), 123–7, 124. The same tendency is seen in the survey of Jewish prayers in Kiley, *Prayer from Alexander to Constantine*, 9–120.

[87] Sauer calls it "ein absolutes Novum in der Literatur der Weisheit" (*Jesus Sirach*, 170–1); similarly, Marböck, *Jesus Sirach 1-23*, 268. Cf. Schreiner, *Jesus Sirach 1-24*, 123.

[88] Translation from Michael E. Stone and Jonas C. Greenfield, "The Prayer of Levi," *JBL* 112 (1993): 247–66, 259. My thanks to Jeremy Corley for this reference.

[89] Ellis, *Hermeneutics of Divine Testing*, 68.

[90] Jon D. Mikalson, *Greek Popular Religion in Greek Philosophy* (Oxford: Oxford University Press, 2010), 50.

for divine aid for the ability to do what is right: "But first glad-hearted men must hymn the god with reverent words and pure speech. And having poured a libation and prayed to be able to do what is right—for these are obvious—it is not wrong to drink as much as allows any but an aged man to reach his home without a servant's aid" (frag. 1,13–15).[91] While it is not clear whether the prayer is asking for help to perform the exact tasks at hand or, more broadly, for help in living morally, the uniqueness of this petition has been widely noted.[92] On the other hand, from a later period, the Stoics could pray for virtue through conformity to the divine will.[93] For example, in Cleanthes' "Hymn to Zeus" he prays "Zeus the all-giver, wielder of the bright lightning in the dark clouds, Deliver mankind from its miserable incompetence. Father, disperse this from our soul; give us Good judgement, trusting in you to guide all things in justice…" (31–34).[94]

Conclusion

In summary, the prayer in 22:27–23:6 provides great insight into Ben Sira's understanding of moral development, especially when appreciated in its Hellenistic context. Ben Sira shares with his contemporaries a number of perspectives: an anxiety about speech and desire, the view that these two are closely associated, the idea that they are liable to get out of control without a vigilant struggle for self-control, and the importance of self-mastery for both internal and external reasons. Where he is unusual is by placing this concern for self-mastery into the framework of a prayer for divine assistance. In doing so, he concedes that the sage, even the idealized one, is never free from temptation and moral struggle. But this unique approach to the struggle for self-mastery flows out of his view of piety, especially insofar as it is characterized by the "fear of the LORD," and his view of God as the supreme pedagogue who instructs and disciplines the sage so that he may conquer his darkest impulses.

---

[91] Translation from James. H. Lesher, *Xenophanes of Colophon: Fragments: A Text and Translation with a Commentary* (Toronto: University of Toronto Press, 1992), 47.

[92] Lesher, *Xenophanes of Colophon*, 52; Mikalson, *Greek Popular Religion in Greek Philosophy*, 50.

[93] Wills, "Greek Philosophical Discourse," 771.

[94] Translation from William Cassidy, "Cleanthes – *Hymn to Zeus*," in Kiley, *Prayer from Alexander to Constantine*, 136.

Bibliography

Adams, Samuel L. *Wisdom in Transition: Act and Consequence in Second Temple Instructions*. JSJSup 125. Leiden: Brill, 2008.

Alderink, Larry J., and Luther H. Martin. "Prayer in Greco-Roman Religions." Pages 123–7 in *Prayer from Alexander to Constantine: A Critical Anthology*. Edited by Mark Kiley. London: Routledge, 1997.

Anderson, Gary A. *Charity: The Place of the Poor in the Biblical Tradition*. New Haven: Yale University Press, 2013.

Avrahami, Yael. *The Senses of Scripture: Sensory Perception in the Hebrew Bible*. LHBOTS 525. London: T&T Clark/Bloomsbury, 2012.

Balla, Ibolya. *Ben Sira on Family, Gender, and Sexuality*. DCLS 8. Berlin: de Gruyter, 2011.

Beentjes, Pancratius C. "Sir 22:27-23:6 in zijn Context." *Bijdr* 39 (1978): 144–51.

Beentjes, Pancratius C. "Some Major Topics in Ben Sira Research." Pages 3–16 in *"Happy the One who Meditates on Wisdom" (Sir. 14:20): Collected Essays on the Book of Ben Sira*. CBET 43. Leuven: Peeters, 2006.

Box, George H., and William O. E. Oesterley. "Sirach." Pages 268–517 in vol. 1 of *The Apocrypha and Pseudepigrapha of the Old Testament*. Edited by Robert H. Charles. Oxford: Clarendon Press, 1913.

Bullard, Roger A., and Howard A. Hatton. *Sirach*. UBS Handbook Series. New York: United Bible Societies, 2008.

Calduch-Benages, Núria. "Ben Sira 23:27—A Pivotal Verse." Pages 186–200 in *Wisdom for Life: Essays Offered to Honor Maurice Gilbert, SJ on the Occasion of His Eightieth Birthday*. Edited by Núria Calduch-Benages. BZAW 445. Berlin: de Gruyter, 2014.

Calduch-Benages, Núria. "Emotions in the Prayer of Sirach 22:27–23:6." Pages 145–60 in *Ancient Jewish Prayers and Emotions: Emotions Associated with Jewish Prayer in and around the Second Temple Period*. Edited by Stefan C. Reif and Renate Egger-Wenzel. DCLS 26. Berlin: de Gruyter, 2015.

Campbell, Keith. "Self-Mastery and Stoic Ethics." *Philosophy* 60 (1985): 327–40.

Cassidy, William. "Cleanthes – Hymn to Zeus." Pages 133–8 in *Prayer from Alexander to Constantine: A Critical Anthology*. Edited by Mark Kiley. London: Routledge, 1997.

Collins, John J. *Jewish Wisdom in the Hellenistic Age*. OTL. Louisville: Westminster John Knox Press, 1997.

Corley, Jeremy. "God as Merciful Father in Ben Sira and the New Testament." Pages 33–8 in *Ben Sira's God: Proceedings of the International Ben Sira Conference, Durham–Ushaw College 2001*. Edited by Renate Egger-Wenzel. BZAW 321. Berlin: de Gruyter, 2002.

Corley, Jeremy. "Searching for structure and redaction in Ben Sira: An investigation of beginnings and endings." Pages 21–47 in *The Wisdom of Ben Sira: Studies on Tradition, Redaction, and Theology*. Edited by Angelo Passaro and Giuseppe Bellia. DCLS 1. Berlin: de Gruyter, 2008.

Corley, Jeremy. "4.3 Greek of Ecclesiasticus/Ben Sira." Pages 214–31 in *The Textual History of the Bible, Volume 2B: The Deuterocanonicals*. Edited by Matthias Henze. Leiden: Brill, 2019.

Crenshaw, James L. "Sirach: Introduction, Commentary, and Reflections." *NIB* 5: 601–867.

Devettere, Raymond J. *Introduction to Virtue Ethics: Insights of the Ancient Greeks.* Washington D.C.: Georgetown University Press, 2002.

Eaton, John. "Memory and Encounter: An Educational Ideal." Pages 179–91 in *Of Prophets' Visions and the Wisdom of Sages: Essays in Honour of R. Norman Whybray on his Seventieth Birthday.* Edited by Heather A. McKay and David J. A. Clines. JSOTSup 162. Sheffield: JSOT Press, 1993.

Ellis, Nicholas. *Hermeneutics of Divine Testing: Cosmic Trials and Biblical Interpretation in the Epistle of James and Other Jewish Literature.* WUNT 396. Tübingen: Mohr Siebeck, 2015.

Eron, Lewis John. "'That Women Have Mastery Over Both King and Beggar' (*TJud.* 15.5) — The Relationship of the Fear of Sexuality to the Status of Women in Apocrypha and Pseudepigrapha: 1 Esdras (3 *Ezra*) 3-4, Ben Sira, and the *Testament of Judah.*" *JSP* 9 (1991): 43–66.

Fox, Michael V. *Proverbs 10-31: A New Translation with Introduction and Commentary.* AB 18B. New Haven: Yale University Press, 2009.

Gilbert, Maurice. "Prayer in the Book of Ben Sira: Function and Relevance." Pages 117–35 in *Prayer from Tobit to Qumran: Inaugural Conference of the ISDCL at Salzburg, Austria, 5-9 July 2003.* Edited by Renate Egger-Wenzel and Jeremy Corley. DCLY 2004. Berlin: de Gruyter, 2004.

Gregory, Bradley C. "Slips of the Tongue in the Speech Ethics of Ben Sira." *Bib* 93 (2012): 321–30.

Hadot, Jean. *Penchant Mauvais et Volonté Libre dans la Sagesse de Ben Sira.* Brussels: University of Brussels Press, 1970.

Haspecker, Josef. *Gottesfurcht bei Jesus Sirach: Ihre religiöse Struktur und ihre literarische und doktrinäre Bedeutung.* AnBib 30. Rome: Pontifical Biblical Institute, 1976.

Hultin, Jeremy F. *The Ethics of Obscene Speech in Early Christianity and Its Environment.* NovTSup 128. Leiden: Brill, 2008.

Kiley, Mark, ed. *Prayer from Alexander to Constantine: A Critical Anthology.* London/New York: Routledge, 1997.

Kister, Menachem. "The *Yetzer* of Man's Heart, the Body and Purification from Evil: Between Prayer Terminologies and World Views." [Hebrew] *Meghillot* 8–9 (2010): 241–82.

Knust, Jennifer. *Abandoned to Lust: Sexual Slander and Ancient Christianity.* Gender, Theory, and Religion Series. New York: Columbia University Press, 2006.

Lesher, James H. *Xenophanes of Colophon: Fragments. A Text and Translation with a Commentary.* Toronto: University of Toronto Press, 1992.

Liesen, Jan. *Full of Praise: An Exegetical Study of Sir 39,12-35.* JSJSup 64. Leiden: Brill, 2000.

Lindenberger, James M. "Ahiqar." Pages 479–507 in vol. 2 of *Old Testament Pseudepigrapha.* Edited by James H. Charlesworth. ABRL. New York: Doubleday, 1983, 1985.

Marböck, Johannes. "Das Gebet um die Rettung Zions Sir 36,1–22 (G: 33,1–13a; 36,16b–22) im Zusammenhang der Geschichtsschau Ben Siras." Pages

93–116 in *Memoria Jerusalem: Freundesgabe Franz Z. Sauer zum 70. Geburtstag.* Edited by Johann Baptist Bauer and Johannes Marböck. Graz: Akademische Druck- und Verlagsanstalt, 1977.

Marböck, Johannes. *Jesus Sirach 1-23.* HThKAT. Freiburg: Herder, 2010.

Mikalson, Jon D. *Greek Popular Religion in Greek Philosophy.* Oxford: Oxford University Press, 2010.

Minissale, Antonino. "The Metaphor of 'Falling': Hermeneutic Key to the Book of Sirach." Pages 253–75 in *The Wisdom of Ben Sira: Studies on Tradition, Redaction, and Theology.* Edited by Angelo Passaro and Giuseppe Bellia. DCLS 1. Berlin: de Gruyter, 2008.

Peters, Norbert. *Das Buch Jesus Sirach oder Ecclesiasticus.* EHAT 25. Münster: Aschendorff, 1913.

Reif, Stefan C. "The Fathership of God in Early Rabbinic Liturgy." Pages 505–25 in *Family and Kinship in the Deuterocanonical and Cogante Literature.* Edited by Angelo Passaro. DCLY 2012/2013. Berlin: de Gruyter, 2013.

Reif, Stefan C. "Prayer in Ben Sira, Qumran and Second Temple Judaism." Pages 321–41 in *Ben Sira's God: Proceedings of the International Ben Sira Conference, Durham—Ushaw College 2001.* Edited by Renate Egger-Wenzel. BZAW 321. Berlin: de Gruyter, 2002.

Reiterer, Friedrich V. "Gott, Vater und Herr meines Lebens: Eine poetisch-stilistische Analyse von Sir 22,27–23,6 als Verständnisgrundlage des Gebetes." Pages 137–70 in *Prayer from Tobit to Qumran: Inaugural Conference of the ISDCL at Salzburg, Austria, 5-9 July 2003.* Edited by Renate Egger-Wenzel and Jeremy Corley. DCLY 2004. Berlin: de Gruyter, 2004.

Satlow, Michael L. "'Try to Be A Man': The Rabbinic Construction of Masculinity." *HTR* 89 (1996): 19–40.

Sauer, Georg. *Jesus Sirach/Ben Sira.* ATD Apokryphen Band 1. Göttingen: Vandenhoeck & Ruprecht, 2000.

Schreiner, Josef. *Jesus Sirach 1-24.* NEchtB 38. Würzburg: Echter, 2002.

Skehan, Patrick W., and Alexander A. Di Lella. *The Wisdom of Ben Sira: A New Translation with Notes by Patrick W. Skehan, Introduction and Commentary by Alexander A. Di Lella.* AB 39. New York: Doubleday, 1987.

Stone, Michael E., and Jonas C. Greenfield. "The Prayer of Levi," *JBL* 112 (1993): 247–66.

Stowers, Stanley K. *A Rereading of Romans: Justice, Jews, & Gentiles.* New Haven: Yale University Press, 1994.

Urbanz, Werner. *Gebet im Sirachbuch: Zur Terminologie von Klage und Lob in der griechischen Texttradition.* Herders Biblische Studien 60. Freiburg: Herder, 2009.

Valentine, Katy E. "First Corinthians 10:1-13 in Light of the Rhetoric of Self-Control over the Desires." *Stone-Campbell Journal* 17 (2014): 47–61.

Wills, Lawrence M. "Greek Philosophical Discourse in the Book of Judith?" *JBL* 134 (2015): 753–73.

Wright, Benjamin G. "Ben Sira on the Sage as Exemplar." Pages 165–82 in *Praise Israel for Wisdom and Instruction: Essays on Ben Sira and Wisdom, the Letter of Aristeas and the Septuagint.* JSJSup 131. Leiden: Brill, 2008.

Wright, Benjamin G. "From Generation to Generation: The Sage as Father in Early Jewish Literature." Pages 25–47 in *Praise Israel for Wisdom and Instruction: Essays on Ben Sira and Wisdom, the Letter of Aristeas and the Septuagint*. JSJSup 131. Leiden: Brill, 2008.

Wright, Benjamin G. "4.1 Textual History of Ben Sira." Pages 187–98 in *The Textual History of the Bible, Volume 2B: The Deuterocanonicals*. Edited by Matthias Henze. Leiden: Brill, 2019.

Yadin, Yigael. *The Ben Sira Scroll from Masada*. Jerusalem: Israel Exploration Society, 1965.

Yonge, Charles D. *The Works of Philo*. Peabody, MA: Hendrickson, 1993.

Zapff, Burkard M. *Jesus Sirach 25-51*. NEchtB 39. Würzburg: Echter, 2010.

Ziegler, Joseph. *Sapientia Iesu Filii Sirach*. Septuaginta: Vetus Testamentum Graecum XII,2. 2nd edition. Göttingen: Vandenhoeck & Ruprecht, 1980.

SPIRITUAL EXERCISES IN SIRACH
AND THE ROLE OF PRAYER

Werner Urbanz

The major theme of the book of Ben Sira/Jesus Sirach (Sir) is the pursuit of wisdom.[1] Seeking wisdom requires a specific way of thinking and living as a whole and, of course, a certain amount of discipline which includes exercise in attitudes and the maintenance of certain practices in daily self-discipline. Strategies for such formation and education are also found in ancient *paideia* and philosophy.[2] The French philosophers Pierre Hadot and Ilsetraud Hadot describe the ancient concept of spiritual exercises.[3]

> According to Hadot, philosophy is first and foremost a way of life, and moreover: one, which is characterised by an existential choice for a 'spiritual life,' which is accompanied by a discourse in which the aforementioned way of life is explained and justified; and which is cultivated by a complete system of spiritual exercises that helps to bring about what this aforementioned life is aiming at, which is: a radical transformation of the person or the self.[4]

---

[1] John J. Collins, "Ecclesiasticus, or The Wisdom of Jesus Son of Sirach," in *The Apocrypha*, ed. Martin Goodman, *The Oxford Bible Commentary* (Oxford: Oxford University Press, 2012), 68–111, 71.

[2] See especially the works of Elisa Uusimäki, "Spiritual Formation in Hellenistic Jewish Wisdom Teaching," in *Tracing Sapiential Traditions in Ancient Judaism,* ed. Hindy Najman, Jean-Sebastien Rey, and Eibert J. C. Tigchelaar, JSJSup 174 (Leiden: Brill, 2016), 58–70 and eadem, "The Formation of a Sage According to Ben Sira," in *Second Temple Jewish "Paideia" in Context*, ed. Jason M. Zurawski and Gabriele Boccaccini, BZNW 228 (Berlin: de Gruyter, 2017), 59–69.

[3] Pierre Hadot, *Philosophy as a Way of Life: Spiritual Exercises from Socrates to Foucault*, trans. Michael Chase (Oxford: Blackwell, 1995) and Pierre Hadot, *What is Ancient Philosophy?*, trans. Michael Chase (Cambridge, MA: Belknapp, 2002). – Ilsetraut Hadot, "The Spiritual Guide," in *Classical Mediterranean Spirituality: Egyptian, Greek, Roman*, ed. A. H. Armstrong (London: Routledge & Kegan, 1986), 436–59.

[4] I largely follow the systematization of the topic in the oeuvre of Pierre and Ilsetraud Hadot by Paul van Tongeren, "Philosophy as a Form of Spirituality with Reference to the Work of Pierre Hadot," in *Seeking the Seeker: Explorations in the Discipline of Spirituality: A Festschrift for Kees Waaijman on the Occasion of His 65th Birthday*, ed. Hein Blommestijn et al., Studies in Spirituality Supplement 19, (Leuven: Peeters, 2008), 109–21, 110–1 (italics were omitted).

Daniel Harrington also situated Sir in such a context as "a handbook for spiritual formation"[5] and a special guide to spiritual exercises.[6]

Elisa Uusimäki also shows the range of such exercises "that can be described as 'spiritual,' i.e., practices that form the sage or sage-to-be spiritually and are undertaken with an aim to attain and / or retain wisdom. They indicate that wisdom's embodiment in everyday life is imagined in pragmatic yet spiritual terms."[7] Important research has been done in Sir as the book of "the praying sage"[8] including the "shaping [of] the scribal self through prayer and *paideia*".[9] So prayer is an important exercise at the interface of religious / spiritual education and education in general.[10]

In the following, I present a few concrete facets of these exercises in prayer (subjects, methods). The foundation of this study begins with the vocabulary for prayer,[11] which is arranged according to different perspectives—without being able to cover all aspects. The presentation is framed by some remarks on the matter of prayer in general and facets and contours of the discourse on spirituality in Sir.[12]

---

[5]   Daniel J. Harrington, "Ben Sira as a Spiritual Master," *Journal of Spiritual Formation* 15 (1994): 147–57, 147.

[6]   Daniel J. Harrington took up the impulse from Hadot in his book *Jesus Ben Sira of Jerusalem* (Collegeville, MN: Liturgical Press, 2005), 101, and he systematized the various topics in the book in the form of ten (spiritual) "exercises" as a model for his pedagogy (102–32) and as a good way of "doing" biblical theology (132).

[7]   Uusimäki, "The Formation of a Sage According to Ben Sira," 60 follows the paths of Hadot and Harrington in an inspiring way. She names the following activities: teaching, scribal activities, contemplation, emulation, prayer, prophecy, self-mastery, prosocial deeds.

[8]   Hermann Spieckermann, *Lebenskunst und Gotteslob in Israel: Anregungen aus Psalter und Weisheit für die Theologie*, FAT 91 (Tübingen: Mohr Siebeck, 2014), 116–40.

[9]   Judith H. Newman, *Before the Bible* (New York: Oxford University Press, 2018), 23–51; the chapter on Sir also in eadem, "The Formation of the Scribal Self in Ben Sira," in *"When the Morning Stars Sang": Essays in Honor of Choon Leong Seow on the Occasion of his Sixty-Fifth Birthday*, ed. Scott C. Jones and Christine Roy Yoder, BZAW 500 (Berlin: de Gruyter, 2018), 227–38.

[10] Uusimäki, "The Formation of a Sage According to Ben Sira," 65; Harrington, "Ben Sira as a Spiritual Master," 153.

[11] Werner Urbanz, *Gebet im Sirachbuch*, HBS 60 (Freiburg: Herder, 2009), 29–30, 133–4. The Greek text forms were used as a starting point for pragmatic reasons, since they provide a continuous textual context of the book and thus can serve as a basic matrix for this thematically oriented presentation. The Hebrew text forms were made visible in critical places, pointing out the differences as far as possible. For more details, please refer to special studies on this issue, e.g.: Maria Carmela Palmisano, "La prière de Ben Sira dans les manuscrits hébreux et dans les versions anciennes," in *The Texts and Versions of the Book of Ben Sira: Transmission and Interpretation*, ed. Jean-Sébastien Rey and Jan Joosten, JSJSup 150 (Leiden: Brill, 2011), 281–96.

[12] In this article, the term "Sir" is used to refer to the texts of the book (also in the different text versions), following Judith H. Newman, "Liturgical imagination in the

Aspects of Prayer in Sir

The book of Sirach often references the subject of prayer. The book not only contains prayers of its own (e.g. Sir 22:27–23:6; 36:1–22; 51:1–12; 51:12a–o; 51:13–30), but also many statements about prayer in practice and reflection.[13] These frequent occurrences qualify the theme of prayer as an important element of a wisdom-based approach to the world, which in this form is a novelty in wisdom literature.[14] Lament and praise, as the two basic relations of biblical prayer, are present in almost half of the book's chapters with a rich variety of relevant vocabulary.[15] The book covers the whole range from Sir 2:10 in a context of lamentation ("or has anyone called upon [ἐπεκαλέσατο] him and been neglected?") to Sir 51:29 with the aspect of praise ("and may you never be ashamed to praise him"/ἐν αἰνέσει αὐτοῦ).[16] In the course of the book, a dynamic is emerging from lament to praise (cf. the Psalter).[17] If terms of lament are distributed more evenly in the book, the vocabulary of praise has

composition of Ben Sira," in *Prayer and Poetry in the Dead Sea Scrolls and Related Literature: In Honor of Eileen Schuller on the Occasion of her 65th Birthday*, ed. Jeremy Penner, Ken M. Penner, and Cecilia Wassen, STDJ 98 (Leiden: Brill, 2012), 323–38, 326 and her "shift in focus from thinking about Ben Sira as intentional author of a single synchronic whole to considering Ben Sira and his role in the book as a constructed authorial voice, and the book itself as a traveling and shifting accumulation of textual traditions."

[13] Maurice Gilbert, "Prayer in the Book of Ben Sira: Function and relevance," in *Prayer from Tobit to Qumran: Inaugural conference of the ISDCL at Salzburg, Austria, 5-9 July 2003*, ed. Renate Egger-Wenzel and Jeremy Corley, DCLY 2004 (Berlin: de Gruyter, 2004), 117–35 and Severino Bussino, "Word and Prayer in the Book of Ben Sira," in *Various Aspects of Worship in Deuterocanonical and Cognate Literature*, ed. Ibolya Balla, Géza G. Xeravits, and József Zsengellér, DCLY 2016/2017 (Berlin: de Gruyter, 2017), 117–40. – Jan Liesen, *Full of Praise: An Exegetical Study of Sir 39,12–35*, JSJSup 64 (Leiden: Brill, 2000) and Michael Reitemeyer, *Weisheitslehre als Gotteslob: Psalmentheologie im Buch Jesus Sirach*, BBB 127 (Berlin: Philo, 2000), focus on the theme of praise.

[14] Maurice Gilbert, "La prière des sages d'Israël," in *L'expérience de la prière dans les grandes religions: Actes du colloque de Louvain-la-Neuve et Liège (22–23 Novembre 1978)*, ed. Henri Limet and Julien Ries, Homo Religiosus 5 (Louvain-la-Neuve: Centre d'Histoire des Religions, 1980), 227–43 and Spieckermann, *Lebenskunst und Gotteslob in Israel*, esp. 117–8.

[15] Cf. Urbanz, *Gebet im Sirachbuch*, for lament (126–32) and for praise (217–24) 20–21 Greek lexemes each.

[16] English quotations from NRSV. Greek and Hebrew from the Standard Editions (Ziegler and Beentjes).

[17] Marko Marttila, "Ben Sira's Use of Various Psalm Genres," in *Functions of Psalms and Prayers in the Late Second Temple Period*, ed. Mika S. Pajunen and Jeremy Penner, BZAW 486 (Berlin: de Gruyter, 2017), 356–83.

a strong presence especially from Sir 39 onwards.[18] As it was common
in antiquity, the theme of prayer is present in collective and individual
forms[19] and as part of everyday religious practice as well as philosophical
reflection.[20] And so it is not surprising that Sir as a book of wisdom and
education/*paideia* takes the topic into consideration.

The Students Who Pray

But which people are, or are associated with, the bearers and subjects of
prayer in Sir?

The "students" are the largest group mentioned.[21] They are the primary target group of messages concerning prayer in the book. The students are addressed as individuals, or as a group. In such contexts, it is
often attitudes of prayer which are presented to them.

A specific form of address (e.g. "[my] child"/בנ/τέκνον in 21:1,
38:9) is rarely found in statements about prayer, but most of the time, we
can conclude from the context that the students are being addressed.[22]
If you look at the references, the following becomes apparent: In the
context of lament, the students' address is mostly in the singular (e.g.
21:1 "ask forgiveness"/δεήθητι), in the context of praise mostly in the
plural (e.g. 39:14 "bless"/εὐλογήσατε).

Forms dominate in the imperative, indicating the educational nature of
the book. Dimensions of lament primarily concern the individual. Encour-
agements to plea, lament and reversion do not take place collectively but
in a more sheltered and solitary setting. On the other hand, praise is not

---

[18] Johannes Marböck, *Jesus Sirach 1–23*, HThKAT (Freiburg: Herder, 2010), 190;
Urbanz, *Gebet im Sirachbuch*, 225–37.

[19] Emmanuel von Severus, "Gebet I," *RAC* 8:1141–5.

[20] Reinhard Feldmeier, ",Geheiligt werde dein Name': Das Herrengebet im Kontext der
paganen Gebetsliteratur," in *Das Vaterunser in seinen antiken Kontexten: Zum Gedenken an Eduard Lohse*, ed. Florian Wilk, FRLANT 266 (Göttingen: Vandenhoeck &
Ruprecht, 2016), 25–47; according to Severus and Feldmeier it should be noted, however, that there were many different opinions on prayer within ancient philosophy.

[21] Based on the (Greek) vocabulary of prayer, 27 references can be counted: Lament and
praise (*italic*) references are graphically distinguished: 4:26; 7:10.14; 13:14+; 17:25;
18:22.23; 21:1; 28:2; *32:13*; *35:10*; 37:15; 38:9; *39:14c.d.15a.b.d.35a.b*;
43:11.28a.30a(2x).c; *50:22a*; 51:29. – For a differentiated perspective on the "students" of Sirach as "addressees" of the book with regard to a general audience and the
readers of his writings, see among others: Frank Ueberschaer, "Jewish Education in
Ben Sira," in Zurawski and Boccaccini, *Second Temple Jewish "Paideia"*, 29–46,
31–3.

[22] E.g. Sir 7:10 ("do not grow weary when you pray"/μὴ ὀλιγοψυχήσῃς ἐν τῇ προσευχῇ
σου); 17:25 ("turn back to the Lord"/ἐπίστρεφε ἐπὶ κύριον).

performed solely, but as a collective movement of prayer that aims at a surplus of voices and register. The aspects of lament turn into praise from 39:14 onwards. It seems that first there is a personal introduction to the dimensions of plea and lament, which then turns into collective praise.

Human Beings in General and in Special Circumstances

In the texts, especially in the context of praise, many passages appear which either make general anthropological statements (17:8, 9, 10, 28; 32:14) or begin with phrases such as "(any)one/human being(s)" (ἄνθρω-πος 28:3, 4 NETS "person"; 38:6), "none/no one" (οὐθείς 18:4) or "who?" (τίς 17:27; 18:5; 43:31). It becomes clear that the living human being is called to sing the praise of his creator (17:8–10, 28), for the dead are no longer able to do so (17:17–28). At the same time, however, no one (18:4) is able to describe to completely all the miracles and mercies of God (18:5; 43:31). Prayer, especially according to the passages in Sir 17, is a decisive characteristic of human beings, laid out in the order of creation.

In some cases, people are specifically qualified because of their actions, conditions or the situation in which they are. Subjects of prayer are the persons honouring their father (3:5), the humble (3:20), the sinner (15:9) and the merciful (32:14). In part, these groups may also overlap with the group of students of Sirach. Here one could also classify the sinful people (15:9), who should not be subjects of praise, but as subjects of repentance and lament, they would of course also be included in the prayer subjects (cf. 21:1). Those who have definitely no way to say any more prayers, neither lament nor praise, are the dead (17:28). Their condition should be a reminder to all those who violate boundaries by sin and yet still have the possibility of repentance and prayer (17:25).

A special group is formed by poor and oppressed people, who bring their distress before God primarily in the context of lament (4:5, 6; 21:5; 35:16–17, 20–21). Especially in Sir 35, with the mention of widows and orphans, this group of people is clearly named, whose prayers, whose cries of distress and oppression have a privileged position with God. With the widow, the text explicitly mentions a woman as the subject of prayer.[23] Apart from this, Sir 48:20 is the only place which refers to

---

[23] Cf. Ibolya Balla, "Ben Sira on the Piety of Men and the Piety of Women: Binary Opposites in the Taxonomy of Piety?," in *Various Aspects of Worship in Deutero-canonical and Cognate Literature*, ed. Ibolya Balla, Géza G. Xeravits, and József

women, sc. the female inhabitants of Jerusalem—while they are not
directly named, this is most probable given the context.

Representatives of different professions also appear in the book as
subjects of prayers. Thus, physicians (38:14) and craftsmen (38:34) are
aware that not only they alone hold the success of their work in their
hands, but that they are also dependent on help and support from the
divine side. Of course, this knowledge of larger relationships naturally
applies to the scribe (38:24 γραμματεύς/ספר). His detailed portrait in
chapter 39 contains compact statements about prayer in the forms of
lament and praise (39:5–6).

The Wisdom Teacher

The figure of the wisdom teacher, who articulates both lament and praise
in the first-person, is (in terms of forms) the third most frequent subject
of prayer in the book.[24] Since he can also be considered the ideal promoted by the author/authors of the book, his role as a praying person
cannot be overestimated. Since most forms are found in Sir 51, this chapter illustrates perhaps the most contoured aspects of a personal journey
of prayer and a personal understanding of prayer.[25] In this line, the "meditation on the activity of the ideal sage" (Sir 38:34c–39:11) also contains
aspects of prayer.[26] The book evokes a "scribal body" as a "mindful
body" which is a "praying body".[27]

Historical Figures and Beyond

Even important figures of the past appear as prayers in the book. In
a collective dimension, they are people like the generations of old (2:10),
who called upon God; the servants of God (36:22) with their supplica-

---

Zsengellér, DCLY 2016/2017 (Berlin: de Gruyter, 2017), 107–16. Cf. other references
where a collective is mentioned and women can be included (Sir 48:20 as inhabitants
of Jerusalem and SirG 47:5–6 people) or are explicitly referred to (SirH[B] 47:6 בנות).

[24] Of the 19 references, most are in the context of praise (lament only 51:8, 9ab, 10, 13,
19): 42:15ab; 51:1abc, 8, 9ab, 10, 11abc, 12cd, 13, 17, 19, 22, 29.

[25] Benjamin G. Wright, "Ben Sira on the Sage as Exemplar," in Praise Israel for Wisdom
and Instruction: Essays on Ben Sira and Wisdom, the Letter of Aristeas and the Septuagint, JSJSup 131 (Leiden: Brill, 2008), 165–82, 177–8; cf. Werner Urbanz, "Sir 51,1–
12: Anhang oder Knotenpunkt," in Texts and Contexts of the Book of Sirach: Texte
und Kontexte des Sirachbuches, ed. Gerhard Karner, Frank Ueberschaer, and Burkard
Zapff, SBLSCS 66 (Atlanta: SBL Press, 2017), 301–22.

[26] Wright, "Ben Sira on the Sage as Exemplar," 178–81.

[27] Newman, Before the Bible, 23.

tions, the people at the time of David (47:6) and the inhabitants of Jerusalem at the time of Hezekiah (48:20). Possibly the "holy ones" (42:17
τοῖς ἁγίοις κυρίου / H^M קדשי אל) can also be enlisted here.

Joshua (46:5), Samuel (46:16), Solomon (47:17),[28] and David (47:5–
10) are prominently displayed in the prayer history of Israel. Apart from
the last two, the aspects of the lament predominate in the small portraits.
In David, lamentation and praise merge.

Text passages already mentioned, Sir 47:6 and 48:20, use plural forms
and thus indicate a prayer movement supported by the community. Similarly, Sir 36 is a collective ("we") prayer that speaks of "servants" at the
end (v.22) and has all of "Jacob" in mind. Carrying on this thought,
Sir 50 offers the scenery of a liturgical action with a larger public and
a distribution of roles. In addition to the high priest Simon, there are the
sons of Aaron (50:16), the psalm singers (50:18; cf. 47:9–10), and
the whole people (50:17–19).

Outside of the congregation of Israel stand the enemies of the people
(36:10), who, however, are also ultimately to be led to the narrative
praise (ἐκδιηγέομαι) of God's deeds. As a cosmic element, the sun
should be mentioned, which with its rising functions as a herald proclaiming (43:2 διαγγέλλω) the glory of God.[29]

Modes of Being Guided in Prayer

The basic structure of the book is didactic in nature with its emphasis on
instruction, character formation and help for a successful life. Prayer is
a factor to be addressed at all these levels. But how does the book bring
the topic home to its disciples? Three kinds of methods can be
discovered.

---

[28] Solomon is usually missing in enumerations of praying figures in the book of Sirach.
However, it is noticeable that he also causes amazement by the poetry of songs and
thus takes up a term from David's "praise movement" (47:9). Both the Hebrew שיר
and the Greek ᾠδή, allow profane (Amos 5:23), religious (Ps 42[41]:9) and cultic song
of the Levites with instrumental accompaniment (Neh 12:27) as interpretation; George
H. Box and William O. E. Oesterley, "The Book of Sirach," APOT 1:268–517, 498.

[29] The examples 36:10 and 43:2 show only in G prayer vocabulary; Urbanz, Gebet im
Sirachbuch, 202–3, 208–9. For a detailed analysis of the differences in Sir 36, see:
Maria Carmela Palmisano, "Salvaci, Dio Dell'Universo!": Studio Dell'Eucologia Di
Sir 36H,1–17, AnBib 163 (Rome: Editrice Pontificio Istituto Biblico, 2006), 191–9,
221–8 and eadem, "La prière de Ben Sira," 281–6.

Role Models

An essential element are clear and concrete examples of praying persons from past and present.[30] As early as the beginning of the prayer theme in 2:10, the reference to the former generations, whose call upon God attracted attention, provides a positive basic signal for acceptance of such behaviour. Prominent figures in the history of Israel, such as Joshua (46:5), Samuel (46:16), David (47:1–11), Hezekiah, and Isaiah, together with the inhabitants of Jerusalem (48:20), show that prayers will not die away in nothingness. God reacts and responds to invocation, petition and plea for help. Likewise, especially with David (47:8–10) and implied by Solomon (47:17), praise and thanks are discernible. In particular in Sir 47, in the context of David, many details worth imitating are given: "calling" (v.5), "giving thanks" (v.8), "proclaiming glory" (v.8), "singing praise with all his heart" (v.8), "giving beauty to festivals" (v.10). The example of famous people—maybe in addition to the wisdom teacher—provide (attractive) role models for the students to find their own gestures of prayer and illustrate ways in which they can confront God with the reality of people in the speech act of (lament) prayer or praise.

Even the wisdom teacher himself, as a direct reference and role model for the student can serve as a "medium".[31] This is particularly evident in the passages in which Sir speaks of prayer in forms of the first person singular (e.g. 42:15), especially in detail in Sir 51:1–12, 13–30 (compare the many similarities with the Davidic pericope).[32] Also in the texts concerning the role of the scribe (15:9–10; 39:1–11) something of the high ideal of Sir for this class becomes clear. Prayer is thereby a total commitment,[33] which expresses a basic attitude, especially in the sensitivity to the realities referred to as "sin." His own example as a direct role model and that of the scribe

---

[30] Núria Calduch-Benages, "Ben Sira's Teaching on Prayer: The Example of the Generations of Old," in *On Wings of Prayer: Sources of Jewish Worship. Essays in Honor of Professor Stefan C. Reif on the Occasion of his Seventy-fifth Birthday,* ed. Michael W. Duggan and Dalia Marx, DCLS 44 (Berlin: de Gruyter, 2019), 37–54.

[31] Cf. the term "intermediary" in Catherine Petrany, *Pedagogy, Prayer and Praise: The Wisdom of the Psalms and Psalter*, FAT 2/83 (Tübingen: Mohr Siebeck, 2015), 68 in recourse to Notker Füglister: "The sage models himself as an intermediary, who has gained wisdom through vertical communication and now dispenses the knowledge he has gained to a human student."

[32] The connection is clearer in Greek; see the different vocabulary in Hebrew: e.g. ἐπι-καλέω in Sir 47:5 (H^B קרא) and 51:10 (H^B רום) or ἐξομολογέω in Sir 47:8 (H^B נתן הודות) and 51:1, 11 (H^B v.1 הלל and ספר, v.11 תפלה).

[33] Cf. Josef Haspecker, *Gottesfurcht bei Jesus Sirach,* AnBib 30 (Rome: Pontificial Biblical Institute, 1967), 230; Otto Rickenbacher, *Weisheitsperikopen bei Ben Sira,* OBO 1 (Fribourg: Universitäts-Verlag; Göttingen: Vandenhoeck & Ruprecht, 1973), 194 speaks of "Engagement total."

(Sir 39) are oscillating and should stimulate the young pupils to a similar shaping of the personality, characterized by clear features of prayer.

The doctors and craftsmen (Sir 38) with their everyday practice of prayer also show attitudes of piety which should be even more particular to a scribe.

Motivation and Instructions

In addition to the examples of people, Sir also endeavours to motivate and stimulate young people through other references and examples to prayer and related actions. He not only encourages prayers in general, but also gives clear guidance about their "when" and "how". One should not be fainthearted in prayer (7:10 μὴ ὀλιγοψυχήσῃς ἐν τῇ προσευχῇ σου; cf. SirH^A בתפלה אל תתקצר "be not brusque in your prayers"),[34] nor make too many words (7:14 μὴ δευτερώσῃς λόγον ἐν προσευχῇ σου). In the face of dangerous and disturbing situations (13:14), in riots (26:5) and, of course, in illness (38:9), one should say prayers. Just as one should turn to God in situations in which one needs help and orientation (37:15), one should also thank and bless him (εὐλογέω / ברך) for positive experiences, such as all the good things that one has received from him (e.g. in the context of banquets, 32:13).[35]

Another area that Sir repeatedly addresses is the theme of sin. How do you behave when you have sinned? Prayer plays an essential role in this, as one should confess one's sins and need not be ashamed (4:26). But the book draws attention to the other steps which must be taken: the first is turning back to the Lord, followed by the cessation of sin and finally the pleading for forgiveness of sins (17:25; 21:1). This is more likely to be granted when one has also forgiven one's neighbour in everyday life (28:2, 4)[36] and does not commit sin again (34:31). Why this is important is described in the context of 17:25, when in 17:27–28 death is to be reckoned with as a threateningly close consequence. But in order not to become a sinner: pray![37]

---

[34] Patrick William Skehan and Alexander Di Lella, *The Wisdom of Ben Sira: A New Translation with Notes*, AB 39 (New York: Doubleday, 1987).

[35] Also in the Greek culture, an act of piety (e.g., libation, chant) was customary at the end of a banquet (Plato, *Symp.* 176); Collins, "Ecclesiasticus, or The Wisdom of Jesus Son of Sirach," 97.

[36] Cf. the similarities to NT texts (e.g. the Lord's Prayer in Matt 6:12) or other Jewish Literature (T.Gad 6:3–7); cf. Skehan and Di Lella, *The Wisdom of Ben Sira*, 363–4.

[37] Núria Calduch-Benages, "Emotions in the Prayer of Sir 22:27–23:6," in *Ancient Jewish Prayers and Emotions: Emotions Associated with Jewish Prayer in and Around the*

Also for the vow practice, Sir gives concrete hints. He urges that vows (εὐχή/εὔχομαι) should not be spoken lightly (18:23), and when spoken, they should also be fulfilled (18:22).

Thus we may conclude that those references speaking of the effectivity of the prayer and supplication of the poor are primarily admonitions to the youth not to neglect the poor, the oppressed, the supplicants, the orphans, and the widows, but to turn to them, because God listens to the cry of those who are unjustly treated. God will hear and will react accordingly to the perpetrators (4:5–6; 21:5; 34:29; 35:16–17, 21). On a second level, however, these statements may also apply to the students if they find themselves in an emergency situation and are themselves suppliants and poor, giving them an impulse to turn confidently to their Creator (4:6) and to trust in the power of prayer (35:21–22), even if one is only able to pronounce a curse (4:5; 34:29).

And here one might also classify the great prayers in the book itself, which are comprehensible prayer movements—one could also speak of prayer models. The prayer for verbal and sexual restraint in Sir 22:27–23:6 opens twice with the question who can assist you in these matters (τίς 22:1; 23:2). Twice the answer is that God as a father (κύριε πάτερ καὶ δέσποτα / θεὲ ζωῆς μου 23:1, 4) is a powerful helper in avoiding sins and their consequences.[38] The common first-person-singular forms make it possible for anybody to use the prayer in any situation. In the collective lament/prayer for deliverance of the people, the city, and the temple (Sir 36:1–22),[39] Israel as a whole is the oppressed/poor (cf. 34:21–35:26) who pleads with God (36:1 H^B אלהי הכל / δέσποτα ὁ θεὸς πάντων) in a lot of imperative forms to intervene in favour of his people. The wisdom teacher and his disciples (in their understanding also as H^B עבדיך / τῶν ἱκετῶν σου 36:22) extend their thoughts to the diverse political and historical dimensions of Israel and the threats God's people have been facing. In the end, they express the hope that at last the whole earth will know the one true God.[40]

Second Temple Period, ed. Stefan C. Reif and Renate Egger-Wenzel, DCLS 26 (Berlin: de Gruyter, 2015).

[38] Harrington, *Jesus Ben Sira of Jerusalem*, 46.

[39] Palmisano, *"Salvaci, Dio Dell'Universo"*.

[40] It is not surprising that elements of Sir 36 were used in Jewish prayer literature (New Year and *Shemone Esre*); cf. Georg Sauer, *Jesus Sirach / Ben Sira*, ATD Apokryphen 1 (Göttingen: Vandenhoeck & Ruprecht, 2000), 249.

The third prayer is the thanksgiving psalm (Sir 51:1–12), which returns to an individual's experience.[41] Through the pleading prayer, he has experienced the saving grace of God, to whom he now dedicates his praise. In different circumstances, these three prayers offer the opportunity to raise one's voice to God along the pre-composed prayer-score of Sir.

The book also mentions how prayers can be performed. In general, one should set out early to seek God, especially in prayer (32:14),[42] and if one's service is pleasing to the Lord, one's plea penetrates to the clouds (35:20). Also prayer pose is an issue, e.g. to spread the hands toward God (48:20), as well as sequences to be observed in public liturgies (with many details in 50:16–21). Cultic action should always be carried out with kindness (35:10). Above all, one should be carried away to marvel and admire praise, spontaneously at the sight of splendid spectacles in nature like the rainbow (43:11) or—as described in many variations—in the knowledge of the wonderful works of God in nature (39:12–15, 35) and in humanity (50:22). Such praise should be spoken vigorously (43:30), and one should never be ashamed of it (51:29). It should continue to work forever (51:30). The students are not alone in this process. The wisdom teacher accompanies them and lets them participate in his prayer exercise, in a common "we" (43:28).

Reflection

As a wisdom teacher, the ideal figure of the book reflects on the subject that concerns him in his teaching and offers these reflections to his students. Already in the context of the motivation to pray, traces of such a reflection become visible; cf. in the considerations on the prayer of the

---

[41] Antonio José Guerra Martínez, *El Poder De La Oración: Estudio De Sir 51,1–12*, Asociación Bíblica Española 50 (Estella, Navarra: Verbo Divino, 2010); cf. also an apocryphal Hebrew psalm (hymn of divine names after Sir 51:12) and the wisdom poem Sir 51:13–30. Cf. Collins, "Ecclesiasticus, or The Wisdom of Jesus Son of Sirach," 109–10 and Matthew J. Goff, "Temple Songs of Simon and Ben Sira: The Accumulation of Hymnic Material to the End of the Book of Ben Sira," *BN* 180 (2019): 31–54.

[42] Cf. the same vocabulary in G ("to rise early," ὀρθρίζω) also in Sir 4:12 ("search for wisdom"); 6:36 ("company of elders" / "wise and intelligent man") and especially in 39:5 in the context of the scribe. This aspect of prayer is more evident in SirH^B 32:14b (ויענהו בתפלתו); Víctor Morla Asensio, *Los manuscritos hebreos de Ben Sira*, Asociación Bíblica Española 59 (Estella, Navarra: Verbo Divino, 2012), 187.

poor (4:5–6; 21:5; 34:29; 35:16–17, 21–22) or in the context of sin and forgiveness (4:26; 17:25; 21:1; 28:2, 4; 34:31).

This would also include the statements in 15:9–10, which is the first place in the book (except for 3:20) where vocabulary of praise is concentrated. They emphasize that praise of God is unseemly in the mouth of the sinner (15:9) and, in contrast, a legitimate pronunciation from the sage's mouth (15:10). But these statements already bear witness to a comprehensive knowledge and reflection on the connections and consequences of sinful speech and the address of the holy God in praise. In addition, the second stich in each verse puts the actions in relation to a divine order and thus deepens the background of this thought. Similarly, such statements reappear later in the portrayal of the scribe and his prayer-movement in Sir 39:5–6.[43]

In the basic anthropological statements of 17:6–10, there are numerous links between several topics such as creation, tasks of man and praise.[44] This requires an awareness of these specific areas and, furthermore, the ability of making an adequate theological connection. Here, praise is the ultimate aim of man (17:9–10 "And they will praise his holy name, to proclaim the grandeur of his works").[45] If the foundations are laid down in Sir 17; Sir 18:4–5 clarifies the limits of this movement, that no-one can fully explain God's works. Sir admits the imperfection of human thought and prayer actions, as Sir 42:17 and 43:28–31 point in this direction: 43:30a "Glorify the Lord and exalt him as much as you can, for he surpasses even that."

Also, the statements about the work of craftsmen and the vocabulary of prayer can be classified in this context of reflection. In SirG 38:34a the craftsmen, by doing their work, support / take part in the creation of the world (ἀλλὰ κτίσμα αἰῶνος στηρίσουσιν). And they are god-related because they (like the physician in 38:14) know the broader horizon for the success of their work and practice supplication / prayer (v.34b καὶ ἡ

---

[43] Cf. the importance of petition and confession of sin as strategies for bringing about self-diminishment vis-à-vis the deity; Angela Kim Harkins, "The Function of Prayers of Ritual Mourning in the Second Temple Period," in *Functions of Psalms and Prayers in the Late Second Temple Period*, ed. Mika S. Pajunen and Jeremy Penner, BZAW 486 (Berlin: de Gruyter, 2017), 80–101, esp. 91–3.

[44] In Sir there are many reciprocal relationships between anthropology and theology; cf. Markus Witte, "'Barmherzigkeit und Zorn Gottes' im Alten Testament am Beispiel des Buchs Jesus Sirach," in *Texte und Kontexte des Sirachbuchs: Gesammelte Studien zu Ben Sira und zur frühjüdischen Weisheit*, FAT 98 (Tübingen: Mohr Siebeck, 2015), 83–105.

[45] Marböck, *Jesus Sirach 1–23*, 215 refers also to Sir 15:9–10; 39:14–15 and 32:13 as well as the Zeus Hymn of Cleanthes.

δέησις αὐτῶν ἐν ἐργασίᾳ τέχνης).[46] In everyday life, in daily work and the striving to fulfil one's tasks—with the help of God—in the best possible way, one action emerges which is society-building and solidifying God's creation.[47]

Especially the prayer-path from Sir 51:1–12 with its different stages from the praising introduction (v.1), the past deliverance (v.2), the description of the emergency situation (v.3–9) with the vows of praise to the rescue from distress (v.10–11) and concluding thanks (v.12) shows many aspects of reflection. Situations of life are analysed in retrospective and interpreted, in and through prayer (cf. in SirG 51:1, 12 with ἐξομο-λογέω) that also shows reflexive actions.

Observations and Considerations on Prayer and Spirituality

After the investigation of the subjects and the modes to initiate and guide prayer experiences in Sir, a few further reflections on the issue of prayer and spirituality are to be tried. I would like to look at some hermeneutical perspectives on how prayer as a spiritual exercise in Sir can be interpreted.

Prayer as Formation of Personality and Piety

According to Oda Wischmeyer, Sir has to be seen as a document of early Jewish-wisdom piety and thus a religious document in the context of Hebrew-speaking Jerusalem Judaism and its adaptation in the Greek Jewry of Alexandria.[48] The importance of religion extends even deeper to the psychic culture of the individual and society. It influences the feelings and thoughts as well as actions of the persons and in this way has a culture-shaping effect. One important part of the religious perspective is prayer as an expression of a personal relationship with God. Prayer is an eminent factor in the formation of the personality of the wisdom teacher, the students and all the other praying persons mentioned

---

[46] Here, many translations follow the Syriac Tradition; e.g. "their concern is for", see Skehan and Di Lella, *The Wisdom of Ben Sira*, 446. Also, Burkard M. Zapff, *Jesus Sirach 25–51*, NEchtB 39 (Würzburg: Echter, 2010), 256 speaks of a "Gebetsgemein-schaft" (prayer community) of a physician and his patient in the context of the Sir 38:1–15 (attitudes to physicians), because both need divine assistance. In a similar fashion, the craftsmen also form such a prayer community.

[47] Cf. Urbanz, *Gebet im Sirachbuch*, 96–7.

[48] Oda Wischmeyer, "Die Konstruktion von Kultur im Sirachbuch," in Karner, Ueberschaer, and Zapff, *Texts and Contexts of the Book of Sirach*, 71–98.

in Sir.[49] But the shaping effect can only be obtained if the religious practice is persistently activated and practiced appropriately. So prayer is close to and part of spiritual exercises.

Prayer as Lived (Religious) Experience of Transformation

In the context of today's modern age, the concept of piety has lost much of its original meaning and relevance. The concept of spirituality has conquered the (religious) field, and it is always necessary to pay close attention to what each term means.[50] Sandra Schneiders defines spirituality "as the lived experience of conscious involvement in the project of life integration through self-transcendence toward the ultimate value one perceives"[51] and articulates many points of contact to ideas of Hadot (ongoing life project; person as a whole, inner and outer; vs. self-absorption, dispersion, and fragmentation) but also to Sir. Spiritualities (plural) "come to expression in the Bible and witness to patterns of relationship with God that instruct and encourage our own religious experience."[52] The facets of prayer (lived relationship with God) in Sir can be understood as elements of spiritual exercises. As modes of thinking / teaching / practicing, they lead to higher understanding and existential change.[53] So also prayer is an element and a medium of a comprehensive understanding of human education.[54]

Especially the texts at the end of the book in Sir 51 reflect a conception of the role model of the teacher "as a sage who encouraged the praise of God"[55] and whose example was followed in a kind of ongoing revelation

---

[49] For the various aspects, see Oda Wischmeyer, *Die Kultur des Buches Jesus Sirach*, BZNW 77 (Berlin: de Gruyter, 1995), 267–70.

[50] Note also the different titles of the book of Pierre Hadot "Exercices spirituels et philosophie antique" (1981) and the varying titles of the translations: "Philosophy as a Way of Life: Spiritual Exercises from Socrates to Foucault" (1995) and the German versions translated in parts by Ilsetraud Hadot "Philosophie als Lebensform: Geistige Übungen in der Antike" (1991) and the 2nd edition with the different subtitle "Antike und moderne Exerzitien der Weisheit" (2005).

[51] Sandra M. Schneiders, "Spirituality," *NIDB* 5: 5:365–8, 366.

[52] Sandra M. Schneiders, "Biblical Spirituality," *Int* 56, no. 4 (2002): 133–42, 134.

[53] Cf. the term of "transformation" in Schneiders, "Biblical Spirituality," 138 or "transformative process" (136) or "transformative engagement" (137).

[54] Harrington, *Jesus Ben Sira of Jerusalem*, 102. For aspects of education, see Frank Ueberschaer, *Weisheit aus der Begegnung,* BZAW 379 (Berlin: de Gruyter, 2007), and Ueberschaer, "Jewish Education in Ben Sira."

[55] Goff, "Temple Songs of Simon and Ben Sira," 35. Goff emphasizes that mentioning the name Ben Sira in 50:27 and the blessings of Simon in Sir 50 "established a textual context in which hymnic material could be and was added to the book" (33).

"obtained in a continuing dialogue through prayer and liturgical performance".[56] The life of the one who cried out to God in great distress was saved (Sir 51:1–12). The requests for support, both to avoid or overcome individual bad habits (Sir 22:27–23:6) and to survive collective threats (Sir 36), are recorded in a prayer model. In Sir, prayer seems to be "at the very center of the intellectual endeavour."[57] The students are being trained for the quest for wisdom as a "quest for the realisation of a meaningful life and society, for a blessed 'full' life, supported by a God who is both its origin and its goal."[58] The students can make their own interpretation and realisation of prayer/s in the form of "actualisation" of the meaning of the text for them as "present readers." This kind of "appropriation" is also a process of transformation.[59]

Prayer as Relation to an Other

The high ethical standards of ancient philosophy led to a sometimes critical view of prayer and to special perceptions of it. Accordingly, the function of prayer is the alignment of the whole life to the Divine. Prayer becomes a kind of philosophical contemplation.[60] In doing so, the divine, or at least the relationship to it, is increasingly located in the self-relation of the worshipers. The interest is not so much the encounter with a counterpart than a kind of "self-discovery" for the purpose of self-

---

[56] Newman, "Liturgical Imagination in the Composition of Ben Sira," 325.

[57] James L. Crenshaw, "The Restraint of Reason, the Humility of Prayer," in *Urgent Advice and Probing Questions: Collected Writings on Old Testament Wisdom* (Macon, GA: Mercer University Press, 1995), 217. What remains unanswered is why in Sir, more than in the other classic wisdom books, the theme of prayer plays such an important role? Philip Sheldrake, *Spirituality: A Brief History*, Wiley-Blackwell Brief History of Religion Series (Malden, MA: Wiley-Blackwell, 2013), 6 describes a process of "reformatting of religion" in modern spirituality discourse. This can be a process "from above" when religious authorities seek to adapt to new cultural-social realities. But more frequently this process is "from below" when "classic themes are reformulated, spiritual practices are adapted, or new ways of life are adopted to re-express a tradition."

[58] Bénédicte Lemmelijn, "Wisdom of Life as Way of Life: The Wisdom of Jesus Sirach as a Case in Point," *OTE* 27 (2014): 446.

[59] Huub Welzen, *Biblical Spirituality: Contours of a Discipline*. Studies in Spirituality Supplement 30 (Leuven: Peeters, 2017), 19 is referring to the work of John R. Donahue, "The Quest for Biblical Spirituality," in *Exploring Christian Spirituality: Essays in Honor of Sandra M. Schneiders,* ed. Bruce H. Lescher and Elizabeth Liebert (New York; Mahwah, NJ: Paulist, 2006), 73–97.

[60] Cf. the steps in the later Christian "lectio divina" with *lectio, meditatio, oratio* and *contemplatio*; Schneiders, "Biblical Spirituality," 140.

optimization.[61] Thus in the Bible, prayer "has a transformative function
as an essential practice that shapes consciousness in relation to an
Other."[62] The person who thanks and praises God does not cease to
think, but he restricts his thinking from self-reflection and object-reflec-
tion through communication with God in prayer.[63]

In Sir, the pursuit of wisdom does not lead to philosophy, but to theology, the discerning love for the Jewish God.[64] This is hereafter described
as the "fear of the Lord" in the sense of reverential and loving devotion
to God by keeping the commandments (cf. Sir 1:11–30; esp. 1:26).
Nowhere in the world is there true wisdom and education unless it is awe
for the God of the Jews. Fear of God / respect for the Lord "opens up
the horizontal dimension to an immediate commitment to God in respect
and fidelity"[65] and makes prayer in Sir "predominantly monotheistic".[66]
Prayer becomes the supreme form of the fear of God and the expression
of a personal relationship with God.[67]

Prayer is a fundamental way of thinking and living a scholarly existence.[68] For Sir "worldly wisdom and spirituality come from God and are
best nurtured in an atmosphere of prayer."[69] Perhaps the strong emphasis
on prayer and the way in which it is taught, in addition to the doctrinal
character of the book, have been an incentive to take it as "Ecclesiasticus" into the particular ecclesiastical use and appreciation as a spiritual
guide.

Bibliography

Balla, Ibolya. "Ben Sira on the Piety of Men and the Piety of Women: Binary
    Opposites in the Taxonomy of Piety?" Pages 107–16 in *Various Aspects of
    Worship in Deuterocanonical and Cognate Literature*. Edited by Ibolya
    Balla, Géza G. Xeravits, and József Zsengellér. DCLY 2016/2017. Berlin:
    de Gruyter, 2017.

---

[61] Feldmeier, "Geheiligt werde dein Name," 38–9.
[62] Newman, *Before the Bible*, 18.
[63] Spieckermann, *Lebenskunst und Gotteslob in Israel*, 135 emphasizes that the hymn is
    a speech act in which the person brings tradition, experienced and discovered knowl-
    edge before God, from whom everything comes and to whom everything is related.
[64] Spieckermann, *Lebenskunst und Gotteslob in Israel*, 119–20.
[65] Lemmelijn, "Wisdom of Life as Way of Life," 449.
[66] Newman, *Before the Bible*, 18.
[67] Marböck, *Jesus Sirach 1–23*, 67.
[68] Spieckermann, *Lebenskunst und Gotteslob in Israel*, 118.
[69] Harrington, *Jesus Ben Sira of Jerusalem*, 81, referring to Sir 39:5.

Box, George H., and William O. E. Oesterley. "The Book of Sirach." Pages 268–517 in vol. 1 of *The Apocrypha and Pseudepigrapha of the Old Testament*. Edited by R. H. Charles. Oxford: Clarendon, 1913.

Bussino, Severino. "Word and Prayer in the Book of Ben Sira." Pages 117–40 in *Various Aspects of Worship in Deuterocanonical and Cognate Literature*. Edited by Ibolya Balla, Géza G. Xeravits, and József Zsengellér. DCLY 2016/2017. Berlin: de Gruyter, 2017.

Calduch-Benages, Núria. "Emotions in the Prayer of Sir 22:27–23:6." Pages 145–59 in *Ancient Jewish Prayers and Emotions: Emotions Associated With Jewish Prayer in and Around the Second Temple Period*. Edited by Stefan C. Reif and Renate Egger-Wenzel. DCLS 26. Berlin: de Gruyter, 2015.

Calduch-Benages, Núria. "Ben Sira's Teaching on Prayer: The Example of the Generations of Old." Pages 37–54 in *On Wings of Prayer: Sources of Jewish Worship. Essays in Honor of Professor Stefan C. Reif on the Occasion of his Seventy-fifth Birthday,* Edited by Michael W. Duggan and Dalia Marx. DCLS 44. Berlin: de Gruyter, 2019.

Collins, John J. "Ecclesiasticus, or The Wisdom of Jesus Son of Sirach." Pages 68–111 in *The Apocrypha*. Edited by Martin Goodman. The Oxford Bible Commentary. Oxford: Oxford University Press, 2012.

Crenshaw, James L. "The Restraint of Reason, the Humility of Prayer." Pages 206–21 in *Urgent Advice and Probing Questions: Collected Writings on Old Testament Wisdom*. Macon, GA: Mercer University Press, 1995.

Donahue, John R. "The Quest for Biblical Spirituality." Pages 73–97 in *Exploring Christian Spirituality: Essays in Honor of Sandra M. Schneiders,* Edited by Bruce H. Lescher and Elizabeth Liebert. New York; Mahwah, NJ: Paulist, 2006.

Feldmeier, Reinhard. "'Geheiligt werde dein Name': Das Herrengebet im Kontext der paganen Gebetsliteratur." Pages 25–82 in *Das Vaterunser in seinen antiken Kontexten: Zum Gedenken an Eduard Lohse*. Edited by Florian Wilk. FRLANT 266. Göttingen: Vandenhoeck & Ruprecht, 2016.

Gilbert, Maurice. "La prière des sages d'Israël," Pages 227–43 in *L'expérience de la prière dans les grandes religions: Actes du colloque de Louvain-la-Neuve et Liège (22–23 Novembre 1978)*. Edited by Henri Limet and Julien Ries. Homo Religiosus 5. Louvain: Centre d'Histoire des Religions, 1980.

Gilbert, Maurice. "Prayer in the Book of Ben Sira: Function and relevance." Pages 117–35 in *Prayer from Tobit to Qumran: Inaugural conference of the ISDCL at Salzburg, Austria, 5-9 July 2003*. Edited by Renate Egger-Wenzel and Jeremy Corley. DCLY 2004. Berlin: de Gruyter, 2004.

Goff, Matthew J. "Temple Songs of Simon and Ben Sira: The Accumulation of Hymnic Material to the End of the Book of Ben Sira." *BN* 180 (2019): 31–54.

Guerra Martínez, Antonio José. *El Poder De La Oración: Estudio De Sir 51,1–12*. Asociación Bíblica Española 50. Estella, Navarra: Verbo Divino, 2010.

Hadot, Ilsetraut. "The Spiritual Guide." Pages 436–59 in *Classical Mediterranean Spirituality: Egyptian, Greek, Roman*. Edited by A. H. Armstrong. London: Routledge & Kegan, 1986.

Hadot, Pierre. *Philosophy as a Way of Life: Spiritual Exercises from Socrates to Foucault*. Translated by Michael Chase. Oxford: Blackwell, 1995.

Hadot, Pierre. *What is Ancient Philosophy?* Translated by Michael Chase. Cambridge, MA: Belknapp, 2002.

Harkins, Angela Kim. "The Function of Prayers of Ritual Mourning in the Second Temple Period." Pages 80–101 in *Functions of Psalms and Prayers in the Late Second Temple Period*. Edited by Mika S. Pajunen and Jeremy Penner. BZAW 486. Berlin: de Gruyter, 2017.

Harrington, Daniel J. "Ben Sira as a Spiritual Master." *Journal of Spiritual Formation* 15 (1994): 147–57.

Harrington, Daniel J. *Jesus Ben Sira of Jerusalem: A Biblical Guide to Living Wisely*. Interfaces. Collegeville, MN: Liturgical Press, 2005.

Haspecker, Josef. *Gottesfurcht bei Jesus Sirach: Ihre religiöse Struktur und ihre literarische und doktrinäre Bedeutung*. AnBib 30. Rome: Pontifical Biblical Institute, 1967.

Lemmelijn, Bénédicte. "Wisdom of Life as Way of Life: The Wisdom of Jesus Sirach as a Case in Point." *OTE* 27 (2014): 444–71.

Liesen, Jan. *Full of Praise: An Exegetical Study of Sir 39,12–35*. JSJSup 64. Leiden: Brill, 2000.

Marböck, Johannes. *Jesus Sirach 1–23*. HThKAT. Freiburg: Herder, 2010.

Marttila, Marko. "Ben Sira's Use of Various Psalm Genres." Pages 356–83 in *Functions of Psalms and Prayers in the Late Second Temple Period*. Edited by Mika S. Pajunen and Jeremy Penner. BZAW 486. Berlin: de Gruyter, 2017.

Morla Asensio, Víctor. *Los manuscritos hebreos de Ben Sira: Traducción y notas*. Asociación Bíblica Española 59. Estella: Editorial Verbo Divino, 2012.

Newman, Judith H. "Liturgical Imagination in the Composition of Ben Sira." Pages 323–38 in *Prayer and Poetry in the Dead Sea Scrolls and Related Literature: In Honor of Eileen Schuller on the Occasion of her 65th Birthday*. Edited by Jeremy Penner, Ken M. Penner, and Cecilia Wassen. STDJ 98. Leiden: Brill, 2012.

Newman, Judith H. "The Formation of the Scribal Self in Ben Sira." Pages 227–38 in *"When the Morning Stars Sang": Essays in Honor of Choon Leong Seow on the Occasion of his Sixty-Fifth Birthday*. Edited by Scott C. Jones and Christine Roy Yoder. BZAW 500. Berlin: de Gruyter, 2018.

Newman, Judith H. *Before the Bible. The Liturgical Body and the Formation of Scriptures in Early Judaism*. New York: Oxford University Press, 2018.

Palmisano, Maria Carmela. *"Salvaci, Dio Dell'Universo!": Studio Dell'Eucologia Di Sir 36H,1–17*. AnBib 163. Rome: Editrice Pontificio Istituto Biblico, 2006.

Palmisano, Maria Carmela. "La prière de Ben Sira dans les manuscrits hébreux et dans les versions anciennes." Pages 281–96 in *The Texts and Versions of the Book of Ben Sira: Transmission and Interpretation*. Edited by Jean-Sébastien Rey and Jan Joosten. JSJSup 150. Leiden: Brill, 2011.

Petrany, Catherine. *Pedagogy, Prayer and Praise: The Wisdom of the Psalms and Psalter*. FAT 2/83. Tübingen: Mohr Siebeck, 2015.

Reitemeyer, Michael. *Weisheitslehre als Gotteslob: Psalmentheologie im Buch Jesus Sirach*. BBB 127. Berlin: Philo, 2000.

Rickenbacher, Otto. *Weisheitsperikopen bei Ben Sira*. OBO 1. Fribourg: Universitäts-Verlag; Göttingen: Vandenhoeck & Ruprecht, 1973.

Sauer, Georg. *Jesus Sirach / Ben Sira*. ATD Apokryphen 1. Göttingen: Vandenhoeck & Ruprecht, 2000.

Schneiders, Sandra M. "Biblical Spirituality." *Int* 56, no. 4 (2002): 133–42.

Schneiders, Sandra M. "Spirituality." *NIDB* 5:365–8.

Severus, Emmanuel von. "Gebet I." *RAC* 8:1134–258.

Sheldrake, Philip. *Spirituality: A Brief History*. Wiley-Blackwell Brief History of Religion Series. Malden, MA: Wiley-Blackwell, 2013.

Skehan, Patrick William and Alexander Di Lella. *The Wisdom of Ben Sira: A New Translation with Notes*. AB 39. New York: Doubleday, 1987.

Spieckermann, Hermann. *Lebenskunst und Gotteslob in Israel: Anregungen aus Psalter und Weisheit für die Theologie*. FAT 91. Tübingen: Mohr Siebeck, 2014.

Ueberschaer, Frank. *Weisheit aus der Begegnung. Bildung nach dem Buch Ben Sira*. BZAW 379. Berlin: de Gruyter, 2007.

Ueberschaer, Frank. "Jewish Education in Ben Sira." Pages 29–46 in *Second Temple Jewish "Paideia" in Context*. Edited by Jason M. Zurawski and Gabriele Boccaccini. BZNW 228. Berlin: de Gruyter, 2017.

Urbanz, Werner. *Gebet im Sirachbuch: Zur Terminologie von Klage und Lob in der griechischen Texttradition*. HBS 60. Freiburg: Herder, 2009.

Urbanz, Werner. "Sir 51,1–12: Anhang oder Knotenpunkt." Pages 301–22 in *Texts and Contexts of the Book of Sirach: Texte und Kontexte des Sirachbuches*. Edited by Gerhard Karner, Frank Ueberschaer, and Burkard Zapff. SBLSCS 66. Atlanta: SBL Press, 2017.

Uusimäki, Elisa. "Spiritual Formation in Hellenistic Jewish Wisdom Teaching." Pages 57–70 in *Tracing Sapiential Traditions in Ancient Judaism*. Edited by Hindy Najman, Jean-Sebastien Rey, and Eibert J. C. Tigchelaar. JSJSup 174. Leiden: Brill, 2016.

Uusimäki, Elisa. "The Formation of a Sage According to Ben Sira." Pages 59–69 in *Second Temple Jewish "Paideia" in Context*. Edited by Jason M. Zurawski and Gabriele Boccaccini. BZNW 228. Berlin: de Gruyter, 2017.

van Tongeren, Paul. "Philosophy as a Form of Spirituality with Reference to the Work of Pierre Hadot." Pages 109–21 in *Seeking the Seeker: Explorations in the Discipline of Spirituality: A Festschrift for Kees Waaijman on the Occasion of His 65th Birthday*. Edited by Hein Blommestijn, Charles Caspers, Rijcklof Hofman, Frits Mertens, Peter Nissen, and Huub Welzen. Studies in Spirituality Supplement 19. Leuven: Peeters, 2008.

Welzen, Huub. *Biblical Spirituality. Contours of a Discipline*. Studies in Spirituality Supplement 30. Leuven: Peeters, 2017.

Wischmeyer, Oda. *Die Kultur des Buches Jesus Sirach*. BZNW 77. Berlin: de Gruyter, 1995.

Wischmeyer, Oda. "Die Konstruktion von Kultur im Sirachbuch." Pages 71–98 in *Texts and Contexts of the Book of Sirach: Texte und Kontexte des*

Sirachbuches. Edited by Gerhard Karner, Frank Ueberschaer, and Burkard Zapff. SBLSCS 66. Atlanta: SBL Press, 2017.

Witte, Markus. "‚Barmherzigkeit und Zorn Gottes' im Alten Testament am Beispiel des Buchs Jesus Sirach." Pages 83–105 in *Texte und Kontexte des Sirachbuchs: Gesammelte Studien zu Ben Sira und zur frühjüdischen Weisheit*. FAT 98. Tübingen: Mohr Siebeck, 2015.

Wright, Benjamin G. "Ben Sira on the Sage as Exemplar." Pages 165–82 in *Praise Israel for Wisdom and Instruction: Essays on Ben Sira and Wisdom, the Letter of Aristeas and the Septuagint*. JSJSup 131. Leiden: Brill, 2008.

Zapff, Burkard M. *Jesus Sirach 25–51*. NEchtB 39. Würzburg: Echter, 2010.

LIST OF CONTRIBUTORS

Samuel E. Balentine is Professor of Old Testament and Director of Graduate Studies at Union Presbyterian Seminary in Richmond, Virginia. His publications include, *The Hiddenness of God* (Oxford University Press, 1983), *Prayer in the Hebrew Bible: The Drama of Divine-Human Dialogue* (Augsburg Fortress, 1993), *The Torah's Vision of Worship* (Fortress, 1999), *Leviticus* (Westminster John Knox, 2002), *Job* (Smyth and Helwys, 2006), *Have You Considered My Servant Job? Understanding the Biblical Archetype of Patience* (University of South Carolina Press, 2015), *Wisdom Literature* (Abingdon, 2018), and *"Look At Me and Be Appalled." Essays on Job, Theology, and Ethics* (Brill, forthcoming).

Beate Ego holds the Chair for "Exegesis and Theology of the Old Testament" at the Protestant Theological Faculty at the Ruhr-University Bochum, Germany. Her main fields of research are Hebrew Bible in the Persian and Hellenistic Time; Apocrypha and Pseudepigrapha of the Hellenistic and Roman Period. She is the author of a recent commentary on the Book of Esther published by Vandenhoeck & Ruprecht in 2017. Her current research is on the book of Tobit and magical and mystical traditions in Ancient Judaism.

Matthew E. Gordley is Professor of Theology and Dean of the College of Arts and Sciences at Carlow University in Pittsburgh, PA (USA). He is the author of *New Testament Christological Hymns: Exploring Texts, Contexts, and Significance* (2018); *Teaching through Song in Antiquity: Didactic Hymnody among Greeks, Romans, Jews and Christians* (2011); and *The Colossian Hymn in Context: An Exegesis in Light of Jewish and Greco-Roman Hymnic and Epistolary Conventions* (2007). His research focuses on early Jewish and Christian psalms, hymns, and prayers with particular attention to their historical, social, and literary contexts.

Bradley C. Gregory is an Associate Professor of Old Testament at the Catholic University of America in Washington, D.C. (USA). His research interests include Second Temple Judaism, sapiential ethics, and the translation, transmission, and interpretation of biblical texts in antiquity. He is the author of *Like an Everlasting Signet Ring: Generosity in the Book of Sirach* (Berlin: de Gruyter, 2010) and is currently working on a commentary on Sirach for the *International Critical Commentary* series.

Jennie Grillo is Tisch Family Assistant Professor of Theology at the University of Notre Dame (USA). She is the author of *The Story of Israel in the Book of Qohelet: Ecclesiastes as Cultural Memory* (Oxford University Press, 2012), which won a Manfred Lautenschlaeger Award, and her current book project is a study of the Additions to Daniel in the history of interpretation.

Noah Hacham is a faculty member in the department of Jewish History and contemporary Judaism at the Hebrew University of Jerusalem, Israel. His research topics are Jewish Diaspora in the Hellenistic-Roman Period, the Jews of Egypt in this Period, and Rabbinic Literature as a historical source.

Angela Kim Harkins (co-editor) is an Associate Professor at Boston College School of Theology and Ministry, Boston, MA (USA). Her work on the lived experience of religion covers a range of prayers and apocalyptic literature from the Second Temple period. She is the author of *Reading with an "I" to the Heavens* (2012, paperback 2018) and more than three dozen articles and essays. She has also co-edited several volumes. Harkins held a Fulbright fellowship for study at Hebrew University in 1997–1998 and a Marie Curie International Incoming Fellowship at the University of Birmingham, England in 2014–2015. She is currently working on a long-term project on the early Christian work known as the *Shepherd of Hermas*.

Andrew R. Krause is the Interim Academic Director at ACTS Seminaries of Trinity Western University in Langley, British Columbia, Canada. He is the author of *Synagogues in the Works of Flavius Josephus* (Brill, 2017) and is currently working on a commentary on 2 Maccabees for the *Society of Biblical Literature Commentary on the Septuagint*.

Joseph P. Riordan, S.J. is a lecturer in Old Testament at the Pontifical Biblical Institute in Rome, Italy. In 2017–2018, he was awarded a Fulbright research fellowship for study at Hebrew University in Jerusalem, Israel. His areas of research include textual criticism, prophetic literature and its ancient Near Eastern context, and the afterlife of prophecy in the theological discourse of Second Temple Judaism. He is currently working on a monograph dealing with aspects of the early reception history of the Book of Isaiah.

Barbara Schmitz (co-editor) holds the Chair of Old Testament and Biblical-Oriental Languages at the Catholic Theological Faculty of Julius-Maximilian University in Würzburg, Germany. Her main research areas are in Jewish Literature in the Hellenistic-Roman Period, Septuagint Studies, and Narrative Literature of the Old Testament. Her most recent publications include: *Perspektiven. Narratologische Zugänge zum Alten Testament* (SBB 75), (co-edited with Ilse Müllner), Stuttgart: Katholisches Bibelwerk 2018; *The Early Reception of the Book of Isaiah*, (co-edited with Kristin de Troyer), (DCLS 37), Berlin / Boston: de Gruyter, 2019. Project: "Local Self-governance in Judea in the second century BCE: Historical and Literary Perspectives", DFG Research Unit 2757: Local Self-Governance in the context of Weak Statehood in Antiquity and the Modern Era.

Werner Urbanz is Professor of Biblical Theology at the Private University of Education, Diocese of Linz, and Senior Lecturer at the Department of Biblical Studies at the Catholic Private University Linz. Since his book *Gebet im Sirachbuch* from 2009 he is interested in various aspects of the book of Ben Sira and the topic of prayer and spirituality in the Bible. His current research relates to the Oracles against Foreign Nations in the book of Ezekiel (especially Egypt).

Lawrence M. Wills is Visiting Professor in Judaic Studies and Religious Studies at Brown University. His book *The Jewish Novel in the Ancient World* was included among the Outstanding Academic Books of 1995 by *Choice* magazine for academic librarians. His commentary on Judith has been published in the Hermeneia series, and *Introduction to the Apocrypha: Jewish Books in Christian Bibles* is forthcoming from Yale Press. His present research addresses the ideal moral agent in Judaism and the relations between Jews and followers of Jesus in the first century.

INDEX